Self - Possession

BEING AT HOME IN

CONSCIOUS PERFORMANCE

MARK D. MORELLI

ISBN 978-0-578-50787-3

LIBRARY OF CONGRESS CONTROL NUMBER: 2016910822

First published 2015

Reprinted 2016

2nd Edition 2019

ENCANTO EDITIONS
LOS ANGELES   CA

Cover Image: Picasso's *Girl Before a Mirror*
Reproduced with the permission of the Museum of Modern Art,
New York

These are the days of turning toward the innerself, of increasingly taking possession of oneself, which, under apparent repose, goes on in the most intimate workings of the heart.

Rainier Maria Rilke, *Selected Letters*

The individual does not, as it were, give himself a task, but rather this is given to him at the same time as his being. Of course, the individual gives it to himself eventually *with consciousness*, but he can do this only because it is given to him originally without consciousness and through his mere being.

J. G. Fichte, *The Facts of Consciousness*

It seems to me that every mortal possesses, very nearly at the center of his mechanism, and well placed among the instruments for navigating his life, a tiny apparatus of incredible sensitivity which indicates the state of his self-respect. There we read whether we admire ourselves, adore ourselves, despise ourselves, or should blot ourselves out; and some living pointer, trembling over the secret dial, flickers with terrible nimbleness between the zero of a beast and the maximum of a god.

Paul Valery, *A Letter to a Friend*

Contents

ACKNOWLEDGEMENTS

This book has been years in the making. I tried out earlier versions of it in my introductory philosophy courses for several years. I'm grateful to the students in those courses for the questions they posed to me and for their thoughtful responses to the questions I asked them. They've alerted me to omissions, unnecessary complexities, and lapses in clarity in those early drafts. Several colleagues have read versions of the manuscript. James Marsh, Betsy Behnke, Doug Hoffman, Neil Ormerod, Michael Sharkey, Mojgan Taheri Morelli, and Richard Dawson have made substantive and editorial suggestions from which I have benefited greatly. Any errors that remain do so despite their efforts. I am also indebted to Mojgan Taheri Morelli and Eric J. Morelli for the interest they've shown in this project, for conversations that always evoked insights, for their editorial advice, and for their kind encouragement and support.

*

PREFACE

This inquiry was inspired by the work of Bernard Lonergan who drew my attention to myself as a conscious performer and introduced me to myself in that regard. I am greatly indebted to him for alerting me to the personal, practical, social, political, cultural, and historical significance of our knowledge of ourselves, and of our ignorance of ourselves, as conscious performers.

Bernard Lonergan's overriding interest was to promote self-knowledge in the practitioners of high-cultural disciplines devoted to the pursuit of explanatory knowledge – natural scientists and human scientists, philosophers and theologians. He was deeply troubled by persisting high-cultural conflicts over the meaning of meaning, objectivity, knowledge, truth, reality, and value. He located the root of these conflicts in the absence of agreement on an account of our own conscious performance as informed and guided by these notions. These conflicts over the meaning of meaning, objectivity, knowledge, truth, reality, and value are in need of resolution. Fruitful collaboration in the pursuit of answers to the complex questions with which the high-cultural disciplines are concerned depends upon their resolution. Even more importantly, fruitful collaboration in the control of our history and the promotion of progress depends upon it. Accordingly, Lonergan devoted his intellectual life to working out a concrete account of conscious performance in high-cultural, intellectual endeavors in the hope that this account might serve as a common ground upon which men and women of intelligence might meet and on the basis of which they might collaborate fruitfully and progress steadily.

In his book *Insight: A Study of Human Understanding*, published in 1957, Lonergan undertook to expose the common core – the invariant dynamic structure – of attentive, intelligent, reasonable, and responsible performance in the high-cultural inquiries of mathematics, natural science, human science, and philosophy.[1] It is a very sophisticated investigation addressed to a very well-informed and intellectually-orientated readership. It invites its readers to engage seriously in the pursuit of meaning, objectivity, knowledge, truth, reality, and value and to catch themselves in the act of doing so. It demands and requires of its readers a perspicuous attentiveness to the 'interior' experience of seeking meaning and value. It expects and encourages its readers to undertake to verify the account he provides of the invariant dynamic structure of attentive, intelligent, reasonable, and responsible performance in and for themselves. Lonergan's overriding aim was to assist his readers to make their conscious performance their own, to appropriate or take possession of themselves as conscious performers.

Lonergan had good reasons for deciding to address *Insight* to highly specialized readers. The contemporary crisis in the control of meaning is related fundamentally, in his view, to high-cultural failure to resolve satisfactorily the ongoing conflicts over the meaning of meaning, objectivity, knowledge, truth, reality, and value. Lonergan aimed to confront this crisis at its source. He aimed, on the one hand, to convince high-cultural practitioners that intelligent, reasonable, and responsible conscious performance is constituted by a common core of related and recurrent operations and, on the other hand, to mediate in those high-cultural practitioners a degree of self-possession that enables them to pursue meaning and value deliberately and methodically. In this way, he hoped, the perduring high-cultural conflicts surrounding the meaning of meaning, objectivity, knowledge, truth, reality, and value might eventually be resolved, clearing the way for truly fruitful, ongoing collaboration.

Lonergan's *Insight*, then, is a demanding and difficult book. Many readers lack the presumed familiarity with state-of-the-art intellectual practices in a wide range of disciplines that is required to follow his argument. Many fail to recognize his requirement of reflective 'inwardness', and many of those who acknowledge it find it puzzling, too difficult to meet, or in conflict with their existing philosophical commitments. For some readers, moreover, the book is rendered even more difficult by Lonergan's style of writing. Some find his writing one-sidedly denotative and scientific and insufficiently connotative and literary. They find him too sparing in his use of the sorts of descriptions that evoke the experience of the

---

[1] *Insight: A Study of Human Understanding*, vol. 3 of the Collected Works of Bernard Lonergan, eds., F. E. Crowe, et al. [Toronto: University of Toronto Press, 1992].

conscious operations whose relations to one another he is under-standably anxious to explain.

Lonergan was not unaware of the challenge his book posed for many readers. To those who found the opening chapters on mathematics and physics over their heads he recommended going directly to the two chapters on intelligent and reasonable conscious performance in the domain of everyday, commonsense living. Everyone, he remarked, is familiar with everyday living, and the same common core – the same invariant dynamic structure – of intelligent, reasonable, and responsible operations may be found in the flow of conscious performance that constitutes our ordinary living. But the bulk of the evidence to be adduced in support of his argument that there is a common core of operations that con-stitutes intelligent, reasonable, and responsible human endeavor in all areas of inquiry is to be found in the experience of the more deliberately methodical practices of mathematicians and scientists. Further evidence can be found in the conscious performance constitutive of ordinary living, but in that domain it is relatively obscured and occluded by the intrinsic spontaneity and practical and social preoccupations of ordinary living. The emergence of the desire to understand and the occurrence of the act of insight, for example, are fairly easily identified in the performance of geometrical exercises, whereas they are often overshadowed in ordinary social and practical living by the desire to live and the affective richness of ordinary practicality and drama. In the conscious flow of ordinary living, they are much more difficult to identify, isolate, and explore. Accordingly, even in those chapters on commonsense conscious performance, Lonergan pro-vides little in the way of description and focuses especially on bringing to light the explanatory relations of operations to one another. Moreover, the thrust of his analysis of commonsense conscious performance is to exhibit the limitations of that mode of performance, its susceptibility to bias and derailment, and the need for men and women of common sense to recognize the declinatory social, cultural, and historical consequences of a disdain for theoretical endeavors and of the unbridled pursuit of practicality.

If highly specialized readers find Lonergan's *Insight* difficult, the ordinary educated reader who lacks the required specialized background and who expects and requires evocative descriptions finds it virtually impenetrable. This is very unfortunate. It is true, I think, that the future course of our history depends heavily upon successful conscious performance in our ever more complex high-cultural pursuits. But it depends as well on successful conscious performance in the pursuit of our practical and social lives. As Lonergan remarked, men and women of common sense run the world. Further, our ordinary practical and social lives are also afflicted by recurrent conflicts over what counts as meaningful, objective, true, real, and valuable. These conflicts seem to become more obvious and more intense as we become more aware of the great variety of meanings and values, often incompatible with one another, that can inform and guide everyday living. They may be rooted in and exacerbated by high-cultural failure to achieve unanimity on the meaning of meaning, objectivity, knowledge, truth, reality, and value; but, until that unanimity is reached, if it is to be reached, we must continue to do the world's work. If it is worthwhile for high-cultural practitioners to take possession of themselves as conscious performers, it is also worthwhile for those of us who are engaged in everyday pursuits to discover the common core – the invariant dynamic structure – of operations constitutive, not only of high-cultural pursuits, but also of our everyday conscious performance and to take possession of ourselves as commonsense conscious performers.

The special interest and limited aim of this book, then, is to promote the type of self-knowledge that would enable us to perform *in our everyday lives* with sufficient attention to our conscious performance as informed and guided by the notions of meaning, objectivity, knowledge, truth, reality, and value. Its aim is to expose the common core of operations especially as it informs and constitutes our everyday conscious performance. Its aim is to articulate an orientating, philosophical foundation that is accessible to the educated layperson, the specialist in ordinary living, as it were, who intends to remain a man or woman of common sense and wishes to be an intelligent, reasonable, and responsible manager of his or her life and an intelligent, reasonable, and responsible contributor to the human community.

With regard to the project of taking possession of ourselves as conscious performers, Lonergan wrote, "The basic step is to give basic terms and relations the meaning they possess as names of conscious events and conscious processes." The proximate aim of this book is to take this first step. In the service of that aim, I employ illustrations and examples from ordinary living, undertake to provide evocative descriptions, and develop very gradually a precise technical terminology by tethering familiar, ordinary words to the conscious operations they identify. In this regard, my procedure is one-sidedly descriptive of the relevant experiences of conscious performance in the interest of enabling the reader to achieve the essential minimum of explanatory understanding – an understanding of the relations of conscious operations to one another and to the notions of meaning, objectivity, knowledge, truth, reality, and value – required to orientate herself in everyday living. The remote aim is to enable men and women of common sense, in virtue of having acquired that self-knowledge, to take possession of themselves as conscious performers. Those familiar with the work of Bernard Lonergan will discern his influence throughout. But this book is not an account of the ideas of Bernard Lonergan. If I may borrow Lonergan's own words: "Your interest may quite legitimately be to find out what Lonergan thinks and what Lonergan says, but I am not offering you that, or what anyone else thinks or says, as a basis."[2] I would not have been able to write the book if I had not encountered the thought of Bernard Lonergan, but the book itself is an independent exercise in *taking possession of oneself* in which the reader is asked to participate.

At the conclusion of his Preface to *The Vocation of Man*, J. G. Fichte offered his readers advice on how to read his book. The same advice may be offered to readers of this book:

> I must, however, remind my reader that the "I" who speaks in this book is not the author himself; but it is his earnest wish that the reader should himself assume this character, and that he should not rest contented with a mere historical apprehension of what is here said, but that during reading he should really and truly hold converse with himself, deliberate, draw conclusions and form resolutions, like his imaginary representative, and thus, by his own labour and reflection, develop and build up within himself that mode of thought the mere picture of which is presented to him in the book.[3]

---

[2] Bernard Lonergan, Collected Works of Bernard Lonergan 17: *Philosophical and Theological papers 1965-1980* [Toronto: University of Toronto Press, 2004]: 372, and Collected Works of Bernard Lonergan 5: *Understanding and Being*, eds. Elizabeth A. Morelli and Mark D. Morelli. Revised and Augmented by Frederick E. Crowe with the collaboration of Elizabeth A. Morelli, Mark D. Morelli, Robert M. Doran, and Thomas V. Daly [New York and Toronto: University of Toronto Press, 1990], 34-35.

[3] Chicago: The Open Court Publishing Company, 1931: xii. Trans. William Smith.

Prologue

AN ELEMENTAL MEDITATION

W hen I feel overwhelmed by the pressures and demands of life; when I feel a vague uneasiness, not just with this or that occasional disruption or unpleasant surprise, but with "the whole situation"; when I become roundly confused, persistently anxious and unsettled, or terribly bored; when I'm faced with a multitude of competing options, or with a vigorously contending few, or with what seem to be no options at all; when I feel unanchored, adrift, de-centered, at odds with myself, an obstacle to my own success – then I'm tempted to try to wash away or drown my uneasiness, confusion, anxiety, boredom, and indecision in a flood of preoccupations and involvements. I accelerate the pace of my living, push outwardly onward, and occupy myself ever more intensely with the things and people and events that surround me. But, in the solitude and inactivity of late nights and early mornings, I discover that my uneasiness and confusion were only muted by my deliberate pursuit of distractions. I can't achieve the relief I'm seeking by diving still more deeply into the very flow that has driven me to distraction.

Then I might withdraw, turn inward, and try to center myself in quiet meditation. I might choose the inward turn and the meditative course. But what do I hope to achieve in meditation? I hope to recover, or to evoke for the first time perhaps, a tranquil mood of thoughtfully guided purposefulness and responsible commitment, a self-feeling of confident orientation and centeredness that endures even as my situation undergoes continuous reconfiguration. I know that my withdrawal can be no more than a brief respite. I know I'll have to reemerge and resume my involvement in the tumultuous flow of life. Still, it's my hope that I'll return calmed and refreshed, re-orientated, re-centered and, perhaps, enlightened in some way.

To realize this hope, instead of submerging myself in activity, I undertake to liberate myself from cares, to arrest the unrelenting flow of everyday worries and concerns, to banish my desires. I seek a temporarily comforting silence and stillness. But, in the course of my meditation, I find that complete silence and stillness always elude me.

In my attempt to free myself from all desire or care, I encounter a tenacious anticipation, desire, or concern that I can't silence or still. This concern motivates my meditative withdrawal; it lingers to enforce and guide it; it persists as an anticipation of my return to the pulsing flow of life. If I were to succeed in banishing *this* concern, my desire to meditate would itself dissolve, and my meditative effort would cease. This enduring care, concern, or desire moves me to meditate. It remains as long as I still care enough to meditate. When I reemerge from my merely temporary meditative cocoon to resume my search for direction in the flow of life, it continues to guide and regulate my living. It seems that my attempt to banish *all* my cares is futile. In my pursuit of silence and stillness, my desire to liberate myself from cares remains, murmuring and fidgeting.

What is this care that defies and defines my efforts to rid myself entirely of cares?

Instead of striving futilely, then, to banish my cares and concerns, I might attempt to detach myself from them and, from a reflective distance, seek to identify them, sort through them, weigh and evaluate them. Perhaps I can realize my hope through a meditative detachment that enables me to attend to my many pressing concerns, sort through them, explore them, and evaluate them without being overwhelmed by them.

But, in my detached attempt to come to terms with the cares and concerns that disrupt my present living, I'm vaguely aware of a concern of mine to which I remain intimately attached. It endures as other, transient concerns arise and recede. In my detached attentiveness to my concerns of the moment, I cannot distance myself from this enduring care. The care without which I would not care to pursue reflective distance, the care I bring with me into my reflective stance, the care that enforces my detachment, looms on the periphery of my attention, unidentified, unexplored, and unevaluated. Throughout my meditative pursuit, this care of mine to make sense of my transient cares endures. It underlies my efforts to make sense of those cares and concerns that come and go. At my reflective distance, a care from which I cannot distance myself persists as other feelings change and come and go.

What is this desire of mine to achieve a reflective distance, to recognize, to sort through, to weigh and evaluate my transient cares? What is this care that endures as other cares and concerns come and go and from which I can't detach myself without abandoning my meditative quest?

In the following meditation, we'll direct our attention to this basic concern that persists, murmuring and fidgeting, even as we pursue meditative silence and stillness, and without which our meditative withdrawal would make no sense and have no value whatsoever. We'll direct our attention to this basic anticipation that moves us to meditate at all. We hope to concentrate our attention upon that anticipatory concern of ours that we find irresistible, irrepressible, and impossible to dispel, unlike the de-centering distractions we rightly aim to banish and the diverse and transient concerns we rightly aim to recognize, sort through, and evaluate.

We'll focus our attention on the elemental concern or basic anticipation that manifests itself in our dissatisfaction with our uneasiness, confusion, anxiety, unsteadiness and disorientation, that tempts us to distraction and leads us to resort to meditation, to persist in it, and to expect from it something of lasting value. Our meditative attention will be guided, not by a vague hope for tranquility, orientation, or enlightenment, but by the very basic questions, *What am I doing when I'm meditating? Why do I bother to meditate at all?* Under the guidance of these questions, we'll turn upon itself this enduring concern to identify, sort through, weigh and evaluate our cares.

In the following meditation, I withdraw from the pulsing flow of life in order to illuminate this basic anticipation or concern. This is why this meditation is called elemental. This basic anticipation or concern of mine doesn't come and go. I can't discard it at will or replace it with another just as deeply rooted. I can't "meditate it away" without robbing my meditative withdrawal of its very meaning and worth. This basic anticipation or concern is so profoundly *my own*, so deeply mine, that I experience myself as *owned by it*. While the roots of this concern are intertwined inextricably with the roots of my personality, they burrow more deeply to tap the underground spring of my humanity. As I seem to be owned by this elemental anticipation or concern, so it seems that I'm not its sole owner. My meditative aim is to take notice of a basic anticipation or concern that is at once intimately mine and not just mine, but ours.

In this Elemental Meditation we shall direct our attention to this elemental anticipation – to our insuppressible interest in making sense of things, in getting things right, in finding direction in life, in living a worthwhile life. We shall attend to the ineradicable concern that moves us into meditation when we feel obstructed by the difficulties and complexities of our lives, and yet defeats our efforts to achieve absolute silence and stillness. In this Elemental Meditation, we shall allow this basic anticipatory concern its voice. We shall discern in the seriousness of its tone *a commitment that is intimately ours*. We shall find ourselves always already bound by it and unable to escape it. In our pursuit of an enlightenment that enables us to commit ourselves wholeheartedly to the pursuit of direction in the flow of our lives, we shall find ourselves already bound by a commitment we already have and cannot escape.

Our meditative aim is to give full attention to our ineliminable anticipation of meaning, objectivity, knowledge, truth, reality, and value. My meditative withdrawal will be mine, yours will be yours, but the basic concern we aim to identify, explore, and evaluate, while intimately mine, is also intimately yours. I'm not alone in preferring meaning to nonsense, objectivity to bias, knowledge to ignorance, truth to falsehood, reality to illusion and what is to what is not, and the worthwhile to the worthless. This is our elemental passion – underpinning any and every life we may lead, motivating every profound and every trivial question we ask, every robust and every frail conclusion we draw, every heartfelt and every half-hearted decision we make – to sift the wheat from the chaff, the *meaningful* from the *meaningless*, the *objective* from the *one-sided or biased*, *knowledge* from *guesses and ignorance*, *truth* from *falsehood* and *the likely* from *the unlikely*, *reality* from *illusion* and *nothing at all* and, above all, *the more valuable* from *the less valuable*, *the most worthwhile* from *the completely worthless*.

I invite you to make the meditative turn with me now but to do so with a concern to bring this enduring and inescapable concern into focus, to identify it, and to come to terms with it. Let's seek silence and stillness in order to bring to light the anticipatory concern we cannot ultimately silence or still, to bring to light the concerned anticipation that motivates, informs, and guides our meditative withdrawal. Let's seek reflective distance and detachment from our transient cares and concerns in order to bring to light our enduring concern to make sense of those transient cares.

Let's attempt to identify this enduring care that defies our efforts to achieve carefree stillness and silence. Let's attempt to understand and evaluate this elemental care that motivates and penetrates our efforts to understand and evaluate our transient cares and concerns.

THE ELEMENTAL MEDITATION

At this moment, *I find myself preferring meaning to nonsense.* I might not find it, but I am looking for it. This preference of mine is so basic that I can't eliminate it, no matter how hard I try. Even if I were to declare a preference for the meaningless, I would do so only because I find it *meaningful* to do so now.

At this moment, *I find myself preferring objectivity to bias.* This is also a basic preference of mine. Even if I were to conclude right now that objectivity is unachievable, that no one can ever be objective, I would draw that conclusion only if I regarded it as the *objective* one to draw, only if I were satisfied that it is not merely an expression of some bias of mine.

At this moment, *I find myself preferring knowledge to ignorance and truth to falsehood.* These, too, are inescapable preferences of mine. Even if it turned out that knowledge of the truth can never be attained by anyone, or is not worth having, I would still think it's worth *knowing* that that is *true.*

At this moment, *I find myself preferring the real to the unreal. I prefer what is to what isn't.* My preference for the real is also inescapable. I prefer a real dinner to a pretend one, and I prefer a real friendship to an imitation. I prefer the real things to fakes and to nothing at all. If I were to conclude right now that I can't reach what's really real, I would not draw that conclusion if I didn't think that that's the way things *really are.*

At this moment, *I find myself preferring what's worthwhile and valuable to the worthless and valueless.* This almost goes without saying. My preference for the valuable over the valueless is also inescapable. Even if I were to claim that what I'm doing now has no value, or that nothing I do has any value, I wouldn't make that claim if I didn't think it was *worthwhile* to do so.

At this very moment, *I find myself committed, without ever having deliberately committed myself, to the pursuit of meaning, objectivity, knowledge, truth, reality, and value.*

This commitment is not mine alone. I notice that others, too, are bothered, annoyed, irritated, frustrated, aggravated, and exasperated by nonsense, by bias, by a cavalier attitude toward facts and truth, and by carelessness about the worth of people and things. Others seem to be just as inescapably committed to the pursuit of meaning, objectivity, knowledge, truth, reality, and value, as I am. No one wants to be regarded as unintelligent, unreasonable, or irresponsible. *Others share this basic commitment with me.*

We have identified and given succinct expression to a deep, inescapable, intimately personal yet shared, commitment to meaning, objectivity, knowledge, truth, reality, and value. This is the elemental concern we cannot silence or still in our pursuit of silence and stillness. This is the enduring care that motivates and penetrates our efforts to make sense of our transient cares.

But this is not the end of our meditative process. For, this Elemental Meditation has brought to light a primordial beginning. This inescapable anticipation is the beginning of all our beginnings. It is our basic anticipation of all the ends to which our thinking and acting can lead us. Superficial distractions and impulses have been swept aside to reveal a concern we can't silence or still. Now we begin to discern vaguely that the enlightenment we thought might be graciously bestowed upon us, if only we could succeed in achieving the complete disengagement and absolute effortlessness of abyssal silence and stillness, can be actively sought by turning this basic commitment loose upon itself, by releasing our concern for meaning, objectivity, knowledge, truth, reality, and value on our own meditative experience of our inescapable commitment to the pursuit of those ideals.

Our Elemental Meditation, then, invites us to undertake a prolonged exercise of radical reflection upon our relationship to the basic ideals that animate our conscious living: meaning, objectivity, knowledge, truth, reality, value. These ideals, it happens, are the very subject matter of Philosophy. Our Elemental Meditation, then, invites us to engage actively in philosophical reflection. If we accept this invitation, we stand to gain a basic clarity about ourselves – a basic knowledge of ourselves – that might enable us to remain tranquil, orientated, purposeful, and centered even while we're subjected to the cacophonous and confusing, disorientating and de-centering pressures and distractions of life. If we identify clearly our basic commitment, describe accurately to ourselves the unfolding of our most basic anticipatory concern, and determine to the extent we can what *meaning, objectivity, knowledge, truth, reality, and value* mean to us and how we are to pursue them, we might reach a dynamic state of ever more enlightened tranquility in our ongoing pursuit of direction in the flow of life – *a still-point-in-motion,* so to speak, or *radical self-possession.*

This book is a prolonged meditative exploration of our shared primordial experience of the elemental passion brought to light by the Elemental Meditation. It is an introduction to the elementally meditative discipline of Philosophy.

Chapter One

THE BASIC NOTIONS

M eaning, objectivity, knowledge, truth, reality, and value are basic notions to which we appeal and upon which we rely for guidance, sometimes explicitly but often covertly, in our conscious living as we seek direction in the flow of our lives. These basic notions are expressions of our basic commitment to the pursuit of meaning, objectivity, knowledge, truth, reality, and value.

1. AN INESCAPABLE COMMITMENT

The fundamental role played in our conscious living by these basic notions can be illustrated by the questions we raise and the directions we issue to ourselves and to others with some frequency.

FAMILIAR QUESTIONS AND DIRECTIONS

What do you mean? Does that have any meaning at all? Are you sure that makes sense? What sense does it make? Do you really mean that? Do you really know that, or is it just your opinion? Do you think it's true? Do you even know what you're talking about? Are you kidding me? Don't you get it? Was that real, or was I dreaming? What's really going on here? Is that the way it really is, or does it just seem that way? Would that really be worthwhile? What good is that? So what? Figure it out! Think about it! Try to

grasp the meaning! Use your head! Be open-minded! Be
objective! Don't be biased! Give me some evidence! Give
me one good reason! Be realistic! Do something worthwhile! Be good now! Don't do anything I wouldn't do. Do
you get what I'm saying? Know what I mean?

But, whether or not we make our commitment to meaning,
objectivity, knowledge, truth, reality, and value explicit in these
ways or in others, and whether or not we do so frequently or only
rarely, it is constantly in force, informing and guiding our conscious
living. Our commitment to meaning, objectivity, knowledge, reality,
truth, and value is an inescapable commitment.

Skepticism Confirms this Basic Commitment. The commitment is so
basic that even our doubt and skepticism about it exhibits it and, in
that way, confirms its ongoing presence.

DOUBTING THE COMMITMENT

What on earth do these notions *mean*? Even if these
notions do mean something, is our appeal to them *truly*
inescapable? Is this so-called "basic commitment" just the
expression of a peculiar standpoint, a personal preference,
a particular cultural background, some ideology, or some
hidden agenda? How can this claim that the commitment is
inescapable be regarded as *objective*? Is it *true*? Are we
really committed fundamentally to the ideals expressed by
these notions? Is this a *realistic* view, or is it just wishful
thinking? And *so what* if all of this is true? And, *so what* if it
isn't? What difference does it make if we are or we aren't
committed in this way? Even if we are, *so what*? And, if we
aren't, what difference does it make? What *good* is all this
talk about basic notions and a basic commitment to
meaning, objectivity, knowledge, truth, reality, and value?
What's the point?

In our skepticism and doubt and disagreement, as much as in
our belief and agreement, we exhibit our inescapable commitment
to meaning, objectivity, knowledge, truth, reality, and the worthwhile. Even if I were to adopt the standpoint of a nihilist, I would

do so only because it *makes sense* to me to do so, only because not to do so would be an intolerable violation of my commitment to what I take to be my *objective knowledge* of the sad *truth* about my *real situation*, and because, at a very basic level, I regard it as *worthwhile* to be a nihilist and to let people know I'm one and why I'm one.

Sometimes my concern about the meanings of things is far from obvious. Sometimes it's not obvious to me that I'm trying to be objective. Sometimes, to others, I'm obviously not being objective even as I proclaim my objectivity. Oftentimes, knowledge of the truth and being in touch with what's really real aren't major concerns of mine. But, even when I'm not deliberately and explicitly pursuing the ideals identified by these basic notions, they still play their roles quietly in my conscious living.

Sometimes, it seems, I'm not concerned at all about the meaning of things, content to accept without question the common understanding of things and situations, not at all attentive to the intrusions of biases into my thinking, not trying very hard to draw knowledgeable conclusions, not worrying about the reality of things, not wondering if some course of action would or would not be worthwhile or more worthwhile. At times it may even appear to others that I am deliberately unconcerned with all this.

When it appears that I'm not concerned at all with the ideals expressed by these basic notions, it's not because they're inoperative in my conscious performance; they're always operative. It's probably because the situation I'm in is already familiar to me. I've already grasped the relevant meanings. I've already acquired the relevant knowledge. I'm already in touch with the reality of my situation. I've already decided that my involvement in it is worthwhile. It's not that I no longer desire meaning, objectivity, knowledge, truth, reality, and value. It's just that my desire for them has been temporarily satisfied.

The more obvious manifestations of my commitment may have receded temporarily, but my commitment hasn't gone away. I'm resting in its temporary satisfaction now, rather than restlessly pursuing it. At any moment something unexpected could happen, something unfamiliar could arise, something unanticipated could occur to make my basic commitment obvious again. Someone might say something I find jarring or ridiculous or absurd, something that doesn't seem to follow, or something that just doesn't make sense or ring true to me. Someone might do something that disturbs me because it seems to me to betray gross ignorance of what, to my mind, is really going on, really happened, or is really likely or unlikely to happen. Someone might propose a course of action that gives me pause and makes me hesitate because it doesn't seem right to me and it's not clear at all to me that it would be the least bit worthwhile.

Even in my seeming lack of concern about meaning, my commitment to meaning remains. Whatever it is that seems to concern me instead does so only if I find it meaningful and only if it remains meaningful to me. When we're dealing with familiar situations our commitment to meaning, objectivity, knowledge, truth, reality, and value persists, but it is more difficult to discern. When we already understand, or think we do, we no longer feel a strong desire to understand. When we already know, or think we do, we don't feel perplexed or confused or puzzled. When we've already evaluated a course of action, found it to be worthwhile, and decided to carry it out, we don't keep second-guessing ourselves. Our commitment can be obscured by the grasped meanings and the known reality and the deliberate conduct of the moment, but it isn't eliminated. On the contrary, it's present in our temporary satisfaction that we've understood, that we know what's going on, that we're doing what we ought to do; it is still quietly operative.

When we're confronted with nonsense, bias, ignorance, falsehood, illusion, nothing at all where we expected something to be, and the worthless and when we encounter the new, the unfamiliar, the unknown, and the prospect of trying the untried, our basic commitment becomes vividly apparent once again. We may experience it as sudden disorientation, confusion, surprise, embarrassment, annoyance, bafflement, perplexity, puzzlement, wonder, skepticism, doubt, reservation, disillusionment, hesitation, suspicion, caution, worry, anxiety, or offense. Our deep concern for meaning, objectivity, knowledge, truth, reality, and value assumes many surface guises. At the heart of all these feelings, the same basic commitment is at work.

Can I Abandon My Basic Commitment? Sometimes our apparent lack of concern with meaning, objectivity, knowledge, truth, reality, and value is not a result of our familiarity with our situation. Sometimes we undertake deliberately to abandon our basic commitment.

Perhaps it serves my interests to be inattentive to some aspects of my experience, to suppress or ignore questions that might lead me to ideas I'd rather not entertain, to twist the truth or to depict what's true as false, to characterize what's worthwhile as worthless or what's worthless as worthwhile. Maybe I just want to win an argument, regardless of what's true or truly valuable, just because I like to be the one who's right or just because I enjoy the experience of power. But, still, I cannot escape my basic commitment to meaning, objectivity, knowledge, truth, reality, and value.

The selectivity of my attention, no matter how narrowly selective it might be, is not an abandonment of my concern for meaning. It's only a restriction of the range of experience in which I allow myself to search for meaning. I justify the suppression or dismissal of questions by declaring that there's no point in asking them because they're meaningless. I steer clear of specific ideas because of the unwanted meanings they contain. When I twist the truth, I twist it to resemble what I'd like the truth to be. When I depict the true as false I affirm, however surreptitiously, the truth of that denial. When I deliberately misrepresent the worth of things, I'm not discarding my notion of value but just manipulating it for my own ends which, at that moment, I regard as more valuable.

Lying and Being Lied To. Even downright lying depends for its effectiveness upon the presence of the basic commitment in myself *and* in those I hope to deceive.

My lying is successful only if what I'm saying sounds sensible and intelligent, only if my presentation of it sounds objective and knowledgeable, only if the idea I'm promoting is made to seem true and to seem to reflect reality. I wouldn't bother lying if I didn't think it was worthwhile, in some meaning of that notion, to do so. I can't lie without knowing that I'm lying. To know that I'm lying and to lie effectively, I must remain committed, in a roundabout way, to meaning, objectivity, knowledge, truth, reality, and value.

Successful deception depends as well on the presence of the basic commitment in those to whom I tell my lies and upon their expectation that I share that basic commitment. I cannot lie effectively to someone who is not concerned about meaning, objectivity, knowledge, truth, reality, and value. If they lack this concern, lying to them is pointless. When I lie I'm attempting to redirect and misdirect, and therefore presupposing, another's interest in meaning, objectivity, knowledge, truth, reality, and value. If they don't care what's true or false, they're immune to my deception. Nor can I lie successfully to someone who doesn't presuppose *my* basic commitment to meaning, objectivity, knowledge, truth, reality, and value. If they didn't make this assumption, I would be to them like the boy in Aesop's fable who cried wolf. They wouldn't take seriously anything I say. To lie successfully, the basic commitment must be present in the person to whom I'm telling my lie, and the person I'm lying to has to presuppose the basic commitment in me.

The notions of meaning, objectivity, knowledge, truth, reality, and value are operative in all of our conscious living. They orientate and guide our conscious performance. Our commitment to the pursuit of them is inescapable. Every attempt to make them inoperative in our living turns out to be just another instance of their operation. If I attend to anything at all, I am anticipating *meaning*. If I ask any questions at all, I am pursuing meaning. If I seek answers to any questions at all, I am pursuing *objective knowledge of the truth* about the *real*. If I do anything with any degree of seriousness at all, I do it because I find some *value* in doing it.

2. MAKING SENSE OF THE BASIC NOTIONS

Our living, at its deepest level, is a pursuit of meaning, objectivity, knowledge, truth, reality, and value. This basic commitment is present even when, from time to time, we seem to be avoiding, abandoning, or fleeing from it. We become uneasy and uncomfortable, nervous, annoyed, frustrated, dismayed, angered by nonsense, bias, ignorance, falsehood, illusion, and the worthless. The basic notions are ideals toward which we strive. Their opposites are to us what a vacuum is to nature. Nonsense, bias, ignorance, falsehood, illusion, and worthlessness are the vacuum *we* abhor. Is all this talk about basic notions just nonsense? Can we make sense of the basic notions? Let's begin to turn our basic commitment on itself.

The Basic Notions Aren't Ideas or Concepts. These basic notions aren't ideas or concepts we come up with. It is because of our prior commitment to them that we come up with any ideas and concepts at all about anything. It is for this reason that I call them 'notions' rather than 'ideas' or 'concepts'. Ideas and concepts are *produced by* our conscious performance. The basic notions *inform and guide us* in our conscious encounters with anything at all. We bring them with us to every encounter we have with anything and anyone. Were it not for these basic notions we would not pay serious attention to anything, we would not ask more than merely rhetorical questions about anything, we would not come up with any ideas at all about what we experience or what we might possibly do. They *inform* our conscious performance, making it the kind of performance it is. They *guide* our conscious performance, giving it its fundamental orientation. Because the informing and guiding role they play in our living is so basic, any attempt to determine and specify their meanings, any effort to come up with precise ideas or concepts of them, must take their already-operative meanings for granted.

The basic notions are constitutive of our conscious performance. They aren't acquired by means of our conscious performance. They are not themselves *products* of our conscious performance. They are at the core of all of our *production* as conscious performers. To them we must always appeal, either tacitly or explicitly, as the main actors in the dramas that are our lives.

The basic notions are prior to ideas and concepts and different from them. Whenever we're awake, these basic notions are in play. But the performance they inform and guide is *conscious*. Our orientation toward meaning, objectivity, knowledge, truth, reality, and value is not unconscious like the growth of our hair and fingernails or the functioning of our metabolism. We are *aware in* our performance. We are *aware in* our pursuit of meaning, objectivity, knowledge, truth, reality, and value. We are *aware in* our basic commitment. This *awareness in* our conscious performance is a basic, largely unexplored, unarticulated experience of the notions at work before we come up with ideas or concepts of them and before we express those ideas and concepts in words like 'meaning', 'objectivity', 'knowledge', 'truth', 'reality,' and 'value'. We already have the notions expressed by these words before we make any attempt at all to form ideas or concepts of them and before we attempt to put them into words. We have *notions* of meaning, objectivity, knowledge, truth, reality, and value *in our conscious performance*. We produce *concepts* of meaning, objectivity, knowledge, truth, reality, and value by reflecting upon our conscious performance. In virtue of the notions *already at work* in our conscious performance, we produce concepts of the basic notions and give these basic notions names.

Before we explore our conscious performance and become familiar with it, we don't have clear ideas or concepts but just *notions* of meaning, objectivity, knowledge, truth, reality, and value. Our mere *consciousness in* our performance is not yet a grasp of the *meaning* of our conscious performance, not yet the achievement of *objective knowledge* of what's *true* about our conscious performance, not yet the determination on the basis of that knowledge of the *value* of our conscious performance.

Our grasp and achievement and determination of the meaning and value of our conscious performance emerge only after we've made our own conscious performance the object or topic of our own conscious performance. It arises only after our basic notions have informed and guided our own exploration of the basic commitment imbedded in our conscious performance. But, before we undertake and carry out this deliberate exploration of ourselves, we are already *conscious in* our performance. We are *aware in* the spontaneous, unreflective, unexplored unfolding of the basic notions that constitute and guide our conscious performance. That *awareness in* our conscious performance is already a *notion* of where we're headed, of what we're aiming for, of what would satisfy us. But, as *merely conscious* in our performance, we haven't yet turned our conscious performance on itself to produce ideas and concepts of our basic commitment as conscious performers.

Our conscious performance is constituted and guided by a desire for meaning, objectivity, knowledge, truth, reality, and value. But I don't have to think about this feeling of myself in my conscious performance and come to realize that meaning, objectivity, knowledge, truth, reality, and value are what I want. To be a conscious performer is already to be aware in my pursuit of what I'm after. It is to be orientated already toward meaning, objectivity, knowledge, truth, reality, and value. As a conscious per-former I already have *notions* – not ideas or concepts – of what will ultimately satisfy me. As conscious performers we already have *notions* of where the flow of consciousness is heading. But, even though I have those notions, I still can't say precisely what I will find meaningful, true, real, and valuable. The basic notions are more than mere feelings that something is missing and less than precise knowledge of what is missing.

Sometimes, when we experience a desire, we have a clear idea of what would satisfy it. I would like a new car, and I know exactly which car I want. I have much more than a notion of what I desire; I already *know* what I desire. Sometimes we don't know what would satisfy the desire we feel. I may feel that something's missing in my life, but I don't know what it is. When I think about this feeling, I may come to realize that I'm lonely. Or, I may feel discomfort and come to realize that I'm hungry. Now I have a clear idea of what I'm after. But, before I ask about the lack I feel and identify it as loneliness or hunger, I have neither a clear idea nor a notion of what I am desiring.

The desire that motivates our conscious performance is not like the desire for companionship or nourishment or the desire for a new car. We don't have to figure out that what we're interested in is meaning, objectivity, knowledge, truth, reality, and value. We're already *aware* of this *in* our conscious performance. But that "already being aware in our conscious performance" is not a clear idea or precise concept of what will satisfy the desire that motivates our conscious performance. It's not a clear or vague idea of what will fulfill our basic desire for meaning, objectivity, knowledge, truth, reality, and value. But it is a *notion* of the fulfillment of that desire, an orientation toward the fulfillment of that desire, *in the very experience of that desire.* In contrast, before we realize we're hungry or lonely, we don't find ourselves already pursuing food or companionship but only experiencing an absence. These desires, as mere desires, are not already notions of what will fulfill them. But in the basic desire that motivates our conscious performance, in our basic commitment, there is already a notion of its fulfillment.

The Operative Meaning of the Basic Notions. The basic notions are constitutive of and operative in our conscious performance. We may produce ideas and concepts of them, but no idea or concept we produce of the notions by our conscious performance, which is itself informed and guided by the basic notions, is the *operative meaning* of those basic notions. No meaningful idea can capture the very meaning of meaning. Again, we may try to assign a specific meaning to reality, but until we know all of reality we will not know what reality really means. The same sort of problem arises when we attempt to assign specific meanings to any of the basic notions. Their operative meanings *always exceed* the specific meanings we assign them. When I seek and then assign a specific meaning to 'meaning', for example, I take for granted in my seeking and assigning the meaning of meaning *already operative* in my seeking and assigning. The fundamental meaning of the basic notions resides in their *constitutive and guiding role in our conscious performance.* Our best clue to the ultimate meaning of the basic notions resides in our conscious performance itself where the basic notions are *already operative.*

So, it is best to speak of these anticipations that constitute and guide our conscious performance as 'notions' in order to avoid confusing them with the ideas or concepts we produce by our conscious performance under their guidance. It is best to say we have *notions* of meaning, objectivity, knowledge, truth, reality, and value, just as we sometimes say we have a notion of where we're heading in life or of an "ultimate purpose" to life, but as yet have no clear idea or precise concept of where we'll end up or what that "ultimate purpose" is. It's important to keep in mind that we don't have to discover or figure out what would satisfy the anticipations that inform and guide our conscious performance. To have those anticipations is to already have the basic notions of what will fulfill us. We already *possess* these notions, and we give expression to them with the words 'meaning', 'objectivity', 'knowledge,' 'truth', 'reality', and 'value'. It is, perhaps, more accurate to say that we are *already possessed by them*, and that's why our reliance upon them is inescapable and our appeal to them is inevitable.

Just how elemental or basic these notions are may be illustrated by attending more closely to what happens when we attempt to give precise and thorough accounts of them. This effort involves us inevitably in a peculiar circularity. For, we are trying to determine precisely *the meaning of meaning*. We are trying to define *objectivity objectively*. We are seeking *objective knowledge of objective knowledge*. We are seeking *the truth about truth*. We are trying to determine *the reality of the real*. We are taking it for granted that it's *worthwhile* to pursue the truth about meaning, objectivity, knowledge, truth, reality, and *value*. The very pursuit of a precise, conceptual understanding of the basic notions obviously requires conscious performance. Conscious performance is constituted by the notions we're attempting to define, permeated by them, already informed by them, and guided by them. The conscious performance of attempting to give precise, conceptual meanings to the notions is itself just another instance of the notions *already at work.*

Performative Self-Contradiction. The fundamental role played by these basic notions is illustrated as well by what happens to us when we try to deny their role. Why is it that, even when we deny the possibility of reaching *objective truth*, we can't avoid affirming the *objectivity* and *truth* of our denial? Why, even when we reject the idea that there are *true values*, do we inevitably affirm the *true value* of our rejection? Why, even when we reject the possibility of *knowledge*, do we claim *knowledge* of this impossibility? More generally, why is it that whenever we undertake, by whatever means we regard as appropriate, to deny the basic informing and guiding role of the notions of meaning, objectivity, knowledge, truth, reality, and value, we find ourselves embarrassed by the requirement to affirm their constitutive and orientating role in our performance of denying it?

This peculiar and troubling *contradiction between what we say and what we're doing when we say it* afflicts every attempt to deny or reject our inevitable appeal to these basic notions and our inescapable reliance upon them.

Let us call this especially self-revealing type of contradiction *performative self-contradiction*. The contradiction in performative self-contradiction is between what I'm saying and my performance in saying it. Performative self-contradictions are the most telling evidence of the futility of any attempt to deny the role and significance of the basic notions in our living. Whatever we say about the basic notions of meaning, objectivity, knowledge, truth, reality, and value, our performance when we say it always stands in a fundamental relation to them, as informed and guided by them. Whenever we attempt to deny or to reject the fundamental role played by the notions, we involve ourselves in performative self-contradiction.

It's fruitless to attempt to define clearly and precisely the meanings of the basic notions. Their meanings cannot be completely contained by any ideas we might form of them or by any concepts we might have of them. They elude every attempt we make to pin them down once and for all, because they underpin and penetrate every attempt to pin them down and penetrate their meaning. It's also futile to deny that the basic notions inform and guide our conscious performance. They are our very anticipations of meaning, objectivity, knowledge, truth, reality, and value. Every attempt to deny or reject their fundamental meaning and significance to us appeals to them and relies upon them for its meaning and significance, and we find ourselves involved in performative self-contradiction.

Normally, when someone catches us in performative self-contradiction, we are embarrassed, non-plussed, and might become anxiously self-conscious. By our involvement in performative self-contradiction we reveal our inattentiveness to our own conscious performance, our ignorance of ourselves in our basic commitment, and our lack of self-possession. But it can happen that we aren't embarrassed when someone points out to us that we're involved in performative self-contradiction. In that case, we're taking *what we're saying* much more seriously than *what we're doing when we're saying it*, and we're taking the products of our conscious performance much more seriously than we're taking our conscious performance in producing those products; our priorities are strangely skewed. If I identify myself with *the products of my conscious performance* – with my present ideas, my present beliefs, my present values – rather than with *my performance as productive and often corrective of my ideas and beliefs and values,* then the only contradictions by which I will be embarrassed are those between the products of my performance – between the ideas, beliefs, and values I have at present or between my beliefs or values and the actions I perform. I may be embarrassed by a lack of consistency and coherence among "my present views and opinions," and I may be still more deeply embarrassed by my hypocrisy. Both forms of inconsistency suggest a certain lack of integrity. But the consistency of my beliefs and values with one another, and the consistency of my beliefs and values with my actions, pertain only the *minor integrity* of consistency of the products of my performance with one another. The integrity of consistency guarantees only that I am either consistently wrong or consistently right. It doesn't guarantee that what I'm saying, however consistent it might be, is in harmony with what I'm doing while I'm saying it. Performative self-contradiction is embarrassing only to those who take themselves seriously as conscious performers, only to those who do not take the products of their performance more seriously than their performance of producing them, only to those who do not rely for their sense of integrity upon their present views and opinions but, rather, identify themselves with their productive performance. Sometimes the ideas, beliefs, and values we produce turn out to be unimportant. But our conscious performance in producing them and in determining their importance is never a trivial matter. To lapse into performative self-contradiction is to display the absence of the *major integrity* without which the minor integrity of consistency means little.

Exploring the Basic Notions at Work. Even though we cannot hope to define clearly and precisely the basic notions, we can achieve some understanding of the fundamental role they play in our conscious performance. The attempt to provide clear and precise definitions of these basic notions by which we are orientated in our living is an inevitably circular procedure. The basic notions upon which we rely and to which we appeal in order to find direction in our lives cannot be defined. Every attempt to define them is to underestimate the informing and guiding role they play in our conscious lives. But we may still achieve a clearer and more precise understanding of ourselves *as basically committed* to meaning, objectivity, knowledge, truth, reality, and value *by catching these notions in the act* of informing and guiding our conscious performance and by giving an account of these basic notions *at work.* Even though we cannot define the basic notions, we still may be able to achieve objective knowledge of ourselves as informed and guided by the basic notions by undertaking a self-attentive exploration of our inevitable appeal to the basic notions and of our inescapable reliance upon them.

There is much to be gained by undertaking such an exploration. If we do come to know our own conscious performance as informed and guided by the basic notions, we will have acquired an intimate knowledge of ourselves that is of the greatest strategic importance for the conduct of our lives. What, as conscious performers, are we doing? How and where in our conscious performance does the constitutive and guiding role played by the basic notions come to light? What is the *operative meaning* of these basic notions? By asking and answering these questions with close attention to our own conscious performance, we may come to know ourselves better as conscious performers. This knowledge of ourselves as conscious performers, like other knowledge, would be empowering. It would enable us to transform our *spontaneous and unreflective commitment* to the ideals expressed by the basic notions into a *deliberate and reflective commitment*. It would enable us to *take possession of ourselves* as committed to meaning, objectivity, knowledge, truth, reality, and value and *to be at home with ourselves* in that commitment. Clearly, mere awareness in our conscious performance – a merely spontaneous and unreflective commitment – is not sufficient to solve the problem of finding direction in the flow of life; for, we have been conscious all along, and we remain disorientated and confused. The identification of ourselves with the products of our conscious performance – with our present views and opinions and values and actions – will not solve the problem; for these are only as good as the performance that produced them.

A BASIC COMMITMENT?

When I make a commitment I usually know I'm making it. Otherwise, why would I call it a 'commitment'? You seem to be saying that I'm committed to the pursuit of meaning, objectivity, knowledge, truth, reality, and value *before* I've actually committed myself to pursuing them, and that seems a little strange. When I say that I'm committed to saving the environment, or that I'm committed to my best friend, I know I've made these commitments, and I can remember making them. But this basic commitment you're talking about seems to be one I may never have even thought about and don't remember ever making. Does it make sense to talk about having a commitment you don't even know you have and didn't ever make? Oh, wait a minute! Here I am trying to figure out why you're calling my interest in meaning, objectivity, knowledge, truth, reality, and value a basic commitment! So, in my trying to figure out why you're calling it a basic commitment I am actually illustrating the commitment you're talking about? I think I'm starting to get this now. It *is* strange. I guess I *am committed* in a way to making sense of things. I hadn't actually thought about it before! And this commitment *isn't* a result of some major decision I made at some point in my past! I think I see now why you call it a *commitment*, and why you say it's *basic*. Even though I'd say that my commitment to saving the environment and my commitment to my best friend are pretty basic in my life, I can see that they're not quite as basic as my commitment to meaning and value. I don't think I would have made those commitments if I weren't committed in the way you're talking about. Oh, I just thought of something else! I took it for granted that I make commitments, didn't I? I guess I'm committed to value, too! This is so obvious, and I didn't even notice it before. Is this what you mean by "the notions already at work"?

Chapter Two

BEGINNING TO EXPLORE CONSCIOUS PERFORMANCE

1. SOME CLUES FROM DAVID HUME

In the long quotation below, the eighteenth-century Scottish philosopher David Hume makes a number of important observations about the difficulties associated with the exploration of our conscious performance. He also illustrates, but not deliberately, how tenacious these difficulties are and how difficult it is to master them. Before we begin to explore our conscious performance and the role played in it by our basic notions of meaning, objectivity, knowledge, truth, reality, and value, let's consider carefully what Hume has to say about the type of project we're undertaking.

> It is remarkable concerning the operations of the mind, that, though most intimately present to us, yet, whenever they become the object of reflection, they seem involved in obscurity; nor can the eye readily find those lines and boundaries, which discriminate and distinguish them. The objects are too fine to remain long in the same aspect or situation; and must be apprehended in an instant, by a superior penetration, derived from nature, and improved by habit and reflection. It becomes, therefore, no inconsiderable part of science barely to know the different operations of the mind, to separate them from each other, to

class them under their proper heads, and to
correct all that seeming disorder, in which they lie
involved, when made the object of reflection and
enquiry. This task of ordering and distinguishing,
which has no merit, when performed with regard
to external bodies, the objects of our senses, rises in
its value, when directed towards the operations of
the mind, in proportion to the difficulty and labour,
which we meet with in performing it. And if we
can go no farther than this mental geography, or
delineation of the distinct parts and powers of the
mind, it is at least a satisfaction to go so far; and
the more obvious this science may appear (and it is
by no means obvious) the more contemptible still
must the ignorance of it be esteemed, in all
pretenders to learning and philosophy. (*Enquiry*, §
1)

2. OUR INTIMATE PRESENCE TO OURSELVES

Hume is talking about the operations of the mind or what I've
been calling conscious performance. He takes it for granted that
our operations are present to us. We're present to ourselves in our
performance. This presence to ourselves in our operations is not
sensible experience, but Hume doesn't seem to be discouraged by
this fact. However, he does refer to our experience of our own
operations as an *intimate presence*. He probably adds this interesting
qualification because our presence to ourselves is so different from
the presence of objects to us in our sensible experience.

ME, CROWS, AND BILLIARD BALLS

The crow I see perched on the wire behind my yard is
present to me, but its sensible presence to me is quite
different from the intimate presence I have to myself while
I'm looking at it. I wonder if the crow is intimately present
to itself? Does it have an intimate, non-sensible experience
of itself similar to mine as it scans my garden? Is it aware
of itself as it sits up there on the wire? If its sensible
experience is anything like mine, I think it probably is
intimately present to itself as it turns its head first this way

and then that way and then this way again. I don't think my sensible experience would be any kind of experience at all if I weren't intimately self-present in my sensing. Could I describe myself as seeing something if I weren't also aware in my seeing? If I weren't intimately present to myself, I don't think *anything* would be present to me. I wonder if the crow senses things without any experience of itself sensing things? I wonder if the crow lacks self-presence. I don't know for sure; I'm not a crow. But it doesn't seem likely. I can only imagine what it might be like to be sensing like a crow. But at least I can imagine it. I can't even imagine what it might be like to be a billiard ball. I'm pretty sure that a billiard ball isn't present to itself. I'm just as sure that nothing at all is present to a billiard ball. So, there's no experience of being a billiard ball to be imagined. I can imagine what it's like to be a sensing human being. But I don't have to imagine that, because I am one. I'm present to myself as a sensing human being, and I'm present to myself when I'm wondering if crows and billiard balls are present to themselves.

I think Hume is right to assume that we are intimately present to ourselves in our operations. I am intimately present to myself in my sensitive operations. I'm intimately present to myself in the other operations I perform as well. I've been intimately present to myself in my performance of all the operations that went into writing the paragraph above, just as you've been intimately present to yourself in all the operations that have gone into reading it and trying to understand it. If you weren't intimately present to yourself in your performance of reading the paragraph, you wouldn't be able to say that you understood it completely, or only partially, or not at all.

Hume says that when he *reflects* upon the operations of his own mind they seem to him to be involved in obscurity. But he takes it for granted that he can reflect upon them. After all, they are intimately present to him. Hume is present to himself in his performance, just as we are present to ourselves in our performance. We're able to reflect upon our non-sensible operations, just as we're able to reflect upon the objects of our sensible experience.

Hume is also intimately present to himself while he's reflecting on his non-sensible operations. His self-presence in his reflecting enables him to reflect on his performance of reflecting on his performance. He says a few things about this *reflective conscious performance*, this reflection upon our operations. Let's give some attention to what Hume has to say about reflection on conscious performance or what I'll name *Conscious Performance Analysis [CPA]*.

3. CONSCIOUS PERFORMANCE ANALYSIS [CPA]

When we reflect upon our conscious operations, we're going beyond our intimate presence to ourselves in our performance. We aren't resting content with the mere experience of ourselves operating with regard to sensible objects. We're overcoming our common preoccupation with sensible objects. When we reflect on our operations, says Hume, (a) we attempt to "know the different operations of the mind." By this, I think Hume means that we should try to *identify and name the different operations* in which we're present to ourselves. When we reflect on our operations (b) we attempt to "separate them from each other." By this, Hume probably means that we should try to *identify the differences of the operations from one another*. Further, (c) we attempt to "class them under their proper heads." Hume is saying that we should try to *organize the operations into groups* once we have discovered their similarities and differences.

Hume stresses the difficulty of conscious performance analysis. His operations seem to him to be involved in obscurity and disorder. He seems a little puzzled by this. Our conscious operations are intimately present to us. Even so, when we turn our attention to them they seem involved in obscurity and disorder. We should note that Hume says that the operations *seem* involved in obscurity and *seem* to lack order. He doesn't say they *are* obscure and *are* lacking order. Hume attributes this seeming obscurity and disorder to the type of object a conscious operation is.

3.1 OPERATIONS ARE NON-SENSIBLE OBJECTS

Hume remarks that "the lines and boundaries" between the different operations cannot be found by "the eye." The experience of our own operations is non-sensible experience. In our sensible experience we can isolate and identify objects and events fairly easily, even when we haven't yet come to understand what they are or what it is that is happening. We may not know the nature of a sensible object, we may not know what its meaning is, we may not even know what to call it. But it can at least be located, isolated from other things, and identified as something to be inquired about. The same is true of sensible events. But the isolation and identification of non-sensible, conscious operations, in comparison, is more difficult.

It isn't that difficult to isolate the operation of *seeing* in the flow of our conscious performance and to identify it, but that may be due to the close connection of seeing to the sensible objects we see. All I have to do is close my eyes and open them again to notice my seeing. I can stop seeing and start seeing at will. It is somewhat more difficult to identify the operation of *questioning* and the operation of *understanding* in our conscious performance and to isolate them both from seeing and from one another. I can decide to ask a question that has arisen for me, but I can't decide to have it arise. I can decide to formulate a discovery, but I can't discover just by deciding to do so.

When I wonder about my sensible experience and begin to ask questions about it, I'm no longer just seeing a sensible object. I'm also asking questions about it. I'm seeing and questioning at the same time. I'm questioning *while* I'm seeing. I'm not just seeing, I'm *observing*. The seeing involved in my observing is more obvious to me than the questioning involved in my observing, just as the object I see is more obvious to me than my seeing. If, suddenly, I come to understand the sensible object I've been observing, I'm coming to understand what I'm seeing. I'm understanding and seeing at the same time; I'm seeing what I'm also coming to understand; I'm seeing *while* I'm understanding. Now I'm no longer observing the sensible object. I've stopped questioning while I'm seeing. Now I'm understanding *while* I'm seeing. But my seeing while I'm coming to understand is still more obvious to me than my understanding. It's not that I don't experience my understanding at all. I stop questioning precisely because I experience my understanding. I'm present to myself when I'm coming to understand, and understanding, unlike seeing, is typically accompanied by a release of tension that's very satisfying and hard to miss. But normally I'm attending to the sensible object or to the idea I've gotten about it. When I come to understand, I'm still inclined to say "Aha, now I see it!" instead of "Aha, now I *understand* it! I've answered the question I was asking!"

The tendency to speak of all our conscious operations as 'seeing' or as similar to 'seeing' is ubiquitous. We use the word 'seeing' indiscriminately to speak of very different operations we're performing *while* we're seeing. We do the same with 'hearing', 'smelling', and even 'tasting'. Sometimes we say "I hear you" when it would be more accurate to say "I understand what you mean." We say "I don't like the sound of that" when it would be more precise to say "I disagree." We say "That leaves a bad taste in my mouth" when it would be more accurate to say "I doubt the value of that." Because our operations cannot be found by "the eye" or by any of our other senses, they *seem* involved in obscurity. It's difficult to find "the lines and boundaries, which discriminate and distinguish them." The farther removed our conscious operations are from the operations of sensing, the more involved in obscurity they may seem.

Conscious operations are *non-sensible*. We can't pick out, isolate, and identify them with ease the way we can pick out, isolate, and identify objects of our senses. They have no locations, no places, no positions. They're not close to me or next to me or far away from me. They aren't above me or below me. They aren't next to or far away from other things. They don't come from over there or over here, from above or from below. They don't move toward me or away from me. They aren't big or small, thick or thin, tall or short. They have no size. They have no shape. They have no weight. They have no color, smell, taste, sound, or texture. They aren't inside me or outside me, internal or external. They don't span or bridge distances between me and objects. They don't close gaps. They don't reach across anything. They don't fill anything up. They don't take up any space. They're nowhere at all.

We have a habit of speaking about conscious operations as though they were *spatial objects*. We have a spontaneous interest in spatial objects, and we are certainly more familiar with them. When we begin to reflect upon our conscious operations we bring with us a spontaneous expectation that we're going to encounter something like spatial objects. This is a mistaken expectation. When we shift our attention to conscious operations and begin to reflect upon them with this expectation, they seem involved in obscurity and disordered. In our initial efforts to achieve clarity about our conscious performance we typically use language more appropriate for talking about sensible objects. We also tend to use the names for those operations most closely related to objects of sense, like 'seeing' and 'hearing' and 'tasting', when we mean to talk about operations that are very different from seeing, hearing, and tasting, such as questioning, understanding, and evaluating.

We spontaneously import into the language we use to talk about our conscious operations the language we use to talk about spatial objects. It is a deeply ingrained habit. It may not be entirely avoidable. It is common-place even among some contemporary philosophers, for example, to speak of concepts as 'thick' or 'thin', like a slab of meat, or 'robust', like a cup of coffee, and of the analysis of concepts as "taking concepts apart" or "breaking them down," as if they were physical structures, or 'dissecting them," as if they were physical organisms. In ordinary conversation we might speak of an idea or thought as 'heavy', like a lump of lead, or 'deep', like the ocean, and we may call an odd or unexpected or ill-formed idea 'spacy' and ask "Where did that come from?" or "Where are you going with that?"

In some cases, it doesn't matter if we import this spatial language into CPA, as long as we know that all of our conscious operations and many of their objects are actually non-sensible and that our depictions of them as 'inside' or 'outside', 'thick' or 'thin', 'heavy' or 'light' are actually inaccurate and misleading. If we don't know this, our use of spatial language can obstruct and undermine our efforts to understand ourselves clearly as conscious performers. It can obscure rather than clarify "the lines and boundaries" that separate conscious operations from one another by misrepresenting these relations as similar to spatial relations. It could even lead us to conclude, before our reflection has begun and despite our intimate presence to ourselves in our conscious performance, that there are no conscious operations at all. It seems like it's possible for us, because of the way we prefer to talk, to convince ourselves that CPA is too difficult a task or even an impossible one.

Hume emphasizes the difficulty the non-sensible character of conscious operations poses for us when we begin CPA. The objects of reflection on conscious performance, he says, are "too fine to remain long in the same aspect or situation, and must be apprehended in an instant, by a superior penetration . . .." Hume's use of the word 'fine' to describe the operations of our minds is intriguing. We may think he's using 'fine' the way we use the word when we distinguish a 'fine' line from a 'thick' one. We have reason to think he's using the word in this sense, because in the same quotation he uses the phrase "lines and boundaries." Obviously, even Hume is not immune to using spatial language to speak about non-sensible things or to speaking of conscious operations as different from spatial objects because they're 'internal' rather than 'external'. His use of 'fine' here probably is a little 'spacy'. But, if Hume were using 'fine' only in the sense of 'thin', he would be ignoring his own point that the operations are non-sensible. We might describe someone as "extremely narrow-minded," but we don't really mean her mind is way too skinny. We mean she doesn't ask very many questions. We might describe people as "closed-minded," but we don't mean their minds have doors that can be opened and shut. We mean they don't ask the relevant questions; we mean they aren't performing objectively. Hume may describe the operations as 'fine', but he doesn't really mean that it is difficult to isolate, identify, and distinguish them because they're so thin and, therefore, very hard to see.

In the 18th Century when Hume was writing, 'fine' also meant "of delicate or subtle composition," "unalloyed or pure," and 'superior'. The operations of the mind are of subtle composition. They are pure and unalloyed with sensible matter. They are not like sensible objects because they aren't composed of material parts that take up space. They are of delicate composition. 'Delicate' can mean "of a highly personal nature" and "requiring careful handling." The composition of the operations of the mind does not involve matter. But it does involve matters of a highly personal nature. The operations of the mind cannot be found by "the eye." They are intimately present to us and require special handling. Further, they are superior to sensible objects. If it weren't for the intimately present operations of the mind, we wouldn't be able to make sense of sensible objects or of anything else. If we weren't present to ourselves in our performance, *nothing at all* would be present to us. Our relationships to sensible objects depend upon our non-sensible conscious performance.

3.2 OPERATIONS ARE PURELY TEMPORAL OBJECTS

The operations of the mind are *purely temporal* objects. They are non-sensible events. If we like, we may call them 'spiritual' events to distinguish them from material things. But we shouldn't think of spiritual events, as the earliest philosophers did, as ethereal, airy events in space. Unlike the billiard ball, they don't just sit in one place until pushed by the cue. Unlike the crow, they don't move themselves from one place to another. Like sensible events, conscious operations happen. But, unlike sensible events, they don't happen in a particular place like the roll of the billiard ball across the surface of the pool table and into the pocket or the alighting of the crow on the electrical wire behind my garden.

We may say that conscious events occur "*in* our heads" or "*in* our brains." We may say "I always like returning to this place, because it's *where* I had the breakthrough that completely changed my understanding of myself." But we'd be speaking imprecisely. Even if I submitted my brain to an exhaustive investigation by a team of neuroscientists, even if I explored every nook and cranny of that place where I had my life-changing breakthrough, no conscious operations would be found. We can find them only if we attend to what is intimately present to us in our performance of such fruitless hunts in space for events that occur only in time. To find conscious operations, neuroscientists must attend, not to the brain they study, but to what they're doing when they're studying the brain, and I must attend, not to the place where I had my breakthrough, but to what I'm doing when I return to and explore that place.

When we reflect upon the operations of the mind they seem involved in obscurity and disorder, because they're purely temporal events. Notice the temporal language Hume employs. Conscious operations don't "remain long," says Hume, "in the same situation or aspect, and must be apprehended in an instant."

One moment I may be *wondering* what a non-sensible object is. In the next instant I may be *imagining* a black crow perched on a swaying wire or a red billiard ball inert on green felt. In the next instant I may be *remembering* being in the place where I had the breakthrough that changed my life. In the next instant, I may be *imagining* white-coated neuroscientists probing my brain. In the next instant I may be *wondering* if my breakthrough was really as big a breakthrough as I thought it was at the time. In the next instant I may be *wondering* if non-sensible, conscious events can really be said to exist if they don't have material parts. In the next instant I may be *concluding* that they must exist if I am *really wondering* if they do. In the next instant I may *decide* to have the stir-fry for lunch. In the next instant I may *remember* that I had the stir-fry yesterday and *imagine* what it tasted like. I may be performing all of these operations *while* I'm *seeing* and *understanding* the words on this page, *hearing* the sound of traffic on the street outside, *feeling* the uncomfortable pressure of the hard chair I'm sitting in. The operations of the mind don't "remain long" in the same situation or aspect. They must be apprehended "in an instant."

Our conscious operations are non-sensible, but they do occur. We can't *deny* that we perform them without lapsing into performative self-contradiction, because that denial is itself a conscious operation. But we don't have to lapse into performative self-contradiction to be present to ourselves in our conscious performance. Because we're present to ourselves in our conscious performance we can reflect upon it, although the reflection is difficult. When we begin the exploration it seems to us that the operations of our minds are involved in obscurity and disorder. The difficulty of reflection upon our conscious operations is due to the fact that they are merely temporal events, they can occur in rapid *succession*, and some of them, as we've already noticed, can occur *simultaneously*. As a result, it is much more difficult to isolate, identify, and distinguish conscious operations than it is to isolate, identify, and distinguish sensible objects. It is difficult to find the "lines and boundaries" by which we might distinguish them and to determine the relationships among them.

To make the operations of our minds "the object of reflection and enquiry," Hume says, requires "a superior penetration." The penetration required is superior, not only because it is an apprehension of non-sensible objects, but also because it itself is not an operation of the senses. This superior penetration is possible, says Hume, because it is "derived from nature." By this he means that, because we are the kinds of things who are intimately present to ourselves in our operations, we are able to explore ourselves as conscious performers. The seeming obscurity of the objects when we begin to reflect upon our own operations can be met and overcome partially by recognizing the differences between sensible objects and merely temporal events and by adjusting our expectations accordingly. Furthermore, says Hume, the superior penetration, the reflective inquiry that is required in the exploration of our operations, can be "improved by habit and reflection." The more we reflect upon and inquire about our operations, the better we become at doing it. The more we do CPA, the better we get at doing it.

3.3 TWO UNMENTIONED SOURCES OF OBSCURITY

There are two other sources of the *seeming* obscurity and disorder of our conscious operations that Hume neglects to mention. The first is that conscious operations can only be experienced when they're performed. They aren't just sitting there like the stars in the sky, the crow on the wire, or the billiard ball on the felt awaiting our attention and inquiry. If we don't perform them, we won't have any experience of them at all. The second is that operations never occur without their contents. It is possible for us to be so distracted by the contents of our operations that we fail to notice the operations themselves.

i. WE HAVE EXPERIENCE OF OPERATIONS ONLY WHEN WE PERFORM THEM.

Suppose that I enjoy *describing* the things I see and that I do so frequently. In that case, I am frequently present to myself in my *describing*. By means of that superior penetration mentioned by Hume I am able to isolate and identify my conscious performance of describing. But suppose that I never try to *define* or *explain* the things I describe. Suppose I readily ask about the sensible qualities of things but never ask why those things have those qualities, never try to define things or to discover the relations in which those things with those qualities stand to one another. I may describe a sunset, for example, but I may never ask for the reasons for that colorful array. If I never try to *define* or *explain* anything, I'm never present to myself as *defining* or *explaining*. No matter how good I become at that superior penetration I shall never be able to isolate and identify my conscious performance of defining and explaining. The source of obscurity here, then, is not the non-sensible nature of these conscious operations. It's the fact that I don't perform them. If I never undertake to define or explain anything, I'll never be present to myself in my defining and explaining. I'll have no experience at all of these operations.

Hume remarks that the superior penetration required for the exploration of our conscious operations can be improved by habit and reflection. But no degree of improvement will pierce the obscurity that results when the operations don't even occur. We have to perform conscious operations in order to have anything at all to reflect upon. The more operations we perform, the more operations we have to reflect upon. The fewer we perform, the fewer we have to reflect upon.

Earlier, we noted that the farther removed our operations are from the operations of sensing and the less directly they pertain to sensible objects, the more obscure they may seem. Now, we can add that the farther removed our operations are from the operations of sensing, the less frequent our performance of them tends to be. There's no conscious performance more obscure to us than what we never or only rarely do.

ii. OPERATIONS NEVER OCCUR WITHOUT THEIR CONTENTS.

Conscious performance is never just the performance. It is performance about, with regard to, pertaining to *something*. I never just see; I see something. I never just inquire; I inquire about something. I never just imagine; I imagine something. I never just understand; I understand something. I never just decide; I decide to do something. My conscious performance is always *a conscious relationship to objects*. Conscious operations never occur without their contents. We're not just present to ourselves in our operations. To be present to ourselves in our operations is always also to be present to ourselves in our relationships to objects. My intimate presence to myself in my performance is simultaneously the presence to me of the objects of my performance. When I'm present to myself, I'm present to myself performing operations about or with regard to or with reference to *something*.

The 'something' to which I am related in my operations can be anything at all. It could be a sensible object, or an image of a sensible object, or a memory of a sensible object. It could be a non-sensible object, like a conscious operation, or an idea about a non-sensible or sensible object, or a memory of a non-sensible object. It could be some aspect of a sensible or non-sensible object. It could be a real or imaginary object. It could be a dynamic image of a course of action I haven't yet undertaken. It could be anything at all that any of my conscious operations can pertain to, refer to, or be about.

In CPA, when we begin to reflect upon our conscious operations, we're *redirecting our attention* from the contents of our operations to the operations themselves. We're shifting our attention from what we are related to by our operations to the operations. The operations *by which* we are related to objects now become the objects *to which* we are related by our conscious performance. Our conscious performance that always relates us to 'something' becomes the 'something' to which we are related by CPA. The memory of the objects to which we *were* related by the operations upon which we are *now* reflecting may distract us from the operations themselves.

SHIFTING MY ATTENTION FROM CONTENTS TO OPERATIONS

In the past I've wondered about the consciousness of crows and billiard balls and drawn some tentative conclusions. Now, having become interested in my own conscious performance, I want to redirect my attention to the *wondering* I was doing when I was wondering about crows. Because I was present to myself when I was wondering about crows, I can recall my experience of that conscious performance. In the memory I try to isolate the operation of asking questions from the questions I was asking about crows. I ask, "What am I doing when I'm *asking a question about crows?*" I answer, "I'm trying to understand *crows.*" But *asking questions* is not just trying to understand crows. My attempt to understand crows is *just one experience* of asking a question. What I'm interested in is what I'm doing when I'm *asking questions,* not just what I'm doing when I'm asking questions *about crows.* I haven't successfully redirected my attention to my wondering, because I haven't yet isolated my wondering from what I was wondering about. My shift of attention is incomplete. I've shifted my attention from crows to asking about crows. I've shifted my attention from the content of my conscious performance to my conscious performance *with* its content. I need to get rid of the crows. If I rephrase my question, perhaps I can complete the shift of attention required by CPA: "What am I doing when I'm *asking a question about anything at all?* What am I doing when I'm *wondering?"*

Earlier, we noticed that, spontaneously, we are more interested in and more at home with spatial objects than we are with non-sensible, purely temporal ones. Now we must notice, as we begin CPA, that we're more inclined to attend to the contents of the operations upon which we reflect than to the operations themselves. Even when, in CPA, an operation we've previously performed becomes the content of the reflective operations we're now performing, our interest in the content to which that previous operation related us tends to overwhelm any interest we might have in the operation itself.

THE TENSION OF CPA

The prospect of self-possession exerts a pull on me. I'd like to be at home with myself in my performance. I think I see the value in that. But my spontaneous interest in objects of my senses exerts a strong counter-pull. It's hard for me even to think of anything that isn't sensible as *meaningful or real.* It's a struggle for me to see how I could attend to myself in this way and still consider myself *objective.* Even if I agree to redirect my attention to my operations, the influence of the counter-pull persists. It seems I'm only willing to give serious attention to my operations if I can think of them as just more *objects of my operations* instead of as *my operating.* It's like I'm spontaneously at odds with myself. I think I see the point of attending to my operations. At the same time, I spontaneously *avoid doing it.* Even after I decide to do it, I seem still to *resist doing it.*

4. "MENTAL GEOGRAPHY": A MISLEADING ANALOGY

For the reasons given by Hume, and for other reasons as well, the operations of the mind, when we begin to reflect upon them, *seem* involved in obscurity and disorder. It is a significant achievement merely to distinguish the operations of our minds and to order them. Hume suggests that there is still more than this to be learned about our conscious performance, but he seems to think that the difficulties inherent in reflection on our operations may prevent us from going farther than this initial distinguishing and ordering. Still, says Hume, "It is at least a satisfaction to go so far." If we get this far, says Hume, we'll have at least a "mental geography" of the human mind.

Hume is envisioning his conscious performance the way a geographer envisions unexplored terrain. He is *imagining* conscious performance to be similar to the unmapped surface of the earth. It is not surprising that Hume would use this image. In his day geography was a fairly new and rising science. Bernhardus Varenius' *Geographia Generalis*, the pre-eminent geographical work of the time, was available in English translation when Hume was studying and writing, and it is very likely that Hume was familiar with it. In his book Varenius distinguished between absolute geography, relative geography, and comparative geography. Absolute geography investigates the mathematical facts about the earth as a whole. Relative geography investigates the effects of the sun and stars on the earth. Comparative geography is concerned with the surface of the earth, its divisions and their relative positions, the construction of globes and maps, and navigation.

When Hume describes reflection on our operations as mental geography, he is thinking of comparative geography. Comparative geography requires venturing into unexplored areas, describing the terrain or physical features, and drawing accurate maps for use in navigation.

Hume's depiction of reflection on our operations as mental geography may seem appropriate at first. Images are often helpful, especially when we're trying to communicate complicated ideas, and imagining seems always to assist us when we're trying to understand.[4] Hume's use of an image may even come as a relief after our brief struggles so far to isolate and identify conscious operations. Reflection upon conscious performance is like exploring new terrain, and we undertake the exploration for the sake ultimately of steering a course through life. But the assistance provided by the image is far outweighed by its perniciousness. The image is radically inadequate and dangerously misleading. It tends to reinforce, rather than to diminish, the influence of our spontaneous preference for sensible objects.

By employing this image without adding a warning about its radical inadequacy, Hume is reopening the door to earlier confusion and misunderstanding. He is obscuring once again what he has been laboring to clarify. He is letting us off the hook. If what he has already said about the operations of the mind is true, he shouldn't be doing that. If he's interested in promoting fruitful reflection on our operations, as he says he is, he shouldn't be letting us off the hook, no matter how difficult and contrary to our inclinations we find the task of isolating and distinguishing purely temporal objects.

Hume has provided a seemingly helpful image, and it is appropriate in some ways. Conscious performance is similar to unfamiliar, unexplored terrain. The conscious operations that make up our conscious performance can be compared to the physical features that distinguish unexplored terrain. Like the surface of the earth, conscious performance has many distinguishing features. Some of them we've already experienced. Others we won't experience until we involve ourselves in further performance. Some of the features of the surface of the earth we've

---

[4] As the philosopher John Locke observed, "Men, to give names which might make known to others any operations they felt in themselves, or any other idea which came not under their senses, were fain [i.e., obliged] to borrow words from ordinary known ideas of sensation, by that means to make others the more easily to conceive those operations which they experimented in themselves, which make no outward sensible appearances." Quoted in *The Works of Thomas Gray: Notes on Aristophanes and Plato*, ed. Edmund Gosse [London: Macmillan, and Co., 1884], p.217 *n.*1.

already experienced in our travels. Some we won't experience unless we do more traveling. In these ways, describing conscious performance is like describing the features of the surface of the earth, and distinguishing and ordering the operations of the mind is like mapping the surface of the earth. As comparative geography is concerned with the surface of the earth, its divisions, and the relations between the divisions, reflection on the operations of the mind is concerned with "the lines and boundaries, which discriminate and distinguish" operations and with "delineating the parts and powers of the mind."

Hume's image, though, is a dangerously misleading one. Hume has reverted to the use of spatial language to characterize reflection on the merely temporal operations of the mind. Despite his own astute observation that the seeming obscurity and disorder of our conscious performance when we begin to reflect upon our operations is due to our inappropriate expectation that purely temporal objects will be like spatial objects, he reinforces that mistaken expectation by depicting reflection on our operations as comparative mental geography. Hume's own points, that the operations of the mind are purely temporal objects and that this can cause us major difficulties when we try to reflect upon our operations, don't seem to have "sunk in," as we say in similarly spatial language.

We may not have explored our conscious performance yet, but it isn't actually unfamiliar terrain. It's all the conscious operations with which we're already intimately familiar, and all the operations with which we will be intimately familiar when we eventually perform them. It's all those operations as already intimately present to us before we have isolated, identified, distinguished, described, and ordered them. We don't need to *travel* anywhere to find our conscious operations. We're always *already on the scene* when we perform them.

Conscious operations are not physical features to be located and distinguished in a landscape. They're non-sensible events to be isolated, identified, distinguished, and ordered in the temporal flow of our conscious performance. We don't have to travel in order to find them. We simply have to perform them in order to find them. Describing, distinguishing, and ordering the operations of the mind is not drawing a map that shows their relative locations and the paths we must follow to get from one to another. There are no paths from one operation to another. There is just one operation after another or one operation at the same time as another. The operations themselves are the paths. There are directions in conscious performance, but they aren't toward the north or the south, the east or the west, the higher or the lower elevation. They are toward meaning or nonsense, objectivity or bias, increased knowledge or persisting ignorance, truth or falsehood, reality or illusion, the worthwhile or the worthless.

Hume's use of the misleading image of doing comparative geography is puzzling. He's using it in an attempt to help us understand what's involved in reflection on the operations of the mind, but it's an ill-conceived effort. It invites us once again to think of conscious operations *as objects in space* and to attempt to order them the way geographers order physical features of a landscape. Hume knows that reflection on our operations is not exactly the same as comparative geography. That's why he calls it *mental* geography. It differs from comparative geography, because it has to do with conscious operations, not with physical features. But he seems to think it's the same as comparative geography in other respects.

Hume is drawing an analogy between comparative geography and reflection on the operations of the mind. When we say that one thing is analogous to another, we're saying that the two things are similar in some ways and different in others. We aren't saying that the two things are the same in every respect. But the difference, for Hume, between comparative geography and reflection on our operations is not that one is geography and the other is not. In Hume's view, the two are similar, because *both* are geography. They differ only in that one is geography of the earth and the other is geography of the mind. Hume is saying that reflection on our operations is *like* comparative geography because it is geography, but it is *unlike* comparative geography because it concerns mental features, boundaries, and divisions rather than physical ones.

Hume doesn't seem to have fully grasped just how radically different mental objects like conscious operations are from physical objects like rivers and mountains. If he had, he would have realized that reflection on our operations *is not like* comparative geography. He has drawn a bad analogy. If there is any similarity at all to be found between comparative geography and reflection on our operations, it can only be found by *imagining* our conscious operations to be like physical features of a landscape. But they aren't like that, as Hume himself has already observed. Strangely, he seems to have almost immediately forgotten his own insightful observation.

This anomaly can't be explained by mere forgetfulness. Hume's memory couldn't have been so poor that what he wrote at the start of a paragraph was forgotten by the time he got to the end of it. The more plausible explanation for Hume's use of a particularly bad analogy, and for his other occasional lapses into spatial language, is that serious reflection on conscious performance was, in his time, still a new endeavor and not yet firmly established. Hume's remarks about the great value of reflection on our conscious performance and on the consequences of ignorance of "this science," as he calls it, reveal his awareness that he is proposing something fairly new and relatively untried. It is not the pursuit of self-knowledge and self-possession that was new and untried. Philosophers since the time of Socrates and Plato have recognized the importance of self-knowledge in the conduct of our lives, and they have consistently pursued it. But they haven't pursued it in the direct and intimately personal way that Hume has in mind.

4.1 THE TRADITIONAL APPROACH TO SELF-KNOWLEDGE

With a few exceptions, the standard procedure before Hume was to approach basic knowledge of ourselves by starting with the kinds of objects with which we concern ourselves or with the contents of our operations. From the various kinds of objects, various kinds of acts were inferred. From the various kinds of acts inferred from the various kinds of objects, various powers or faculties of the mind were inferred. The standard procedure was to approach knowledge of ourselves by proceeding inferentially from objects to acts to potencies or powers or faculties. This inferential procedure is sometimes called the "metaphysical approach" to self-knowledge.

Sensible objects are present to us, so we must perform acts of sensing. If we perform acts of sensing, we must have a faculty of sensibility. Imaginary objects are present to us, so we must imagine. If we imagine, we must have a faculty of imagination. Ideas and truths are present to us, so we must understand and make rational judgments. If we understand and make rational judgments, we must have an intellect or rational faculty. We pursue good things and bad things, so we must deliberate, evaluate, and decide. If we deliberate, evaluate, and decide, we must have a faculty of will. Before Hume's time, we came to know ourselves in a basic way by inferring our operations from the objects present to us and by inferring our powers from the inferred operations.

The main problem with the standard approach is not that it leads to grossly inaccurate conclusions but that it is excessively abstract. It offers us only a minimally accurate, bare-bones account of ourselves as having certain powers, and that account is grounded in the objects we experience instead of being grounded more directly in our experience of the performance by which we relate ourselves to objects. It seems to provide a minimally accurate account of ourselves. We do sense things, understand things, grasp truths, make choices and decisions. It's true enough that we have the powers to perform these operations. The knowledge that I have these powers is a degree of self-knowledge. But knowledge of *myself as able to perform* conscious operations of certain types is not knowledge of the operations or of *myself in my actual performance of them*. This minimal account of ourselves is not reached by *attending to* our conscious performance, *isolating and distinguishing* the conscious operations, *ordering* them, and *describing* the informing and guiding role of the basic notions in our performance. It is reached by inferring operations from objects present to us, and by then inferring powers from the inferred operations, as though we are not present to ourselves as conscious performers at all. Notice the preference for sensible objects and for the contents of our operations that marks this approach.

The standard or traditional approach is not pure or groundless speculation, because it appeals to our experience of the objects that are present to us and with which we concern ourselves. It appeals to our experience of the contents of our operations. But it results in an excessively abstract account of ourselves. What we can infer about ourselves from the objects to which we are related in our operations is much less than we can learn about ourselves from reflection on our performance of the operations by which we are related to objects. The self-possession to be achieved on the basis of this abstract self-knowledge is equally abstract. For example, to be at home with myself as merely capable of being reasonable differs greatly from being at home with myself as actually performing reasonably. It is one thing to be at home with myself in my *powers or potentialities*, whether or not they are actualized or realized. It is quite another to be at home with myself in my *actualization or realization* of them.

SPEAKING ABSTRACTLY ABOUT MYSELF

I am a certain kind of thing among other things in the world. I have faculties or powers that are part of my nature. These faculties or powers distinguish me from other kinds of things. I am, for example, essentially a rational animal, and so is everyone else, or so I'm told.

SPEAKING MORE CONCRETELY ABOUT MYSELF

Sometimes I perform conscious operations informed and guided by the notions of meaning, objectivity, knowledge, truth, reality, and value fairly well. Usually I perform these operations spontaneously and not very well. My adequate or inadequate performance of them may be more or less spontaneous or deliberate. I may perform some conscious operations frequently or even excessively, and others rarely or not at all. Sometimes I don't perform operations I should perform, and sometimes I perform some operations when I should be performing others. Sometimes I can be described accurately as actually reasonable. Sometimes I'm more accurately described as careless in my conscious performance or biased. Whatever my powers or faculties might be, what I am *concretely* and what is *concretely possible* for me, are to be known only by reflecting on my actual conscious performance and describing the roles played in my performance by the basic notions.

4.2 A NEW APPROACH TO SELF-KNOWLEDGE

Hume is on the cusp of a major change in the way we attempt to come to know and take possession of ourselves. He has one foot in the traditional approach and one foot in the new one. Previously, we thought of ourselves as *substances or things among other substances or things*, as affected by objects and as affecting objects, as being caused by things to do this or that and as causing things to do this or that. We wondered what kind of substances or things we are and where we stand in relation to all the other substances or things around us. We approached knowledge of ourselves by inferring operations from the objects affecting and affected by us, and by then inferring powers to perform those operations from the inferred operations. We paid little attention to the fact that the operations are *conscious* operations and that we're *present to ourselves* in our performance of them. We could have taken notice of our concrete experience *in* our operations. But, in virtue of our approach, we attended only to the contents of our operations, and we made logical inferences instead.

In Hume's time we had just begun to think of ourselves as *subjects* who are intimately self-present in our operations, rather than as *substances* among other substances. We began to wonder what kind of subjects we are and how we stand in relation to all the objects of our operations and to other subjects. A new approach to knowledge of ourselves had begun to emerge. Instead of inferring what we are from our experiences of other things, we were beginning to approach self-knowledge by *describing ourselves as present to ourselves* in our conscious performance. The fact that our operations are conscious, that we're present to ourselves in our performance of them, had begun to receive closer attention. We began to take advantage of our concrete experience in our operations, instead of inferring what we are from the objects to which we're related by our conscious operations. We began to think of ourselves, not just as being caused to do this or that and not just as causes of this or that, but as thoughtfully and more or less deliberately *authoring* our lives. Hume is contributing to this transition and promoting it, but he hasn't yet completed it.

Hume promotes reflection on the operations of the mind that are intimately present to us. I've given this new approach to self-knowledge the name Conscious Performance Analysis. Hume wants to distinguish CPA with its interest in the *subject-as-subject* from the standard or traditional approach to self-knowledge with its interest in the *subject-as-object* that is just another substance or thing or object among substances or things or objects. He draws an analogy between this new approach to self-knowledge and comparative geography. He calls this new approach to the subject-as-subject "[comparative] mental geography," and he describes mental geography as the "delineation of the parts and powers of the mind." Hume's attempt to promote and to clear the way for CPA is almost immediately crippled by the analogy that characterizes reflection on operations as comparative geography, by his lapsing now and then into spatial language when he means to speak of purely temporal operations, and by his adoption from the abstract, metaphysical approach to self-knowledge of the language of "parts and powers of the mind" when he intends to speak of conscious operations and of the conscious performance in which we are concretely and intimately present to ourselves.

Hume may be excused for having an inadequate and partial grasp of the dangers associated with his geographical analogy and the use of spatial language in CPA. After all, even today the traditional approach is still widely practiced. His adoption of the language of "parts and powers" which was employed for centuries before him, while misleading, is understandable. But his lapses into spatial language and into the language of the traditional abstract approach threaten to corrupt CPA and to leave us, in the end, with less than adequate, merely abstract knowledge of ourselves as conscious performers. To navigate through our lives we must pre-suppose our power to do so. But navigation requires more than the knowledge that navigation is possible. To assume authorship of our lives, we must assume the capacity to write our own stories. But successful authorship of our own stories requires knowledge of the conscious performance through which our authority is exercised.

4.3 DETERMINING LINES AND BOUNDARIES

In CPA we're seeking to determine, as Hume says, "those lines and boundaries" which distinguish conscious operations from one another. We know now that Hume's conception of the kind of lines and boundaries to be discovered in CPA is probably influenced by his conception of CPA as comparative mental geography. What kinds of lines and boundaries does Hume expect to find? Does he expect to find the kinds of lines and boundaries that distinguish sensible objects from one another? Clearly, it would be a mistake to expect purely temporal objects to be distinguished from one another in that way. What sorts of lines and boundaries could distinguish conscious operations from one another?

Conscious operations are always operations with contents. So they may be distinguished by their different kinds of contents. But this is barely one step removed from the traditional approach that infers different types of operations from different types of objects, as if we were not conscious in our operations. This approach has to be abandoned as we shift from inquiry about the subject-as-a-substance or subject-as-object to reflection on the subject-as-subject.

CPA anticipates the discovery of the types of lines and boundaries that could distinguish conscious operations and relate conscious operations to one another. On the basis of what we know already about conscious performance we can identify four ways in which conscious operations could be distinguished from one another and related to one another.

i. THE OPERATIONS ARE *CONSCIOUS*.

We are present to ourselves in our performance of conscious operations. They could be distinguished from one another and related to one another by differences and similarities in *the quality of our presence to ourselves in our performance of them.* If I am conscious *in* my operations, and my operations differ from one another, I could be conscious differently in my performance of different operations.

For example, my presence to myself in my *questioning* is qualitatively similar to my presence to myself when I'm only *wondering* without having yet asked a question. I'm present to myself as either articulately or inarticulately puzzled or perplexed. My presence to myself in my *seeing* seems to be qualitatively different from my presence to myself in my *deliberating.* When I merely see something, I'm not perplexed at all, and I have one kind of self-experience; when I wonder what I'm going to do, I have another kind of self-experience. The differences in the quality of my presence to myself may be described as differences in the tension, intensity, or feeling of striving in my performance of different operations. Perhaps we can distinguish and relate conscious operations by differences and similarities in the quality of our self-feeling in our performance of them.

ii. THE CONSCIOUS OPERATIONS ARE *PURELY TEMPORAL OBJECTS.*

Conscious operations could be distinguished from one another and related to one another *sequentially,* as occurring before or after one another, or as occurring *simultaneously.* They could be distinguished from one another or related to one another as occurring at different times or at the same time. For example, *understanding,* when it occurs, always occurs *after I've asked a question,* and asking a question, if it's not a merely rhetorical question, always occurs *after I've begun to wonder.* But *understanding* normally occurs *while I'm seeing or hearing or imagining or remembering.*

iii. THESE PURELY TEMPORAL OBJECTS ARE *OPERATIONS.*

Conscious operations could be *dynamically and functionally related* to operations that precede them, follow them, or occur at the same time. Some operations may call forth, evoke, or anticipate others, or be called forth, evoked, or anticipated by others. Subsequent operations may transform the prior operations that we continue to perform. All of our operations could be dynamically and functionally related to one another. *Witnessing* something I don't understand evokes my *effort to understand*; my *inquiry* evokes and anticipates my *understanding*; my *understanding* evokes my *doubts* about the adequacy of my understanding and anticipates a judgment of truth or falsity;

my *judgments* about what's really going on call forth and anticipate my *deliberation* about what I ought to do about it. Just as the images I produce when I do geometry differ from the images I produce when I'm deliberating about possible courses of action I might take, so my *imagining* functions one way in the service of my *understanding* and another way in the service of my *deciding*.

iv. THE FLOW OF CONSCIOUS OPERATIONS IS *INFORMED AND GUIDED BY THE BASIC NOTIONS.*

Conscious operations could be distinguished from one another or related to one another by *the roles played by the basic notions* in their performance, by their various relations to each of the notions, and by their relations to all of the notions taken together or to my basic commitment.

Conscious performance is a continuous flow of purely temporal operations with contents. It is not an aggregate or collection of sensible objects related only because they form parts of a single terrain. It is an integrated flow of purely temporal operations constituted and guided by the basic notions and performed by me.

In his comparative mental geography, Hume anticipates finding lines and boundaries that *distinguish* conscious operations from one another. This is consistent with the unfortunate geographical analogy. In CPA, on the other hand, we anticipate not only distinctions but also, and especially, *relations*. The distinctions between the operations, the lines and boundaries, are most significant in the early stages of the exploration. They enable us to isolate, identify, and name the different operations. Ultimately, it will be the relations that will be of greatest interest to us. The relations described by us may reveal a flow that is spontaneously and not yet deliberately integrated, but it will exhibit integration nonetheless. The one who unites my spontaneous conscious performance is the same one who unites my deliberate conscious performance. My performance, whether spontaneous or deliberate, whether acknowledged or unacknowledged, is always mine. This is to say quite a bit more than that my conscious operations are united only because they are features of the same impersonal terrain, which is all the geographical analogy enables us to say. I am the *one* who performs all of my operations, and it is *my relation* to the basic notions that relates my operations to one another.

Distinguishing Types of Subjects. In addition to anticipating distinctions and relations between conscious operations, CPA anticipates distinctions and relations between types of performing subjects. I have already distinguished *unreflective and spontaneous performance* and *reflective and deliberate performance*. But conscious operations don't perform themselves. You and I perform them. It is you or I who performs unreflectively and spontaneously or reflectively and deliberately. When I'm performing spontaneously, I can be described as a *spontaneous subject*. When I am performing deliberately, I can be described as a *deliberate subject*. Before I come to know myself as a conscious performer, I am an unreflective and spontaneous subject. If I take possession of myself as a conscious performer, I will have become a reflective and deliberate subject. Besides different conscious operations, besides the distinctions and relations between those conscious operations, there are different ways of performing all of the operations. There are *different ways of being a subject*, because there are different ways in which I can be *related to myself* as a conscious performer.

The unreflective and spontaneous subject and the reflective and deliberate subject are two types of performing subject. CPA aims to make it concretely possible for us to make the shift from being unreflective in our performance to being reflective in our performance, and from performing spontaneously to performing deliberately. These two types of subject are distinguished from one another by their different relations to themselves as conscious performers. But we may find that we can make further distinctions between types of subjects in terms of the more specific relations we have to the basic notions that inform and guide our conscious performance. We may be able to distinguish types of subjects by the kinds of *meaning* they're most interested in, the kinds of *knowledge* they most desire, the domains of *reality* they inhabit and in which they're most comfortable, the kinds of *values* that concern them most. We may be able to distinguish types of subjects by *the specific meanings they assign to the basic notions* of meaning, objectivity, knowledge, truth, reality, and value. Once these distinctions have been made, we can go on to explore the interpersonal relations of the different types of subjects to one another.

The Value of CPA. Our dialogue with Hume has brought to light a number of important issues surrounding CPA. Hume concludes his extremely fertile remarks with a comment about the *value* of reflecting upon our conscious performance. He says that no one can call herself learned or a philosopher who has not attempted the task of ordering and distinguishing the operations of the mind. The task increases in value, he says, as it increases in difficulty. Hume is anticipating the application of the self-knowledge acquired by reflection upon the operations of the mind toward the solution of long-standing philosophical problems that have a bearing on the conduct of high-cultural pursuits like the human sciences. Hume had a strong interest in the human sciences, and the fruits of CPA would certainly be of value to practitioners of those disciplines. The more self-possessed human scientists are, the better it will be for all of us who are their objects of study. But knowledge of our conscious operations has a wider application as well.

The self-knowledge to be acquired by CPA is not just for professional philosophers and practitioners of the human sciences. It is for *everyone*. We're all conscious performers engaged more or less deliberately in authoring our own lives. Ultimately, the value of CPA resides in the power it gives us to transform our unreflective and spontaneous basic commitment to meaning, objectivity, knowledge, truth, reality, and value into a reflective and deliberate commitment in any endeavor in any walk of life. No one, we may say, can call herself enlightened or self-possessed who has not attempted the task of ordering and distinguishing the operations of her own mind.

Chapter Three

Conscious Performance Analysis

If we become familiar with ourselves as committed to meaning, objectivity, knowledge, truth, reality, and value, we will empower ourselves to be ourselves more attentively, more intelligently, more reasonably, more deliberately and responsibly. Knowledge of the world enables us to manage our environment more attentively, intelligently, reasonably, deliberately, and responsibly, even if we don't always manage our environment in those ways. Similarly, *self*-knowledge enables us to conduct ourselves more attentively, intelligently, reasonably, deliberately, and responsibly. It enables us to elevate our *spontaneous and unreflective commitment* to the level of *deliberate and reflective commitment*.

As spontaneous performers who have not yet undertaken serious and prolonged reflection upon our conscious performance, our performance goes on behind our own backs, so to speak, and it is fairly easily disordered and derailed. Our adherence to our basic commitment is fragile, and we're easily driven off course. Our performance doesn't go on entirely behind our backs, of course. We're *conscious in* our performance. But being conscious in our performance is not *being attentive to* our performance, *inquiring about* our performance, *describing* our performance, *discovering relationships* among the various elements of our performance, or *knowing what we're doing* when we're performing. If we don't know ourselves as conscious performers, we can't claim legitimately to be in possession of ourselves or to be at home with ourselves as conscious performers.

When our situation requires us to distinguish the meaningful from the meaningless, the objective from the merely one-sided, knowledge from mere opinion, truth from falsehood and fact from fiction, real from illusory or unreal, value from disvalue, authentic living from unauthentic living – and our situation seems always to carry this requirement – we may find ourselves at a loss and disorientated. We can turn to others for assistance, but they could be just as lacking in self-knowledge and self-possession as we are and just as disorientated. We can't tell whether they're credible advisors and counselors or not. We can draw upon conventional opinion or upon a long-standing tradition, but we only encounter the same problems again, this time on a grander scale. But we can't simply dismiss our disorientation either. Our feeling of disorientation is itself a manifestation of our basic commitment. Our appeal to the basic notions is inevitable. Our reliance upon them is inescapable. Our spontaneous orientation toward meaning, objectivity, knowledge, truth, reality, and value is ineradicable. On the other hand, if our commitment remains merely spontaneous, it remains fragile, and we can easily be derailed.

If we are to become capable of *self*-orientation, *self*-determination, and *self*-direction, we must come to know and take possession of ourselves as already spontaneously motivated and orientated by the basic notions. We must transform our unreflective and spontaneous commitment into a reflective and deliberate one. We make this important transition from spontaneous and unreflective commitment to deliberate and reflective commitment by getting hold of these basic notions *as operative in our conscious performance* and by *taking possession* of our own conscious performance as informed and guided by them.

The *operative meaning* of the basic notions may be brought to light by careful description of our conscious performance in which they are already implicit and inevitably and inescapably at work. This deliberate pursuit of self-knowledge for the sake of self-possession and self-direction in the flow of life is Conscious Performance Analysis [CPA].

CPA Is Not Conceptual Analysis. The approach taken by CPA is not the usual approach to solving the problem of self-knowledge and self-possession. As I indicate in Appendix I at the end of this book, it is not an approach that is widely accepted. The favored approach at present is conceptual analysis of the variety of explicit meanings we happen to have assigned to the basic notions. In other words, the basic notions are typically treated as though they were conceptual products rather than as at work in the very production of concepts. This conceptualist approach is taken without regard for the historical embeddedness of the various meanings assigned to the basic notions, without regard for the peculiar circularity encountered in the attempt to assign specific meanings to these notions, and without regard for the coherence or incoherence of these explicit meanings with the performance of pursuing them, entertaining them, affirming them, or rejecting them. It assumes that these *notions* are ideas or concepts and then tries to unpack their meanings by analyzing them. For example, what, one may ask, is Plato's *concept* of the soul? Or, what is Lao Tse's *concept* of self-cultivation? Or, what is Aristotle's *concept* of virtue? Or, how is the *concept* of truth used in contemporary Oxford or Webster English? The analytical procedure of conceptual analysis, despite its popularity and wide employment, is a backward procedure, and it is radically unacceptable. It puts the cart before the horse. It fails miserably, because it ignores the *operative meaning* of the notions, the meaning of the notions already at work in our conscious perfor-mance. In short, it is an unreflective procedure. As such, it is at best a subsidiary philosophical technique that is preoccupied more with *how we speak* about ourselves than with *what we're doing* when we're being ourselves.

Conceptual analysis, despite its popularity among con-temporary philosophers, is inappropriate for our purposes, because it aims to be a strictly logical procedure, the sort of procedure that is carried out solely with conceptual products of our conscious performance. First, it pays no mind to conscious performance, but focuses attention exclusively on already-formulated concepts found ready-made in the language we happen to use. Secondly, because it pays no mind to conscious performance it is insensitive to the circularity of every attempt to define the basic notions. It doesn't notice the notions already at work in its pursuit of definitions of the notions. Thirdly, because it is inattentive to conscious performance and attends only to ideas or concepts, it cannot hope to address the peculiar and troubling contradiction between what is expressed and the performance of expressing it, and so it lapses into the incoherence of performative self-contradiction, although typically without being troubled or embarrassed by the fact that it does so. Fourthly, while it aims to be a merely logical procedure that escapes the vicissitudes of history and culture, conceptual analysis regularly seeks support and justification for its conclusions in historically- and culturally-embedded 'intuitions' about ordinary living, but it does this without acknowledging the historical and cultural embeddedness of these 'intuitions'. Consequently, it is incapable of accomplishing more than a clarification of the way concepts just happen to have been used or happen to be used in a particular place at a particular time.

Conceptual analysis, as the name implies, is not analysis of our conscious performance but analysis of concepts. Concepts may pertain to, may be about, and may even be products of attempts to describe our conscious performance, but they are not the performance they pertain to, are about, or attempt to describe. Concepts are *products* of conscious performance. Conscious performance is the *producer* of concepts of itself as well as of everything else. "The concept of mind," for example, receives a lot of attention from conceptual analysts, and well it should. But their conceptual analyses of "the concept of mind" are typically unmindful of the mind they really have in mind and which is at work when they undertake to analyze "the concept of 'mind." This is not at all the procedure we have in mind when we're doing CPA.

CPA is the exploration of the *operations* that generate all concepts, including our concepts of those basic guiding notions of meaning, objectivity, knowledge, truth, reality, and value. It aims to expose those basic notions *as already operative* in our performance before we conceive specific meanings for them and before we affirm or reject the various meanings that have been given to them at various stages in history and in a variety of cultural contexts. It aims to describe *the activity or performance of pursuing meaning, pursuing objectivity, pursuing knowledge, pursuing truth, pursuing the real, pursuing value*. CPA aims to describe conscious performance and to expose in that performance the operative meaning of the basic guiding notions of meaning, objectivity, knowledge, truth, reality, and value. CPA is the attentive description of the conscious performance referred to vaguely and misleadingly as "the mind."

1. THE LANGUAGE OF SELF-POSSESSION

To say that CPA is not conceptual analysis is not to say that we can do without concepts altogether in our approach. Conscious Performance Analysis is not just *being conscious in* our performance. It is not just pre-conceptual and pre-linguistic experience of the basic notions at work; it's not just spontaneous immersion in the felt but unarticulated pursuit of meaning, objectivity, knowledge, truth, reality, and value. If it were, then we could rightly claim to be engaged in CPA whenever we're awake. But this is obviously not the case. CPA goes beyond *mere experience* of the notions at work to attempt to speak with descriptive precision about our conscious performance and to describe the notions in operation. If we wish to talk about conscious performance, we have to use language. If we use language, we use concepts. The description of conscious performance reached by CPA will be linguistically expressed, and so it will be a collection of related concepts.

We cannot avoid the use of concepts, and we would not wish to do so. What we do want to avoid is the confusion of concepts of conscious performance with our concrete conscious performance. What we want to avoid is the confusion of conceptual analysis with the description of the actual conscious flow *by which* concepts are generated, criticized, analyzed, clarified, accepted, rejected, and distinguished. We don't want to confuse concepts of our conscious performance with the actual performance *about which* they are concepts. We want to avoid the confusion of concepts of our performance with the performance itself which we are trying to conceive clearly and precisely with the aid of concepts.

I've already introduced a set of terms that I think are central to understanding ourselves as conscious performers. They are: *conscious performance; meaning, objectivity, knowledge, truth, reality, value; basic commitment; notion; concept.* In my discussion so far I have used many other terms as well. In the course of this book, I shall introduce and make use of still more terms to speak about aspects of our conscious performance that I find especially significant. For the most part, these are words with which we are already familiar and upon which we already rely to talk about ourselves as conscious performers. It will be helpful to give a name to this language we commonly use to talk about our conscious performance in which the guiding notions play their informing and guiding role. Let us name it the Language of Self-Possession to distinguish it from the various ordinary and specialized languages we use to talk about everything else.

A Marginal Language. Although everyone speaks the Language of Self-Possession, it lies unexamined for the most part on the fringes of our thinking and expression. Yet, our use of the Language of Self-Possession, however obscured it may be by intimate familiarity, habitual use, or the deliberate dismissal of its significance, is our public revelation to ourselves and to one another of how we find our way in the ever-shifting flow of our lives. It is our expression of our inescapable reliance upon and inevitable appeal to the basic notions imbedded in our conscious performance. It is a public manifestation of our interest and effort to find and give ourselves direction in the flow of life.

We frequently and regularly employ words signaling the performance in which the basic notions are operative. But we don't usually pay much attention to them. We attend more readily and easily to the products of our conscious performance than to our performance itself. We also give more attention to the language that refers to those products than we do to the language that refers to the conscious flow of performance out of which they arise.

Even though we cannot do without it, our employment of the Language of Self-Possession is usually casual, off-hand, and inadvertent. Even philosophers with expertise in the technique of conceptual analysis, who might regard CPA's shift of attention from concepts to conscious performance as pointless or wrong-headed, employ the Language of Self-Possession. They do so, not only in their ordinary living, but also in their carefully crafted conceptual analyses. It is not at all unusual to be asked by the author of a philosophical work if we've *understood* the question at hand, if we've *gotten the point*, if we *agree* or *disagree*, and if we recognize how *true* or *worthwhile* the approach being taken, conclusions being drawn, and the position being promoted are. The words and phrases in italics here are part of the inventory of the Language of Self-Possession. But, typically, the conscious performance these authors are obviously attempting to evoke in their readers and to which these words and phrases allude is simply taken for granted and constitutes an unexplored background to the conceptual analysis being pursued in the foreground. There are even extreme cases in which conceptual analysts of a particular philosophical persuasion fall blithely into performative self-contradiction by asking their readers if they've *understood* that there are *no mental acts at all*! This is no different from asking their readers *to get the idea* that there's no such thing as *getting ideas* or *to understand* that no one ever *understands* anything.

Casual, off-hand, and inadvertent appeals to conscious performance are made, then, not only in everyday conversation, but even in the sophisticated treatises of expert analysts of concepts. As in everyday life, so also in high-cultural analyses, the Language of Self-Possession is used consciously but usually inadvertently, and so it remains marginal and receives only fleeting attention. In a way, this is surprising, because the use of this language pertains to the very performance by which meaning and direction are given both to our ordinary living and to our sophisticated high-cultural pursuits. However, given our spontaneous preoccupation with the products of our conscious performance, perhaps it's not that surprising. If my basic commitment is unreflective and spontaneous, my use of the Language of Self-Possession will probably be equally casual, off-hand, and inadvertent. On the other hand, if my basic commitment becomes reflective and deliberate, my use of the Language of Self-Possession will also become reflective and deliberate. The care or carelessness with which we use the Language of Self-Possession reveals just how self-possessed or lacking in self-possession we are.

The conduct of our lives is bound up so closely with the basic notions that we rarely take notice of their influence. Like the earth under our feet and the force of gravity, we live on them and within the field of their inevitable and inescapable influence. These rise vividly into our field of attention only when we risk a dangerous leap, suffer an unexpected fall, or attempt a perilous climb. Similarly, the notions at work in our conscious performance attract our attention when meaning, objectivity, knowledge, truth, reality, and value elude us; they become conspicuous by their absence. Then, our basic commitment attracts our attention as *puzzlement, confusion, perplexity, disorientation, a feeling of loss or that something's missing, boredom, frustration, wonder, or anxiety*. The Language of Self-Possession pertains to that intimately felt conscious flow, and the words we use to talk about it are normally given a merely marginal and subsidiary position in our speech and writing. Only when the flow of our conscious performance is seriously disrupted, derailed, or impeded do we feel a pressing need to speak about it with precision and clarity. Then we may begin to wonder what it means to 'understand', to "overcome a bias," to "make a judgment," to "discern a value." Then, too, we may ask for more clarity and precision from those who offer us such well-intentioned but vague pieces of advice as "You need to get serious!", "Think about it!", "Be open-minded!", "Try to work it out!", "You have to rely on yourself!", "Just go with the flow!", "Just be yourself!".

The Language of Self-Possession is commonly employed in a casual and ordinary way, rather than in a deliberate and technical way. That doesn't mean that its grammar and vocabulary are free of high-cultural influences. The Language of Self-Possession is shot through with the historical sediment of high-cultural technical meanings. It carries a lot of baggage, some of it useful and some of it useless. Sometimes what's in the baggage is useful, because it fits our conscious performance well. Sometimes it doesn't fit at all and obscures rather than clarifies our conscious performance. Conceptual analysis, because it tends to ignore the historical embeddedness of words and concepts, typically fails to notice this. In this respect, the analyst of concepts is no different from other inhabitants of the world of ordinary living. We usually employ the Language of Self-Possession without taking note of the influences that have deter-mined its current meanings. But in CPA it is important to be sensitive to these influences, because we wish to use the Language of Self-Possession to clarify and understand ourselves, not to make ourselves still more obscure to ourselves or to reinforce some traditional misunderstanding of ourselves.

If we remain content with the ordinary usages of these words, we invite misunderstanding and confusion, and we deprive ourselves of the benefits afforded by articulate self-understanding. The ordinary usages, as such, have arisen from *ordinary attention* to conscious performance. Ordinary self-attention is typically divided by the imperious pressure of our spontaneous preference for the sensible objects of our performance, as we shall see in § 2 of this chapter. Ordinary attentiveness normally produces the kinds of descriptions that enable us to evoke in conversation with others a general idea of what we're talking about. It produces descriptions that are good enough to serve our ordinary practical and social purposes, but these descriptions are still fairly vague and merely allusive.

The ordinary usages may also have been constituted partially by high-cultural technical meanings, but those technical meanings, even if they were clear and precise to begin with, often have been reduced in ordinary usage to imprecise and unclear remnants, to mere shadows of their originals. Plato, for example, distinguished clearly between "understanding ideas" and "seeing images," and he went to great pains in his dialogues to expose their differences. This distinction altered radically our understanding of ourselves and of how to go about introducing order and direction into our lives. It changed the course of Western history. But, despite our being beneficiaries of that clarification, ordinarily we don't distinguish clearly between these two different ways of performing, just as we don't always distinguish clearly between 'seeming' and 'being', and even some contemporary philosophers still fail to notice their differences from one another.

Those original technical meanings, of which our everyday usages contain only the shadowy remnants, may have arisen from perspicuous attention to our conscious performance. But it is also possible that they originated from sophisticated oversights of key moments in conscious performance and have left traces in our everyday Language of Self-Possession of what is just ungrounded, inattentive high-cultural speculation. Insufficiently self-attentive philosophers have invented mysterious 'intuitions', conjured up complicated unconscious processes, and posited convenient "innate ideas" in their attempts to solve the problem of finding direction in the flow of human life. Sometimes the remnants of high-cultural speculation radically misrepresent our conscious performance, relieve us of the need to attend to and to explore our conscious performance, or divert our attention from it altogether.

Purification of the Language of Self-Possession. The ordinary Language of Self-Possession, with its ordinary imprecision and its high-cultural baggage, cannot be adopted safely as it stands by CPA. It must be critically corrected and carefully clarified. It must be *purified.* The effort to come to know and to take possession of ourselves as conscious performers requires that we pull the Language of Self-Possession from the periphery to the center of our attention, from the background to the foreground. It requires that we sensitize ourselves to our own casual and uncritical use of it. Instead of employing this language casually and relatively inattentively, we must try to employ it carefully and deliberately. In order to accomplish this, we must undertake to reinforce its existing connections to the conscious performance it's meant to describe, and we must attempt to forge real connections where these are missing. We must tether the existing Language of Self-Possession more closely to the flow of our conscious performance by careful, self-attentive description.

As we give closer attention to our use of the Language of Self-Possession, familiar words will acquire initially an aura of unfamiliarity. We will find ourselves using familiar words more carefully and precisely and putting them together in new and perhaps unfamiliar, uncommon, and unexpected ways. We will begin to use them in a more complex fashion. We will also become more vigilant so that we don't revert to our old habits of inaccurate and imprecise speech about ourselves. Ultimately, if we're successful, we will find ourselves in possession of *a basic lexicon and a basic grammar*, as it were, upon which we can draw to speak precisely and fruitfully to ourselves and to others about our conscious performance and about the basic notions that inform it and guide it. With this transformed and purified Language of Self-Possession we may find ourselves capable of speaking clearly and precisely, and so also more fruitfully, to ourselves and with others about the highly personal, universal problem of finding direction in the ongoing flow of life.

As in any serious investigation, it is important in CPA to develop a clear and precise language. The existing Language of Self-Possession is our starting-point, but it can't be adopted just as it is. That language must be brought into tighter connection with the conscious performance about which it purports to speak. As we tether the Language of Self-possession more tightly to our actual conscious performance, the traces of high-cultural inattentiveness and speculation will be shed, the remnants of high-cultural insight and perspicuity will be retained, and the amorphous core of meaning produced by everyday practical and social self-understanding will be given a definite shape. CPA requires this purification of the ordinary Language of Self-Possession in the interest of providing a clear and precise vocabulary and grammar for use in our pursuit of articulate self-knowledge and self-possession.

As we take this essential step we must not forget that CPA is much more than merely attention to and analysis of our use of the Language of Self-Possession. If we ignore this caveat and permit our use of language and the meanings imbedded in it to become our primary concern, we risk diverting our inquiry into the *cul-de-sac* of merely conceptual analysis of the unpurified Language of Self-Possession. We must not let CPA degenerate into *merely talking about how we and others just happen to talk* about our conscious performance. We must resist the allure of merely conceptual analysis and resist the temptation to mistake words or concepts or descriptions for the conscious occurrences, operations, and processes which, with the aid of the Language of Self-Possession, we aim to describe and to understand. The Language of Self-Possession, used critically, carefully, and precisely, may serve as an essential set of handholds to support us as we venture beneath the linguistic surface into the frequently ignored, largely unexplored, often obscured, and poorly illuminated realm of our own conscious performance where the basic notions are already at work before they're noticed and named.

As we grow accustomed, through the medium and with the assistance of the Language of Self-Possession, to our own conscious performance – as we become familiar with our own operations, their sequences, their relations, their disconnections and disruptions, their orientations, and their proper objects – the Language of Self-Possession will begin to serve for us, it is hoped, a more powerful communicative and self-revelatory function than it does at present in our daily lives. It will undergo a transformation, not into a logically consistent and coherent 'system' of clearly defined and thoroughly unpacked concepts, but into a fundamental lexicon and grammar of self-direction. It will begin to serve us as the linguistic expression of a reflective and critical understanding of the *flow* of our conscious performance *as we live that flow* and of the *operative meaning* of the basic notions. Then, it is hoped, when we instruct ourselves or are advised by others to "pay attention," to "be intelligent," to "be reasonable," to "be responsible," we'll have a clear idea of what's involved and how to go about it. More generally, the often repeated, well meaning, seemingly profound and pointed, but frustratingly vague, indeterminate, and therefore ultimately unhelpful advice to "Be yourself!", "Be authentic!", "Go with the flow!", "Give it your all!", "Give it everything you've got!", and "Be natural!" may take on profound, pointed, precise, determinate, and truly helpful meaning.

The purifying transformation of the Language of Self-Possession, while it will serve our purposes and is essential to them, is not the final aim of CPA. It's just one important step in our pursuit of the self-knowledge that will enable us to take possession of ourselves as conscious performers. Further, even if we manage to achieve the self-possession made possible by CPA, even if we become at home with ourselves as conscious performers, each of us must still face the intimately personal problem of determining the specific direction of the flow of her own life. Self-possession of the sort made possible by CPA is a solution to the problem of *how I should perform* in the pursuit of a solution to a problem of living that is *uniquely my own*. CPA can assist us in obtaining the self-knowledge required to make our unreflective and spontaneous basic commitment into a reflective and deliberate one. But the specific manner and direction in which that reflective and deliberate commitment will be lived out is a matter that is to be settled entirely by oneself and on one's own. I take possession of the humanity of the person I am, in the style and manner of my own personality. I take possession of what I am as who I happen to be and hope to be.

2. EXTROVERSION: OUR ORDINARY PREFERENCE FOR SENSIBLE OBJECTS

The flow of our conscious performance is the ever-present background of our day-to-day occupations and preoccupations. Like the Language of Self-Possession in which it is expressed accurately or inaccurately, precisely or vaguely, it falls for the most part outside the range of our ordinary practical and social concerns.

No one would deny that the vocabulary of, say, 'experiencing', 'inquiring', 'understanding', 'thinking', 'formulating', 'reasoning', 'expressing', 'evaluating', 'deciding', and so on, identifies, even if only vaguely and obscurely, performance we know ourselves to engage in regularly. No one is willing to claim that she never 'understands', 'thinks', or 'decides'; to do so would be to admit to being stupid, thoughtless, and slavish. Nor would anyone deny, after a moment of reflection, that the occurrence of this conscious performance contributes to and is of considerable importance for the successful conduct of our lives. Still, there seems to be little inclination in our ordinary living to give the field of conscious performance the focused attention it certainly deserves.

One reason why we tend to give only cursory attention to our conscious performance is the nature of ordinary day-to-day living itself. In ordinary living we're beset by a steady flow of practical and social demands that are best met if we give them our undivided attention. Even when they abate, we tend to use our free time to relieve the accumulated stresses and fatigue that meeting them and trying to meet them create in us. We may exclaim, "TGIF!" as the workweek comes to a close. But our gratitude is not normally for a weekend we shall devote to taking possession of ourselves as conscious performers, but for a few mornings of sleeping-in and a few evenings of diverting recreation. CPA is a luxury that requires leisure time, but most of our leisure time is consumed with recovering from the labor required to live a successful everyday life. In short, we're usually too involved in conscious performance – either of the sort required to meet prac-tical and social demands or of the sort that relieves the fatigue and stress created by those demands – to give much serious attention to our conscious performance.

Let's consider another reason why we may find ourselves disinclined to take our own conscious performance seriously and to take the time to undertake seriously the project of CPA. It is a basic assumption of this prolonged meditation that the truly fruitful future of human exploration doesn't lie in the distant, cold, and currently uninhabitable reaches of interplanetary or intergalactic space, despite the fascinating attraction exerted by those mysterious expanses. It lies in the most proximate and familiar habitat wherein we are most intimately ourselves and which is always warmed, even when we're isolated and alone, by our intimate presence to ourselves. In our scientific inquiries we seem always to be reaching farther and deeper into the so-called "outer world" revealed to us by our senses. We rarely inquire with the same detached seriousness into the so-called "inner world" of our own performance. When we do turn our attention to our own performance, it's usually because we've been driven by recurrent practical and social failures to do so. After enough missteps or a long enough run of bad luck, I might eventually ask, "What am I doing wrong?" and I might "turn inward," as we say. 'Outer' and 'inner', 'outward' and 'inward', and 'external' and 'internal' are just metaphors, of course, and their use in the existing Language of Self-Possession is characteristically vague and misleading. When we speak of "turning inward," we really mean to say we're shifting our attention from *the actual and possible objects of our senses* (the 'outer') to *the intimately experienced flow of our conscious performance* (the 'inner').

There is a notable preference for attention to and inquiry into our sensible experience. We seem to turn our attention and inquiry to our conscious performance only when we're forced by recurrent disruptions of our living to do so. When I'm misled repeatedly by my perceptions, when others are always correcting my inaccurate memories, when my bright ideas repeatedly prove to be unfounded, when my decisions embroil me over and over in unanticipated difficulties and entanglements, then I might turn my attention to my conscious performance and begin to wonder about it.

Clearly, the manner in which we manage our conscious lives has a significant bearing upon the guidance both of our ordinary practical and social lives and of our high-cultural pursuits. Whether we're river-boat captains or research scientists, marketing strategists or metaphysicians, baseball players or biologists, financiers or physicists, anchorwomen or anthropologists, politicians or political scientists, nurses or neuroscientists, thespians or theologians, the 'decisions' we take or fail to take, the deliberate or careless 'evaluation' and 'deliberation' by which we arrive at our 'decisions', the nature and adequacy of our 'reasoning' and of the 'judgments' we make, our attentiveness or inattentiveness in our 'experiencing', and the occurrence or non-occurrence of 'understanding' of our experience, all bear directly upon the success or failure of our endeavors.

But the history of human inquiry is for the most part a story of the exploration of *everything but* the flow of our conscious performance and of the basic notions at work in our performance. Our interest, historically, has been, more often than not, an *extroverted interest*, an intelligent interest in the experience we acquire through our five senses and through our technological extensions of our five senses. For the most part, we have been preoccupied with the sensible objects of our performance. Even our interest in ourselves is often an interest in ourselves *as objects* visible in mirrors or other reflective surfaces, as seen by others, as observable and observed by others while we're engaged in practical tasks, social interactions, and recreational activity. We, the ones who perform, are inclined to regard ourselves merely *as sensible objects* of our own and others' conscious operations. Only rarely, and usually only under duress, do we attend to ourselves *in* our conscious performance *as conscious performers*, that is, *as operating subjects*.

Throughout what has been an extremely fruitful process of extroverted inquiry, our conscious lives have proceeded simultaneously, of course. If we had not 'inquired' and 'understood', 'hypothesized' and 'experimented', 'learned' and "come to know," 'evaluated' and 'decided', how could we have achieved such successes in our ordinary practical and social lives and in our high-cultural pursuits? Nevertheless, our conscious performance has for the most part escaped the sort of serious and prolonged attention, investigation, and precise description that results in a clear and precise Language of Self-Possession. We may be able to speak clearly and precisely about *objects of* our conscious performance and about *ourselves as objects of* our own and others' conscious performance, but we don't yet speak very clearly and precisely about ourselves *as subjects of* our conscious performance, that is, *as conscious performers*. We're quite articulate when it comes to discussing *the subject-as-object*, the one who is looking back at us when we look into the mirror, or the one who is observed by others. We are not nearly as articulate when it comes to discussing *the subject-as-subject*, the one who is herself looking into the mirror, or the one who is observing others while she is being observed.

Spontaneous extroversion, the preoccupation with objects of our five senses and with ourselves as sensible objects, is characteristic of those who remain in the everyday life-world and, for the most part, also of the practitioners of high-cultural pursuits. In our ordinary living this extroversion finds a readily accessible and fairly non-controversial justification in our experience of imperious biological needs, in the persistent demands of social life, and in our success in meeting these needs and demands by giving our undivided attention to our sensible experience. We cannot meet our biological needs, discern and accomplish our practical tasks, and meet our social obligations without attending to our sensible experience. We ignore the testimony of our five senses at our own risk, and to give it close attention is normally to our physical, practical, and social advantage. In the realm of high-cultural pursuit, especially in the pursuit of the natural sciences (e.g., physics, chemistry, biology, neuroscience), the spontaneous preference for sensible experience is erected into *a methodological rule*. The spontaneous extroversion that serves ordinary practical and social living so well is laid down by natural scientists as a rule for the governance of serious intellectual inquiry into all of nature.

3. A DELIBERATE RESTRICTION OF OUR ATTENTION

CPA violates not only the spontaneous restriction of ordinary attentiveness to immediately-present sensible experience but also the deliberate restriction of our attention to sensible data that is expressed in *a basic canon or methodological rule* of natural scientific procedure.

Our violation in CPA of the norms of procedure of the ordinary life-world is easily justified. The immediate interests of CPA are only remotely practical and social, and so our procedure need not be governed, either implicitly or explicitly, by the criteria appropriate to the immediately practical and social pursuits of everyday life. CPA doesn't bake bread or establish friendships. It pertains to the conscious performance without which I would find no meaning or value in baking bread, making friends, or doing anything else. It may be said that CPA is practical, but it is so in a way that far exceeds the contracted and narrow practicality of everyday life. It may also be said that CPA has social consequences. However, these far exceed the limited sociality of everyday living. For, they pertain to the way we collaborate as conscious performers in anything and everything we human beings decide to do together.

CPA's transgression or violation of a widely accepted and apparently uncontroversial rule of scientific procedure is more difficult to defend. The enterprise we're undertaking is a pursuit of knowledge. While it is not natural science, it is nevertheless an intellectual inquiry and quite different from ordinary practical and social living. In view of the fact that both in ordinary living and in the most prominent scientific practice a restriction of inquiry to the field of sensible experience is strongly recommended and even dictated, I shall offer a brief defense at the outset for the view that such a restriction is entirely inappropriate for a study of conscious performance and must not be adopted by CPA.

It is not unusual to hear the natural scientific inquirer and those especially enamored of or deferential toward the empirical scientific method proclaim that it is the sole *objective* method of inquiry, that it is the one and only acceptable manner of pursuing *knowledge*, that whatever connection we are likely to have with *reality* will be had through the application of empirical scientific method, and that, consequently, it is the only *worthwhile* method to employ in the pursuit of knowledge of anything at all. In effect, what is being claimed by these practitioners and proponents of scientific method is that *objectivity* is at least, and perhaps even essentially, attentiveness to sensible data, that *knowledge* is to be attained only by way of attention to sensible experience, that the *real* is coextensive with what can be sensed and that the non-sensible is not real, and that the *good* investigator, therefore, ought to attend to and inquire into sensible data alone. No other kind of inquiry, it is claimed, is really as *worthwhile*. Notice the basic notions at work here, and notice the specific meanings that are being assigned to them.

From the standpoint of the present exploration, such proclamations must be regarded as uncritical and dogmatic claims to know once and for all the correct meanings of the guiding notions of meaning, objectivity, knowledge, truth, reality, and value. These claims prejudge the issue we're calling into question and hope to settle in CPA. These claims aren't results arrived at by CPA; they aren't reasonable conclusions reached by CPA. They are unreasonable presumptions about conscious performance made before CPA has been carried out, before we have thoroughly explored our conscious performance.

A little reflection reveals that these proclamations by the advocates of the superiority of the natural scientific approach are nothing more than declarations of their faith in the correctness of the meanings given the basic guiding notions by scientific investigators and those who agree with them. We are under no rational obligation to share this prejudice, no matter how successful scientific investigators may have been in enabling us to control sensible objects and to predict sensible events. On the contrary, given the aims of the present investigation, we are obliged to hold these specific meanings, no less than others assigned to the basic notions by other types of conscious performers, in suspension until such time as CPA has revealed their proximity to or distance from the operative meaning of the notions in their concrete role of informing and guiding conscious performance in all walks of life and fields of inquiry.

The restriction of attention and inquiry to sensible experience is, in fact, a deliberate exclusion of our own conscious performance from the field of occurrences and objects to be seriously investigated. Our conscious performance is *not sensible*. We can't see it, hear it, taste it, smell it, touch it, or even imagine it. Obviously, the imposition of such a restriction does not, by some scientific magic, eliminate the conscious performance that constitutes both our ordinary and our high-cultural pursuits, including all of the natural sciences. The advocate of the restriction of inquiry to sensible data, in fact, appeals to her experience of that non-sensible, conscious performance in the very formulation and issuance of the restriction. The rule "Attend only to sensible data!" exhorts us to exercise control over our *attending*. But attending is conscious performance we neither see, nor hear, nor touch, nor taste, nor smell, nor detect with the aid of special instruments that extend the range of our senses. We can't scientifically observe attending. This is one serious difficulty, then, with the restriction: it cannot be issued, and it cannot be abided by, without actually *violating* it.

The preference for the method of natural science cannot be at the same time a denial of the existence of non-sensible data. The command to restrict our attention to sensible data is superfluous if there is no non-sensible data to which we might attend instead. If there were actually nothing for us to attend to besides sensible data, then it would be pointless to order us to restrict our attention to sensible data. It's a fair assumption that those who issue the pre-scription to attend only to sensible data don't do so because it is pointless to issue the prescription. The restriction to sensible data requires the affirmation of some non-sensible experience to which we could attend instead. Without this affirmation of non-sensible experience, the prescription lapses into utter meaninglessness, and it's hardly worthwhile to issue utterly meaningless prescriptions.

The natural scientific prescription makes sense, then, only as the expression of *a preference for sensible data*. Behind this preference there lies a reasonable and respectable disdain for groundless speculation about sensible objects. But it happens that it is also a devaluation of attention to the non-sensible flow of conscious performance and a devaluation of the serious exploration of it. In order to issue the restriction, some serious attention must be paid to non-sensible conscious performance. If no attention at all is given to non-sensible conscious performance, the prescription can't be formulated and issued or understood and obeyed. The rule of procedure that dictates the restriction of our attention to sensible data alone is itself a violation of the letter of the rule, for it derives its meaning in part from serious enough attention to non-sensible data to enable us to distinguish it from sensible data. It is also a violation of the spirit of the rule, for the value it promotes cannot be realized without attention to non-sensible performance. Behind this preference lies an assignment of *specific meanings* to the basic notions *before* the *operative meaning* of the notions has been thoroughly explored.

The natural scientific method, which is governed by the restriction to sensible data, *is itself conscious performance*, but of a deliberately restricted type. If it weren't a type of conscious performance, there would be nothing upon which to impose the restriction to sensible data, and all the other canons of scientific performance would also be senseless, pointless, and superfluous utterances. As a deliberately restricted kind of conscious performance, scientific method itself falls outside the range of our senses. But scientific method is obviously something we can experience ourselves doing when we're doing science. If we weren't conscious in the performance of the operations that make up scientific method, the rule that restricts attention to sensible data would be meaningless and pointless. We wouldn't be able to tell if we were following it or not. We wouldn't even be able to tell if we were doing science or not.

The restriction to sensible data rules out the exploration of natural scientific practice itself. Because it limits serious inquiry to sensible data, it denies the value of exploring even the restricted conscious performance that constitutes *scientific observation, inquiry, hypothesis, and verification or falsification by experiment*. Again, the very issuance of the restriction is found to be a violation of the restriction, for it is an implicit denial of the value of inquiry into the conscious performance to which the restriction is to be applied.

The conclusion we must draw, then, is that scientific method is neither a comprehensive method nor a method that admits the possibility of describing and justifying its own employment. It is not a comprehensive method, because human affairs, insofar as they are constituted by the non-sensible conscious performance of human beings, fall outside the effective range of its inquiries. It cannot justify its own employment because, according to its own rules, it has nothing significant to say about conscious performance, not even about that restricted conscious performance called scientific method, that is, not even about itself. However, this does not prevent advocates of natural scientific method from totalizing their restricted method, that is, from attempting to make the full range of existing things conform to the limitations of the restricted conscious performance they have chosen. Nor, obviously, does it prevent them from commenting on their own method, identifying at least generally the operations appropriate to natural scientific procedure, and denigrating other methods that violate their own preferred canons of conscious performance. Notice the conspicuous performative self-contradiction in which they are involved, and notice also that they seem to be oblivious to it.

When natural scientific method is totalized, human affairs are pared down to their sensible components. The non-sensible experience that is the conscious performance that informs and guides the affairs of human beings is declared irrelevant, sheared off, and cast aside. Inquiring attention is paid only to the truncated sensible object that remains, only to the human *subject-as-object*. In spite of their own ongoing appeals to the non-sensible experience of conscious performance, totalizing practitioners of natural science make no clear distinction between, for example, the literal meaning of the mythic speculation of Hesiod about the origins of the separation of the heavens from the earth, for which there is no evidence at all, sensible or non-sensible, and a statement about conscious performance such as "I've come up with a new hypothesis," for which there is apparently ample non-sensible evidence in many a respected scientific practitioner. To them, the claims of mythic speculation and claims about our conscious performance are equally groundless and equally unworthy of our attention, because no sensible evidence can be found for either.

Ultimately, the natural scientific restriction of attention to sensible data is just an expression of a restricted interest in understanding sensible experience and of a desire to avoid groundless speculation about the meaning of sensible experience. While groundless speculation has no place in CPA, just as it has no place in natural science, the interest of CPA is not an interest in understanding *sensible experience* at all. It is *an interest in understanding our interest in understanding* the entire range of our experience. The interest of CPA lies in making sense of non-sensible conscious performance.

CPA must reject the natural scientific rule that would restrict serious investigation to sensible data alone. We make the assumption, one that even those who would restrict inquiry to sensible data alone must also make, that when we use the Language of Self-Possession we are talking meaningfully, although often vaguely and imprecisely, about our non-sensible experience of our own conscious performance in which we are intimately present to ourselves.

4. HIGH-CULTURAL INFLUENCES ON EVERYDAY LIVING

The widespread, ordinary use of the Language of Self-Possession suggests that our abandonment of the natural scientific restriction of inquiry to sensible experience is not likely to outrage the ordinary reader who daily employs this language without similar inhibitions and without lapsing into performative self-contradiction. When, in ordinary living, we ask someone to "pay attention" or to "consider a possibility," we aren't violating our own ordinary rules of procedure. It is of some interest that it is the practitioners of the high-cultural disciplines who seem to have the stronger propensity to fall into performative self-contradiction. In fact, the widespread implementation of the natural scientific restriction to sensible data would entirely undermine our practical and social lives, including the practical and social lives to which natural scientists always return when they shut down their electron microscopes, lock up their labs, pick up their paychecks, and drive home. But even the ordinary reader who ventures rarely into the thought-world of scientific culture may be somewhat troubled by the serious turn to non-sensible conscious performance required by CPA. Besides the pressure of spontaneous extroversion in ordinary practical and social living, there is the influence of high-cultural pursuits and their conceptual products on our everyday expression and conduct. Something needs to be said about these influences so that they don't undermine our exploration of our conscious performance even before we've begun.

Everyday living is not immune to the influence of high culture. On the contrary, it is permeated by that influence. The meanings of the notions of objectivity, knowledge, and reality assigned and promoted by scientific practitioners filter down and sediment in the culture-at-large. Sometimes we're rebuked or admonished, by those with whom we're collaborating in a practical task, or by those with whom we're enjoying a personal relationship, to emulate the natural scientist, to contract the range of our attentiveness, to limit the range of our conscious performance, by imposing the restriction to sensible data. Sometimes we even prescribe the restriction to ourselves inappropriately, in uncritical imitation of natural scientific procedure. Like the advocates of scientific method, when we do this, we do it without noticing that we're lapsing into radical incoherence.

OBSERVING MY ROOMMATE

Suppose, for example, that I'm coming to the end of my first week in a course on Experimental Psychology. I've been impressed by my professor's seemingly unshakeable faith in the procedures of natural scientific method. My own confidence in my ability to make sense of things is not nearly as strong. I'm inclined to defer to the high-cultural expertise of my professor. On my way back from class, I decide to adopt toward my roommate an attitude of "scientific observation." After all, I *do* want to get to know her, and knowledge, I've been told, is attained by "scientific observation." When I enter our room, she's reading at her desk. I settle quietly into a chair across the room. "I've got a test tomorrow. I'm almost finished studying," she says. I remain silent. I discount the significance of what she says about herself, about what she's doing and why she's doing it; her neurological processes are producing sounds. I deliberately avoid putting myself in her shoes to discover what my own conscious performance in a similar situation might reveal. I attend only to her observable behavior. I try not to see her as the friend with whom I've shared concerns, questions, interests, ideas, decisions, happiness, and sadness. I pare her down in properly scientific fashion. Her non-sensible performance is irrelevant to my understanding of her actions. I've sheared it off and tossed it aside. Her sensible body is moved by unconscious events in her brain that I could detect if only I had the proper instruments. I watch her as she sits. I recall the large diagram of the human brain that hangs on the wall of the classroom. I wonder what kind of brain activity learning is. From time to time she casts a glance in my direction. I think she's probably wondering what I'm doing. I banish that thought. I can't see any wondering. She's just moving her head and her eyeballs. I feel an impulse to say something, but I maintain my scientific objectivity and remain silent. I don't want to contaminate my observations with her first-person reports. Eventually, with a puzzled expression she turns to face me and inquires, "What is *with* you today? Why are you *looking* at me like that? Is there something you want to *know*? Did I *do* something or *say* something? What's going on? Ohmygod, are you depressed?!" I struggle to maintain my scientific attitude, taking note of the agitation my presence seems to be stimulating in the organism before me. I remain silent. "Are you listening to me?" she asks, somewhat urgently. "Did something happen? Are you *OK*?" I'm touched by her concern. I don't want her to think something terrible has happened. This has gone on too long. I abandon my scientific stance and attempt to reassure her. "No, no, I'm fine, I was just being 'scientific'. Don't worry. Nothing's wrong. It's my Experimental Psych class. You know." Her relief is evident as she says, "You were looking at me so strangely, it was weird, like I wasn't even here."

In our ordinary living, we're susceptible to other sedimented influences of high-cultural investigations as well. The prominent facts of psychological, social, economic, political, cultural, and religious diversity issuing from high-cultural studies are known to virtually everyone within range of contemporary print and electronic media. In light of these facts, we may be tempted to conclude that the conscious performance underlying the multitude of diverse manifestations in human affairs must be as diverse as the manifestations themselves. For example, we might regard exploration of the flow of conscious performance as nothing more than immersion in the particular, the individual, the unique, the idiosyncratic, the peculiar, the one-of-a-kind. Inquiries into that ineluctably private domain may fascinate and even titillate, but they are unlikely, we might assume, to reveal a similar flow of conscious performance, governed by the same basic commitment, in every human being. Or, we might assume a similarity within a particular cultural or historical context but conclude that no transcultural or trans-historical similarity is to be found.

But the universal use of the Language of Self-Possession, despite its everyday imprecision, belies these expectations. There is no compelling reason to become fixated on diversity while ignoring the unavoidable presupposition of fundamental similarity that we in fact reveal with every effort we make to communicate with one another about ourselves and about anything else. We would probably not be struck so forcefully by our differences from one another and so puzzled by them, were it not for this expectation of fundamental similarity that is validated time and again by others' comprehension of what we have in mind when we say "Pay attention!", "Consider this possibility!", "Go ahead and ask!", "Think about it!", "Make a decision!", "Don't decide yet!", "Do you agree or disagree?", and so on. What is given attention, what is considered possible, what is asked about, what is thought about, what is decided, and what is agreed upon may vary from culture to culture, as they may vary within a single culture. But the attending, the considering, the asking, the thinking, the deciding, and the agreeing or disagreeing are done by all. The conceptual products of conscious performance may vary widely from culture to culture and across historical periods. But the flow of conscious performance that generates these products, revises them, and sometimes discards them, we assume to be the same.

It is impossible to say, prior to our having carried out our précising and purification of the Language of Self-Possession and our exploration of the flow of conscious performance, in what ways our basic commitments are identical in their operative origins. But it would be incoherent to expect to discover that in our conscious performance the basic notions play no role at all. The radical relativist lapses into performative self-contradiction. The relativist's assertions that meaningful means only "meaningful to me," that objectivity means only "objective to me," that knowledge means only "knowledge for me," that truth means only "true for me," that reality means only "real to me," and that value means only "worthwhile to me" are worth making and worth taking seriously by all of us only if these claims are *not only true for the radical relativist*, only if the radical relativist *presupposes* the basic commitment to meaning, objectivity, knowledge, truth, reality, and value in herself and in her listeners or readers.

If it is assumed from the start that there is no common operational structure and orientation to human conscious performance, that the *operative meaning* of the basic notions is not fundamentally the same in all of us, then we must add "for me" or "to me" whenever we appeal to the basic notions. 'Meaning' must be indistinguishable from "what's meaningful to me." 'Objectivity' must be indistinguishable from "the way I prefer to think." 'Knowledge' must be indistinguishable from "my thoughts and my opinions." 'Truth' must be indistinguishable from "true for me." 'Reality' must be identical with "my reality." 'Value' must be the same as "valuable for me." Given these particularized, idiosyncratic, and arbitrarily determined meanings of the guiding notions, the performing subject becomes a nihilist, and direction in human living becomes a function of accident and whim, of arbitrariness and caprice, of fluctuating desires and fears. Guiding ideas and beliefs, decisions and choices, become indefensible and uncommendable. Serious public discourse on what matters most to us becomes impossible. Individual living becomes drifting. The course of history becomes a mere aggregate of events with no discernible direction. Any interested attempt to 'explain' why humanity drifts this way or that way at any particular moment must be regarded as just one more shift in the direction of the winds in the radically inexplicable atmosphere of human existence. Of course, this dismissal of *explanation* is itself an attempt to *explain* why an attempt to *explain* shouldn't be taken seriously, and we can recognize in it all the elements of the now familiar performative self-contradiction.

CPA can certainly benefit from the cumulative achievements of high cultural pursuits. It can also be undermined by a lack of critical sensitivity to the influence exerted on us by high-cultural pursuits and their products. Two influences in particular are insidious. We may recognize the performative self-contradiction in the natural scientific restriction of our attention to sensible data and still find ourselves inclined to abide by it. We may discern the performative self-contradiction in the anthropological proclamation of radical cultural difference and diversity and still find ourselves inclined to dismiss the possibility of finding a common ground. To engage in CPA is to take our conscious performance seriously and to anticipate the discovery of a unity of conscious performance beneath the great diversity of the products of our conscious performance. CPA undertakes to describe the ways in which the basic notions inform and guide the conscious performance of *all* human beings.

5. An Invitation

The description of conscious performance offered in this book is, of course, my own. I'm not present to myself in anyone else's performance; I'm not a mind reader. Accordingly, I invite you to set off with me from our meditative starting-point and to accompany me on this exploration. I invite you to consider carefully the nature of my invitation, its radical difference from an invitation to engage in conceptual analysis or in natural scientific inquiry, its bearing upon the issue of human difference and diversity, and its bearing especially on our efforts to find direction in the flow of life.

The Meaning of the Invitation. I'm not inviting you to accept uncritically the account I shall give of conscious performance. If I did that, I'd entangle myself in the very performative self-contradiction we wish to avoid.

I'm inviting you to attend to *your own* conscious performance as I attempt to describe *my own* conscious performance. I'm inviting you to consult your own conscious performance and to ask yourself if I've noticed everything that should be noticed or if I've overlooked something, if I've asked and answered the questions that should be asked and need to be answered, if I've stayed on course by keeping my exploration focused on the question of the informing and guiding role of the basic notions of meaning, objectivity, knowledge, truth, reality, and value in my own conscious performance.

I'm inviting you to give your attention to the non-sensible experience of your own performance, to employ the Language of Self-Possession carefully and to produce accurate descriptions of your own performance, to go ahead and ask your questions about your performance and about the adequacy of the language you're using to describe it, to attempt to answer those questions for yourself, to try to stay on course by keeping your own exploration focused on the question of the informing and guiding role of the basic notions in your own conscious performance, to ask if the role played by the basic notions in your conscious performance is similar to the role I say they play in mine. If you find that your performance is not like mine, I hope you will identify the differences, describe them, and attempt to explain why they exist. If you find that it is as I describe it, I hope you will ask yourself what difference that makes.

I'm inviting you to join me in turning the basic commitment encountered in our elemental meditation on itself. I'm inviting you to attend to your own conscious performance, to try to *make sense* of your own conscious performance, to try to do so *objectively* in the hope of coming to know the *truth* about it, the *reality* of it. I'm also inviting you to ask yourself, once you've done that, if what you've learned about your own conscious performance enables you to take firmer possession of yourself as a conscious performer, if it enables you to be more at home with yourself, and if that is of any *value* to you, to those close to you, to the world at large, and to the course of history. Perhaps, in receiving this invitation, you will wonder whether or not your acceptance of it would really be worthwhile, but I hope you will notice that this reservation, if you have it, expresses your own basic commitment and at least a general understanding of the relationship of my invitation to that commitment.

CPA is an exploration of the largely unexplored, non-sensible domain of conscious performance. It is an attempt to get to know ourselves and, ultimately, to take possession of ourselves and be at home with ourselves. It is an essay in *self-knowledge* for the sake of *self-possession, self-determination, and self-direction.*

The pursuit of self-knowledge and the quest for self-possession are the traditional provinces of Philosophy. The notions of meaning, objectivity, knowledge, truth, reality, and value are the traditional foci of philosophical attention and reflection. CPA, then, may be regarded as an Introduction to Philosophy. But it differs significantly from the usual introductions to philosophical reflection. Two noteworthy approaches at the present time are the Argumentative Approach and the Critical Thinking Approach. The reader who is interested in the differences between these approaches and the approach of CPA may consult Appendix I at the end of this book. Briefly, CPA differs from the usual approaches in its guiding conception of the self to be known. Because its guiding conception of the self to be known is different, the meaning it gives to self-possession is different. The self to be known is *oneself as a conscious performer* or what I have referred to as *the subject-as-subject*. Self-possession is reflective and deliberate conscious performance that is made possible by knowledge of myself as a conscious performer. It is the transformation of my spontaneous and unreflective commitment to meaning, objectivity, knowledge, truth, reality, and value into a deliberate and reflective one. Because the conception of the self to be known is different, the method of CPA is different. Instead of analyzing concepts readily available in the existing Language of Self-Possession, CPA attempts to describe the conscious performance that produces those concepts and that those concepts are meant to identify and clarify.

6. THE LIMITED AIM OF CPA

The descriptive aim of CPA is strictly limited. There is more involved in achieving *self-possession* than just *knowledge* of myself as a conscious performer. I may come to know myself in new ways, even in a new and fundamental way, but I don't have to *do anything about it.* I can ask, "So what?" and I can answer, "It makes no difference to me" or "I just don't care." I may be newly empowered by this new knowledge to take possession of myself in a new way, but I don't have to exercise my new power.

Self-Knowledge and Self-Possession. There is also more to self-knowledge than descriptive clarity about our own conscious performance and about the informing and guiding role played by the basic notions in our performance. There is much more to knowing ourselves than that, even if there's nothing else quite as basic as that to be known about ourselves. Besides the activities, operations, processes, and practices by which I make sense of the world around me and give meaning and direction to my life, there is my past and present relationship to my own conscious performance revealed in the meanings and the meaningless I've meant and still mean and in the values and disvalues I've pursued and still pursue. In my attentiveness to my conscious performance I encounter not just my performance but also the specific contents and specific objects and specific objectives of my past and present conscious performance. If I ignore the specific contents and objects and objectives of my past and present performance, I cannot claim to have adequate knowledge of *myself.* CPA may give me fundamental insight into *what I am*, but it doesn't tell me *who I am or who I am to be.* Besides descriptive knowledge of myself as a conscious performer, there is the story of my own performance, *my story*, and it is ongoing and still under construction.

CPA can illuminate the conscious performance in which all of us engage. But it cannot answer the more personal questions that each of us must ask and answer for herself.

PERSONAL QUESTIONS

What meanings have I been seeking? What have I meant? What have I been trying to be objective about? What have I been trying to know? What have I come to know? What do I care to know the truth about? What truths have I found? Are these 'truths' really true? What aspects of reality have I been most concerned about? What aspects of reality do I consistently ignore or avoid? What courses of action have I found worthwhile, and are they really worthwhile? What have I done? Why have I done those things and not

> others? What should I have done? What am I doing? Why
> am I doing it? Should I continue to do what I've been doing,
> or should I do something else instead? What direction shall
> I give to my life? What direction have I been going? What
> story has been unfolding? What story would I like to live?
> What would I put in my autobiography if I were to write it
> now? What would I like my biographer to say about me?
> What would I like my epitaph to say?

The questions, "What's the story to be told about me so far?"
and "What will the rest of my story be?", cannot be answered by
CPA. These are strictly personal questions. CPA can't answer these
questions, and it doesn't attempt to answer them. To answer them
I must turn my attention to the specific contents, objects, and
objectives of my past and present conscious performance. On the
other hand, if I attend only to the specific contents, objects, and
objectives of my conscious performance and give no attention to
my conscious operations I will continue to perform unreflectively
and spontaneously. I will lack the basic knowledge of myself as a
conscious performer that can be acquired by CPA.

The haphazard and half-hearted pursuit of meaning and value
is better than no pursuit of meaning and value at all. But the
deliberate and whole-hearted pursuit of meaning and value is still
better. The deliberate and wholehearted pursuit of meaning and
value requires knowledge of the role of the basic notions that
inform and guide us in all our dealings with the contents and
objects of our performance. It requires knowledge of *the basic criteria*
we employ when we assign these contents and objects their places
of honor and dishonor in the expanding field of our lifelong
concern with meaning, objectivity, knowledge, truth, reality, and
value.

CPA enables us to take possession of ourselves, but it doesn't
guarantee that we will. Through CPA we come to know ourselves
as conscious performers, but CPA doesn't tell us what the contents
and objects and objectives of our performance thus far have been
or what they ought to be. For adequate self-knowledge we need
basic knowledge of ourselves in our commitment to meaning and value.
This we can achieve through CPA. But we also need *personal
knowledge* of the way that commitment has been unfolding in us up
to this point in our lives. We all have our own stories to tell about
the contents, objects, and objectives of our conscious living so far.
To attain adequate self-possession we need to transform our

unreflective and spontaneous commitment into a reflective and deliberate one. CPA doesn't accomplish this, but it makes it *concretely possible*. We still have to make that deliberate commitment and live up to that commitment by living the stories we'd like our biographers to tell. What those stories will be depends not just on *how* we pursue meaning, objectivity, knowledge, truth, reality, and value but also on *what* meanings we pursue, *what* we try to be objective about, *what* we come to know, *what* truths we hold dear, *what* realities we discover, and *what* values we discern and *what* we do about them.

Chapter Four

CONSCIOUSNESS

I've spoken of conscious performance and conscious operations with great frequency in the preceding chapters. It's time to pause and reflect upon the meanings I've been giving to the words 'conscious' and 'consciousness'. It is of the highest importance that we come to agree on precise meanings of key terms if we are to make any headway in our efforts to understand and take possession of ourselves. The meaning we give to the term 'consciousness' is crucial to our success when we attempt to do CPA.

'Conscious' and 'consciousness' are commonly employed when we speak about ourselves. They belong to the standard vocabulary of the Language of Self-Possession. They are especially important terms, because they pertain to the *accessibility* to us of the performance we wish to describe in CPA. They're often used when we talk about *why* we're able to explore our performance at all and why, in the opinion of some philosophers, we aren't able to explore it fruitfully. Despite Hume's assumption that we are intimately present to ourselves, our access to ourselves as conscious performers remains a disputed issue among philosophers, and it requires careful clarification.

The words 'conscious', 'consciousness', and 'consciously', and the phrase "being conscious," are used in many ways. Here are some of the usages. We say: (1) "I'm conscious," and mean "I'm *awake*"; (2) "I'm conscious of what's happening," and mean "I *know* what's happening," or "I'm *paying attention*"; (3) "I did it consciously," or "I was conscious of doing it," and mean "I did it *deliberately or on purpose*"; (4) "I've become more conscious of those things," and mean "I've been *noticing* those things," or "I've gotten to *know* more about them"; (5) "I'm raising my consciousness," and mean "I'm growing in my *understanding* of myself or the world."

The words 'unconscious', 'unconsciousness' and 'unconsciously', and the phrase "not being conscious," are also used in many ways. For example, we say: (i) "I was unconscious," or "I wasn't conscious," and mean "I was knocked out or *in deep sleep*"; (ii) "I did it unconsciously," or "I wasn't conscious of doing it," and mean "I didn't do it *deliberately*," or "I didn't *mean* to do it"; (iii) "I wasn't really conscious of her feelings," and mean "I wasn't *paying attention to or considering* her feelings." These words and phrases are used in other ways as well. They're words and phrases we use regularly when we speak the unpurified Language of Self-Possession.

1. Consciousness Is Self-Presence

By 'consciousness' let us mean simply 'self-presence' rather than 'knowing' or "paying attention" or 'deliberateness' or 'noticing' or 'understanding' or 'meaning'. Clearly, I must be present to myself if I'm to *come to know* anything at all, *pay attention* to anything at all, *deliberate about* any course of action at all, *notice* anything at all, *understand* anything at all, or *mean* anything at all. If I'm paying attention or noticing anything, I'm present to myself. If I'm understanding, I'm present to myself. If I'm acquiring knowledge, I'm present to myself. If I am deliberating, I'm present to myself. If I'm intending anything at all I'm present to myself. Were it not for my presence to myself in these operations, the word 'conscious' would not have been given so many different meanings. All of these operations, then, are *conscious* operations. Consciousness, we can say, is a quality of all of these operations. But consciousness is not identical with any of them, and it is not all of them taken together. Still, none of them occurs without it.

Consciousness seems to be a *quality* of these operations and others. Let us mean by 'consciousness' our *presence to ourselves in the performance* of these operations and of any others we can name, and let us call those acts we perform while and as present to ourselves *conscious operations*. Because our operations are conscious, because we're present to ourselves in our performance of them, we can name them, and we're able to confuse them with our presence to ourselves in them.

When we say that consciousness is self-presence we're not merely substituting one word for another word. We are attempting to get beneath or behind the language we use in order to focus our attention on an especially significant quality or property of our performance. Our performance is conscious; in our performance, as Hume noted, we're intimately present to ourselves. To get beneath our language together, we must use language. In CPA there is a permanent danger of mistaking the words we use for the things to which we're trying to direct our attention by using those words. When I say that consciousness is self-presence, I'm "talking around" the object in order to bring the object to light, in order to bring it to the center of our attention. Once we've identified for ourselves what it is we wish to understand, the specific words we use become a little less important. We can use other words, within limits, as long as we know what it is we're talking about. Commonly, once we've identified and understood an object, we can formulate that understanding in language in a great variety of ways. But there already exists a Language of Self-Possession. We serve communication better if we retain its familiar vocabulary and attempt to link that vocabulary more closely and tether it more tightly to what it purports to identify and describe.

Let's attempt to bring our consciousness to light. The object in question, we must remember, is *the subject-as-performing-subject*, not *the subject-as-observed-object*. Besides being the observed or imagined objects of our own or others' performance, we are the conscious subjects of our performance, present to ourselves in our performance, even when we're observing ourselves in mirrors, or imagining witnessing ourselves or being witnessed behaving this way or that way.

We distinguish being awake from being asleep. How do these differ? When I'm asleep, no one is home. When I wake up, I'm back. But how do I know I'm back? I know I'm back because I'm present to myself again. When I'm awake, I'm able to say that I'm awake. When I'm asleep – in deep sleep, that is, and not even dreaming – I'm not present to myself. I can't give you a report of my *experience* of sleeping, neither while I'm asleep nor after I've awakened. I may be present to someone else who is awake and in my room while I'm sleeping, but I'm certainly not present to myself. I can draw the confident conclusion that I was lying in my bed all night, but this is the conclusion of an inference from my recollection of going to bed and my presence to myself in the morning light. I have no experience of being in deep sleep. I'm not present to myself in deep sleep. I'm unconscious.

In my dreaming, though, I'm minimally present to myself. My self-presence when I'm dreaming is fragmentary and intermittent and odd. It's often difficult even to remember my dreams, so close am I to unconsciousness when I'm dreaming. When I do remember them, what I remember is often full of gaps, incoherent, anomalous, fantastic. When I try to report my dreams, I am often struck by how incongruous and inexpressible my self-experience when I'm dreaming is. Much more is possible in my dreams than in my waking life. Even the impossible is possible in my dreams, and the improbable is commonplace. My presence to myself when I'm awake reveals a more controlled flow of experience and activity than my presence to myself in my dreams. What sorts of controls are these that are operative in my waking life but virtually absent in my dreams and completely absent when I'm in deep sleep?

In deep sleep, I have no experience at all. I am not present to myself, no one's home, and nothing at all is present to me. I'm a substance or thing among other substances or things, nothing more than a potential subject and actually only an object. To myself, I'm nothing at all; to those who are awake, I'm a human being on a bed. When I'm dreaming, I'm minimally present to myself, and the flow of my experience is often incongruous and inexpressible. When I'm awake, I'm present to myself in a different, more controlled and expressible way. If I'm called upon to do so, I can describe the self-present flow of my experience. It will be more difficult for me to describe my operations than to describe their contents, but at least it's concretely possible for me to do so. I'll make use of the existing Language of Self-Possession to do so, and initially my descriptions might be somewhat vague and imprecise.

We may wonder if it's enough to say that consciousness is self-presence. My presence to myself in my dreaming is quite different from my presence to myself when I wake up. Is the self-presence of being-awake *of just one kind throughout*, no matter what I'm doing when I'm awake? Is waking consciousness homogeneous self-presence? Or, are there *significant variations or significant differences* in my presence to myself while I'm awake.

2. SELF-PRESENCE IS A QUALITY OF OPERATIONS

We can distinguish, then, between (1) deep sleep, or simple absence of consciousness, or unconsciousness, (2) dreaming or fragmentary or minimal consciousness, and (3) being awake or waking consciousness. But, just as there is a difference between dream consciousness and ordinary waking consciousness, so there are also important differences to be noticed in waking consciousness. It is commonly assumed that there are no significant differences in waking consciousness, that waking consciousness is homogeneous, because the differences in waking consciousness are much subtler than the difference between dreaming and being awake.

When I'm awake, I'm not always awake *in the same way*. My presence to myself when I've just awakened from a dream differs significantly from my presence to myself when I'm wrestling with a decision that might affect the rest of my life. When I wake up to the buzzing of the alarm or to the ringtone on my cell phone and I sit, still somewhat dazed, on the edge of my bed, I'm certainly present to myself. I can report that I've just awakened. I can do that because I've returned, so to speak. I'm not just *a thing or substance*, a human being, balanced precariously on the edge of another thing or substance, a bed. Now I'm *a subject*, present to myself in my recollecting of remnants of my dreams and in my imaginative anticipation of my projects for the day. If I had been awakened out of a deep sleep, I might have said, "Where am I?" or "What time is it?" or "What day is it?" I might experience a temporary disorientation when I re-emerge suddenly from a deep sleep. The sudden transition from unconsciousness to consciousness leaves me disorientated. The transition from minimal dream consciousness to waking consciousness is gradual and less disorientating, but the change in my presence to myself is obvious to me as residual dream-feelings and dream-images are replaced gradually by waking experience and anticipation. But transitions and changes in my waking self-presence attract less attention and easily go unnoticed.

Momentarily disorientated self-presence and my presence to myself when I'm just waking up differ radically from my presence to myself when I'm trying to solve a problem or trying to make a decision about my future and trying to decide upon an appropriate course of action. When I'm trying to solve a problem or to make an important decision, my self-presence is heightened, so to speak; I'm *more awake* than I am when I've just been awakened by the ringing of my alarm clock or my cell phone. We often say, even when we're already awake, that we still need to "wake up." Sometimes we suggest to others that they should "wake up," even though they're obviously neither in deep sleep nor dreaming. A fragment of writings from the 6th century B.C.E., attributed to the philosopher Heraclitus, reads: "We must not act and speak like men asleep" [Fr. 73]. What sense can be made of this notion of "waking up" after I've already awakened, of heightening my waking consciousness? Can we identify differences in our presence to ourselves in our waking consciousness? Can we describe them? Once we've described them, can we explain these differences in our waking self-presence?

Presence to myself is always presence to myself "as doing something." When I'm first awakened, I'm present to myself as *hearing* the alarm, as *noticing* the morning light filtering through the drawn curtains, as *wondering* what time it is, as *feeling* tired, as *remembering* fragments of my dreams, as *envisioning courses of action* to be pursued during the day, as *deciding* to stay in bed for ten more minutes, *etc*. Even when I'm dreaming, I'm *imagining*. The activity of imagining is related to occurrences in my nervous system. Sometimes, when I report my dreams upon waking, they seem to have been little more than imaginative and emotive releases of nervous tension. Sometimes, as I try to recount what I was dreaming about, I get the sense that there's some deeper meaning to my dream-experience. Psychologists and psychoanalysts have hypothesized that some types of dreams just "knit the raveled sleeve of care," as Shakespeare put it, while other types are subtle and indirect communications to ourselves of things we cannot or will not tell ourselves directly. Some theorize that dreams that occur very near to the time of waking are carriers of symbolic meaning that, when interpreted, proves to be pertinent to the future conduct of our lives in the short term or in the very long term. Whatever the complete account of dreams turns out to be, it is clear that our presence to ourselves in our dreaming is a minimal consciousness that accompanies the activity of imagining. But, when I'm in deep sleep, I'm not doing anything at all, and so I'm not present to myself at all.

Changes in Self-presence. Let's suppose, then, that consciousness, my intimate presence to myself, is *a quality or characteristic or property of my operations*. But, not only do I imagine and feel in dreaming sleep, but I perform a still wider variety of operations when I'm awake. We should expect to discover that our self-presence varies with variations in the operations we perform. We should expect our self-experience in waking consciousness to change with changes in the operations we're performing.

Upon reflection, it does seem to me that my presence to myself in my waking performance changes with changes in the operations I perform. The prevalent assumption that waking consciousness is homogeneous inclines me to overlook these changes in my waking self-presence. My presence to myself in my *inquiring*, for example, is different from my self-presence when I'm *evaluating*. When I'm inquiring, I experience myself as concerned especially with *meaning*. I want to know what something is, what makes it what it is, what it's related to, how it came to be, why it happened, or how often it happens. In my evaluating, in contrast, I experience myself as concerned especially with *value*. I want to know if something's worthwhile, what good it is, what difference it makes, what I ought to do, or what I ought to do about it. The difference between my self-presence in my mere experiencing and my deliberating seems to be still greater. In merely experiencing, I'm present to myself as unconcerned about either meaning or value. There seem to be noticeable differences in my presence to myself along the whole spectrum, from my fragmentary and minimal presence to myself in my dreaming to my more controlled and intensified or heightened presence to myself in my decision-making and deliberate acting, and these changes seem to coincide with changes in the operations I perform.

There is a tendency to assume that the only distinctions to be made in our presence to ourselves are those between unconsciousness, dreaming consciousness, and ordinary waking consciousness. It is commonly assumed that, once we've awakened, we're *fully conscious or fully present to ourselves* and that there are no significant differences to be noticed in our presence to ourselves once we're awake. When the ascent from dream consciousness to ordinary waking consciousness has been completed, we tend to assume we've reached the apex of possible self-presence.

We might be inclined to *imagine* ordinary waking consciousness as something like an unchanging medium or atmosphere or arena or theater, separate from our operations, *into which* we enter and from which we depart, *in which* our operations are performed, and *in which* we observe our operations while they're being performed. We might imagine this unchanging medium or atmosphere or arena or theater to exist even when we're not performing any operations, even before we've begun to operate, like the Roman Colosseum before the arrival of the spectators and the gladiators. But when I'm not performing any operations at all, I'm not present to myself. My consciousness changes with changes *in* the operations I perform. My presence to myself seems to be *in* my operating, not something separate from my operations, and not something that my operations are in, as spectators and gladiators are in the Colosseum. It's a quality of my operations, and *by operating* I'm conscious. I *remain* conscious by continuing to operate, even when I'd rather go to sleep. To get to sleep, I have to stop noticing, wondering, asking questions, deliberating, trying to make decisions, and so on. I have to *stop operating*. When I stop operating, I lose consciousness.

My self-presence may be expected to change, not just with my performance of different operations, but also with my performance of the same operations recurrently over time. It may be expected to change with the recurrent performance of the same operations. My pursuit of meaning, objectivity, knowledge, truth, reality, and value over time *changes my relation* to meaning, objectivity, knowledge, truth, reality, and value. That changing relation is also experienced in my performance of conscious operations.

My conscious operations are performed recurrently. The same operations *occur over and over again*, but their contents vary. The flow of conscious performance is constituted and guided by the basic notions. I pursue meaning, but I don't pursue the *same* meaning over and over again. I pursue knowledge, but I don't pursue the *same* bit of knowledge repeatedly. I pursue truth, but I don't pursue the *same* truths time and again. I seek to determine what's worthwhile for me to do, but I don't settle on one course of action and do it robotically in *every* situation that arises. The recurrence of my operations is not a repetition of the contents of my operations. It is an ongoing development of myself as constituted and guided by the notions. As I develop in virtue of the recurrent performance of operations, I become more experienced, more knowledgeable, more skilled, wiser, and I am present to myself as more experienced, more knowledgeable, more skilled, and wiser in the performance of my operations.

In what specific ways does my presence to myself vary with changes in my operations? How am I present to myself differently in the performance of different operations? Can I describe myself as more fully present to myself in some operations than I am in others? Is there a heightening of my consciousness that accompanies changes in the operations I perform when I'm awake? Is there a raising of my consciousness over time as I engage in the recurrent performance of the same operations? What do we mean when we distinguish higher from lower, more from less, deeper from shallower, broader from narrower consciousness?

Heightening Consciousness. When we speak of heightening or raising our consciousness, we're using spatial language to speak about differences in our presence to ourselves. What does 'heightening' mean? What does 'raising' mean? These are spatial terms we use to talk about differences in our presence to ourselves that result from our conscious performance of different operations and of the same operations over time. Can we replace this spatial language with language more appropriate to speaking about our merely temporal operations?

'Heightening' and 'raising' have positive connotations. We assume these changes in our presence to ourselves to be worthwhile. Hidden in our use of these words we use to describe changes in our self-presence is our basic commitment to meaning, objectivity, knowledge, truth, reality, and value. We take it for granted, in our performance of operations, that we're getting somewhere, that we're growing or developing and not merely changing, and we seem to take it for granted that in the performance of some operations we are approximating more closely to the realization of the ideals expressed by the basic notions.

Changes in self-presence are related to the roles of the basic notions in our performance. The basic notions inform and guide our performance of the different operations. We experience the constitutive and guiding role of the notions differently in our performance of different operations. They also inform and guide our recurrent performance of operations over time. We experience the results of their informing and guiding role in the recurrent performance of our operations. But there is no guarantee that I will seek meaning, objectivity, knowledge, truth, reality, and value whole-heartedly. There is no guarantee that my performance will be reflective, deliberate, and methodical rather than unreflective, spontaneous, and haphazard. There is no guarantee that I will be successful in the performance of particular operations. There is no guarantee that I will develop in relation to meaning, objectivity, knowledge, truth, reality, and value over the long term.

If I do perform operations successfully, and if I do develop in my relationship to the basic notions, there will be a change in my presence to myself in my performance over time that can be appropriately described as a 'heightening' or a 'raising' of my consciousness. I will have changed as a conscious performer, and the change will be for the better. I will be differently present to myself as being more attuned to the meanings of things, as being more open-minded, as being more knowledgeable, as living more fully in the truth, as being more realistic, as being engaged in more worthwhile courses of action, and as being more worthy of my own respect and of the respect of others for being that way.

But it seems we can also distinguish among operations between those that are more removed from the ideals expressed by the basic notions and those that are more proximate to those ideals. Besides the heightening of consciousness that comes with the recurrent performance of operations over time, there are changes in my presence to myself that occur as I make the transition from performance of more remote operations to performance of more proximate ones. In merely seeing an object that I don't yet understand, I'm more remote from the ideal of knowledge than I am in grasping a possible meaning of that object. In merely grasping a possible meaning of an object of my inquiry, I am more remote from the ideal of value than I am in deliberating about the best course of action to take in relation to that object. There seems, then, to be a heightening of consciousness that occurs in the performance of different operations in addition to the heightening of consciousness that comes with the recurrent performance of the same operations over time.

In order to achieve greater clarity on these issues, we must give serious attention to the relevant data. But where is this data to be found? It is to be found only in our presence to ourselves in our performing, sometimes unreflectively, spontaneously, and haphazardly, and sometimes more reflectively and deliberately. It is to be found, not only in our presence to ourselves in our recurrent performance of the same operations over time, but also in our presence to ourselves in our performance *now*. Not only are we able to recollect ourselves as conscious performers years ago and to detect a heightening of our presence to ourselves over the intervening years, but we're also able to attend to our present performance and to detect a heightening of our presence to ourselves as we perform different operations. We gain access to the data we need in order to come to know ourselves as conscious performers by attending to ourselves in our performance. We have been and remain present to ourselves in our performance, because consciousness is a quality of our operations.

3. SHIFTING ATTENTION TO OUR OPERATIONS

We're always present to ourselves in our operations, but we're normally preoccupied with the objects or objectives of our operations. We're usually more attentive to what we're acting on or pursuing than we are to the performance itself. If we are to locate the relevant data, we must shift our attention from the objects of our operations to our operating.

For example, instead of attending to *what* we're seeing, hearing, tasting, touching, and smelling, we must shift our attention to the seeing, hearing, tasting, touching and smelling. Instead of attending to *what* we're asking about or trying to understand, we must shift our attention to the asking and the effort to understand. Instead of attending to the ideas we're weighing and criticizing and the courses of action about which we're deliberating, we must shift our attention to the critical and evaluative operations in which we are engaged. In order to get hold of the data we're after, we must accomplish a shift of attention *from the objects and objectives of our operations to the operations themselves.*

We may put this issue in another, more precise and technical way. When I am awake, I am experiencing. That experiencing is at one and the same time an experience of something and an experience of myself experiencing something. To be awake is at once to have something present to me and to be present to myself. If I weren't present to myself, I wouldn't be awake, and I wouldn't be having any experience at all. If I weren't having any experience, I wouldn't be awake, and I wouldn't be present to myself. Every experience involves an object experienced and the one who has the experience, the experiencing subject.

Let's represent "seeing something" by the symbol AA^* where A represents the "something seen" and A^* represents the 'seeing'. "Seeing something" is a combination of A, the content of an operation, and A^*, the operation. Again, "seeing something" is an operation with a content. Similarly, "asking about something" can be represented by the symbol AA^* where A represents "what I'm asking about" and A^* represents the 'asking' that I'm doing. "Asking about something" is a combination of A, the content of an operation, and A^*, the operation. "Asking about something" is an operation with a content. Again, "deliberating about a possible course of action" can be represented by the same symbol AA^* where A represents "a possible course of action" and A^* represents the 'deliberating' that I'm doing. "Deliberating about a possible course of action" is a combination of A, the content of an operation, and A^*, the operation that I am performing.

Any conscious experience, then – whether it's an experience of seeing something, or of asking about something, or of deliberating about a possible course of action – offers us three possible objects for our attention. We can attend (i) to the combination, AA^*, as when I say, "I'm trying to solve (A^*) a problem (A)"; or (ii) to A alone, as when I say, "This is a mathematical problem (A)"; or (iii) to A^* alone, as when I say, "Asking questions can be very frustrating (A^*)." Again, we can attend (i) to "seeing (A^*) something (A)" or "asking about (A^*) something (A)" or "deliberating about (A*) a possible course of action (A)," or we can attend (ii) to the 'something (A)' we're seeing or to "what we are asking about (A)" or to "what we're deliberating about (A)" without regard for the seeing or the asking or the deliberating, or we can attend (iii) to the seeing (A*) or the asking (A*) or the deliberating (A*), without regard for the 'something' seen or "what we are asking about" or "the possible course of action." What happens when we attend in these different ways?

In ordinary living we typically attend to the combination AA* without distinguishing A and A*. We don't normally attend to A alone or to A* alone, but to AA*.

AN ACCIDENT

Suppose I report to a friend that I witnessed a terrible accident yesterday while I was driving, and my friend invites me to describe the experience. My friend has asked me, "What was it like to experience that?" She has asked me for an account of AA*, the combination. I describe hearing the screeching tires and the sound of the impact, the sight of the cars involved spinning and veering off the road, the shock I felt, how scared I felt, *etc.* My friend didn't ask me about just A or just A*. My description is not simply of A, the contents of my operations, and not simply of A*, the operations, but of AA*, my experience of "seeing something," "hearing something," "feeling something," "being shocked or frightened by something." In ordinary living we typically attend to the combination, to our "operations with their contents."

But sometimes we separate the contents from the operations and attend to them alone. Suppose I also happen to be a mechanical engineer, and I'm employed a week later by an insurance company to determine if the injuries suffered in the accident I also happened to have witnessed were due to a mechanical or structural flaw in the design of one or both of the cars involved. I drive out to the wrecking yard, examine the cars in question, and write up my observations. I describe the points of impact, the bent frames, the collapsed roofs, the shattered

windows, the caved-in doors, *etc.*, and I draw a conclusion
about the adequacy of the design of the passenger
compartments. My attention has shifted from AA*, the
combination of the content of my experience with the
operations I perform, to A alone and to the relations
between the various contents of a number of operations of
seeing and asking and understanding.

Further, sometimes we separate the operations from
the contents and attend to them alone. Suppose I now
receive a summons to appear in court as an expert witness
in a lawsuit filed against the company that manufactured
one of the cars. I take my seat on the witness stand, and
an attorney for the defense proceeds to question me. His
questions draw my attention and the attention of the jury
to my performance of operations, to A*: "Did you do a
thorough examination of the car in question? Did you
examine the car in the daytime or at night? Did you assume
there would be a mechanical defect before you examined
the car? Did you draw your conclusion strictly on the basis
of your examination of the car? Did you ask the relevant
questions about what you saw? What makes you an expert
in this field? Do you have training in scientific procedure?
What makes you think your conclusions are correct? Have
you received any payments or gifts from the manufacturer
of the car in question? Have you ever met the driver of the
car before?" My attention and the attention of the jury are
drawn by the attorney's questions to A*, to the operations I
performed and to how I performed them. Recall that I also
happened to witness the accident when it occurred, but the
attorney is not interested in AA*. He is interested in A*
alone, my examination of the car, the way I examined it,
and the adequacy of my examination, because my
performance of my operations will either lend credibility to
my account of A, the car and its mechanical and structural
integrity, or reduce its credibility. It will make me either
credible or not credible.

Now, suppose that, subsequent to my testimony, as
I'm descending the courthouse steps, I begin to reflect on

the questions the attorney asked me and upon the answers I gave. I think about the attorney's special interest in how well I performed my investigation. He was interested in my objectivity or lack of objectivity. It occurs to me that, while I was in the wrecking yard, I wasn't really paying much attention to the objectivity of my performance. I begin to review my experience in the wrecking yard now with an interest in the objectivity of my performance. I'm fairly sure I performed objectively, but I begin to wonder what it is, exactly, about objective performance that distinguishes it from biased performance? My interest has shifted again to A*, to my conscious operations without regard for their content. But the shift is now so emphatic that I raise a more far-reaching question about the objectivity of conscious operations in general, and not merely the question about the objectivity of my own performance on that day in the wrecking yard. What was a cursory shift of attention to A*, provoked by the attorney's questions during my courtroom testimony, has become a deliberate shift of attention to A*. I'm on the threshold now of Conscious Performance Analysis. But I can't maintain this deliberate attentiveness to the performance of conscious operations and pursue the philosophical question of objectivity now. Not only do I find conscious operations to be extraordinarily ethereal objects, but I have to get back to work. After all, I'm not a philosopher; I'm a mechanical engineer and, occasionally, an expert witness.

In ordinary living, we typically attend to AA*, to the combination, to the operation with its content. This is the kind of attending we do as ordinary men and women in our everyday lives. Our practical and social involvements more or less determine that we preoccupy ourselves, not merely with the objects of operations and not just with our operations, but with the relationship of the objects to ourselves as operating subjects. But, if we move out of ordinary living and into the natural sciences, for example, we are expected to develop the skill of 'observation' (A*). Scientific observation is developed attentiveness to A alone, to the content alone and to its relationships to other contents of our operations, to other A's.

Notice that it is easiest and seemingly most natural for us to attend to AA*, the combination, the operation with its content, just as it is easiest and seemingly most natural for us to live ordinary lives. It is a bit harder for us to attend to A alone, to the content without regard for the operation, and this requires a deliberate shift of attention and some training. It is a challenge to depart from our ordinary way of attending and to begin to observe scientifically. It's an even bigger challenge to attend to A* alone, to the operations without regard for their content. To attend to A* alone requires that we overcome our ordinary preoccupation with the objects and the practical, social, and scientific objectives of our operations, considered either together with our operations or in isolation from them. This, too, requires a deliberate shift of attention and some training.

In CPA, in order to get hold of the data relevant to our investigation we must attend to A* alone, to the operations and to their relations to one another, without being distracted either by their contents or by the relations of their contents to our practical, social, or scientific objectives of the moment. This confronts us with a special difficulty. As the natural scientist has to develop the skill of "scientific observation" in order to attend consistently and without distraction to A alone, to the contents of experience alone and their relations to one another, so the philosopher engaged in CPA has to develop the skill of "philosophical reflection" in order to attend to A* alone, to the operations alone and their relations to one another. This requires an extraordinary shift of attention from AA*, operations in combination with their objects, not to A alone, the objects of our operations, but to A* alone, ourselves as operating subjects. We've already noticed that we seem to spontaneously resist this shift of attention and, even when we do make this shift, it is easily reversed by the demands of ordinary living.

4. RESISTING THE SHIFT OF ATTENTION

The shift of attention to ourselves as operating subjects is obviously possible, because we're conscious. As in the illustration above, it is taken for granted that attorneys, juries, witnesses, and judges are able to accomplish this shift of attention in the interest of determining the credibility of courtroom testimony. We also accomplish this shift of attention intermittently and for brief periods of time before we ever undertake anything like CPA. But a prolonged shift of attention is often resisted. The resistance may be spontaneous. It may be rooted (1) in our spontaneous preference for sensible objects and, more generally, in our spontaneous interest in and preoccupation with the contents of our operations. The resistance may be slightly more sophisticated and slightly more deliberate. It may be rooted (2) in our uncritical adoption of the meaning commonly given to the distinction between subjectivity and objectivity in the existing Language of Self-Possession. Finally, it may have its source (3) in a mistaken high-cultural conception of consciousness as itself another operation with a content or object.

Let's consider these three sources of resistance to the prolonged shift of attention required by CPA, even though it will involve us in a bit of repetition. The roots of resistance to CPA are deeply imbedded. If they aren't unearthed, we may not be willing to undertake CPA, or we may even think CPA is impossible. Either way, we won't derive the benefits it has to offer.

4.1 OUR PREFERENCE FOR SENSIBLE CONTENTS (AGAIN)

In addition to the ordinary preoccupation with AA*, there is an ordinary preference for A's in that combination that can be *sensed*, for objects that can be seen, heard, tasted, touched, smelled. There are contents of operations other than the operations involved in sensing. There are contents of understanding, or ideas, and these can't be sensed. There are contents of deliberation, or future courses of action. These can be imagined, but, as future possibilities, they can't yet be sensed. Even though we experience having ideas and experience deliberating upon future courses of action, there remains a preference for the contents of acts of sensing. It is as though, in our ordinary living, we assume that if something isn't immediately available to one or more of the five senses, or to some extension of those senses, or at least imaginable, it cannot possibly be real. Because we all have a basic commitment to the pursuit of the real, if we think only sensible objects are real we aren't likely to be very interested in exploring non-sensible ones.

This ordinary preference for sensible data is strongly reinforced by the tremendous success natural scientists have had as a result of their insistence upon attending only to sensible A's, to contents of acts of sensing. We have already discussed the natural scientific restriction to sensible data. Natural scientists adhere to a rule of procedure that restricts their attention to data that can be sensed. But operations are not sensible data. They are not given to the five senses or to our extensions of them. They are given only in our presence to ourselves as performing operations with contents.

Because A* is not sensible data, it is more or less naturally left in the background in our everyday living, and it is often deliberately ignored in our natural scientific practice.

Ordinary and scientific inattentiveness to A* alone, to the operations of the operating subject, may be justified by the practical and social aims of everyday living and by the limited scientific aims of natural scientists. But the aims of philosophical reflection are not those of ordinary living or natural science. In our ordinary living we're interested in surviving, in getting things done, in meeting the demands our environment makes upon us, and in developing and maintaining social relations. As natural scientists, we're interested in understanding the natural world and in predicting occurrences in that world. As philosophers, we're interested in coming to know and take possession of ourselves as subjects of the operations by which we constitute and guide our practical and social lives, pursue our natural scientific understanding, and do everything else we do. If we restrict our attention to sensible data, we ignore the experience of the operations to which we must attend and that we must understand if we are to come to know and take possession of ourselves as operating subjects.

If the advisability of attending to our conscious operations is questioned by highly practical and social or narrowly scientific people, there can be no question that, if we choose to do so, we can attend to our operations. We are conscious or present to ourselves in our operating. Just as we can isolate and consider A, the content of an experience, so we can isolate and consider A*, the operation in an experience.

The fact that a conscious operation is non-sensible does not mean that it is beyond the reach of our attention. The accessibility of conscious operations is taken for granted, in fact, both in ordinary living and in scientific practice. Ordinary experience involves attentiveness to AA*, so A* already falls within the range of our possible attentiveness even if it doesn't receive our undivided attention. Scientific experience involves a shift of attention from AA* to A exclusively, but exclusive *attention to A*, in obedience to the scientific restriction to sensible data, is yet another experience of AA*. So, A* always falls within the range of possible attentiveness of the practicing scientist, even if only A receives her undivided attention. In ordinary waking consciousness it is taken for granted that A* is accessible. The scientific mode of waking consciousness is a deliberate departure from that ordinary mode in which the accessibility of A* is also taken for granted. It is a deliberate shift of attention from AA* to A exclusively.

A shift of attention from AA* to A* also already occurs intermittently in both ordinary living and in scientific practice. In ordinary living a shift of attention from AA* to A* is made when corporate officers gather to reflect upon the way they make their decisions or when corporate employees sit through a seminar on improving their creativity. In scientific practice a shift of attention from AA* to A* is made when scientific investigators stipulate that observation should be restricted to sensible data and that scientific method should be followed. It seems that when we really want to take ourselves seriously in our ordinary practical and social living, we attend to our operations, to our own performance as practical or social subjects. It seems that when we really want to take ourselves seriously in our scientific practice, we attend to our operations, to our own performance as scientific subjects.

Initially, it may seem that our conscious operations are inaccessible to us, because we tend to assume that we encounter real things only through operations of sensing. Before we have explored the notion of reality at work in our conscious performance, we spontaneously assign a specific meaning to it. We come up with a determinate *concept* of reality without regard for the fundamental role played by the basic notions in all of our conscious performance. We specify the meaning of the notion of reality without regard for its *operative meaning* in the full range of our conscious performance. When we reflect upon our actual practice, it becomes quite clear that our conscious operations are accessible to us, and that our assignment of a specific meaning to the notion of reality is premature and unjustified.

4.2 'SUBJECTIVITY' AND 'OBJECTIVITY'

Besides our spontaneous preference for sensible contents, there is another obstacle to taking ourselves seriously enough to turn our attention deliberately to our conscious operations. That obstacle is the familiar distinction between 'subjectivity' and 'objectivity', between "being merely subjective" and "being objective."

We prescribe objectivity for others and ourselves. We warn others and ourselves against being merely subjective. In issuing these prescriptions and warnings we exhibit our basic commitment. But we do so without having explored the unfolding of our basic commitment in our conscious performance. To be subjective, we commonly assume, is to be biased, prejudiced, one-sided, ideological, and so on. To be objective, we also assume, is to minimize or even to eliminate the influence of our subjectivity on our conscious performance. There's something very wrong with these assumptions, despite their praiseworthy intent.

When we turn our attention to A*, to our operations, we're turning our attention from A, the contents or objects of our operations, to our performance as subjects, to what I have referred to as the subject-as-subject. If we take seriously the advice that is commonly given, we might see little value in that shift of attention and maintain our attentiveness to AA*, the operations with their contents or, as may seem even better, restrict our attention to A, to the objects of our operations, in imitation of the natural scientist.

What point would there be to turning our attention to the *merely subjective* domain in which bias and prejudice find their home and out of which they arise to cripple or destroy our objectivity? If there is any point at all to shifting our attention to our subjective performance, it is assumed, it can only be for the sake of reducing, minimizing, and even extirpating the influence of that subjective performance in our lives. But, if we were to succeed in extirpating the influence of that subjective performance, we would no longer be able to pursue objectivity because we'd no longer have conscious lives.

Insofar as their purpose is to reduce, minimize, or eliminate bias and prejudice in our thinking and acting, the precepts "Be objective!" and "Don't be subjective!" as commonly understood are excellent pieces of advice, redolent of our basic commitment to objectivity, knowledge, truth, the real, and value. Of course, we should be objective. Of course, we should not be biased or one-sided or prejudiced in our thinking. We have a basic commitment to objectivity. Typically, though, the commitment is only spontaneous, it can escape our attention, we can forget about it, we can violate it, and we benefit from reminding ourselves and being reminded by others of our basic commitment.

But, if we follow these precepts as they are commonly understood, we may see little value in shifting our attention to our operations. We may neglect to do so, or fail to do so with seriousness, and deprive ourselves of adequate self-knowledge. The 'objectivity' that the precepts encourage us to pursue is portrayed as *opposed to subjectivity*. When we are advised *to be objective*, we are being advised *to not be subjective*. But if being objective is *a way I'm supposed to operate and act,* then it cannot be strictly *opposed to* subjectivity. It has to be *a kind of subjectivity, a way of being a performing subject.* It has to be a subjective operation or some set of subjective operations performed a certain way.

Again, if the recommendation is that I should eliminate all intrusions by my subjective performance in order to be objective, then it seems that the best way for me to achieve objectivity would be to slip into a deep sleep. If I'm not in a deep sleep, I'm conscious. If I'm conscious, I'm operating. If I'm operating consciously, I'm operating in the only way I can operate, as the subject of my conscious performance. If I'm a performing subject, I'm being subjective. It is obviously absurd to recommend falling into a deep sleep or losing consciousness as the best way to achieve objectivity. It is absurd to suggest that I can be objective in my subjective performance without engaging in subjective performance.

The word 'subjective' must be cleansed of its misleading connotation of bias, one-sidedness, and arbitrariness if we are to recognize that the shift of our attention to our performance as subjects is something worth doing. The word 'objective' must not be understood to be the antonym of 'subjective'. The advice "Be objective!" must be understood as a recommendation *to be subjective in a specific way*. We have to figure out what that way is. We have to determine what is involved in *objective subjective performance*. In order to determine whether or not we are *objective subjects*, we have to attend to our conscious operations, become familiar with them, discover their relations to one another, to the objects to which we are related through them, and to the basic notions. We have to explore the notion of objectivity *at work* in our subjective conscious performance.

The invitation to engage in CPA is not an invitation to abandon our commitment to objectivity and to immerse ourselves in an exploration of a domain that is characterized only by bias, prejudice, personal preferences, and other obstacles to the achievement of objectivity. It is an invitation to discover the type of conscious performance that deserves to be called objective conscious performance. Naturally, CPA will have to include a critical account of biased and one-sided conscious performance, but that account can't be given until we've completed our exploration   of the informing and guiding role of the basic notions in the flow of conscious performance.

4.3 CONSCIOUSNESS ISN'T ANOTHER CONSCIOUS OPERATION

It's evident now that we can shift our attention from the contents of our performance to our performance. We do this with greater or less frequency in our ordinary practical and social living and in our high-cultural intellectual pursuits. We can do this because we're conscious, present to ourselves in our performance. But these facts don't prevent those who theorize about human consciousness from concluding that the shift of attention I've been describing is impossible and that, therefore, the entire project of CPA is impossible.

The conclusion that it is impossible to reflect upon our operations is rooted in a conception of consciousness quite different from the one I've offered. We should give this conception of consciousness serious attention, even though it flies in the face of the facts and involves its adherents in embarrassing performative self-contradiction. It is a conception that is deeply ingrained in contemporary high culture. It has been and is still held by highly educated philosophers who produce complex arguments to support and defend it. It has filtered down and sedimented in our Language of Self-Possession. When we use the word 'conscious' and feel ourselves compelled to add 'of' – as in "I wasn't conscious of …" – the influence of this conception is quietly, effectively, and maliciously at work. The implication of this conception, inadvertently validated by our casual employment of the existing Language of Self-Possession and fully grasped by its high-cultural adherents, is that we are incapable of coming to know ourselves as conscious performers. Obviously, if we can't come to know our own conscious performance, we can't take possession of ourselves as conscious performers, and we can't become reflective and deliberate in our conscious performance. This competing and widely held conception of consciousness has dire implications, and it has to be acknowledged and addressed before we proceed.

Let us suppose, then, that consciousness is one operation among the many others we perform. Suppose that we are present to ourselves or conscious only when we perform *this* operation. In this usage of the word 'conscious', sometimes I am "conscious *of*" what I'm doing, and sometimes I'm not "conscious *of*" what I'm doing. There no verb form of 'consciousness' we can use to name this operation that consciousness is supposed to be. The word 'consciousing' is not part of the vocabulary of the Language of Self-Possession. As we shall see, there's a good reason why it isn't.

A word that is often used to name the operation that consciousness is thought by some to be, is one that I've used already in my discussion of the quotation from Hume in Chapter Two. It is one that Hume used himself: 'reflection'. Neither I nor Hume, though, uses 'reflection' as a synonym for 'consciousness'.

Recall that Hume spoke of 'reflecting' on the operations of the mind. For Hume, 'reflection' is the name for the set of operations we perform when we explore our conscious performance. Reflection involves *attending to our performance, describing it, raising questions about it, discovering order in it,* and so on. We can reflect upon our operations and, as the quotation from Hume illustrates, we can reflect upon our reflection on our operations. We can attend to our reflective performance, describe it, ask questions about it, and so on.

For Hume, reflection is the performance of operations with regard to *what is already intimately present to us*. We are intimately present to ourselves in our operations. We are also intimately present to ourselves in the set of operations we perform when we reflect upon our operations. They're just more operations in which we're intimately self-present. Our intimate self-presence makes reflection possible, and it also makes reflection on our reflection possible. It is not itself the set of operations we perform when we reflect upon the operations in which we're intimately present to ourselves. It's not one unusual, automatic, continuously performed operation either, like the inward gazing of a lidless inner eye. Our intimate self-presence is not an operation at all.

I agree with Hume about this. Like him, I've distinguished between my intimate self-presence and reflection. I've identified consciousness and defined it as my presence to myself in my operations. I've identified reflection with attending to my operations, describing them, and asking questions about them. But many people think of consciousness as an operation, and they identify consciousness with reflection upon our operations.

This mistaken identification of consciousness with reflection is revealed in the way we sometimes use the Language of Self-Possession. We might say, "I wasn't *reflecting upon* what I was doing, so I wasn't *conscious that* I was doing it," or "I was doing that *unconsciously*; I should have been *conscious of* it; I should have *reflected on* what I was doing," or "I wasn't *conscious of* that until I *reflected on* it," or "I play piano better when I'm *unconscious of* what I'm doing; when I *reflect upon* my playing, I start to make mistakes." We misidentify consciousness with reflection when we speak of an outstanding athletic performance as 'unconscious'. "Did you see Kobe Bryant play last night? He couldn't miss! He was *unconscious!*"

When we speak in this way, despite the vagueness and imprecision, we know well enough what we mean to be saying and what we don't mean to be saying, and others understand us well enough. When I say, "I wasn't *reflecting upon* what I was doing, so I wasn't *conscious that* I was doing it," I don't mean I wasn't present to myself while I was doing it. I mean I wasn't attending, or paying attention, to what I was doing, describing it, and asking questions about it. When I say, "I was doing that *unconsciously*," I don't mean I had no experience at all of what I was doing. I mean I wasn't attending to that experience. When I say, "I didn't become *conscious of* that until I reflected on it," I don't mean I was unaware of having any experience at all until I began to pay attention to it. I mean I wasn't paying attention to the experience I was actually having. When I say, "I play piano better when I'm *unconscious of* what I'm doing," I mean I'm a better pianist when I'm playing the piano without thinking about my playing. When I say, "Did you see Kobe Bryant play last night? He was *unconscious!*" I don't mean to say that Kobe was playing so well because he was playing while in a deep sleep. Imagine his interview with the commentator after the game: "Kobe, thirty points in the second half! You were unconscious out there! How did you do that?" And imagine him responding, "I have no idea. Just like you said, I was asleep the whole time." He is more likely to respond, "Sometimes you just get into the zone. I wasn't thinking about it." If consciousness is reflection, how could Kobe have reported this experience of his performance? Like the skilled pianist, he wasn't *thinking about* his performance while he was playing. But he certainly was *present to himself* while he was playing.

The casual, everyday identification of consciousness with reflection invites the creation of amusing, imaginary scenarios involving talented and highly accomplished somnambulists, and its impact on ordinary communication is fairly harmless. But the high-cultural insistence that consciousness is reflection is a different story, and it has a sad ending. It leads to the conclusion that knowledge of ourselves as conscious performers can't be achieved. If knowledge of ourselves as conscious performers can't be achieved, we can't hope to take possession of ourselves as conscious performers.

When consciousness is identified with reflection, it is conceived as an operation or set of operations. Our operations are operations with contents. They relate us to objects. If consciousness is another operation, it is an operation with a content. It relates us to something, just as seeing relates us to something, just as questioning relates us to something, just as deciding relates us to something, and so on. If consciousness is an operation with a content, then when I'm conscious I'm performing an operation with regard to something.

Now, the immediately preceding statement is radically ambiguous, and its ambiguity pertains directly to the issue at hand. From one standpoint – the one maintained in CPA – it is true to say that when I'm conscious I'm performing an operation with regard to something, because I'm only conscious when I'm operating; consciousness is a quality of operations. But this is not the claim being made here. The claim being made here is that consciousness *is itself another operation with a content.* "Consciousness is *consciousness of* ..." is an oft-repeated dictum of many philosophers nowadays. The point of the dictum is to assure us that our conscious operations always have contents or objects, that by our conscious operations we are related to objects, and this is all true. But the dictum also suggests, perhaps inadvertently but nevertheless very problematically, that consciousness, too, is an operation with a content, that consciousness is what is referred to in the technical language of philosophers as an 'intentional' operation, an operation that relates us to objects, and this isn't true.

If consciousness is an operation with a content, if consciousness is always "*consciousness of,*" then consciousness *of* my conscious performance must be an operation that has my operations as its content. The only way I can have any experience of my operations at all, then, is to make them the objects of consciousness, that is, by performing the supposed operation called 'consciousness' on the other operations I perform. Without "*consciousness of*" my operations, it seems, I may be operating, but I won't have an experience of any operations to talk about. I can only gain access to my own operations, before I even begin to describe them, if I make them the objects of the supposed operation called 'consciousness'. In other words, I can't gain access to my operations *in and as* my performance but only to them *as objects of* my performance. But my operations are operations with contents, or performances. They can be the contents of other operations, but that is not all they are, and that is not what they are insofar as they are conscious. Consequently, when I am "conscious of" my operations, my performance is present to me only as other things are present to me, and I am not present to myself *in* them. They are present to me only *as objects of my performance and never as my performance,* which is what they actually are.

According to this conception of consciousness, then, when I am conscious of my operations, I cannot avoid *misrepresenting* them as *objects of an operation.* I cannot gain access to them *as* my operations, or as what they actually are. My presence to myself is not understood to be my self-presence *in* my performance. It is conceived as presence to myself *of* my performance. It is conceived as another operation. My self-presence so conceived, then, inevitably misrepresents my operations by which I am related to

objects as themselves objects of an operation, because it is thought
to be another operation with a content. The conclusion I must
draw is that I simply cannot know my conscious performance as
my conscious performance but only as yet another content of my
conscious performance. Knowledge of myself as a conscious performer is impossible. Knowledge of the subject-as-subject is
impossible. Only knowledge of the subject-as-object is possible. But
that's not the knowledge we're after when we undertake to come to
know and take possession of ourselves as conscious performers.

There's another vitiating implication of the identification of
consciousness with reflection. Even if my performance were not
misrepresented when it is made the content of another operation,
there would always be one operation I could *never* make an object
of my performance, namely, the operation that 'consciousness' is
taken to be. The operation I'm supposed to be performing when
I'm present to myself in my other operations cannot simultaneously
be the object of itself. I can't be conscious *of* my operation of being
conscious *of* other operations. Keep in mind that consciousness,
according to this view, is not my presence to myself *in* my
operations. It is not my self-presence *as* the performing subject. It is
supposed to be the operation through which my operations are
present to me, not as relating me to contents, but as themselves
contents of an operation. The operation of which all other
operations may be contents cannot be the content of itself. The
conclusion I must draw is that, even if my performance were not
misrepresented when it is made into the content of the supposed
operation called 'consciousness', the operation called 'consciousness' could never be attended to, described, or asked about.
Reflection on reflection is simply impossible, and so knowledge of
myself as reflecting on my performance is impossible. One aspect
of my performance, the operation by which my performance is
presented to me, not as my performance but as an object of
performance, inevitably eludes me in my effort to know myself as a
conscious performer. Not only can we say nothing about ourselves
as actually performing, but also we can say nothing about ourselves
as actually performing reflectively with regard to our performance.

The identification of consciousness with reflection has its
source in the confusion of two characteristics or qualities of our
conscious operations. In addition to being conscious, our
operations always have contents or relate us to objects. We are
present to ourselves in our operations, and our operations make
objects present to us. In technical philosophical language, our
operations are both conscious and intentional. When consciousness

is assumed to be an operation, it is taken to be yet *another way in which we are related to objects or another instance of intentionality.* The conclusions that reflection on our conscious performance as performance is impossible and that reflection on our reflection as one type of performance is impossible follow from this fundamental confusion. We are conscious *in* our operations, and *in* them we are related to objects. Our operations relate us to objects, *and* they are conscious. Our presence to ourselves is not another operation by which we relate ourselves to objects. Our relation to objects is *conscious*, but it is not *consciousness*. In our operations we are conscious, present to ourselves, *and* related to objects.

The critical question, then, is this: Am I present to myself *in* my operations, are my operations conscious? Or, am I conscious, present to myself, only when I make the operations I perform the objects of another operation? If I am present to myself in my operations, if self-presence is a quality of my operations, then when I attend to my performance, describe it, and ask about it, I am coming to know it *as* my own performance. On the other hand, if I am present to myself only when I make the operations I perform the objects of another operation, then I have no experience of my performance *as* my performance to which I can attend, which I can describe, and which I can ask about. But if that's the case, what, then, could I be asking about when I ask, as I am now, about my own conscious performance?

According to this confused view, I'm not self-present when I'm performing operations unless I reflect upon them. But how can I reflect on something I'm not aware of? If I am allowed any experience at all of myself as a performer, that experience would always be of myself as an object, as the content of my operations, and never as the subject of my operations that I really am. My experience of myself would seem always to be only of objects I'm intending, or recollective only of objects I've intended, of myself as the object of my own operations, and never the experience of myself previously or now intending objects. I would not be able to know myself as a performing subject, because I would be forced by the supposed operation called 'consciousness' to apprehend myself as an object of an operation instead of as the subject of all my operations.

In the final analysis, if it really were the case that we can't avoid a denaturing 'objectification' of our own operations and are never present to ourselves as performers *in* them, we would have no experience of our operations to reflect upon before and until we reflected upon them. We wouldn't be having any experience at all. There would be no performing subject to reflect upon.

The confusion of consciousness with reflection infects the existing Language of Self-Possession. The infection has its source, I think, in the viral influence of the spontaneous extroversion we've already examined. In the existing Language of Self-Possession, self-presence is not merely conceived mistakenly as an operation but is modeled spontaneously on the operation of seeing. In the high-cultural, theoretical languages of many philosophers, this spontaneous imaginative construction persists to frame and distort analyses of the relations of operations, consciousness, and the contents of operations with the consequence that, instead of eliminating the attendant error, it authoritatively reinforces it. Again, instead of challenging and remedying the imprecision of the existing Language of Self-Possession, it works out its dire impli-cations and provides sophisticated arguments for the futility of trying to take possession of ourselves as conscious performers. It provides a high-cultural rationalization for not taking ourselves as conscious performers seriously. More generally, it arrests the movement from the traditional approach to knowledge of ourselves, that is justly maligned for its abstractness, to the new concrete approach to self-knowledge and self-possession. Either it reinforces the old procedure of thinking of ourselves as substances among other substances and reduces our presence to ourselves as subjects to just another instance of the presence of objects to us, or it rightly discerns that there is no *sensible* subject to be discovered in the flow of consciousness but then goes on to conclude that there is no subject at all. If this conception of consciousness as another operation is not displayed as erroneous and abandoned, the pursuit of knowledge and possession of ourselves as conscious performers will be declared futile before it is even tried.

5. SELF-PRESENCE IS NOT YET SELF-KNOWLEDGE

We have considered several ways in which we may be misled by our use of the existing Language of Self-Possession. Meanings imbedded in the Language of Self-Possession, if left unpurified, can lead us to the conclusion that what we are attempting to do is pointless or even impossible, that CPA is not worth attempting or simply cannot be done.

Before we move on to describe our conscious performance, there is one more unfortunate confusion to be considered. If it isn't exposed and dissolved, we may be inclined to regard reflection on our performance, if not as impossible, then as simply superfluous and unnecessary.

Consciousness, because it is self-presence, is often confused with self-knowledge. If we think we *know ourselves as conscious performers* just because we're *present to ourselves in our performance*, reflection on our performance will seem like a superfluous task. Let's imagine how this confusion might be expressed.

Don't I Know Myself Already?

OK, I agree with Hume that I'm present to myself in my performance. That seems right to me. So I already *know* what I'm doing. Sure, I can always get to know what I'm doing better. I'm not saying I can't do *that*. Isn't it like practicing something you already *know* you can do? But you *already* know you can do it. What would you practice if you didn't? Anyway, I'm not a philosopher, but I still know myself pretty well. Some philosophers or whatever might think I can't do it. They're entitled to their opinion. I know they make logical arguments and all. I'm not a logician or a concept analyst or whatever, so I don't really know if they actually prove it. I kind of doubt it. How can they say that? Do *they* know what *they're* doing? Why can't *I* know what *I'm* doing? They probably think I'm just guessing or speculating about what I do. Anyway, I know what I'm doing, mostly anyway, so I don't see why exactly I ought to do CPA if I already know. It's just so obvious I do things. I'm conscious already, so why do CPA?

Does our presence to ourselves in our conscious performance make the task of CPA unnecessary and superfluous? Is our presence to ourselves in our performance the same as knowledge of ourselves as performers?

The confusion of mere consciousness with self-knowledge has several sources. It may be due to the fact that we have previously engaged in reflection on our performance and have already come to know to some extent what was originally only an unexamined experience of ourselves in our performance. When we use the Language of Self-Possession, we often know, at least generally if not specifically, what we're talking about. Over the years we've learned and employed the existing Language of Self-Possession to aid us in understanding ourselves. We've gone beyond mere presence to ourselves, attended to our performance, asked questions about it, and come to know a bit about ourselves as conscious performers. When I say, "I wonder if …, " or "I think that…," or "I don't know whether…," I do know, at least generally, what I'm talking about. I know how to use these words meaningfully, and I also know generally what the words mean and that they refer to things I'm doing.

There was a prior time when we were merely present to ourselves in our performance, when we hadn't attended to ourselves as performing, when we hadn't yet learned the existing Language of Self-Possession, hadn't named any of our operations, and hadn't asked any questions about them. Now we're present to ourselves as already having acquired some knowledge of ourselves. Because we have acquired some knowledge of ourselves already, we may be inclined to think that our mere presence to ourselves is knowledge of ourselves. But self-knowledge is acquired by reflecting on our performance, that is, by attending to, asking about, identifying, isolating, and understanding our conscious operations. Before we've reflected on our performance, we're present to ourselves in it, but we don't yet know it.

We've been present to ourselves in our performance all our waking lives. While we've been pursuing the meaning of things and events, we've been present to ourselves in that pursuit. Our own performance has always been available to us for investigation, and intermittently we have reflected upon ourselves as conscious performers. We may have been driven to reflect upon ourselves by challenges posed by our situations, by seemingly insurmountable practical obstacles, by problems we couldn't solve, by disrupted relationships, by conflicts with others about what's meaningful or worthwhile and what isn't. We may have been nudged into reflection by others to whom we appeared to lack direction and to need guidance. We may have been drawn into reflection by our own suspicion that we lack direction in the flow of our lives. We may have been lured into reflection by a feeling of being out of touch with ourselves, by a vague sense that we really don't know well enough what we're doing or what we're supposed to do. We may have been led to reflect upon ourselves because we detect our own value as conscious performers and find ourselves interesting.

Sometimes, despite the pressures exerted upon us by our circumstances, by others, and by ourselves, we don't take advantage of our presence to ourselves and begin to reflect upon our own performance. Instead, we let others tell us what we are and how we should act; we're content to imitate what others have done; we're happy to have others tell us what to do. But none of us has rested content with mere self-presence. We have a basic commitment to meaning, objectivity, knowledge, truth, reality, and value. From time to time, we pursue the meaning of our ongoing experience of ourselves as performers and wonder about our own worth.

We've all done some reflecting and, over and above our presence to ourselves, we have some knowledge of ourselves, a basic familiarity with ourselves as conscious performers that is much more than the intimately felt familiarity afforded by mere presence to ourselves in our performance and much less than the sort of familiarity we might attain through the prolonged and perspicuous self-examination involved in CPA.

Recognizing Myself in CPA. The confusion of consciousness with self-knowledge may also be due to the peculiar nature of consciousness itself. Even if it isn't another operation, it does seem to be a kind of *knowing*. When I experience sensible objects, I am not present to myself in them; they're just present to me. I'm not present in the billiard ball on the green felt or in the crow on the wire; they're just present to me. When I attend to them, name them, ask questions about them, I don't have any sense of recognizing something I already know. I don't recognize *myself* in them as I begin to make sense of them. My starting-point, when I begin to make sense of them, is not like my starting-point when I begin to make sense of myself. When I begin to make sense of myself, I begin from *my intimate presence to myself in my operations.*

When I attend to my conscious performance, name my own operations, ask questions about my own performance, I *recognize* myself. I have moments of recognition as I attend to my operations, identify them, give names to them, and understand their relations to other operations. It does seem like I'm just remembering something I already know but had temporarily forgotten. But before we analyze carefully our conscious performance, we may not notice the significant differences between remembering, on the one hand, and attending, identifying, naming, and understanding, on the other. Coming to know our own operations isn't the same as remembering performing them. *Reflection on* our conscious performance isn't the same as *remembering* what we already know about it.

The set of operations we perform when we reflect upon our operations – attending, identifying, naming, inquiring, relating them, distinguishing them, and ordering them – are all different from the operation we call 'remembering'. Reflection may also involve remembering prior performance. If I had no memory of myself in my prior performance, I wouldn't have anything to reflect upon other than my present performance of reflecting. But there's more involved in reflection on our performance than just remembering ourselves performing.

What I now remember, and what I can forget, are things I once had never attended to, identified, named, inquired about, or understood. The content of remembering can be something I know already but just forgot. The content of remembering can also be something that I still don't understand when I remember it. But whether the content is something I know already or something I've experienced but never bothered to ask about, while it's forgotten it's not present to me and I'm not present to myself in it.

Self-presence in our performance isn't knowledge of ourselves as conscious performers. Reflection on ourselves as conscious performers isn't remembering something we already know. If we wish to get to know ourselves as performers and take possession of ourselves as conscious performers, we must attend to our performance, identify and name the operations we perform, ask questions about them, distinguish them from one another, and relate them to one another. We must ask about the constitutive and guiding role of the basic notions in our performance and discover the basic notions at work. In order to achieve adequate self-knowledge we need to supplement the knowledge we've already acquired of ourselves with the serious pursuit of Conscious Performance Analysis.

Chapter Five

CONSCIOUS OPERATIONS AND THEIR ORDER

L et's resist the temptation to *imagine or visualize* what we're doing when we're doing CPA. It's tempting to imagine some interior space, perhaps inside our heads, in which operations appear, float around, zip this way and that way, perhaps cross paths, and then disappear. It's tempting to imagine ourselves gazing into this "inner space" with the intention of isolating and capturing these fleeting events, of imposing some order upon their haphazard movements, or possibly of finding some order already in them. When we try to *imagine* what we're going to do, we always put a distance between our own performance and ourselves. Imagined objects always have some size and shape, and there's always a distance separating the imagined from the imaginer. But my own conscious performance is merely temporal, and it is actually as close to me as anything can possibly be. My very experience of myself is *in* my performance. There is no distance at all between my conscious performance and me.

Our operations aren't fast- or slow-moving objects in space. They're purely temporal events. Our performance of specific operations may be brief or prolonged, but prolonged performance doesn't make them any easier to see, and the brevity of our performance doesn't make them any harder to see. We can't see our operations by "looking inward" into some imaginary space. CPA isn't what is usually meant by 'introspection'. It isn't "looking inward" with a "mind's eye" at operations "in our minds." We can create images to depict the operations to be explored by CPA, but the operations aren't actually imaginable objects, and we don't gain access to them by performing an imaginary operation called 'consciousness'. We're present to ourselves *when* we perform our operations and *in* our performance of them.

Even more obviously, CPA is not "looking outward" with the physical eye at our appearance and our behavior as seen through our own eyes or others'. Conscious operations aren't to be found

by observing our own behavior, the behavior of others, or the behavior of others toward us. We might be able to draw a fairly confident conclusion from someone's behavior that she is performing, or has performed, a particular conscious operation or set of operations. If she adopts a posture like that of Rodin's *The Thinker*, we may conclude that she's probably thinking about something – asking a question and trying to answer it – and probably has been for some time. But she may not be inquiring at all; she may be daydreaming or worrying. We may discern orderliness in someone's behavior that *suggests* that some discernment of meaning and value has gone or is going into it. But she may just be "behaving herself" by doing dutifully what someone told her to do or behaving automatically and out of habit. She may not mean what she's doing at all, and she may not discern the value or disvalue of it. Whatever the connection is between our observable behavior and our basic commitment, it is certainly a loose one that can be tightened up or become even looser. Now and then we deliberately exploit the looseness of the connection between our observable behavior and our present conscious performance to impress others or to deceive them, as when we present ourselves as pensively attentive to mask the fact that another's present stream of talk is, at that moment, just noisy background to our recollections of past events or our anticipations of future possibilities.

Looking Like I'm Thinking

If I adopt the posture of Rodin's *The Thinker,* I look like I'm thinking. But I might be more like Rodin's statue than you think. I might not be thinking at all. Sometimes I look like I'm paying attention when I'm not; I'm daydreaming or feeling hungry. Sometimes I hope others will think I'm paying attention, even though "my mind" is really "somewhere else." Sometimes I appear uninterested when my curiosity is piqued but I don't want you to know that it is. Sometimes I smile with understanding when I don't understand at all, or I nod my head in agreement when I'm actually plagued by doubts. Sometimes I appear credulous when I'm very suspicious. Sometimes I play dumb when I'm pretty sure I know what's going on. Sometimes my behavior is routine and habitual and now thoughtless, and my present conscious performance bears almost no relationship to it at all.

My behavior would be meaningless without my present and prior performance of conscious operations. But often the operations it appears to incarnate or express are neither the operations I'm performing nor operations I've previously performed. I may not be able to explain just what the complex relation is between my behavior and my conscious operations, or between what I casually refer to as "my body" and "my mind." What is clear to me is that the connection can be loosened enough to enable me to make sure at times that what's present to me in my own performance is not known to be present to me by anyone who is observing me. It can also be tightened up enough to ensure that others, if they pay attention, can get a very good idea of what sort of conscious performance I'm engaged in. When a teacher directs a question to an apparently attentive and thoughtful, but actually daydreaming pupil, for example, the transformation of the pupil's facial expression from earnest attentiveness into glassy-eyed incomprehension is immediate and there for all to see. But it seems that, normally, the connection between observable behavior and conscious performance is never completely eliminated. An attentive and experienced poker player, for example, can usually find the tell that reveals another player's assessment of her own hand.

Our sensible experience of the subject-as-object is not experience of the subject-as-subject. My sensible experience of myself-as-object is not experience of myself-as-subject. The subject-as-object is present to me the way crows and billiard balls are present to me, and the way billiard balls are probably present to crows. Our inquiries into our experience of the subject-as-object result only in guesses, hypotheses, suppositions, and speculations about the unobservable conscious performance of the subject-as-subject who, while present to herself, is present to others only as another sensible object, as the subject-as-object.

It will not serve our purposes here to watch the behavior of others, to view ourselves in mirrors and other reflective surfaces, to view videos of ourselves, or to ask others what they think we might be doing. We can pursue knowledge of ourselves as conscious performers in that manner, but we'd be approaching ourselves by an unnecessarily circuitous route, and we'd never quite arrive. The subject-as-subject is myself looking into the mirror, not the one who is looking back at me. It is the one who's watching the movie, not the one who appears in it. It's the one who notices being observed by others, not the one who's observed by others. It is the one who is present to herself, not the one who is present to others the way the crow is present to me or the way the billiard ball is present to the crow and me. We have to reflect on our own operations, identify them, describe what it's like to perform them, and discover their relations to the basic guiding notions.

A JOKE

What did one behaviorist say to the other when they met
on the street?
"You're doing fine! How am I?"

Our presence to ourselves is a quality of the operations we perform. We are *present now* in the performance of our operations. We experience their differences from one another and their relations to one another. We experience the role played by the guiding notions of meaning, objectivity, knowledge, truth, reality, and value in our performance of them. In the performance of the different operations, we should be able to notice changes in the quality of our self-presence. All we have to do is take advantage of our presence to ourselves, pay attention to ourselves in our conscious performance, identify the operations we perform, and describe the qualitative changes in our experience of performing them. That may seem like a tall order. But we have in stock right now everything we need to fill it.

1. IDENTIFYING AND ORDERING OUR CONSCIOUS OPERATIONS

The number of observable activities in which we engage is indefinitely large. Even if we were to devote a lifetime to the effort, we wouldn't be able to list them all. The number is constantly increasing. As we pursue and grasp new meanings, achieve more knowledge, discern and create new values, we also invent and carry out new activities. Some of these activities are repeated over and over. Some are performed once or twice and never performed again. Activities that appear the same to observation may differ widely in their meanings. All of these observable activities are carried out by conscious subjects. At times, it may look to us like the same activity is being repeated. But, when we begin to ask questions about it, we discover that it doesn't have the same meaning or isn't motivated by the same value and is really not the same activity at all.

The number of conscious operations seems, in comparison, to be very small. We perform the same set of operations over and over again. Their contents may differ every time we perform them, but the set of operations is always the same.

What I wonder about may vary from one moment to the next. However diverse the objects of my wondering are, however innovative my choices of questions to ask may be, in each of those moments I'm *wondering* or *asking a question*. The ideas I get in answer to my wondering, in most cases, are new to me. It's hard to see the point of wondering about what I already know or think I know. But every time I obtain what I call a "possible answer," I am *understanding*. I may deliberate about performing new courses of action or about engaging again in actions I've previously performed. No matter what courses of action I deliberate about and decide to do, my performance of them and my refusals to perform them result from my *deliberating and deciding*. All of our operations are operations with contents. The contents vary. The set of operations seems always to be the same.

The conscious operations we perform in our everyday living seem to be strictly limited in number, despite the indefinitely large variety of objects with regard to which we perform them and despite the indefinitely large range of objectives for the sake of which we perform them. The same operations seem to be performed over and over. We don't ask the same question over and over again, but it's always a question we're asking. We don't invent new conscious operations as a result of our ongoing pursuit of meaning and our discovery of new meanings and replace the ones we've been performing with these new ones. We may get better at performing the operations we perform. We may become more discriminating about when to perform specific operations, with regard to what sorts of objects to perform them, and with what sorts of aims to perform them. But we don't replace any of our conscious operations with brand new ones, the way we might replace an observable activity, like playing billiards, with a new one, like hunting crows.

Our conscious operations are informed and guided by the basic notions. Our performance of them can't result in the discovery that asking questions, for example, can be replaced by something else. We may discover better ways to ask questions, but we don't discover in our pursuit of meaning that asking questions is not the way to pursue meaning and that we should do something else instead. We may get better at evaluating, but we don't discover in our pursuit of values that evaluating is not the way to determine the value of something and that we should do something else instead. Even if we tried to do this, we'd still have *to ask if it makes sense* to pursue meaning and value in those new ways, and *if it's more worthwhile* to do so.

The operations we perform in our pursuit of meaning and value can be refined, but they can't be replaced. We can ask questions better, more astutely, more keenly, more precisely, more pointedly. We can evaluate with more discernment, and we can deliberate more imaginatively and effectively. Our operations can lead us to abandon some of our observable activities and to replace them with other observable activities we regard as more mean-ingful or more valuable. But our operations *cannot replace themselves* with different operations or substitute other operations for them-selves. We perform a limited number of conscious operations in everyday living, we always perform these same operations, and we perform them recurrently. The contents of the operations are always changing, but we're performing the same set of operations over and over again.

It would be unreasonable to attempt to list all of the observable activities we engage in. There are too many, and the list would go on and on. It doesn't seem unreasonable to attempt to make a list of all the conscious operations we ordinarily perform. They seem to be limited in number, and they recur. A complete list of our conscious operations, if we can come up with one, would be a major step toward a thorough and adequate account of our conscious performance. It would provide us with a basic set of operations whose relations to one another we could then explore.

Listing Conscious Operations. Usually, we can tell fairly quickly approximately how long a list will be. If we were asked to list the real numbers, we would begin – 1, 2, 3, 4, 5 – and very quickly we would realize that this is going to continue forever. We would add the sign of that realization – ... –, the three dots, and save ourselves an infinite amount of time. With those three dots we express our understanding that the counting can go on forever. If we were asked to list observable activities of human beings, we might begin – sitting in a chair, standing in the living room, walking to the store, talking to a friend, eating pizza, laughing at a joke, feeding the cat, cleaning the garage, cleaning the attic, washing dishes, turning on the dishwasher, negotiating with a dictator, demonstrating for human rights, playing billiards, hunting crows, boarding a bus, reading a book – and we would realize fairly quickly that this list is going to be very long and that it will keep getting longer. We don't add the symbol of infinitude. The list is not endless, but the number of observable activities is indefinitely large and as long as we keep inventing new things to do it will remain unfinished. Instead of continuing, we would add an indication of the indefinite length of the list. We might say "and so on," "and so forth," or '*etcetera*.'

When we attempt to make an exhaustive list of conscious operations, will we have either of these realizations? Will we realize, soon after we begin, that the list is infinite or that it is indefinitely long and that it is pointless to continue listing items? Or will our intimate familiarity with ourselves as conscious performers, and our experience of performing the same operations over and over, incline us to persist until we have a complete list? The answer to these questions lies in the attempt. There are reasons to expect that we won't have to resort to the conveniences of the three dots or the "and so on" when we attempt to list all of our conscious operations.

1.1. A PROVISIONAL AND INCOMPLETE LIST

When we attempt to produce even a partial list of conscious operations, we discover that, before our list gets very long, we begin to repeat ourselves. Even in the short, provisional, and incomplete list of conscious operations below, which we might produce off the tops of our heads, there seems to be some repetition.

A PROVISIONAL LIST OF CONSCIOUS OPERATIONS

Reasoning, inquiring, experiencing, remembering,
thinking, seeing, discovering, judging,
understanding, listening, attending, concluding,
evaluating, visualizing, considering, imagining,
deciding, questioning, choosing.

Let's pause to consider this list more closely, with attention not merely to the words in the list but also to our own performance. Several interesting characteristics of the list come to light when it's considered in this self-attentive way.

Repetition in the List. My provisional and incomplete list contains what appear, at first glance, to be different names for the same operations. Questioning and inquiring, if they are not names for the same operation, are names for very similar ones. Judging and concluding, imagining and visualizing, and discovering and understanding also seem to be virtually synonymous pairs. My provisional list is repetitive.

Mixing Names for Specific Operations and Groups. My list also appears to contain general names for groups of operations in addition to names for individual ones. Thinking seems to include inquiring, discovering, judging, understanding, concluding, evaluating, considering, and questioning. 'Thinking' is not really a name for a specific operation. It's a name for a whole range of operations. We say we're 'thinking' when we're performing any of these operations or several of them one after another. 'Thinking', like the word 'mind', is one of the vaguest words in the lexicon of the Language of Self-Possession. Further, experiencing seems to include listening, seeing, and even imagining and remembering. Moreover, when we recall that we're present to ourselves *in all of our operations,* experiencing could be said to include all of the operations in the list and any others we might add to the list, because they're all *conscious operations.* But, as we've seen, experiencing in the special sense of self-experience or self-presence isn't an operation. If that's what is meant by 'experiencing' in my list, it shouldn't be in the list.

A Lack of Order in the List. The names for specific operations and groups of operations in the list do not seem to be in any particular order. There doesn't seem to be any pattern in the list. Recall that Hume complained about the *seeming disorder* of our operations when he began to reflect upon them. We found this seeming disorder to be related to the difficulty of reflecting upon purely temporal operations. When we bring with us to our reflection the assumption that what we're looking for is something like spatial objects, we run into difficulties, and things seem very obscure. Once we've been alerted to our mistaken expectation, those difficulties can be satisfactorily overcome, and things become clearer. We can proceed to attend to our conscious performance, isolate, identify, and distinguish our operations, and relate our operations to one another. The disorder encountered by Hume, and also encountered by us when we begin to reflect upon our operations, is a *seeming disorder*. It's not disorder in our conscious performance. It's natural to expect some sort of order in the performance of our conscious operations. It would be very strange if the operations by which we make sense of things – by which we discover the order, arrangement, and organization in things – were to make no sense or have no order themselves. What is the pattern or order that we expect and that seems to be missing in our provisional list?

Why do we expect to find a pattern in a list of conscious operations? As we've seen, our conscious performance is always already informed and guided by the basic notions. Before we impose any order on our conscious performance, our operations are already ordered spontaneously by their relations to the basic notions of meaning, objectivity, knowledge, truth, reality, and value, and by our basic and inescapable commitment to these ideals. This spontaneous orderly performance of our operations, in which we are present to ourselves, is not represented by the list. It is not surprising, then, that we would notice that the spontaneous orderliness of our self-present performance of operations is not exhibited clearly by the list.

When confronted by a puzzle or problem, do we first *reason* and then *inquire* and then *experience* and then *remember*? Do we first *judge* and then *understand* and then *listen* and then *attend*? Do we first *imagine* and then *decide* and then *question* and then *choose*? We can perform these operations in these sequences if we wish, but we would probably be judged scatter-brained by anyone who noticed how we are performing, and it isn't likely we'd make much headway in our pursuit of meaning, objectivity, knowledge, truth, reality, and value by performing this way.

The lack of order in my provisional list suggests that it wasn't made with very close attention to my own conscious operations. This is true. I created the list by simply writing down the names of operations as they came to mind. Because our conscious performance is informed and guided by the basic notions, we expect a list of conscious operations to have some pattern or order. My provisional list is just a list of some words we use when we speak about conscious operations in the Language of Self-Possession. I pulled them out of the Language of Self-Possession and listed them in the order in which they happened to occur to me. The words express concepts we already have of operations. The multiple ways we use the words are recorded in our dictionaries. If there were such a thing as a *Self-Possession Dictionary*, I could have consulted it to make the production of my list even easier, the way someone who wishes to list body parts might consult an *Anatomical Dictionary*. If I had been able to do that, my list would probably have a discernible order, but that order would be the merely alphabetical order of words as we find them arranged for our convenience in dictionaries. The alphabetical order of the words isn't the order that we expect and find to be missing in our provisional list.

Introducing Merely Logical Order into the List. We could introduce order into the list by appealing to the dictionary definitions of the words in the list. These definitions can be logically related or logically ordered. The list could be rearranged to reflect whatever logical order is discovered by linguistic or conceptual analysis. But that logical arrangement is not the order that CPA anticipates and attempts to describe. The *logical and conceptual order* of existing definitions of words may be quite different from the *concrete spontaneous order* in the performance of our conscious operations.

The logical order of the meanings we happen to give to words in the existing Language of Self-Possession is not an order in which I'm present to myself. If I were actually present to myself in that order, I wouldn't need to do any conceptual analysis to discover it. I could simply appeal to my experience of it and describe it. In an effort to introduce order into the list we might undertake a conceptual analysis to discover if the concept we have of questioning, for example, 'contains' the concept we have of understanding, or if the concept we have of understanding 'contains' the concepts we have of imagining or remembering. But then we'll find ourselves talking about how we happen to talk about our conscious operations without regard for our self-present performance of the operations we claim to be talking about. We will find ourselves substituting the abstract relations of static, unchanging concepts to one another for the concrete and dynamic relations of operations to one another.

The logical relations of the concepts we have at present of our operations might provide us a clue or two about the concrete relations of the operations to one another in our actual performance, but they shouldn't be assumed to represent them with any real accuracy. It may happen that the concept of 'understanding' can be "analyzed out of" the concept of 'questioning' but not *vice versa*. But real questioning isn't, as the Merriam-Webster Dictionary would have us think, just "subjecting something to analysis," and real understanding isn't reached simply by analyzing the concepts in the questions we ask. The concrete transition from questioning questioning to understanding questioning isn't made by analyzing the static concepts of questioning and understanding. The order in our performance isn't a static or motionless 'geographical' arrangement determined by the logical proximity to one another of the concepts we happen to have of our operations. It is a dynamic pattern determined by the concrete relations of our operations to one another and to the basic notions that constitute and guide them. To substitute conceptual analysis for CPA is to forget that we are dealing, not with concepts we formulate or words we utter, but with conscious operations we perform. The only way to resolve the problem of the missing order or pattern in the list is to attend to the spontaneous orderly performance of our conscious operations. Let's try this.

1.2 SELF-ATTENTIVE DESCRIPTION OF THE SPONTANEOUS ORDER

The description we're attempting to provide here is of the spontaneous order of occurrence of conscious operations *when we're anticipating and pursuing meaning, objectivity, knowledge, truth, reality, and value.* It won't serve our purposes to shift our attention to just any arbitrarily delimited sequence of operations in the ongoing flow of conscious performance. Our reflective attention must be directed to those dynamic segments of the ongoing flow of our conscious performance in which our basic commitment is most prominent. Accordingly, if we are to get hold of the relevant range of data, we must isolate in the ongoing flow of our conscious performance a dynamic segment that is demarcated by a 'beginning' in presence to ourselves *as not having objective knowledge of the true meaning of some situation in which we find ourselves and as not discerning the true value of some possible course of action in response to the same situation* and by an 'ending' in presence to ourselves *as having objective knowledge of the true meaning of the situation and as discerning the true value of a course of action in response to the situation and acting accordingly.* In other words, our interest here lies in describing the spontaneous order of operations in dynamic segments of conscious performance in which we're present to ourselves as pursuing and attaining meaning, objectivity, knowledge, truth, reality, and value. The data to be described can be found in our recollection of past pursuits and attainments. Ideally, however, it is to be found in our immediate self-presence in the present dynamic segment of conscious performance. The conscious performance in which we're presently engaged began with our presence to ourselves as troubled by a lack of order in the provisional list of conscious operations and as wondering what difference the discovery of a spontaneous order of operations could make to our own conscious performance in the future. The ending of this dynamic segment is still only anticipated, and in our performance of completing the dynamic segment we will have immediately available for our reflection all the relevant data.

In my pursuit of *meaning*, some of the operations in the list seem to occur before others. Experiencing, seeing, listening, attending, remembering, and imagining all seem to occur *before* questioning and inquiry. *First* I see or hear or notice or remember or imagine something I haven't understood, *and then* I ask a question. A question is always about something and, if it's a real question, it's always about something I don't yet understand. I can ask questions about what I've already understood, about possible experiences I haven't yet had, or about experiences I can't possibly have. But, when I do that, I'm present to myself as asking rhetorically or merely speculating or musing about meanings I can't hope to pin down, because I'm not really asking, or I don't really have anything to ask about. I don't *first* think of an experience I've never had *and then* ask a question about it. It might be worthwhile to ask a question about the experience of doing that sort of thing, as I am now. But *first* we have to remember or imagine the experience of doing that sort of thing *and then* we can ask that question.

In my pursuit of *objective knowledge of the real*, some of the operations in the list also seem to occur before others. Attending, questioning, inquiry, understanding, and considering all seem to occur *before* judging or concluding. If they don't, I might be justly accused of jumping to conclusions. *First* I attend to something, ask questions about it, get an idea and consider its implications *and then* I draw a conclusion or make a judgment. A judgment is about the correctness of an idea. I won't have an idea on which to pass judgment if I haven't *first* sought one by asking questions. I can't make a judgment if I haven't reached any understanding at all in answer to questions I've asked. What would such a judgment be about? What conclusions could I possibly draw about the correctness of ideas I haven't gotten yet?

Some of the operations in the list seem to occur before others when I'm pursuing *value*. Inquiring, visualizing and imagining, understanding, considering, judging, and evaluating all seem to occur *before* choosing and deciding and acting. If they don't, I might be justly accused of deciding prematurely and acting thoughtlessly or irresponsibly. *First* I inquire about possible courses of action, imagine them, understand what would be involved in performing them, consider their implications and consequences, judge my ideas about them to be probably true or probably false, evaluate them *and then* choose from among the courses of action open to me the best one *and then* decide and act. I don't decide to carry out actions I've never imagined doing. How could I? I don't choose to do things I haven't found some value in doing. Why would I? I certainly don't choose and decide to do things if I haven't even asked if there is anything I should do.

1.3 THE FRAGILITY OF THE SPONTANEOUS ORDER

Our conscious performance never occurs without some relation to the basic notions. That doesn't mean that our everyday conscious performance can't be disorderly. It does mean that it can't be entirely disordered, completely haphazard, without any semblance of order at all. For example, when I ask a question without wanting or anticipating an answer, either I just seem to be asking a question but am not really asking one, or my operations have, so to speak, become disorderly.

Sometimes I ask what we call "a rhetorical question." I already know or think I know the answer to it, and I assume my listeners already know or think they know the answer to it, too. I'm just drawing their attention to the answer they already know or think they know, and I'm doing so in such a way as to emphasize that it is an answer. Sometimes I express judgments in the form of questions, as when I ask, "Is there anyone who hasn't got more to learn? Does anyone know absolutely everything?" or "Can pigs fly?" or "Is the Pope Catholic?" These 'questions' are just disguised versions of the very concise statement, "Duh." In these cases, I express *my possession of knowledge* in the guise or behind the mask of *a pursuit of meaning.* Judging I've already done is disguised as a question I'm just now asking, and my performance isn't really disorderly. But, if I raise a question I haven't answered and then neglect to seek an answer to it myself or refuse to entertain any possible answers offered to me by others, my performance has become disorderly. I'm suppressing or violating my basic commitment. My questioning is no longer tethered securely to the notions of meaning, objectivity, knowledge, truth, reality, and value that inform and guide it. It becomes the mere utterance of words.

My relationship to the basic notions, which imposes the spontaneous order on my performance, can be temporarily weakened, and the spontaneous orderly sequence of my operations can be disrupted. I can explore mere possibilities without the desire to uncover realities. When I'm asking questions about what I've never experienced, I'm present to myself as speculating. When I'm having experiences or remembering them *and then* asking questions about them, I'm present to myself as approaching achievable meaning and possibly even objective knowledge of the truth. I may not discover the meaning I'm seeking; I may get no farther than having a bright idea; I may not reach objective knowledge of my experience. But I'm present to myself as doing more than just speculating or musing. If I go on to reflect upon my musing, I'm inclined to call it that; I notice my tenuous relation to the notion of reality. Even if I don't go on to reflect upon my musing and don't identify it as musing, I'm still present to myself as doing what I would probably call 'musing' if I did happen to take a moment to reflect upon it and name it. On the other hand, sometimes my pursuit of knowledge isn't interrupted or derailed but merely prolonged by my exploration of meaningful, but merely possible, relations, on my way to determining what is possibly true. My relation to the basic notions isn't weakened in this case; my prolonged exploration of possibilities is actually a sign of the enduring strength of my relation to the notions of meaning, objectivity, knowledge, and truth.

It is possible, though, in that part of our living that is purely temporal, to waste our time. Our conscious operations are constituted and guided by the basic notions. Their relationship to the basic notions imposes upon them a spontaneous order. The degree of our commitment to meaning and value can be reduced, but the commitment can't be eliminated. When we perform operations with a weakened concern for meaning and value, they become less orderly.

Even impeccably logical reasoning can be disorderly performance if my relation to the basic notions is weak, if my interest in meaning, objectivity, knowledge, truth, reality, and value recedes, diminishes, fades. Any sequence of operations performed with a weakened commitment to the basic notions is disorderly performance. It is pointless, in the same way that arguing for the sake of arguing or arguing for the sake of winning the argument are pointless. Of course, we see some point in arguing in this way, but the point is not the achievement of meaning, objectivity, knowledge, truth, reality, and value. Disorderly conscious performance is not entirely directionless and without order. It's not chaotic; it's just disorderly. The relations of the operations to the basic notions haven't been eliminated entirely, but they're tenuous. The person who argues for the sake of arguing no doubt thinks it's worthwhile to do so, but her performance isn't tethered securely to the pursuit of objective knowledge of the truth about the real. As the phenomenon of performative self-contradiction reveals, my relation to the basic notions is inescapable. Like disorderly conduct, disorderly conscious performance is still ordered, but the ordering anticipation of the basic notions has become mere background for other, more prominent, personal interests.

1.4 RECONSTRUCTING THE LIST

Now, let's compare the provisional list of conscious operations, which was relatively chaotic, with the same list of operations reconstructed to reveal the repetitions, the differences between names of specific operations and names of groups of operations, and the bare indications of the spontaneous order in our conscious performance that we've noticed in our brief self-attentive reflection.

THE ORIGINAL LIST

Reasoning, inquiring, experiencing, remembering, thinking, seeing, discovering, judging, understanding, listening, attending, concluding, evaluating, visualizing, considering, imagining, deciding, questioning, choosing.

THE RECONSTRUCTED LIST

First experiencing, which is a name for a group that includes seeing, listening, attending, remembering, imagining or visualizing,
and then thinking, which is another name for a group of operations:

> *First* questioning or inquiring,
> *and then* understanding or discovering,
> *and then* considering,
> *and then* reasoning,
> *and then* judging or concluding,
> *and then* evaluating,
> *and then* deciding or choosing.

The original list and my attempt to reconstruct it have provided us with only a first, faint taste of what is to be achieved by CPA. The list of operations we've been considering is merely illustrative. It is provisional and incomplete. The Language of Self-Possession contains more names for operations than are contained in the list I provided. The names for operations are used imprecisely. Some seem to have the same meaning. Some seem to have only slightly different meanings. Some seem to have completely different meanings. The reasons for traditional groupings of operations are not clear. Can we come up with a list that is definitive and complete? Can we come up with a precise and thorough list of the conscious operations we perform? Can we distinguish the operations clearly from one another? Can we expose their relations to one another? Are the groupings simply for the sake of convenience? Are they merely an expression of our inattention to our conscious performance and of our lack of precise knowledge of ourselves? Or, is there something about our actual conscious performance that justifies the organization of our operations into groups?

The Language of Self-Possession is in need of purification. The purification is achieved only gradually as the casual and vague connection of our use of the language to our performance is transformed by CPA into a deliberate and precise one. If we begin by trying to list all the operations we perform, we run the risk of diverting our attention from our conscious performance to the language we use to talk about it. It is best to maintain our attentiveness to our conscious performance and to borrow words from the Language of Self-Possession as the need arises. As we use those words with close attention to our conscious performance, we will attempt to give them the precision and clarity they currently lack.

2. THE BASIC MOODS OF SELF-PRESENCE

We've made an initial attempt to identify conscious operations and to discover the spontaneous order in our conscious performance. It appears that Hume was right about the difficulty of this reflective task. It's easier to describe the changes we experience in *the quality of our consciousness* as we perform different types of operations than it is to isolate and identify the operations we're performing. It's easier to identify and describe changes in our self-feeling when we perform different types of conscious operations than it is to identify and describe the conscious operations we're performing. What it feels like to be a conscious performer is more conspicuous to us than the details of the performance in which we feel that way. Changes in our self-presence are more conspicuous than the changing operations in which we're present to ourselves. But changes in the quality of our self-presence don't happen without changes in the operations we perform and, unless our performance becomes disorderly, changes in the operations we perform don't occur without changes in the quality of our self-presence. When our performance is tethered securely to the basic notions, neither happens without the other. But, if we press on immediately to isolate and to identify all the operations we perform, we risk lapsing into merely linguistic and conceptual analysis. So, let's take a moment to reflect on the changing quality of our presence to ourselves in the performance of various types of operations. After reflecting upon the changing quality of our self-presence, we can resume our effort to provide an account of our conscious operations, their similarities, their differences, and their relations to the basic notions.

My presence to myself is a quality of the operations I perform. My operations are constituted and guided by the basic notions of meaning, objectivity, knowledge, truth, reality, and value. My self-presence in the performance of my operations is my presence to myself *in my relation to* meaning, objectivity, knowledge, truth, reality, and value. It is my presence to myself as being-in-relation-to-meaning or *caring about meaning*, as being-in-relation-to-objectivity or *caring about objectivity*, as being-in-relation-to-knowledge or *caring about knowledge,* as being-in-relation-to-truth or *caring about truth,* as being-in-relation-to-reality or *caring about what's real,* as being-in-relation-to-value or *caring about what's worthwhile.* It is my presence to myself in my relation to the basic notions. My presence to myself changes with changes in my relations to the basic notions. These changes occur with changes in the operations I perform. Let's call these changing qualities of my presence to myself *the basic moods of self-presence.*

2.1 PRAISE, BLAME, AND THE BASIC COMMITMENT

The basic moods may be brought to light by considering how we praise and blame others for their conscious performance. We often praise one another for orderly performance and blame one another for disorderly performance. We approve of those who exhibit their adherence to the basic commitment to meaning, objectivity, knowledge, truth, reality, and value. We disapprove of those who seem to us to be straying from or violating that commitment either inadvertently or deliberately.

We praise others for *paying attention.* We chastise them for their *inattentiveness.* We praise others for *asking questions* when they should, and we praise them still more highly for asking questions when many think they shouldn't. We frown on them for *failing to ask.* We praise *open-mindedness and tolerance* and condemn *closed-mindedness and intolerance.* We praise *the admission of ignorance* and blame *the refusal to admit ignorance.* We approve *the critical spirit* and condemn *naiveté and gullibility.* We praise *measured consideration* and condemn *rash judgment.* We praise *the proficiency that comes with knowledge* and condemn *incompetence.* We praise *honesty and truthfulness* and condemn *lying and deception.* We praise *realism and facing facts* and condemn *wishful thinking.* We praise *whole-hearted deliberateness* and condemn *haphazard spontaneity.* We praise one another for performing *attentively, intelligently, reasonably, and responsibly.* We blame one another for performing *inattentively, unintelligently, unreasonably, or irresponsibly.* We smile on adherence to the basic commitment to meaning, objectivity, knowledge, truth, reality, and value, and we frown upon the careless relation to it and violations of it.

We're often more ready to give expression to our praise than to our condemnations. We're often more willing to let others know that we think they're being attentive or intelligent or reasonable or responsible than we are to tell them we think they're being inattentive or stupid or silly or irresponsible. Whether or not we give public expression to these evaluations of the performance of others, we perform them. Publicly we may proclaim ourselves to be relativists when it comes to truth and value. In public we might condemn the "judgmental attitude" that presumes to know what's true or false or right or wrong, and we might advocate tolerance. But the tolerance we advocate is not indiscriminate. Privately, we take it for granted that there is a basic commitment to the basic notions by which we ourselves and others are bound, regardless of psychological, social, political, cultural, and historical differences. Our private adherence to the basic commitment is revealed in the performative self-contradiction in which we involve ourselves but which usually escapes our notice. So concerned are we to respect the commitment to the pursuit of meaning and value in others, so concerned are we to realize the ideal of objectivity in ourselves, that we inadvertently deny our own commitment to truth and to the truly worthwhile. But we cannot eliminate those concerns. Privately, we make the judgments that the "judgmental attitude" threatens the pursuit of objectivity and that tolerance of diverse values is truly valuable. Despite our public proclamations, our private commitment finds public expression when we praise the attentiveness, intelligence, reasonableness, and responsibility of those who aren't 'judgmental' and who exhibit the tolerance we prize. Our public proclamation may appear to be one of indiscriminate tolerance for differences, but privately we're inescapably intolerant of inattentiveness, stupidity, silliness, and irresponsibility and of the unacceptable differences they make. We still find attentive, intelligent, reasonable, and responsible performance worthy of our praise and inattentive, unintelligent, unreasonable, and irresponsible performance intolerable.

We take for granted the basic commitment to the basic notions in others, just as we take it for granted in ourselves. We expect others to perform attentively, intelligently, reasonably, and responsibly. We don't expect them to perform that way all the time. We realize that the basic commitment in others is like the basic commitment in ourselves. It can be more or less unreflective and spontaneous or more or less reflective and deliberate. It can be explicitly rejected even while it's being adhered to implicitly. It can be spontaneously or deliberately disordered or deliberately violated.

Just as we praise and blame others for their actual relations to the basic notions, so we are subject to praise and blame ourselves. We are sensitive to others' sensitivities, but we're also sensitive to how others regard us. Do others regard me as performing attentively, intelligently, reasonably, and responsibly, or do they regard me as performing inattentively, unintelligently, unreasonably, and irresponsibly, or do they regard me as somewhat unpredictable and flighty or even volatile in my conscious performance?

2.2 FOUR DEGREES OF PERSONAL RISK

The basic moods of self-presence can be discerned still more clearly in the variations in the degree of risk we feel when we express ourselves to others.

The feeling of risk here is not a fear of physical or psychological harm. It is a fear of being found by others to be a disorderly conscious performer. It is a fear of being regarded as only weakly related to the basic notions or in violation of the basic commitment. It is a fear of being judged to be inattentive, stupid, silly, and irresponsible. We assume the basic commitment in others, and they assume it in us. We're inclined to trust that they will be alert to our relation to the basic notions and that, despite the unobservability in our present behavior of our present conscious performance, they will be able to discover in what we say and how we say it, in what we do and how we do it, the real relation in which we stand to our basic commitment. We fear that we won't meet the basic anticipations in others of meaning, objectivity, knowledge, truth, reality, and value. When I express myself to others, I run the risk of disappointing their basic expectations of attentive, intelligent, reasonable, and responsible performance. I feel this risk I run. It is my presence to myself as related especially to the notion of value. It is my concern with my worth, not only as an observable actor in the public arena, but also as the subject of conscious performance of which those actions in the public arena are the expression and culmination.

The First Degree of Risk: Being Inattentive. When I describe to others what I see, hear, taste, touch, smell, remember, imagine, or feel, I don't feel like I'm putting myself at serious risk. Sometimes I misperceive. "Look," I say to my companion, "there's John!" When she responds, "No, that's not him," I look more closely and realize that it's not John after all. "Oh, you're right, it's not. For a second, it looked like him," I say, as though the one I thought was John were shape-shifting and bears the responsibility for looking like John. I'm not embarrassed by my mistake. Sometimes I remember badly. I may be frustrated by my bad memory, but I don't feel responsible for its inaccuracy. I might as well attribute the cause of my mistake, however obliquely and unreasonably, to the one who looked like John. I'd feel just as little responsibility for his misleading, momentary transmogrification into John. Often my remembering requires that I imagine things and events I've encountered in the past. To my companion I say, "Remember when you introduced me to John? How did he look that night? Remember? We were standing outside Starbucks." She responds, "That was a different time, outside Coffee Bean. You were already dating him by then. Someone else introduced you." "Oh, that's right, it was Amy," I say. "Starbucks, Coffee Bean, whatever. I remember now." Again, I'm not embarrassed or worried about my companion's estimation or evaluation of me as a person. I may feel some frustration over my misremembering. I may be inclined to make a token effort to explain my mistake. But I don't feel like I'm seriously at risk.

If I misperceive with great frequency, if my memories are almost always inaccurate, if the events I imagine never occurred, I might come to be known by others as someone who is easily distracted and whose attention is easily diverted. This may begin to concern me. I may wonder if I'm suffering from a neurological disorder. I'm not embarrassed or ashamed by this. I have no control over such things. But I might entertain the possibility that it's not a neurological problem. Maybe I just don't pay close enough attention to my surroundings. Maybe my perceiving and remembering are only weakly related to my basic commitment to the basic notions. If I suspect that this is true, I experience a mild sense of being at risk. I may become hesitant to describe what I see or to recount my memories. I don't want to risk exposing myself as *inattentive*.

I don't mind if others know I suffer from Attention Deficit Disorder. That's not my fault. But I'd rather they not know that I very seldom perceive or remember with any attention to the accuracy of my perceptions or memories. I don't explain to myself why I don't want to be regarded this way. I'm just present to myself as worried about being regarded this way. I just feel like I'm taking a risk now when I describe my experiences or recount my memories. The feeling of risk isn't very strong, and it's easily dismissed. Even when it isn't dismissed, the risk I feel is never felt as a serious threat to my worth. Often I can defend myself with ease against the accusation that I'm inattentive. If I can't claim physical disability or a neurological disorder, I can always deflect the accusation by observing that my inattentiveness to one thing was the result of my attentiveness to something else. After all, I can't give undivided attention to two things at once. If my errors are in fact due to my failure to pay close attention to much of anything, it's enough for me to say, "I know, sometimes I do get distracted," to illustrate *my attentiveness to my inattentiveness* and, in that way, to fend off a bad evaluation for being inattentive.

The Second Degree of Risk: Being Unintelligent. The sense of risk that accompanies the revelation of my conscious performance in the presence of others increases when I ask questions and express the ideas I get in answer to them. It is one thing to be regarded as careless in my sensing, perceiving, remembering, and imagining. It's another to be regarded as careless in my inquiring and understanding. It is one thing to be regarded as inattentive. It's quite another to be regarded as *unintelligent*.

My attentiveness is my alertness to things and events in which meaning might be found. It is a readiness to begin pursuing meaning. My intelligence is my engagement in the pursuit of the meaning of things and events I sense, perceive, remember, or imagine. I could ask a stupid question. I could reveal myself as struggling too long to find a simple answer. I might appear slow and thickheaded. The ideas I propose in answer to my questions might be superficial and obviously flawed. Their defects might be painfully obvious to others. I might come across to others as thoughtless, as a little dense, or as incredibly stupid. The risk I feel when I ask questions and express my ideas is greater than the risk I feel when I recount what I sense, perceive, remember, imagine, or feel.

I'm not entirely unable to defend myself against the accusation that *my relation to meaning* is weak, haphazard, and uncontrolled. If my ideas are shown very quickly to be inadequate, to fail to address the question I asked, to be superficial, ill-conceived, or just the stock answers anyone might give, I can always say, "They're just ideas. I'm just thinking out loud. I never said they were true! I was only kicking them around." I can appeal to my familiarity with the exploratory nature of questioning, to my experience of the tentative and hypothetical character of even the brightest ideas, to the difference between proposing a possible answer and claiming to know the truth, all in order to defend myself against the accusation, if anyone dares to make it, that my relationship to meaning is disorderly.

I run a risk when I ask and answer questions before others. It's greater than the risk I run when I describe what I perceive or recount what I remember. If I think others are drawing the conclusion from my performance that I'm unintelligent, I might even make a preemptive accusation against myself: "Wow, that was so stupid! What an idiot I am! Where did that crazy idea come from!?" Of course I don't mean I'm always stupid or always an idiot or that my ideas arise independently of my own performance and aren't my own. This was just a momentary and exceptional lapse on my part, a rare occurrence, really not like me at all. In fact, by declaring myself stupid in this instance, I show others that I, too, can recognize stupidity when I see it, even when that stupidity is my own. I fend off the accusation of being unintelligent by exhibiting that I'm at least *intelligent enough about my lack of intelligence* to understand how unintelligent I was.

Given the choice, I'd rather be regarded as inattentive than as unintelligent. But I really don't want to be seen as either. This isn't because I heard or learned somewhere that being attentive and intelligent is better than being inattentive and unintelligent. It's more basic than that. I would have had to have been attentive and intelligent to learn that they were better. I would have already taken them to be better.

The Third Degree of Risk: Being Unreasonable. I feel that I'm putting myself at still greater risk when I express to others, not just what I think, but what I judge to be true. My experience of risk when I claim knowledge before others is still more intense. I am revealing *my relationship to objectivity, knowledge, truth, and the real.* I don't hesitate to describe what I perceive or to recount what I remember unless I'm very frequently mistaken. Even then, my sense of risk is minimal. Others might think I'm inattentive, but I can deflect that accusation fairly easily. I'm a bit more hesitant to share with them my questions and my tentative answers. My investment in my questions and ideas is greater. Others might think I'm unintelligent or even stupid, and that accusation is more difficult to deflect. I can't claim color-blindness or some other disability over which I have no control, or claim that I am indeed attentive but that my attention was elsewhere. I've moved beyond that earliest stage of the unfolding of my basic commitment.

When I share the judgments I've made about what I take to be true and false, real and unreal, I take a risk. Others might think I'm biased, uncritical, unreasonable, silly, or deluded. I don't want them to think I'm closed-minded, that I don't care if my inquiry has been objective or if my questioning is uncritical, that I don't bother to ask if the bright ideas I get are any good and really true. I don't want others to conclude that I have no idea what counts as evidence and what doesn't, that I can't tell a good reason from a bad one, or that I have no regard for evidence at all. I don't want others to dismiss my judgments and conclusions as arbitrary, half-baked, ungrounded, unjustified, unsupported by any good reasons. I don't want them to write me off as biased, opinionated, and ignorant. It is one thing to be regarded as inattentive. It is another thing to be regarded as unintelligent. It is yet another to be thought of as *unreasonable* and to be regarded as a fool.

When I express my judgments to others it might become clear that my conclusions are groundless, that I don't really know what I claim to know, that what I judge to be true is not true at all. I may discern in others a growing suspicion that I'm an uncritical and unreasonable person, that I'm oblivious to my own biases, that I lack sensitivity to my own ignorance, that I think things exist that don't exist at all. I can't deflect this rising accusation by saying, "It was just an idea." A judgment isn't just an idea. Judging isn't understanding or getting a bright idea; judging and understanding are different operations. Before I make a judgment my idea is just an idea. I haven't yet committed myself. When I make a judgment I declare my idea true or false. I make a claim to know one way or the other, and I make a personal commitment. When I make a judgment, I'm saying that this is the way things really are. If it becomes evident that things are really not that way at all, I can't claim that I was only hypothesizing, just thinking out loud, or just kicking around ideas. I could stubbornly persist and cling to my judgment, despite the mounting evidence that my judgment is false. But if I realize that this tactic is likely to confirm rather than to allay others' suspicions that I don't really care about the truth, then I might just admit that I judged badly and that, in this instance, I'm wrong.

The accusation of unreasonableness, when I am actually being unreasonable, can be resisted, but it can't be deflected. I'm humbled by my failure to detect my biases. I feel foolish for being convinced of the truth of what is really false or for being so sure that what is really false is true. I feel unsettled by the discovery that what I took to be true isn't true at all. But at least the commitment I made in my judging was only an intellectual one; I haven't yet acted upon it. I can still "change my mind." By doing so, I reveal that I am, after all, a reasonable person. I do care about objectivity, knowledge, truth, and reality. In this particular case I was wrong, but I'm not wrong all the time. I'm not a clown. I'm a critical person. I even criticize my own judgments and correct them. I care about truth. I'm *reasonable enough about my own unreasonableness* to correct myself. I'm a *reasonable* person after all.

The Fourth Degree of Risk: Being Irresponsible. My sense of being at risk increases yet again when I reveal *my relation to value* by sharing my evaluations, by expressing my judgments about what's worthwhile and what isn't, by announcing my decisions, and by speaking frankly to others about my hopes and aspirations for myself. The risk associated with the revelation of my relation to value already lurks in my revelations of myself as attentive or inattentive, as intelligent or unintelligent, and as reasonable or unreasonable. I reveal my relation to the notion of value whenever I express myself to others. My relation to value is also intimately revealed to me in my presence to myself as at risk in my expression of myself to others; I am present to myself as related to the value of myself. Others' evaluations of me as attentive or inattentive, intelligent or unintelligent, or reasonable or unreasonable are at root evaluations of my relation to value. When this ever-present relation to value comes to the fore in my dealings with others, my sense of being at risk seems to reach its greatest intensity.

My expression is always at once a revelation of my basic commitment and of my relationship to it. When I express myself to and with others I'm sharing the results of my conscious performance with them. If they're paying attention, they can discern the presence or notice the absence of attentiveness, intelligence, and reasonableness in my performance. But I'm not just sharing the results of my present and previous performance. I'm also performing now in their presence. I'm revealing in my performance in the moment the strength or weakness of my basic commitment and the nature of my relationship to the basic notions. When I express my questions about what ought to be and what I ought to do, when I share my deliberations and my evaluations, when I make public my judgments on the value of courses of action and announce the decisions and choices I've made, and when I express my deepest aspirations for myself, my relationship to value is most prominent and most easily discerned. My relationship to my basic commitment is most exposed, and I feel most vulnerable and sensitive to evaluation by others.

My relation to value includes in its sweep my attentiveness or inattentiveness, my intelligence or lack of intelligence, my reasonableness or unreasonableness. It's not only my responsibility or irresponsibility in the actions that flow from my deliberating, evaluating, deciding and choosing. It also includes my responsibility or irresponsibility in the performance of all the conscious operations that lead up to my deliberations, evaluations, decisions and choices. Primarily, my relation to value is my responsiveness or lack of responsiveness to my basic commitment. Secondarily, it is the orderliness or disorderliness of my deliberating, evaluating, deciding, and observable conduct. It is my discernment or lack of discernment of what is really and truly worthwhile. But my discernment of what is worthwhile depends upon my attentiveness or inattentiveness in my perceiving, remembering, and imagining. It depends upon my intelligence or unintelligence in my questioning and answering. It depends upon my reasonableness or unreasonableness in my critical questioning and judging. My decisions and the conduct that flows from them depend upon my relationship to meaning, objectivity, knowledge, truth, and reality, and this relationship is always already a relationship to value.

In the questions I ask about what ought to be done and about what I ought to do, I reveal how much or how little I care about value. I reveal my presence to myself as deeply concerned or relatively unconcerned with value. I exhibit the strength or flimsiness of my relationship to value and the narrowness or breadth of my concern with value. When I inquire about what's worthwhile and what isn't, others may discern in me an enthusiasm for asking about what's *worthwhile for me* and a tendency to become bored with questions about what might be *worthwhile for others*. My concern for value may appear to them egoistic or self-centered. My lack of concern for what's worthwhile for others may appear anti-social. I may appear excessively self-interested and hard-hearted or even heartless. The way I raise the question of value may appear cavalier, lacking in seriousness, or disdainful of such questions. I may appear to have almost no conscience at all. I risk being regarded as *irresponsible*.

In my deliberations about possible courses of action, I reveal how much and how little I know about what's real and what's not, about what's possible or impossible, about what's feasible and what's unfeasible, about what's likely to be effective and what isn't. My deliberations may be very brief, unimaginative, unrealistic, fantastic, sensitive only to the likely consequences of possible courses of action for myself, or insensitive even to those. My evaluating may reveal that I make no distinctions between what I or others like, what pleases me or others, what I or others happen to prefer at the moment, and what is truly worthwhile. It may reveal that whatever I find to be painful or unpleasant or uncomfortable or inconvenient I assume to be valueless, or that whatever I find to be pleasant or satisfying or convenient I assume to be truly valuable.

My deciding and choosing may come across as arbitrary and hasty, as whimsical and thoughtless, as careless or desperate leaps in the dark. It may appear to others that I have no clue at all that my questions about value, my deliberating, my evaluating, my choosing and my deciding introduce into the world conduct with which others will have to deal. It may appear to them that it has never occurred to me that what I do is always a more or less meaningful, objective and critical, knowledgeable, truthful, realistic, and worthwhile addition to the world in which we all must live and find direction. I may appear to others as though I just don't take myself as a conscious performer seriously at all and that I pay no heed to the effects of my actions on others. Others may even get the feeling that, because of my disorderly relation to value, I could be dangerous and should be avoided or even forcibly restrained.

When I reveal to others my relationship to value, it may become clear to me through their reactions that I am being hard-hearted, self-centered, unrealistic, uncritical, unquestioning, and inattentive. I sense the risk of being regarded not only as inattentive, unintelligent, and unreasonable but also as deeply careless and dangerously irresponsible, as tied by only the thinnest thread to the basic notions. When I notice that others may be drawing the conclusion that I'm irresponsible, I might attempt to preserve myself in the face of that most feared evaluation. My worth as a conscious performer is at stake. It is one thing to be regarded as inattentive or unintelligent or unreasonable. It is another to be seen as caring so little about value, as so weakly related to the basic notions, as so disorderly in my conscious performance, as to be dangerous. I don't want to be despised by others. I may attempt to defend myself by proclaiming that value is relative, but this tactic is self-defeating. I can't convince others that my performance is truly worthwhile by convincing them that worth is truly relative. I can't persuade others that I do take my relation to value seriously by declaring that the notion of value should not be taken seriously. If they are right about the defects in my deliberating, evaluating, deciding, and the conduct that flows from them, I have no recourse but to admit my irresponsibility. But irresponsible conduct is not just an inaccurate perception or memory. It's not just a poorly conceived idea. It's not just an uncritical judgment. I can't deflect the charge of irresponsible conduct by claiming that I was attending to something else or just kicking around ideas or by agreeing to "change my mind." The ill-conceived, self-centered, shortsighted, hard-hearted, irresponsible deed has been done, and others have to deal with a *fait accompli*. I have no recourse now but to apologize and to announce my intention to perform more responsibly in the future. "I'm so sorry. I wish I could undo it, but I can't. I hope you will forgive me." In the act of apologizing and asking for forgiveness I reveal the renewal of my basic commitment and of my relationship to the notion of value. I feel better now for having done that. That was a good thing to do. I am at least *responsible enough to acknowledge and atone for my irresponsibility*. I'm a *responsible* person after all.

We seem to be most ready and willing to share with others *descriptions* of our experiences of things, people, events, and situations. When we settle for mere description, we run only the minimal risk of being found inattentive. We are often somewhat hesitant to share our tentative *understandings* of our experiences. When we express our ideas about our experiences, we run the greater risk of being found unintelligent. We are usually still more reluctant to declare publicly the *truth* of our understandings of our experiences. When we reveal to others our judgments on the truth of our ideas, we run the still greater risk of being found unreasonable and uncritical. It seems that we are most reluctant to express publicly our *evaluations, choices, and decisions*. When we reveal to others what we take to be more valuable or more worthwhile, less valuable or less worthwhile, valueless or worthless, we run the even greater risk of being found irresponsible. The memories of those times when I've been found to be inattentive may fade quickly. Memories of my public thick-headedness may linger a bit longer. Memories of those times when I've been found to be unreasonable may last longer still. My memories of being justly accused of irresponsible conduct seem to stay with me forever. They seem to be more than mere memories. They become regrets. They're unforgettable episodes in the story I'm authoring as my relationship to my basic commitment to meaning, objectivity, knowledge, reality, truth, and value unfolds and fluctuates.

2.3 FOUR MOODS OF CONSCIOUS PERFORMANCE

Others and their evaluations of us are not our present concern. Our present concern is our own relationship to the basic notions. That relationship is manifested to others when we express ourselves to them and with them. In that self-expression we experience varying degrees of risk. I've identified four degrees of risk we experience when we expose to others our relationship to the basic notions. The degree of personal risk seems to increase with my performance of different operations. It is lowest when I reveal my performance of operations that merely provide me with something I could ask about. It is greater when I reveal my performance of operations by which I pursue the *meaning* of my experience. It is greater still when I reveal my performance of operations by which I pursue *objectivity, knowledge, truth, and reality*. It is greatest when I reveal my performance of operations by which I pursue *value*. Our experience of degrees of personal risk gives us a clue to four basic moods of conscious performance and their spontaneous order.

Whenever we're awake, we're present to ourselves in our relationship to the basic notions. We are present to ourselves as attentive or inattentive, intelligent or unintelligent, reasonable or unreasonable, responsible or irresponsible. Let us name the four basic moods of self-presence (1) Question-free Self-Presence, (2) Wondering Self-Presence, (3) Critical Self-Presence, and (4) Evaluative Self-Presence.

Mood One: Being Attentive or Inattentive. Question-free Self-Presence is our presence to ourselves in the conscious performance of seeing, hearing, tasting, touching, smelling, feeling, perceiving, imagining, and remembering. In Question-free Self-Presence I'm just *attentive or inattentive*. I'm neither intelligent nor unintelligent, because I'm not yet pursuing meaning. I'm neither reasonable nor unreasonable, because I'm not yet pursuing truth. I'm neither responsible nor irresponsible, because I'm not yet pursuing value. I'm not wondering about meaning, about reality, or about value. I'm not wondering at all. I'm just having sensitive, imaginative, recollective, or affective experiences.

There seem to be two kinds of question-free consciousness. First, there is my self-presence in the performance of these operations *before* I've asked about and understood what I'm seeing, hearing, tasting, touching, smelling, feeling, perceiving, imagining or remembering. I'm having experiences about which I haven't yet asked any questions. Secondly, there is my presence to myself in the performance of these operations *after* I've asked about and understood what I'm seeing, hearing, tasting, touching, smelling, feeling, perceiving, imagining, or remembering. I'm having experiences about which I've already asked and answered questions, so I'm not inclined to wonder about them or even to give them much attention.

When I'm seeing, hearing, tasting, touching, smelling, perceiving, or feeling something I've never sensed or perceived or felt before, and do not ask what it is, I'm present to myself as question-free. When I'm remembering or imagining something I've seen before or heard about but haven't yet understood, I'm present to myself as question-free. There are questions to be asked, but I'm not asking them. I don't usually remain long in this question-free mood. In my encounters with the unknown and unfamiliar and strange, I spontaneously try to make sense of things. I may experience this budding interest in making sense negatively as a vivid fear of the unfamiliar and unknown. Very soon, though, I experience it as my positive commitment to meaning, and my pursuit of meaning is superimposed upon my seeing, hearing, touching, tasting, perceiving, remembering, and feeling as I begin to ask questions. The distractions of biological stress or physical threat may temporarily prevent me from trying to make sense of the unfamiliar and from pursuing knowledge of the unknown. Fatigue, hunger, sexual discomfort, and a range of desires and fears may overwhelm my basic commitment to finding meaning in what I haven't yet understood. But in the absence of these distractions and attractions, or when they begin to subside, I find myself compelled to ask a question. Before I begin to wonder and ask questions, though, I'm present to myself as question-free.

When I'm sensing, perceiving, feeling, remembering, or imagining something I've previously asked about and understood, I'm also present to myself as question-free. I'm question-free, not because I've never asked, but because I've already asked, and I've gotten some answers. There are always more questions I could ask, but I'm familiar enough with my situation to get along, so I don't ask them.

WASHING DISHES

I'm just washing the dishes. I've done it many times before. I'm not perceiving anything I feel I need to ask about and come to understand. That's water. That's soap. Soap and water remove grease. That's a faucet. These are plates. I don't feel compelled to ask any questions. I already know well enough what I'm experiencing. I already know it's worthwhile to wash the dishes. I'm feeling the warm water on my hands, watching it slide off the glasses and plates, watching the shifting mounds of bubbles. I don't have any questions about this. I don't feel the impulse to ask any questions. I already understand all this well enough, but I suppose there's plenty more to know about it. There are lots of questions I could ask. There are people who ask about the formation of bubbles, about the effectiveness of dish soap in dissolving grease, about the relation of dishwashing to health, about the impact of the way we wash dishes on the water shortage and ocean life, about the chemical residue left by dishwashing detergent. I can imagine all these people asking all these questions in their labs or wherever. These plates are kind of slippery. I'd better be careful. I've often wondered in the past about the feeling of impatience and boredom I always have when I wash dishes. There it is again. Sometime I might ask why it always makes me feel that way. Right now, I just want to get the dishes done. I'm just washing the dishes.

In my question-free presence to myself I can be *attentive or inattentive*. I can see something I've never seen before and take no notice of it. I can see something I've previously understood and take no notice of it. If I take no notice of something new in my experience, I won't ask about it and won't come to understand it. If I don't attend to experience that is familiar enough to me for my present purposes, I won't gain more detailed knowledge of it and its relations to other things. If I perform familiar tasks inattentively, I run a greater risk of making mistakes. If I wash dishes inattentively, I'm more likely to wash them badly or to break a few. If someone hears the sound of breaking glass coming from the kitchen, she might call out to me, "What are you doing in there? Be careful!" Sensing the minimal risk that accompanies performing before others, I might reply, "It was an accident! The glass slipped out of my hand." In my seeing, hearing, tasting, touching, smelling, perceiving, feeling, remembering, and imagining, I can pay attention or fail to pay attention. In my Question-free Self-presence I am *attentive or inattentive*.

Mood Two: Being Intelligent or Unintelligent. Wondering Self-Presence is our presence to ourselves in the conscious performance of asking questions about what we haven't yet understood, coming to understand or grasping possible answers or getting ideas, and conceiving and formulating the ideas we've gotten. I notice lots of things, but what are they, what do they mean, how are they related to other things? What sense can I make of them?

In Wondering Self-Presence I'm present to myself as *intelligent or unintelligent*. I'm doing more than paying attention. I'm concerned about meaning. I'm wondering what, why, how, what for, how often, how come. On my experience of sensing, perceiving, feeling, remembering, and imagining I superimpose an emerging concern for meaning. I begin to wonder.

BEING INTELLIGENT

I want to know what it is and what it means and why it is the way it is. I want to know what and how and why and how often. I feel frustration. I feel puzzled, perplexed, bewildered, confused. I feel ignorant, uninformed, unclear. I'm dissatisfied with my lack of understanding and troubled by it. I just don't like being confused. I don't like being in the dark. I feel the tension of inquiry. I feel like I'm on the verge of understanding. I wonder why I can't seem to get it. I'm impatient to understand. I feel like I have a clue. I feel stuck and unable to get anywhere. Now I feel like I have no clue. I sense the personal risk that others, if they were to realize I have no clue, might think I'm stupid. I feel intellectually frustrated and slow-witted. I feel annoyance and irritation. I'm smarter than this. I feel a need for enlightenment. I feel hopeless. I can't make sense of things. What difference does it make anyway? Does it really matter if I understand this? I wish someone would just tell me the answer. I fear I might not have the brains for this. But I don't want anyone to tell me. I want to figure it out for myself. I feel that it's too hard. Aha! I've had a sudden breakthrough of understanding. I feel elated. I feel relieved and enlightened, insightful, intellectually satisfied and smart. This is a pretty good idea! It seems so obvious to me now. I feel relief and satisfaction. I get it now; I understand. I don't know why I didn't get it sooner.

In my wondering presence to myself I can be *intelligent or unintelligent*. When I notice the emergence in myself of a desire to understand I can give expression to that wonder in a question, or I can treat my sense of wonder like a feeling of indigestion and hope that it will soon subside. I might hesitate to venture beyond my mere experience of things, to abandon the security of my sensible and imaginable and affective connections to what I can see and touch and imagine and feel. I can take up the challenge posed by my own incomprehension, I can ignore it, or I can flee from it. I can face head-on the possibility that a new idea may force a minor adjustment or major renovation of my viewpoint and alter slightly or disrupt radically my present way of life. I'm present to myself in my commitment to meaning, and I know, even if only vaguely, what that commitment means. If I find new meaning and it turns out to be true, I'll feel bound to live by that knowledge. My anticipation of having to adjust my living to what I discover may intimidate me and weaken my resolve to understand. When I ask the questions that arise in me, I can do so precisely, or I can settle for vague and noncommittal formulations like "What the heck is going on?" or "I wonder what on earth that is." I can formulate my questions well or badly, with a stronger or weaker commitment to the pursuit of meaning. When I get an idea in answer to a question, I can attempt to express it, nail it down, retain it, and take it with me, or I can fail to express it, let it slip away, lose it, and wish later that I'd put it into words or written it down. I can struggle to express my ideas clearly and precisely, or I can settle for opaque and vague allusions to what I've understood. I can try to say precisely what it is I've understood, or I can rest content with the idea without expressing it. I can take the answers I get to my questions seriously, or I can trivialize them. In my questioning, coming to understand and grasping ideas, conceiving my ideas and formulating them, I can be *intelligent or unintelligent.*

Mood Three: Being Reasonable or Unreasonable. Critical Self-Presence is our presence to ourselves in the conscious performance of asking critical questions about the adequacy of the ideas we get, assembling and weighing the evidence for their correctness, grasping that the evidence we've found is sufficient or insufficient, and making the judgment that our ideas are true or false, probably true or probably not true, or that the evidence needed to determine their truth or falsity is not yet in. I get lots of ideas, but are they true?

In Critical Self-Presence I'm present to myself as *reasonable or unreasonable* or as *critical or uncritical.* I'm concerned with objective knowledge of what's really true and really real. I'm wondering about the correctness or incorrectness, the truth or falsity, of my ideas. The wonder that nudged me out of unquestioning self-presence and into the wondering self-presence of the pursuit of the meaning of my experience is redirected now to the meanings I've discovered. My concern for meaning becomes a concern to know whether or not the meaning reached is the right meaning, if my pursuit of meaning has been an objective one, if I can claim now to know the truth about some aspect of reality. My wondering becomes critical and reflective doubt about the objectivity of my inquiry and the correctness of the understanding I've achieved.

BEING REASONABLE

I wonder if the idea I got is just another bright idea and nothing more. Is it really true? I think my idea is pretty good. It sure feels like it's true. It seems like my question has been answered. I had that "aha-experience," but I'm still skeptical and suspicious. I've had insights before that turned out to be wrong. I'm suspicious of my idea, and I'm suspicious of myself. What are the defects and strengths of this idea? Maybe I just want it to be true, but it really isn't. Like everyone else, I have a background, an upbringing, biases, preferences. I wouldn't mind if this idea I have were true. But I wouldn't mind either if other ideas I know are true were false. I can't go on what I would or wouldn't mind. What was the original question I asked? Did I ask it well? Was it what I meant to ask? Was the way I asked it misleading? I need to be sensitive to my biases. I know I have them. We all have them. Are they at work here? I wonder if I've smuggled the answer I wanted into the question I asked. I wonder if I'm even able to notice all my biases. That seems impossible, so why try? I'm probably not even aware of all of them. How can I be sure this idea is any good? What would have to be true or false for me to conclude that this idea is true or false? What conditions would have to be met for this idea to be true? I wonder if I've identified them all. How will I know if I've identified them all? How will I know if they've been met? I wonder if this persistent uneasiness I feel is an inkling that there are other questions I have to ask and answer before I can judge that this idea is true or false. I wonder if my growing feeling of conviction is premature. I wonder if my persisting doubts are excessive and if I'm nitpicking and being hyper-critical. Are these other questions really relevant? Now I'm vacillating. One moment I feel pretty sure, and the next moment I feel unsure again. One moment I really want to know what's true, and the next moment I feel like the whole pursuit is pointless. Can we ever know what's true about anything? I feel the persistent pressure of further questions. Now I feel like my questions are drying up. I wonder if they're drying up because I'm just naive, overlooking something, or missing something I should notice. I wonder if I should ask other people what they think. They have different backgrounds. They have biases too, but their biases are probably not the same as mine. I wonder what others might say about my critical abilities and my judgment if I discuss this idea of mine with them. It would be a risk. I might be making an obvious mistake. I'm not yet ready to claim I know the truth. I'll keep my idea and my concerns about its adequacy to myself for now. Now I feel a surge of confidence that I've assembled all the relevant conditions and that they've all been met. I feel my doubts dissolve. I wonder if I've just discarded them. I'm pretty sure my idea is more than just another bright idea. I feel intellectually sophisticated and confident. There's ample evidence. I *do* have good reasons, and I can state them. I feel an impulse to go public, to share the truth I've found, and prepared to run the risk of being thought unreasonable. I feel like I have some authority to speak about what's true and false in this case. I know what I'm talking about, at least in this case. I can back it up; I've got good grounds. No, wait, I'm not quite ready to make a judgment yet. I want to be really sure before I make it.

In my critical presence to myself I can be *reasonable or unreasonable*. When doubts about the adequacy of my ideas begin to emerge I can express them in critical questions or I can minimize them and squelch them. My critical questions about my ideas can be formulated carefully or carelessly. I can raise or fail to raise questions about the influence of my own biases and preferences. I can take measures to counter my likely prejudices or neglect to take those measures. I can let the risk associated with sharing my critical reasoning with others deprive me of the benefits of discussion. Out of fear of exposing my critical performance to evaluation by others, I can remain silent. I can identify or fail to identify the conditions that have to be fulfilled for my idea to be correct. I can be sensitive to the pressure of further relevant questions, or I can dismiss the feeling that there's something I'm missing or something I'm not taking into account. I can avoid making a judgment, or I can judge rashly. I can refuse to make a judgment even though all the evidence is in, or I can claim to know despite my lingering doubts. I can claim to know because I'm reasonably satisfied that all the evidence is in. In asking critical questions about my ideas, assembling and weighing the evidence for their correctness, grasping that the evidence is sufficient or insufficient, and making judgments on their truth or falsity, I can be *reasonable or unreasonable.*

Mood Four: Being Responsible or Irresponsible. Evaluative Self-Presence is our presence to ourselves in the conscious performance of asking questions about what's worthwhile, deliberating about possible courses of action, evaluating possible courses of action, deciding and choosing, and engaging in conduct that flows from and is orientated and controlled by our performance of these operations. I make lots of judgments about what's true and false. So what? What difference do they make?

In Evaluative Self-Presence I am present to myself as *responsible or irresponsible.* I'm concerned with what is worthwhile, with what is truly valuable. The wonder that pulled me out of unquestioning self-presence into wondering self-presence, that underwent a transformation into reflective doubt in critical self-presence, undergoes another transformation into what is loosely referred to as conscience. My concern for meaning became concern about my objectivity, the truth of my ideas, and what's really real. Now, my concern about my objectivity, the truth of my ideas, and what's really real becomes concern about what, in light of what I know to be true and real, is really valuable and really worthwhile.

BEING RESPONSIBLE

Given what I know, what should I do, and what should I avoid doing? Now that I know these things, am I obliged to act a certain way? What would be worth doing and what wouldn't? What would be moral or immoral, good or evil, constructive or destructive, beneficial or injurious? Can I even discern what's truly worthwhile? I can easily see what would be to my advantage, at least in the short term. But is what's good for me in the short term always good for me in the long term? Is what's good for me always truly valuable? Are my motives really pure? I wonder if my motives are mixed or merely self-serving. I always seem to have mixed motives. I'm hesitant to put myself on the line. I wonder if it's worth it. Anyway, does what I do make any difference at all? I wonder if I even know enough about the situation to make a responsible choice. What about the conse-quences of what I might do? I can't foresee them all! I can imagine being appreciated and praised if things work out. I'm worried; I can't be sure things will work out the way I'd like them to, or the way they should. I don't want people to think I'm bad. I don't want them to despise me or hate me. I'd like to be able to take pride in what I do. I want to be regarded as a reputable person and to be respected. I don't want to feel ashamed of myself or seem disreputable, thoughtless, uncaring, or malicious. Now I feel confident I'm on the right track. I think this might be a good thing to do. I have to be free and self-determining. I'm authoring my own story after all. I don't want to be slavish and act just because of the pressures imposed by others or by circumstances. I want to be autonomous. I can't live my life on autopilot. I've got these habitual ways of acting; I keep on doing what I always do. How do I break these habits? Should I break them? Are they all bad habits? I'm attracted by values I've never pursued before. I feel the risk of doing things I won't be able to undo. I anticipate being account-able for what I do. I remember doing things I've been ashamed of. I could apologize and make amends. Maybe it

wasn't really my fault. I feel like blaming someone else. No,
what I really feel is regret. It was my fault. I didn't do the
best I could. Well, I still feel good about a lot of what I've
done. I'm pleased with what I did. I feel like taking credit
for it. I feel I've made a worthwhile contribution, even if it
was just a small one. But what should I do now? Is there
something I ought to do? I can imagine doing all kinds of
things or doing nothing at all. What course of action seems
most valuable to me? Which one really is most valuable?
What would really be most worthwhile for me to do in this
situation? I can't go on deliberating forever. I've got to
decide. OK, I've decided. It's a big risk, but I'm going to do
it anyway. Given what I know, I'm pretty sure it's the right
thing to do. I still feel anxious. I hope things work out well.

In my evaluative presence to myself, I can be *responsible or
irresponsible*. When the question of value begins to emerge, I can
give expression to it or dismiss it. My questions about what's
worthwhile and what isn't can be formulated well or badly. I can
contract them into questions about what would best serve my
present purposes, what would be most pleasant for me, what would
cause me the least discomfort, what would be most convenient,
what would be most to my personal advantage. I can extend them
into questions about what would be worthwhile regardless of the
impact on my present purposes, my pleasure, and my comfort. I
can envision a number of possible courses of action, or I can settle
for the first one I imagine. I can imagine courses of action without
concerning myself with their consequences, or I can explore the
possible consequences at length or even interminably. I can
deliberate realistically or unrealistically. I can evaluate the worth of
possible courses of action half-heartedly or thoroughly. I can be
sensitive or insensitive to differences between what I'd like to do
and what is really worth doing, and between what I have to gain
and what is worth achieving through a particular course of action.
I can make an effort to sort out the worthwhile from the worthless
and the more worthwhile from the less worthwhile, or I can make
little effort at all to do this. I can make judgments of value critically
or uncritically, objectively or unobjectively, knowledgeably or
ignorantly, with or without sufficient concern for their truth,
realistically or unrealistically. I can avoid making them at all. I can
be sensitive or insensitive to the intrusive influence of prior

decisions and long-standing habits. I can relieve myself of the burden of evaluation and settle for what others would prefer or what others happen to think is good, or I can assume the burden of determining for myself what would be most worthwhile regardless of others' preferences or mine. I can refuse to bring my deliberation and evaluation to a conclusion. I can deliberate and deliberate and never decide. I can be so intimidated by the personal risk and the risk to others of deciding and acting that I won't decide at all. I can be foolhardy and take the leap into action before I've really thought things through. I can be as wise as I can be, select from among the options I've explored the one I judge to be most worthwhile, assume the risk, make my decision, and act. I can forsake careful deliberation and sensitive evaluation and do what everyone does. I can assume authorship of my own story, or I can drift. I can let my story be written by the good and bad decisions of others and by the pressures of circumstance, or I can undertake deliberately to give direction to my life. In asking the question of value, deliberating about possible courses of action, evaluating them, deciding and acting, I can be *responsible or irresponsible.*

We've identified and isolated four basic moods of conscious performance: (1) Question-free Self-Presence, (2) Wondering Self-Presence, (3) Critical Self-Presence, and (4) Evaluative Self-Presence. In Question-free Self-Presence I notice things or fail to notice them; I'm *attentive or inattentive.* In Wondering Self-Presence I'm more or less concerned about meaning. I'm trying wholeheartedly or halfheartedly to understand what I've attended to. I'm *intelligent or unintelligent.* In Critical Self-Presence I'm more or less concerned about objective knowledge of the truth. I'm trying wholeheartedly or halfheartedly to find out if my ideas are correct. I'm *reasonable or unreasonable.* In Evaluative Self-Presence I'm more or less concerned about what's worthwhile. I'm trying wholeheartedly or half-heartedly to decide what is most worthwhile to do. I'm *responsible or irresponsible.*

The Four Moods and Our Basic Commitment. Our basic commitment to meaning, objectivity, knowledge, truth, reality, and value is operative in all of the basic moods. Our basic moods are our presence to ourselves *in* our basic commitment. In Question-free Self-Presence our basic commitment is only incipient. In our minimal wakefulness and inattentiveness it is relatively dormant. It begins to reveal itself in our attentiveness that sets the stage for the emergence of our Wondering Self-Presence. In our Wondering Self-Presence our basic commitment to *meaning* comes to the fore and sets the stage for the emergence of our Critical Self-Presence. In our explicit pursuit of meaning, our anticipation of objectivity, knowledge, truth, reality, and value are implicit, and our attentiveness is preserved. In our Critical Self-Presence our basic commitment to *objectivity, knowledge, truth, and reality* comes to the fore and sets the stage for the emergence of our Evaluative Self-Presence. In our explicit pursuit of objective knowledge of the true and the real, our anticipation of value is implicit, and our concern for meaning is preserved. In our Evaluative Self-Presence our basic commitment to *value* comes to the fore. In our explicit pursuit of value, our concern for meaning and our interest in objectivity, knowledge, truth, and reality are preserved.

Attentiveness sets the stage for wonder and inquiry. Attentiveness and intelligence together set the stage for critical doubt. Attentiveness, intelligence, and reasonableness together set the stage for conscience and the question of value and responsibility. The basic moods are our presence to ourselves in our relationship to our basic commitment. That relationship may be deliberate or spontaneous, strong or weak. Consequently, the mood of Question-free Self-presence can be attentiveness or inattentiveness, the mood of Wondering Self-presence can be intelligence or unintelligence, the mood of Critical Self-presence can be reasonableness or unreasonableness, and the mood of Evaluative Self-presence can be responsibility or irresponsibility.

The Orderly Sequence of Moods. The four moods of conscious performance stand in an orderly, sequential relation to one another. The attentiveness of Question-free Self-Presence is transformed by further operations into intelligent Wondering Self-Presence. To my attentive sensing, perceiving, imagining, remembering, and feeling I add *intelligent inquiry*. What I attend to is what I ask questions about. The intelligence of Wondering Self-Presence is transformed by further operations into reasonable Critical Self-Presence. To my intelligent inquiring, understanding, conceiving, and formulating I add *critical inquiry*. What I understand is what I ask critical questions about. The reasonableness of my Critical Self-Presence is transformed by further operations into responsible Evaluative Self-Presence. To my reasonable inquiry, weighing of evidence, grasping of the sufficiency of evidence, and judgments of truth and falsity I add *evaluative inquiry*. In light of what I know objectively to be true and real, I ask what would be most worthwhile for me to do.

In the ideal case, attentive performance becomes attentive and intelligent performance. Attentive and intelligent performance becomes attentive, intelligent, and reasonable performance. Attentive, intelligent, and reasonable performance becomes attentive, intelligent, reasonable, and responsible performance. There is a spontaneous order to the sequence of moods of our conscious performance.

The tie that binds the four moods is our basic commitment to the pursuit of meaning, objectivity, knowledge, truth, reality, and value. That basic commitment unfolds as a dynamic orientation that transforms inattention into attention, attention into wondering, wondering into critical doubt, critical doubt into conscience. That dynamic orientation receives articulate expression in our formulation of *the question of meaning, the question of truth*, and *the question of value*. Only by raising the question of meaning, the question of truth, and the question of value do we discover what is truly meaningful, really real, and truly valuable. These questions are our operative clues to the answers we seek by asking them. Only by our adherence to the basic commitment in the unfolding of our conscious performance do we find answers to these questions. The operative meaning of the basic notions resides in the unfolding of that basic commitment.

The *operative meaning* of meaning, objectivity, knowledge, truth, reality, and value is found in our presence to ourselves in our actual pursuit of meaning, objectivity, knowledge, truth, reality, and value. Our only clue to the meaning of the basic notions is the orderly unfolding of our basic commitment. We discover the operative meanings of the basic notions only by reflecting upon the orderly unfolding of that basic commitment. We discover the meaning of our basic commitment *by turning that commitment on itself,* by asking the questions of meaning, truth, and value about our experience of ourselves in pursuit of meaning, truth, and value. What we discover is that meaning is what we discover when we understand in answer to our question of meaning, that the true and the real are what we discover when we discover an answer to our question of truth, that the truly worthwhile is what we discover in answer to our question of value.

---

4. RESPONSIBILITY: Evaluative Operations

⇑ Explicit Commitment to Value

3. REASONABLENESS: Critical Operations

⇑ Explicit Commitment to Objectivity, Knowledge, Truth, and Reality

2. INTELLIGENCE: Wondering Operations

⇑ Explicit Commitment to Meaning

1. ATTENTIVENESS: Question-free Operations

⇑ Incipient Basic Commitment

THE SPONTANEOUS ORDERLY SEQUENCE OF MOODS OF
CONSCIOUS PERFORMANCE

Disorderly Sequences of Moods. The unfolding of our four moods of conscious performance may be disorderly. I don't have to be attentive, intelligent, reasonable, and responsible in my performance. I can be inattentive, unintelligent, unreasonable, and irresponsible. I can spin my wheels in Question-free Self-Presence. I can slip into a dream world of inattentiveness. I can be attentive and still fail to ask about the objects to which I attend. I can stall in Wondering Self-Presence. I can play intellectual games, argue for the sake of arguing, revel in the hypothetical, amuse myself with the pursuit of the logical implications of merely abstract possibilities, tarry with the trivial. I can try to be intelligent about what I haven't really attended to. I can leap from Wondering Self-Presence to Evaluative Self-Presence without passing through Critical Self-Presence. I can leap to Critical Self-Presence without passing through Wondering Self-Presence. I can try to criticize ideas I haven't understood. I can try to make judgments without attention to the relevant data. I can stop myself short in Critical Self-Presence and never ask what difference the truth I've found should make in my living. I can deliberate and evaluate and act unreasonably, unintelligently, and inattentively.

The four moods of conscious performance are spontaneously ordered by their relations to the basic notions of meaning, objectivity, knowledge, truth, reality, and value. The spontaneous order is:

> *First* Question-free Self-Presence
> > *and then* Wondering Self-Presence
> > > *and then* Critical Self-Presence
> > > > *and then* Evaluative Self-Presence.

This order is initially only spontaneous. It isn't deliberately imposed. It is the spontaneous orderly unfolding of ourselves as conscious performers before we've come to know and take possession of ourselves as conscious performers. The spontaneous order of our conscious performance, because it isn't deliberately imposed and maintained, is fragile, and it easily becomes disorderly performance. But, even when the unfolding of our conscious performance becomes disorderly, we are present to ourselves as disorderly in one or more of these four moods of conscious performance. Even in our disorderly performance we're present to ourselves as inattentive and/or unintelligent and/or unreasonable and/or irresponsible.

3. FOUR MODES OF CONSCIOUS OPERATION

The four moods of conscious performance are the four ways in which we're present to ourselves when we're awake. They are our consciousness in the various types of operations we perform. We've already had occasion to mention many of these operations in our discussion of the four basic moods. Let's shift the focus of our attention now from the changes in our presence to ourselves in the performance of different operations to the operations themselves of which attentiveness or inattentiveness, intelligence or unintelligence, reasonableness or unreasonableness, responsibility or irresponsibility are qualities.

Just as there are four distinguishable *basic moods of conscious performance*, so also there are four distinguishable *modes of conscious operation*: (1) the Question-free Mode of Operation, (2) the Wondering Mode of Operation, (3) the Critical Mode of Operation, and (4) the Evaluative Mode of Operation. Like the four moods, the four modes unfold in a spontaneous orderly sequence. Each of the four modes of operation consists of *a set of operations*. The operations in the Wondering, Critical, and Evaluative modes also occur in spontaneous orderly sequences. The sequences of operations in these three modes of operation can become disorderly, and the sequence of the four modes can become disorderly.

Mode One: Question-free Performance. The operations that constitute the Question-free Mode of Operation are *seeing, hearing, tasting, touching, smelling, perceiving, imagining, remembering, and feeling*. For ease of reference we may call operations in the Question-free Mode *experiential operations*. The mood of performance in the Question-free Mode of Operation is the Question-free Self-Presence already described. When I respect and adhere to the basic commitment incipient in the Question-free Mode of Operation, I am attentive. When I fail to respect and adhere to the basic commitment incipient in the Question-free Mode, I am inattentive.

EXPERIENTIAL OPERATIONS

Seeing, hearing, tasting, touching, smelling, perceiving, imagining, remembering, feeling

Mode Two: Wondering Performance. The operations that constitute the Wondering Mode of Operation are *questioning, imagining, understanding, conceiving, formulating*. For ease of reference, let's call operations in the Wondering Mode *intellectual operations*. But we don't want to be misled by this shorthand. When I call these operations 'intellectual', I don't mean that only intellectuals perform them. All of us perform these operations in our ordinary living. I mean only that they all pertain directly to our intelligent or unintelligent pursuit of meaning. The mood of performance in the Wondering Mode of Operation is Wondering Self-Presence. When I respect and adhere to the basic commitment in this mode of operation, I am intelligent. When I fail to respect and adhere to the basic commitment in the Wondering Mode, I am unintelligent.

INTELLECTUAL OPERATIONS

Questioning, imagining, understanding, conceiving, formulating

Mode Three: Critical Performance. The operations that constitute the Critical Mode of Operation are *reflective or critical questioning, marshaling and weighing the evidence, grasping the sufficiency of the evidence, and judging.* For ease of reference let's call operations in the Critical Mode *critical operations*. When I call these operations 'critical', I don't mean that they're always performed reasonably. I mean only that they all pertain directly to the reasonable or unreasonable pursuit of truth. The mood of performance in the Critical Mode of Operation is Critical Self-Presence. When I respect and adhere to the basic commitment in the Critical Mode of Operation, I am reasonable. When I fail to respect and adhere to the basic commitment in the Critical Mode, I am unreasonable.

CRITICAL OPERATIONS

Reflective or critical questioning, marshaling and weighing the evidence, grasping the sufficiency of the evidence, judging

Mode Four: Evaluative Performance. The operations that constitute the Evaluative Mode of Operation are *moral questioning, deliberating, evaluating, and choosing and deciding.* For ease of reference let's call operations in the Evaluative Mode *moral operations*. To call this set of operations 'moral' is not to say that they're always performed responsibly or that we're always moral when we perform them. It just means that they all pertain directly to our responsible or irresponsible pursuit of value. The mood of performance in the Evaluative Mode of Operation is Evaluative Self-Presence. When I respect and adhere to the basic commitment in the Evaluative Mode of Operation, I am responsible. When I fail to respect and adhere to the basic commitment in the Evaluative Mode, I am irresponsible.

EVALUATIVE OR MORAL OPERATIONS

Moral questioning, deliberating, evaluating, choosing and deciding

Transformation of Earlier Operations by Later Operations. I have identified a specific set of operations for each Mode. But notice that both the Question-free Mode and the Wondering Mode include the operation of imagining. This seeming repetition alerts us to a characteristic of our conscious performance that we must not ignore. Just as later moods preserve and augment earlier moods in the spontaneous orderly sequence of moods, so too later modes of operation go beyond but preserve operations in earlier modes of operation in the spontaneous orderly sequence of modes.

In the spontaneous orderly sequence of moods, the Wondering Mood of intelligence goes beyond, preserves, and transforms the Question-free Mood of attentiveness, the Critical Mood of reasonableness goes beyond, preserves, and transforms both the Wondering Mood of intelligence and the Question-free Mood of attentiveness, and the Evaluative Mood of responsibility goes beyond, transforms, and preserves the Critical, Wondering, and Question-free Moods that precede it in the orderly sequence. The later moods go beyond the earlier moods, but the earlier moods are preserved and transformed by the later. Question-free attentiveness becomes intelligent attentiveness and then reasonable attentiveness and then responsible attentiveness. Wondering intelligence becomes reasonable intelligence and then responsible intelligence. Critical reasonableness becomes responsible reasonableness.

But these moods are our presence to ourselves in our performance of operations of different types. In the spontaneous orderly sequence of modes of operation, then, earlier operations are similarly surpassed, preserved, and transformed by our performance of later operations in the sequence. While I'm seeking understanding I continue to perform Experiential Operations. But these Experiential Operations are transformed by my performance of later operations. Seeing in the Question-free Mode may be hopeful watching or just staring blankly. But seeing in the Wondering Mode becomes intelligent observation and scrutiny. Remembering in the Question-free Mode may be just trying to recall a name or daydreaming. In the Wondering Mode it becomes intelligently selective recollection of situations similar to the one I'm trying to understand. Imagining in the Question-free Mode is merely representative of real or merely imaginary objects and situations. It may be attentive imagining of previous situations for the sake of remembering someone's name. But imagining in the Wondering Mode has been put in the service of the pursuit of meaning. It has become intelligent imagining for the sake of understanding, and it may be no more representative of the object I'm trying to understand than the Periodic Table is of the chemical elements it intelligently organizes. Later modes of operation are superimposed upon earlier modes. Later modes of operation go beyond, preserve, and transform operations in earlier modes in the orderly sequence of modes.

The relationship of later modes of conscious operation to earlier modes is an unusual one. It isn't merely the stacking of sets of operations on top of other sets of operations. It is true that the later sets presuppose the performance of the earlier sets, but in our performance of the later sets we don't leave the earlier sets behind. The later sets absorb, so to speak, the earlier sets into ever more complex sets of operations. Neither is it merely the addition of sets of operations to sets of operations and the creation of ever larger sets. It isn't the mere aggregation or gathering together of operations of different kinds into a bigger set. It is not merely a quantitative change but a change in qualitative complexity. The quality of my presence to myself in my performance of the earlier operations undergoes a change as the earlier operations are absorbed in my performance of the later operations.

The German philosopher G. W. F. Hegel was the first philosopher to identify this unusual relationship of later modes of conscious operation to earlier modes, and he gave it the German name *Aufhebung* which is usually translated into English as 'sublation'. 'Sublation' is an invented technical term for the unusual kind of relation we discover when we investigate our conscious performance. Later modes of operation *sublate* earlier modes: they go beyond them; they don't leave them behind but preserve them; they transform them. They go beyond them, as being intelligent goes beyond mere question-free experiencing. They don't leave them behind but preserve them, as perceiving doesn't cease when we begin to ask questions about our experience but continues while we inquire. They transform them, as merely gaping at the sky is transformed into scrutiny of the sky when we begin to wonder if a storm is brewing. Again, later moods *sublate* earlier moods. They go beyond them, as my critical self-presence or concern for truth goes beyond my concern for meaning. They preserve them, as my responsible self-presence or concern for value isn't an abandonment of my concern for truth and meaning but preserves it. They transform them, as my responsible self-presence transforms my intelligent and critical attentiveness into moral attentiveness. The sublative relation of later modes and moods to earlier modes and moods is not a stacking or an aggregation of sets of operations. It is an unimaginable relation of sets of operations where the later sets go beyond, preserve, and transform the conscious performance of the earlier sets. As our conscious performance governed by the basic notions unfolds, our question-free attentiveness becomes intelligent attentiveness and then intelligent and critical attentiveness and then intelligent and critical and responsible attentiveness.

4. ORDER AND DISORDER IN CONSCIOUS PERFORMANCE

The Orderly Sequence of Modes. The four modes of operation are constituted and guided by the basic notions. Like the four moods of conscious performance they are spontaneously ordered by their relations to the basic notions of meaning, objectivity, knowledge, truth, reality, and value. The four modes of operation unfold in the following spontaneous orderly sequence:

> *First* the Question-free Mode of Operation
> *and then* the Wondering Mode of Operation
> *and then* the Critical Mode of Operation
> *and then* the Evaluative Mode of Operation.

Again, here is the spontaneous orderly sequence of modes of operations, this time using our convenient shorthand:

> *First* Experiential Operations
> *and then* Intellectual Operations
> *and then* Critical Operations
> *and then* Moral Operations.

MOODS			
ATT/INATT	INT/UNINT	REAS/UNREAS	RESP/IRRESP
↓ →	↓ →	↓ →	↓
Q-f →	W →	C →	E
MODES OF OPERATION			
➡ ➡ ➡ ➡	BASIC COMMITMENT	➡ ➡ ➡ ➡	

THE SPONTANEOUS ORDERLY SEQUENCE OF MOODS AND MODES

The Orderly Sequences of Operations Within Modes. The various operations that constitute the Wondering, Critical, and Evaluative Modes unfold in spontaneous orderly sequences. But there is no spontaneous orderly sequence in the performance of Experiential Operations. The basic commitment is only incipient in this mode.

We can't say that our basic commitment, as merely incipient, requires that we *first* see *and then* hear, *first* feel *and then* taste, *first* see *and then* imagine, and so on. Some Experiential Operations are always performed simultaneously. What we call 'perceiving', for example, seems to be the simultaneous performance of remembering, imagining, and operations of sensing. Normally, when we're seeing we're also imagining and remembering. When our sensing is unaccompanied by remembering and imagining, and when it is accompanied by inaccurate remembering or imagining, we experience isolated, shocking, and surprising sensations. When we descend a familiar flight of stairs in the dark and reach the landing while we're expecting another step, we're surprised by touching that is not accompanied by accurate remembering and imagining. Remembering and imagining enable us to sense with anticipation and expectation. Sometimes Experiential Operations occur in an orderly sequence, but this happens only when our performance of those operations has been transformed by our performance of Intellectual, Critical, or Moral Operations. But, before their transformation by the emergence of intellectual, critical, or moral questions, they don't occur in a spontaneous orderly sequence.

Intellectual Operations are spontaneously ordered in the Wondering Mode:

> *First* I express my wonder by asking a question
> > *and then* I imagine
> > > *and then* I understand
> > > > *and then* I conceive the idea I grasped
> > > > > *and then* I formulate my conception.

Critical Operations are spontaneously ordered in the Critical Mode:

> *First* I express my doubt by asking a reflective and critical question
> > *and then* I marshal and weigh evidence
> > > *and then* I grasp that the evidence is sufficient
> > > > *and then* I make a judgment.

Moral Operations are spontaneously ordered in the Evaluative Mode:

> *First* I express my conscience by asking what is worthwhile
> > *and then* I deliberate about possible courses of action
> > > *and then* I evaluate the possible courses of action
> > > > *and then* I decide and act.

Disorderly Sequences of Operations. Intellectual, Critical, and Moral Operations can become disorderly. Deliberate jumbling of the sequences of operations in these modes illuminates, by contrast, the spontaneous orderly sequences in which we are already intimately present to ourselves. Some of the disorderly sequences of operations that result from these rearrangements are impossible to carry out. Others are concretely possible, but it's obvious that our performance of operations in those sequences is disorderly. This obviousness to us of disorder when we encounter it is not the obstructive obviousness of ungrounded preconceptions that stand in the way of understanding and are rightly to be suspected. It is the revelatory obviousness of our operative and inescapable basic commitment.

In the examples to follow, the disorderly sequence proceeds vertically, from top to bottom. The spontaneous orderly sequence is indicated by numbers in brackets.

Consider these two disorderly permutations of Intellectual Operations:

> *(First)* I formulate my idea [5]
> *(and then)* I ask a question [1]
> *(and then)* I conceive my idea [4]
> *(and then)* I understand [3]
> *(and then)* I imagine [2].

First, I articulate clearly an idea (I somehow already have without having previously asked and understood), *and then* I ask a question in pursuit of understanding (I've already gotten), *and then* I conceive the idea (I had prior to asking) by connecting it to the essential aspects of some creative image (I haven't yet imagined), *and then* I understand (what I've already understood), *and then* I produce a creative image to assist me in gaining understanding (I already have). There's obviously something wrong here.

> *(First)* I understand [3]
> *(and then)* I formulate my idea [5]
> *(and then)* I conceive the idea [4]

(*and then*) I ask a question [1]
(*and then*) I imagine [2].

First, I grasp an idea (without having asked a question), *and then* I articulate my idea clearly, *and then* I connect my idea to just the essential aspects of an image (I haven't yet conjured up and which, therefore, couldn't possibly have provoked an understanding), *and then* I ask the question (after having already understood), *and then* I creatively imagine (in order to evoke an idea I already have). Again, there's obviously something seriously wrong.

Here are two disorderly permutations of Critical Operations:

(*First*) I marshal and weigh the evidence [2]
(*and then*) I make a judgment [4]
(*and then*) I grasp the sufficiency of the evidence [3]
(*and then*) I ask a reflective and critical question [1].

First, I assemble the evidence in support of my idea (before I've asked if it's correct), *and then* I conclude that it is sufficient (without having understood that it is), *and then*, (already having gathered the evidence) I ask if there is any evidence for the truth of my idea and what evidence would be required for me to judge that it is true. Again, something is obviously amiss.

(*First*) I make a judgment [4]
(*and then*) I ask a reflective and critical question [1]
(*and then*) I grasp the sufficiency of the evidence [3]
(*and then*) I marshal and weigh the evidence [2].

First, I conclude that my idea is true (without having asked if it is), *and then*, (already having concluded that my idea is true) I ask if my idea is true or false, *and then* I grasp the sufficiency of evidence (I haven't yet assembled), *and then* I gather the evidence for the truth of my idea and ask if it is sufficient. Again, the operations are obviously out of sequence.

Here are two disorderly permutations of Moral Operations:

(*First*) I deliberate about possible courses of action [2]
(*and then*) I decide to act [4]
(*and then*) I evaluate possible courses of action [3]

(and then) I ask what I ought to do [1].

First, I envision a range of actions I could perform (without having asked what I ought to do), *and then* I decide to perform one of them (without evaluating the possibilities), *and then* I ask which action would be most worthwhile to perform (after having already decided to perform one), *and then* I ask what I ought to do (after having already decided to what to do).

(First) I decide on a course of action [4]
(and then) I ask what I ought to do [1]
(and then) I evaluate possible courses of action [3]
(and then) I deliberate about possible courses of action [2].

First, I decide to perform a specific action (without having evaluated any possible courses of action), *and then* I ask what action I ought to perform (without having envisioned any courses of action), *and then* I evaluate a range of actions (I haven't yet envisioned), *and then* I envision possible courses of action I could take.

Disorderly Sequences of Modes. The spontaneous orderly sequence of modes of operation can also become disorderly. Here are three disorderly permutations:

(First) the Critical Mode [3]
(and then) the Question-free Mode [1]
(and then) the Evaluative Mode [4]
(and then) the Wondering Mode [2].

First, I am suspicious about the truth of an understanding (I haven't yet gotten) about a situation (I haven't yet attended to), *and then* I attend to my situation, *and then* (not having understood my situation) I ask what I ought to do, *and then* I wonder about the situation.

(First) the Evaluative Mode [4]
(and then) the Wondering Mode [2]
(and then) the Critical Mode [3]
(and then) the Question-free mode [1].

First, (without having come to know the truth about the situation I'm in) I ask what I ought to do, *and then* I ask a question (about nothing in particular), *and then* I doubt the correctness (of an idea I can't possibly have gotten yet), *and then* I attend to the situation I'm in.

> *(First)* the Question-free mode [1]
> *(and then)* the Critical mode [3]
> *(and then)* the Wondering Mode [2]
> *(and then)* the Evaluative Mode [4].

First, I experience something, *and then* I ask if what I experienced is true (without having grasped an idea that could be true or false), *and then* I wonder and seek understanding of what I experienced, *and then* (without having determined if my idea is true or not) I ask what I ought to do.

The Basic Commitment Governs the Orderly Sequences. My Experiential Operations present me with sensed or imagined or remembered contents to which I can attend or not attend. When I begin to wonder about my experience, I might ask a question. My attentiveness is *to* the given and *for the sake of* inquiry. My basic commitment to meaning is *emerging*.

My Intellectual Operations present me with contents about which I can be intelligent or unintelligent. My questioning is *about* my experience and *for the sake of* understanding. My questioning has a content, but it is also constituted and guided by the notion of *meaning*. My basic commitment to meaning is *at work*.

In the pursuit of understanding of my experience, I imagine. My imagining, when I'm wondering, is not the kind of imagining I do in the Question-free Mode of Operation. It is imagining governed and transformed by my desire for understanding. It is not the imagining I do when I'm daydreaming. It is not imagining for the sake of diversion or amusement. It is imagining *for the sake of understanding*. The images I produce to assist my effort to understand may not resemble at all the experience I'm trying to understand. What I'm trying to understand may not even be imaginable; it may be, as in our present pursuit of understanding, purely temporal operations and their dynamic relations. These images are created *for the sake of* bringing to light the meaningful pattern, organization, structure, and relations in the experience about which I'm asking. If I'm trying to understand why a car tire rolls so smoothly, I may draw a simple image of a circle. The color and texture of the rubber, the design and thickness of the tread, the magnesium wheel, and the Michelin logo are all irrelevant. If I incorporated them into my image, they would distract me, and my effort to understand would be inhibited rather than promoted by my imagining. Imagining in the Question-free Mode of Operation is *representative imagining*. Imagining in the Wondering Mode of Operation is *heuristic imagining* or imagining adapted to the aim of understanding. My imagining in the Wondering Mode of Operation is transformed by my relationship to the notion of meaning. My imagining is *of* images and *for the sake of* getting an idea. My commitment to the notion of meaning is *unfolding*.

If I'm attentive and intelligent in my performance of these operations, if I adhere to my basic commitment, I might have the 'aha!' experience; I might have an insight. My intelligent inquiring and intelligent imagining might evoke understanding. The content of my understanding is an idea. My understanding is *of* ideas and *for the sake of* objective knowledge of the real. As merely the content of understanding, my idea has not yet been conceived and formulated. It is pre-conceptual and pre-linguistic. I'm present to myself as having understood, but I haven't yet attempted to conceive the connection between my idea and the image that evoked it. But my notion of meaning is *fully operative*, and my notions of objectivity, knowledge, truth, and reality are *coming into play*.

My conceiving is *of* my idea and *for the sake of* formulating it. The content of my conceiving is the set of aspects of the image that are essential to the occurrence of my understanding. When I formulate my idea, I pin it down. The content of my formulating is my idea. My formulating is *of* my idea and *for the sake of* critical judgment on the truth or falsity of my idea. The understanding I've formulated may or may not be a correct answer to the question I asked. My commitment to objective knowledge of reality is *surfacing and becoming explicit*.

My Critical Operations pertain to contents about which I can be reasonable or unreasonable. When I adhere to my basic commitment, my critical doubt is *about* my conceived and formulated idea and *for the sake of* knowing what's true and being in touch with what's real. It has its own content, but it is constituted and guided by the notions of truth and reality. When I assemble evidence in support of my idea, I perform again Experiential and Intellectual Operations, but I perform them now under the governance of my notions of knowledge, truth, and reality. My Experiential Operations are now neither question-free, nor merely incipiently orientated toward meaning, nor governed explicitly only by my notion of meaning. Their contents are the same contents with which I began, but now the Experiential Operations are *for the sake of* critical and reflective judgment. I weigh the evidence I've assembled. The content of my weighing of the evidence is the collection of the relevant contents of my original Experiential Operations, of my questioning, of my imagining, of my understanding, of my conceiving, of my formulating, of my critical questioning, and of my reflective assembling *and* of my performance of the whole set of operations that relate me to those contents. My weighing of the evidence is in the Critical Mode. It is under the governance, not only of my notions of knowledge, truth, and reality, but also of my notion of objectivity. It is *of* the evidence, but the relevant evidence always includes my own attentive or inattentive, intelligent or unintelligent, reasonable or unreasonable performance, and so it is *for the sake of* objectivity. My notions of objectivity, knowledge, truth, and reality are now *fully operative.*

When I grasp the sufficiency of the evidence for the truth of my idea, I critically and reflectively understand. The content of my reflective and critical understanding is my realization that the complete set of the conditions that must be fulfilled for my idea to be true is present and that there are no further relevant questions to be asked and answered. My reflective understanding is *of* the fulfillment of the conditions or the sufficiency of the evidence and *for the sake of* judgment. The content of my judging, though, is twofold. It is both the formulated idea about which I had critical doubts and my affirmation or denial of the truth of that formulated idea. Judging is not merely formulating an idea in the Wondering Mode; it is not merely the formulation of the idea I reached through understanding. It is the affirmation or denial of the truth of the formulation of an idea in the Critical Mode. In my affirmative judgment, my pursuit of objectivity, knowledge, truth, and reality is *satisfied temporarily*, that is, with regard to the single issue or object or situation by which I was originally perplexed.

My Moral Operations present me with contents about which I can be responsible or irresponsible. My judging in the Critical Mode is *for the sake of* worthwhile performance and action. If I adhere to my basic commitment, the content of my moral questioning is *about* what I might do and *for the sake of* doing what is worthwhile. To my wondering pursuit of meaning and my critical pursuit of truth is added my moral pursuit of value. My Experiential Operations are transformed by moral intent. My imagining now is not of representative images for the sake of diversion or amusement, and it is not of heuristic images for the sake of understanding in the Wondering Mode. It is *of* possible courses of action and *for the sake of* deliberation. My deliberation is *about* courses of action I envision and could or could not perform and *for the sake of* evaluation. My evaluating is *of* the relative worth of the actions I could perform and *for the sake of* moral judgment. The content of moral judgment, like the content of critical judgment, is twofold. Moral judgment is *about* a proposed course of action and *on* the value of the proposed course of action. It is *for the sake of* choosing, deciding, and acting. The content of my choosing and deciding is the action I will perform. My choosing and deciding are *for the sake of* doing what's worthwhile. In my choosing and deciding I begin to act. My notion of value is *fully operative and now takes precedence* [See Diagrams I and II in Appendix II].

5. BELIEVING: DEPENDING ON OTHERS' PERFORMANCE

I've made no mention of the conscious performance we call 'believing'. The account of conscious operations I have given is an account of the process by which we attain understanding, gain knowledge, and discern values *by ourselves* on the way to making our decisions. But we don't conduct our lives alone and simply on the basis of what we ourselves have come to understand and judged to be the case.

In the existing, unpurified Language of Self-Possession the words 'knowledge' and 'belief' are employed ambiguously. We often say we 'believe' when we mean to say we 'know'. We often say we 'know' when we mean to say we 'believe'. Much of what we say we believe, we actually know. Much of what we claim to know, we actually believe. What is the difference between the performance of coming to believe and the performance of coming to know?

If, in our conscious living, we relied only on what we have come to know by performing Experiential, Intellectual, and Critical Operations, we would find ourselves severely restricted. My experience is limited. What I can come to know for myself is strictly limited by the range of my experience, by the range of questions I have asked, by the range of understandings I've gotten, by the range of judgments I've been able to make. I overcome this crippling personal limitation by "borrowing from" the conscious performance of others whose experience is not as limited as mine or is limited differently, whose questions have been different, and so on. In my spontaneous adherence to my basic commitment I don't do all the driving myself. Frequently, I hitch a ride on the conscious performance of others. We benefit from others' experience, understandings, and judgments. We benefit from what others have learned by carrying out decisions we've never made ourselves. We also suffer the consequences of our uncritical and irresponsible reliance upon others in whom the basic commitment is especially weak or by whom it is deliberately violated.

In coming to believe, as in coming to know and decide for myself, I perform Experiential, Intellectual, Critical, and Moral Operations. I attend to my experience of the person upon whose conscious performance I might rely. My Wondering Operations are *about* whatever pertains to their trustworthiness and credibility as conscious performers and *for the sake of* critical judgment on their trustworthiness and credibility. My critical judgment is a judgment on the adequacy or inadequacy, correctness or incorrectness, of my understanding of their trustworthiness. If I conclude that they are credible and trustworthy, I decide to believe them. If I conclude that they are untrustworthy performers, I decide not to believe them. Believing, then, is not a suspension or putting aside of my own conscious operations; it is not a blind leap of faith. In believing, the four modes of operation unfold in the same spontaneous orderly sequence, but they pertain to the credibility or trustworthiness of another person. They pertain to another's adherence or failure to adhere to their basic commitment.

6. PROGRESSIVE AND DECLINATORY CYCLES OF PERFORMANCE

The four modes of operation unfold in a spontaneous orderly sequence. The operations that constitute the Wondering, Critical, and Evaluative Modes occur in spontaneous orderly sequences within those modes, and they transform the quality of the performance of operations in the modes that precede them in the sequence. Recall the way imagining is transformed as we move from the Experiential Mode to the Wondering Mode, and from the Wondering Mode to the Evaluative Mode. But the entire sequence of modes of operation is repeated in the course of our living. We engage in the modes of operation in their orderly sequence over and over again. The same modes of operation are performed repeatedly in the same spontaneous sequence, but the contents change. This recurrence of the four modes in their orderly sequence is not just pointless repetition. It is either *a cycle of development* constituted by repeated attentive, intelligent, reasonable, and responsible performance or *a cycle of decline* constituted by repeated inattentive, unintelligent, unreasonable, and irresponsible performance, or *some blend of progressive and declinatory performance.*

By my conscious performance I constitute myself as a certain kind of subject. The repetition of the sequence may be a progressive cycle of self-constitution or a declinatory cycle of self-constitution. In my conscious performance over time, I author the unique story in which I am both the protagonist and the antagonist. I make myself into the kind of person I will become. Attentive, intelligent, reasonable, and responsible repetition of the four-mode sequence is a cycle of personal development. Inattentive, unintelligent, unreasonable, and irresponsible repetition of the four-mode sequence, or repeated disruption of the orderly sequence, establishes a cycle of personal decline. I *develop* by adhering to and respecting my basic commitment to the pursuit of the basic notions over time. I *decline* by failing to adhere to and honor my basic commitment to the pursuit of the basic notions over time. My basic worth as a conscious performer is augmented by my adherence to my basic commitment or diminished by my failure to adhere to it. Over time, the range of my experience and understanding expands, my knowledge of myself and the world grows, my capacity to envision and carry out worthwhile actions increases, and I become ever more self-determining. Or the range of my experience and understanding remains the same or contracts, I fail to grow in knowledge of myself and my world, I become ensconced in familiar routines and my range of action becomes ever narrower, and my living becomes ever more effectively and thoroughly determined by circumstantial personal, social, cultural, and historical pressures.

Typically, conscious performance over the long term is a blend or mixture of the progressive and the declinatory. We have our ups and downs. We have our progressive phases when we're consistently adventurous, daring, and brave, interested and open, thoughtful, insightful and creative, incisively critical, intrigued and excited by the unfamiliar and unknown, in love with the truth and protective of it, finely attuned to value and disvalue, inspired by the worthwhile, appalled by the worthless, angered by injustice, determined to make something worthwhile of ourselves, unruffled by the risks involved, and eager to act and to make our mark. We have our declinatory phases when we're fear-ridden, hesitant and insecure, bored and uninterested, uncreative and dull, uncritical, unreflective and gullible, unaccepting of our ignorance, careless of the truth and willing to play fast and loose with it, skeptical about the value of anything at all, intimidated by the prospect of departing from the norm, depressed by our limited prospects, too anxiety-ridden to act, and content to drift through life.

My progressive conscious performance over time is my personal development. In my attentive performance of Experiential Operations I challenge my spontaneous or habitual selectivity and expand the range of my experience. I give myself more to notice, and I notice more. As the range of my experience expands, I have more to ask about. My attentive, intelligent and reasonable performance of Intellectual and Critical Operations expands my knowledge of the world and of others. It expands my knowledge of myself as a conscious performer and as attentive or inattentive to my preferred and chosen ranges of meanings and values. As my knowledge of reality increases, the range of actions I can reasonably and responsibly contemplate performing expands. My attentive, intelligent, reasonable, and responsible performance of Moral Operations attunes me to new ranges of value and engages me in new ranges of conduct. My engagement in new ranges of ever more attentive, intelligent, reasonable, and responsible conduct supplies me with new ranges of experience to which I previously couldn't attend. I have more to notice, and I notice more with regard to which I can now intelligently, critically, and responsibly inquire and act.

My Question-free, Wondering, Critical, and Evaluative performance is also transformed. These are now the performance of someone whose understanding of the world, of others, and of herself is broadening and deepening and whose power to act intelligently, reasonably, and responsibly is increasing. I'm not stagnating. I'm not merely "going through changes." I'm not just drifting through life. I'm not just more or less passively and automatically 'evolving'. I'm not merely adjusting myself to the demands and requirements others make upon me, attending when I'm told to attend, asking when I'm invited or told or permitted to ask, seeking truth and value only when my critical and evaluative performance don't make me uncomfortable or ruffle others' feathers. I'm becoming an increasingly more competent and effective conscious performer; I'm developing [See Diagram III in Appendix II].

We have attempted to isolate and identify the conscious operations we perform and to discover their spontaneous order. We began by considering an incomplete and provisional list of names for conscious operations and groups of conscious operations found in the existing Language of Self-Possession. In order to address the lack of order in our list, we shifted our attention to our conscious performance and to the spontaneous order in its unfolding. As a way of approaching an account of our conscious operations and their order, we turned our attention to our experience of personal risk when we expose ourselves as conscious performers to others. We identified four degrees of risk we may experience when we express ourselves in the presence of others. Our identification of these four degrees of risk led us to identify and to distinguish four Moods of Self-presence: Question-free Self-Presence, Wondering Self-Presence, Critical Self-Presence, and Evaluative Self-Presence. We went on to identify and distinguish four Modes of Conscious Operation in which we're present to ourselves in the four Moods: the Question-free Mode, the Wondering Mode, the Critical Mode, and the Evaluative Mode. We identified a spontaneous order in the unfolding of the four Moods and in the unfolding of the operations that constitute the Wondering, Critical, and Evaluative Modes of Operation. To highlight the spontaneous order we discovered, we considered some examples of disorderly sequences of Modes of Operation and of operations within the Wondering, Critical, and Evaluative Modes. We noted that the spontaneous order or the disorder of the Modes of Operation and the order or the disorder of operations within the Wondering, Critical, and Evaluative Modes are due to and determined by our relationship to our basic commitment. We briefly considered the conscious performance involved in believing. We found that believing is not a suspension of our own conscious operations but performance of the same four modes of operation with regard to the credibility and trustworthiness of others. Finally, we considered progressive and declinatory cycles of conscious performance over time and their relationship to our constitution of ourselves as the main actors in our unfolding personal stories.

Chapter Six

MOTIFS OF CONSCIOUS PERFORMANCE

We've turned our basic commitment on itself. We've been seeking the meaning of our basic commitment to the pursuit of meaning, objectivity, knowledge, truth, reality, and value. We've explored the variations in our presence to ourselves in our conscious performance, and we've identified four Basic Moods of Conscious Performance. We've carried out a preliminary exploration of the operations we perform. We've found that we perform these operations in spontaneous, orderly dynamic sequences, and we identified four Basic Modes of Conscious Performance. We've come a long way since our basic commitment was brought to our attention in our opening Elemental Meditation [See Diagram IV in Appendix II]. But we have to push our meditative inquiry still further.

Our operations are not just conscious. They also relate us to objects. Our operations always have *contents*; they are always *of* or *about* something. In my Question-free Operations I don't just attend or fail to attend. I attend to what interests me, and I ignore what is of no interest to me. In my Wondering Operations I don't just ask questions. I ask specific questions about specific things in specific ways and for specific purposes. In my Critical Operations I reach specific judgments about the correctness of specific ideas. In my Evaluative Operations I deliberate about specific courses of action I might undertake in light of specific judgments I've made. In our conscious performance we experience ourselves as attentive or inattentive, intelligent or unintelligent, reasonable or unreasonable, and responsible or irresponsible *with regard to what is of interest to us.* In addition to the basic moods and basic modes of conscious performance, there are salient themes or *motifs of our conscious performance.*

1. ATTENTION AND INTEREST

My basic commitment is my fundamental concern for meaning, objectivity, knowledge, truth, reality, and value. But that fundamental concern begins to unfold with regard to *what I attend to* in the ever-changing flow of my experience.

The Demands and Invitations of the Given. What I experience when I perform Experiential Operations of seeing, hearing, tasting, touching, smelling, imagining, and remembering is merely *given for* my attention. Similarly, what I experience in my presence to myself as a performer is merely *given for* my attention. As merely given for my attention, as experienced but not yet attended to, what I experience *invites* my attention by its mere occurrence. Sometimes what I experience also *demands* and virtually captures my attention. As merely occurring and inviting my attention, it sometimes receives my attention, and I go on to ask about it and come to understand it. But sometimes I don't give it my attention. When what I experience demands my attention, normally I do give it my attention, but I don't have to, even when the demands are pressing, persistent, painful, or otherwise disruptive of my living. I attend to what is given to me in my Experiential Operations and in my presence to myself only if I'm sufficiently interested in what is given. I attend to what interests me. I don't attend to everything I experience. I don't attend to everything I could attend to. I'm not interested in *everything* I experience.

Reacting to Demands and Responding to Invitations. My basic commitment to meaning and value *begins to surface* as I make my selection from what is given for my attention. I make my selection in light of my interests. My basic commitment *begins to unfold* in questions about what I'm interested in and attend to. I wouldn't attend to anything at all if I weren't committed to meaning and value. But why do I accept the invitation or bow to the demand to attend to some things and events and decline the invitation or dismiss the demand to attend to others? Why do I select *this* thing or event and give it my attention, instead of giving my attention to something else? Why do I ignore *those* things and attend to *these*?

Why do I sometimes resist the pressing demands of the given and fail to attend even to those things and events that collide with my present concerns? Why do I force myself to attend to some things and events even when they don't force themselves on my attention? Why do I go on to perform Intellectual, Critical, and Moral Operations with regard to some things and events and rest content with inattentive Question-free Experience of others? In addition to my basic commitment to the basic notions, I have interests. I select from the full range of my experience, from what is given for possible attention, from what merely invites my attention and from what demands my attention, what I will attend to and ask about. I select those contents of my experience whose meaning and value I will take the trouble to pursue.

The basic notions play a constitutive and guiding role in our conscious performance. But they play that role with regard to what we find interesting. We pursue *meaning*, but we pursue the meaning only of what interests us. We pursue *objectivity*, but we try to be objective only about what interests us. We pursue *knowledge*, but we seek knowledge only of what we're interested in. We pursue *truth*, but we seek the truth only about things of interest to us. We want to be *realistic*, but we try to be realistic only about what interests us. We pursue *value*, but we concern ourselves only with what might be worthwhile for us to do within our own sphere of interest. My shifting and alternating interests determine the *direction* my personal development will take and how my personal story will unfold. The breadth and depth, or the narrowness and shallowness, of my interests determine the actual course of my developing relationship to meaning, objectivity, knowledge, truth, reality, and value.

Knowledge of our interests and of the role they play in determining what we attend to and what we ignore enables us to become *deliberately selective* in our inevitable selectivity. It enables us to attend deliberately to what we think requires our attention, warrants our attention, and ought to receive our attention. Ignorance of our interests and of their role in determining what we attend to leaves us victims of the spontaneous interests that we *just happen to have or that just happen to be evoked in us* by the demands of what is given for our attention, including the demands others make upon us.

Our performance over the long term is the progressive or declinatory unfolding of our lives. Our knowledge or ignorance of our interests, and of the ways in which they specify or focus our basic commitment to meaning and value, has implications for our conscious performance over the long term. Without this knowledge we are more or less at the mercy of the situations in which we find ourselves, and we're pulled this way and that way by what we happen to sense, perceive, imagine, remember, and feel. But if we possess this knowledge we can approach and deal with the situations in which we find ourselves intelligently, reasonably, and responsibly. We can determine deliberately the interests we will bring to our experience. We can bring to our situations the interests we discover to be appropriate to them. We can *deliberately attend* and *deliberately withhold our attention*.

It is not sufficient for us to reflect upon our Basic Modes of Performance and our Basic Moods of Self-presence in our performance. We have to take CPA still further. We must reflect as well upon the selective interests we have in what is given to us for our attention and inquiry and action. We need to broaden the sweep of our self-attention and pay closer attention to the selectivity of our attention, to the interests that determine what we pay attention to and what we ignore, what we readily ask about and what we hardly ever ask about, what we come to know and what we remain ignorant about, what we envision ourselves doing and what we don't or won't or can't possibly envision ourselves doing. In addition to the four Moods of our conscious performance and the four Modes of our conscious operation, there are interests that determine the prevalent themes of our conscious performance. Let's attend now to our selective attention to what is given for our attention and to the themes or Motifs of our conscious performance as it unfolds with regard to what we find interesting.

2. PATTERNS OF ATTENTION AND EMERGING MOTIFS

Recall that we found that the operations which constitute the Wondering, Critical, and Evaluative Modes of Operation unfold in spontaneous orderly sequences, and we observed that the operations of the Question-free Mode do not. We discovered that, spontaneously, *first* we ask questions *and then* we understand, *first* we grasp that the evidence is sufficient *and then* we make a judgment, *first* we evaluate a possible course of action *and then* we decide and act. But we didn't discover that, spontaneously, we *first* see *and then* hear *and then* remember *and then* imagine, or that we *first* hear *and then* imagine *and then* remember. In our presence to ourselves as performing Wondering Operations, for example, we find in our questioning a conscious anticipation (wonder) of understanding and in our understanding the conscious anticipation (doubt) of

Critical Operations. Again, in our presence to ourselves as performing Critical Operations, we find in our assembling and weighing of evidence the conscious anticipation of critical judgment and in our critical judgment the conscious anticipation (conscience) of Evaluative Operations. But, in our presence to ourselves as seeing, for example, we don't find a conscious anticipation of hearing or imagining or feeling, except in those cases when these Experiential Operations *have already been transformed* by our performance of subsequent Modes of Operation. A spontaneous ordering of operations appears only in our Wondering, Critical, and Evaluative performance. No spontaneous ordering comes to light in our performance of operations in the Question-free Mode. In the Wondering, Critical, and Evaluative Modes our basic commitment to meaning, objectivity, knowledge, truth, reality, and value unfolds explicitly. In the Question-free Mode of Operation our basic commitment is still implicit, anticipatory, and incipient. The spontaneous order we find in our performance of the operations that are explicitly related to the basic notions is not found in the performance of our Experiential Operations. In our performance of them, the conscious flow is not qualified by wonder or by doubt or by conscience.

Our operations in the Question-free Mode, prior to their transformation by subsequent modes of operation, are more receptive than active. We perform them, but our seeking in them – our pursuit of meaning, objectivity, knowledge, truth, reality, and value through them – is only incipient, implicit, and anticipatory. I see, hear, taste, touch, smell, perceive, imagine, and remember. But, before I *try to* see, *try to* imagine, or *try to* remember this or that, I'm *already* seeing things and imagining and remembering. My purely Experiential Operations are not the explicit seeking of wondering, inquiring and understanding, of doubting, pursuing evidence and judging critically, of conscientiously deliberating, evaluating and deciding. Our Experiential Operations merely provide us with *something we could wonder about, something we could ask about, and something we could possibly understand.*

Our Experiential Operations are nevertheless operations we perform, however spontaneously and effortlessly we may perform them. We who perform them have a basic commitment to meaning and value. In the performance of our Experiential Operations, we're always already committed to meaning and value, even if that basic commitment has yet to unfold explicitly in the present moment. We should expect our basic commitment in its incipient, implicit, and anticipatory phase to make an appearance, even if only indirectly and obscurely, in our performance of purely experiential, Question-free Operations.

2.1 THE BASIC COMMITMENT IN THE QUESTION-FREE MODE

Our basic commitment makes an appearance in the Question-free Mode of Operation. But it doesn't make its appearance directly and explicitly in a spontaneous orderly sequence of operations as it does in the other modes. It makes its appearance indirectly and implicitly in *the patterned or configured flow of the contents* of our Experiential Operations. It comes to light as ordered temporal sequence *on the side of the contents* rather than as ordered temporal sequence *on the side of the operations*. In our performance of Experiential Operations our basic commitment in its incipience is revealed, not in the spontaneous order and explicit seeking we discovered in the flow of our Wondering, Critical, and Evaluative Operations, but in a dynamic configuration of the flow of the contents of our Experiential Operations. It makes its appearance in *the temporal flow of our attention. First* I attend to this *and then* I attend to that *and then* to that *and then* to that, and so on. This temporal flow is not just the inexplicable occurrence of one content after another. It is a series of connected contents. As attending or neglecting to attend, I constitute the order of the flow of contents. There are dynamic configurations to be discovered in the flow of my attention from one experiential content to another. In the temporal flow of experiential contents to which I attend, my basic commitment to meaning and value makes its first appearance as a patterned or dynamically configured flow of attention to specific contents.

These configurations of the flow of our attention to contents of our Experiential Operations are our first anticipations of meaning, objectivity, knowledge, truth, reality, and value. But they are anticipations of *specific ranges* of meaning, objectivity, knowledge, truth, reality, and value. They are temporal sequences of specific contents selected from what is given to us and about which we will go on to ask questions. They are the salient themes or motifs of our conscious performance *in their most rudimentary form* before their unfolding as the contents of Wondering, Critical, and Evaluative Operations. These motifs of conscious performance make their first appearance in the patterning of the contents of the Question-free Mode of Operation, in the temporal sequences of contents of our Experiential Operations of seeing, hearing, tasting, touching, smelling, feeling, imagining, and remembering. The spontaneous order in our conscious performance of Wondering, Critical, and

Evaluative Operations is imposed by our spontaneous commitment to the basic notions. But the configuration of the flow of the contents of our Experiential Operations is imposed directly by the interests that govern the selectivity of our attentiveness. It is imposed by spontaneous interest in the meaning and value *of this and that (and not of everything else)*.

The dynamic configuration of the flow of experienced contents *remains throughout our performance of subsequent operations.* It isn't left behind as we go on to perform subsequent operations. As we go on to perform Wondering, Critical, and Evaluative Operations, we continue to perform Experiential Operations. Whenever we're awake, we're experiencing, just as whenever we're awake we're also present to ourselves. Sometimes we're only performing Experiential Operations; sometimes we're performing only in the Question-free Mode. Sometimes we're performing in other modes as well. Our performance in the other modes is superimposed upon and simultaneous with our performance of Experiential Operations; it subordinates our Experiential Operations to our explicit pursuit of meaning, objectivity, knowledge, truth, reality, and value and enlists them in that pursuit. Our Experiential Operations don't cease when we wonder, criticize, and evaluate. They are transformed and put into the service of our wondering, criticizing, and evaluating. For example, our seeing may be transformed into observation and scrutiny, our hearing into listening, our smelling into detecting odors, our remembering into recollection of similar events, and our imagining into the production of schematic diagrams. We continue to perform Experiential Operations when we're inquiring, criticizing, and evaluating. But in the continuing performance of these Experiential Operations we remain selectively attentive, and the flow of experiential contents retains a dynamic configuration established and governed by some interest.

The interests that pattern the flow of contents of our Experiential Operations, and determine what we attend to, remain in force when we move on to the performance of Wondering, Critical, and Evaluative Operations. They persist throughout our performance of these operations and continue to specify the contents of our performance. That specifying influence can be found, not only in the contents of subsequent modes of operation, but also in *the way we perform the operations in the subsequent Modes and in the shifting Moods of our performance* in those Modes. These interests establish Motifs of Conscious Performance.

Our relationship to meaning and value *begins* with the selective flow of our attention to contents of our Experiential Operations. Our basic commitment to the basic notions *unfolds* with regard to *what we attend to*, and we attend to *what we're interested in*. My experience is the point from which I started as a wailing infant. It is the point from which I begin again and again throughout my childhood, adolescence, and adulthood. The cycle of my conscious performance recurs over time as I wonder again and again about the constant flow of changing contents to which I selectively attend. But my experience is just the starting-point.

What I *understand* about the world and myself is not discovered by sensible experience or self-presence alone. It might seem that it is, because much of my present sensible experience I already understand, and because I've been present to myself in my performance all my waking life. But what I've come to understand was originally *just an experience* to which I attended without understanding. What I come to *know* about the sensible world of my experience is not attained by sensible experience alone, and what I come to *know* about my own conscious performance is not attained by self-presence alone. I had to ask about and come to understand my sensible experience and judge critically the ideas I got about it. Similarly, my knowledge of myself as a conscious performer is not acquired by self-presence alone. Self-presence is not self-knowledge. I have to ask about and come to understand my experience of myself as a performer. What I know of the sensible world and of myself as a performer is what, before I came to know it, I merely attended to. The *realities* in terms of which I live my life are not known by me through sensitive experience and self-presence alone. I'd never have discovered them without my sensible experience and self-presence. Those realities are the ones to which my attentiveness first exposed me before I knew if they were really real or not, but I didn't come to know that they are real by merely attending to them. The *worthwhile courses of action* I pursue are not determined by my sensible operations and mere self-presence alone. What I can conceive of doing depends upon the selective attention I have brought so far, bring now, and will bring to my sensible and self-present experience, but my decisions to act aren't made on the basis of my selective attention alone.

Our conscious performance is constituted and guided by the basic notions. The basic notions give my Wondering, Critical, and Evaluative performance a spontaneous order. But they don't impose a spontaneous order on my Experiential Operations. They don't determine the order of the sequence of the flow of the contents of my experience. No doubt, my basic commitment plays a quiet role in the selection of the motifs of my conscious performance, but it doesn't determine spontaneously *the specific objects of my attention* and what, therefore, I'm able to ask about. It doesn't determine spontaneously *the specific ranges of objects* with regard to which I'll pursue meaning and objective knowledge. It doesn't determine spontaneously *the sphere of activities* I consider valuable or worthwhile. It constitutes and guides my conscious performance in my dealings with *any objects* I might attend to. But it doesn't spontaneously *select* the specific objects of my attention for me. That selection is made by me, either spontaneously or deliberately, and either intelligently, reasonably, and responsibly, or unintelligently, unreasonably, and irresponsibly, under the guidance and direction of *my interests*. My interests introduce dynamic configurations into the flow of the contents of my purely Experiential Operations. My interests dynamically configure the flow of my attention.

2.2 THE PATTERNING OF THE FLOW OF CONTENTS

The Motifs of Conscious Performance make their first appearance in the configurations of the flow of contents of my attentive Question-free experience. These patterns are temporal flows of successive contents of my sensing, imagining, and remembering, accompanied by feelings and organized and governed by a prevailing interest. They are *temporal sequences* of sensations, images, memories, and feelings, with a direction determined by an interest. As flows of sensible contents, they're linked to my bodily movements. My bodily movements are part of the experiential pattern. I turn my head, crane my neck, lean forward, back away, run after, run away from, step around and over, reach out, cup my ears, squint, and so on. I move, and move myself around, as my interest dictates. As I move and move myself around, my sensations, images, memories, and feelings change, but the configuration of the entire flow, imposed by the interest that governs the flow, remains. These already organized flows of successive contents, determined by our interested attention, are what we ask about when we ask about our sensible experience.

When we reflect upon our conscious operations, we find not only the four Basic Modes and the four Basic Moods, but also variations in our performance of the four Modes of Operation and variations within each of the four corresponding Basic Moods. These differences and variations are due to differences in the prevailing theme or motif of our conscious performance. The conscious performer we discover in CPA is ourselves as committed to the basic notions. But the basic commitment operative in our performance is always specified or focused by some interest. Concretely, the conscious performer I discover when I do CPA is the *selectively interested* conscious performer I am. My basic commitment to meaning, objectivity, knowledge, truth, reality, and value is not a commitment to these notions *in the abstract*. My commitment to the basic notions isn't a commitment to pre-existing and unchanging *categories* into which I can pack the experiences I have, or under which I can arrange the under-standings I get. It is a concrete, operative commitment to the pursuit of the meanings and the values of the concrete things and courses of action *in which I have some interest*. In CPA I discover myself as a conscious performer who is intelligent or unintelligent, reasonable or unreasonable, responsible or irresponsible *in relation to a flow of contents governed and configured by a prevailing interest*. I discover a conscious performer whose conscious performance always already has a *motif*.

3. IDENTIFYING MOTIFS OF CONSCIOUS PERFORMANCE

Motifs of Conscious Performance are prevailing themes of our unfolding basic commitment. They are themes of our unfolding conscious performance. They first emerge as the configuration of the flow of contents of our experience by interests. The configur-ations are flows of sensations, perceptions, images, memories, and feelings, involving and linked to bodily movement. The flows of contents are configured by some prevailing interest. These interests are either demanded by our experience or invited by our experience. The configurations are the motifs in their earliest manifestation in our conscious performance. The motifs make their first appearance in the ordered sequences of contents that result from the confluence of our interests with what is given to us for possible attention.

A Purely Temporal Configuration. The configuration of the flow of contents of Experiential Operations is fairly difficult to identify in Question-free performance. It is not to be found in any *single* sensation, perception, image, memory, or feeling to which we find ourselves attending. It is not even to be found in the *entire collection* of contents. It is to be discerned in *the sequential flow* of our attention to specific sensations, perceptions, images, memories, and feelings. The configuration is a purely temporal sequence. The temporal sequence of contents is not just a series of unrelated sensible contents. It is governed by a prevailing interest. The prevailing interest introduces an order into the temporal sequence. In that pattern we discern a budding Motif that will become a persistent, prominent theme of the conscious operations that follow upon, are superimposed upon, and transform our ongoing Experiential Operations.

The order in the flow of contents of my experience, contrary to our spontaneous expectations, is *not a sensible pattern* that is discerned by experience alone. If we turn our attention to the flow of our experience with the expectation of finding a sensible pattern, we'll be missing the point, and we'll be disappointed. The pattern to be discovered is not a visible or audible relationship of the contents to one another, like the visible pattern of wallpaper or the audible pattern of a melody. It is a pattern *to be discovered* in the flow of experience; it's a pattern of experience, but it's *not an experienced pattern*. The relationship that binds all the contents together in the flow is not a sensible relationship. It is an order or organization or configuration that is grasped only by asking questions about the experienced *flow* and discovering the interest that accounts for the temporal sequence of the contents of the experienced flow or explains why those contents are occurring in that sequence.

The interests that determine the motifs of our conscious performance are much more easily identified in our performance of Wondering, Critical, and Evaluative Operations, when our basic commitment is explicitly operative. They come to light most vividly in *the types of questions* we ask about the flow of our experience and in *the kinds of actions* we envision and carry out. But it is worthwhile for us to explore briefly the working of these interests at the earliest stage of our conscious performance so that we understand clearly how they establish the prevailing themes of our subsequent modes of operation early on and at the level of our mere attention to the contents of our experience, before we ask any questions about them. These interests come into play before we wonder, before we come to know, and before we decide on a course of action.

Identifying Purely Experiential Configurations. It's difficult to gain the rudimentary perspective that enables us to identify the very early influence of these interests in our conscious performance. Because we normally move on so quickly to subsequent operations, it's very difficult to isolate our presence to ourselves in our performance of merely Experiential Operations. Our Wondering Operations are quickly and spontaneously superimposed on our Experiential Operations, and the configured flow of purely experiential contents becomes a background that is simply taken-for-granted as our concern for meaning and value becomes explicit. To help us understand how interests pattern our attention to experiential contents even before we begin to wonder about those contents, let's try an unusual and fairly complex thought-experiment.

The Fantastic EFR: A Thought-Experiment

Let's imagine we're able to do something that's actually impossible. Let's imagine that we're able to make a complete, real-time documentary record of the sequential flow of contents of a person's purely experiential operations over a period of, say, a half-hour. In order to make our documentary we must make use of a device that's designed in such a way as to serve our specific purpose. The device we're going to use is very unusual and extremely complex. The software application and storage capacity required for its operation are so enormous that the team charged with developing the hardware struggled for many years without success until, finally, with the aid of additional funding by the Department of Homeland Security, a single functioning prototype of the device was produced. After lengthy negotiations with Submicro Subjective Supersystems, Inc., and after signing sheaves of waivers releasing the corporation from legal liability, we've been given access to the only existing Experiential Flow Reduplicator, or EFR.

The EFR is capable of recording the purely experiential flow of the subject-as-subject. It can record a person's experience *as it is experienced by that person*. It can record not only all of the visual and acoustical elements of the flow of experiential contents, as in a movie, but also images as they are imagined, memories as they are remembered, and feelings as they are felt. It can record a subject's experiential flow in real time *just as* that flow is experienced and *exactly as* the experience of that subject.

With the EFR we can produce a complete documentary record of the stream of contents of a person's merely experiential, Question-free performance, precisely as it is experienced by that person. You can see why the Department of Homeland Security was anxious to accelerate development of the EFR.

Of course, the EFR has the additional capacity to play back the recorded flow of contents. It can play back a complete temporal sequence of sensations, perceptions, images, memories, and feelings, involving and linked to bodily movements. It can play back the recorded flow for others or for the person whose experiential flow has been recorded. But it is important to note that it plays back the documentary record in such a way that, while the temporal sequence of contents is preserved, *the selective interest* of the subject whose experience was recorded is *removed*. That selective interest is absent from the recording, because a recording of the flow of experience of a conscious subject is not, of course, itself a conscious subject. As a result, the person for whom the recording is played back, whether that is the subject who was recorded or someone else, is free to reflect upon the temporal sequence of contents with an interest *different from* the one that patterned the recorded flow. In this case, the different interest that is called for is our reflective philosophic interest in identifying and understanding patterns of attention, that is, the interest of the subject engaged in CPA.

This unusual playback feature of the EFR is actually regarded as a defect by its developers, but this is only because they *have no interest* in the reflective advantage it affords to practitioners of CPA. Nevertheless, it makes the EFR a perfect device for *our* purposes, even if it isn't quite what the Department of Homeland Security had hoped for. We want to be able to play back a recorded flow of contents of purely Experiential Operations in such a way that we can bring to it an interest *different from* the one that originally patterned the contents. This enables us to explore *the configuring done by interest* in the recorded flow without bringing to the flow *the same interest in the contents* that originally gave the flow its configuration. It enables us to bring *our reflective interest* as practitioners of CPA to the flow *as a configured flow* without bringing to it the same interest in the contents that gave the flow its configuration. In other words, the EFR is not a Conscious Performance Reduplicator, or CPR. That even more complicated device is still in the earliest stages of its development by Submicro Subjective Supersystems, Inc. (While the neuroscientific community is optimistic, others in the religious and philosophical communities are not convinced that the envisioned CPR is actually possible.) The EFR reduplicates the flow of purely Experiential Operations without the Wondering, Critical, and Evaluative Operations being superimposed upon them as typically occurs in ordinary conscious performance.

Now let's suppose we make use of the EFR to record the flow of *your attention* to specific sensations, perceptions, images, memories, and feelings, involving and linked to your bodily movements, for a period of a half-hour. Select any half-hour of your experience for recording. It doesn't matter what you're doing or where you are, as long as you're awake. Choose a time when you're engaged in the normal business of everyday living. The EFR operates invisibly and remotely and can record your experience wherever you are and while you're doing anything at all.

Let's activate the EFR. You go about your business and, when a half-hour has elapsed, the EFR is switched off. Now we have a real-time record of your configured experiential flow from which the interest that prevailed for that recorded half-hour has been removed, enabling us to bring to that configured experiential flow our reflective interest in configured experiential flows.

Now let's play the recording *for you* so that you can bring your reflective interest in the ordered sequence of the contents of the flow to the recorded flow of your own experience *exactly as it was recorded*, without altering the contents and corrupting their given order with your present reflective interest as a practitioner of CPA. You relive, but now with a "reflective distance," only the flow of experience you were having while the EFR was operating. You relive a temporal sequence of sensations, perceptions, images, memories, and feelings, involving bodily movements, but your presence to yourself in the specific interest that organized the recorded sequence is absent.

Now, ask yourself these questions: *Why are the contents of the flow I now experience occurring in this temporal sequence? Why did I attend to this perception and then to that perception and then to this image and then to that memory and then to these feelings and then to this image and then to this feeling, and so on?* The recording isn't being played back for me, so I don't know what the temporal sequence of contents is that you're re-experiencing and reflecting upon. But I think you'll find that there's *no sensible pattern* in the sequence, no matter what the sequence is. It's a *purely temporal sequence* of experienced contents.

There's no sensible pattern to be found, for example, in seeing a dog crossing the street *and then* seeing a man walking *and then* hearing a song lyric *and then* seeing a red light *and then* feeling impatience *and then* imagining having lunch *and then* feeling tired *and then* remembering a time when you got a speeding ticket *and then* seeing the digital readout on a gas gauge *and then* imagining having the oil changed in your car *and then* imagining going to the bank *and then* imagining riding to the hospital in an ambulance *and then* feeling irritated *and then* seeing the time on your digital watch *and then* seeing a green light *and then* imagining the pile of bills on your desk at home, and so on.

These seemingly unrelated contents are tied together into a temporal sequence by what you're doing, and you were doing what you were doing because you were doing something you were interested in doing. There is a *direction* in the temporal sequence of seemingly unrelated

contents. Were it not for the direction supplied by some
interest in doing something, the temporal sequence of
contents would not have occurred. But notice that the same
interest in doing something could have selected an entirely
different set of contents and pulled them into a sequence.
For example, the same configuring interest can be
discovered in the following temporal sequence: seeing a
green light *and then* seeing a child on a bicycle *and then*
hearing a car horn *and then* feeling impatient *and then*
seeing the blinking lights on the back of a bus *and then*
remembering snippets of a phone conversation *and then*
hearing a siren *and then* feeling thirsty *and then* imagining
being at the beach *and then* feeling irritated *and then*
feeling your hand rubbing your neck *and then* feeling your
fingertips tapping the console, and so on. All of the contents of the temporal sequence can change while the
ordering interest which explains the existence of the
specific sequence remains the same.

With the perspective afforded by the EFR recording,
you've been able to discover that the configuration in the
experiential flow is not a sensible pattern, that it doesn't
reside in the sensible relationship of the contents to one
another, and that it is not tied to the specific contents.
You've been able to discover that the configuration is in the
temporal sequence of contents that can vary widely, and
that the temporal sequence is due to the direction given to
the flow of contents by a prevailing interest. The prevailing
interest is not a special interest in any of the contents
except incidentally. It is an interest that governs your
attention through a variable range of contents and, in doing
so, makes those contents available to you for the
performance of subsequent Wondering, Critical, and
Evaluative Operations. A shift in interest will guide your
attention through another variable range of contents and,
when it does so, it will make that temporal sequence of
contents available to you for your questioning and
understanding.

Try using the EFR again, this time to record a different half-hour of your performance of purely Experiential Operations. Notice how the contents and the sequence of contents change. Reflect upon the sequence. Try to determine what interest is responsible for the temporal sequence this time. It may happen that it's the same interest. As we shall see, much of our living is governed by *a practical interest in completing tasks or getting things done*. Notice, too, that the temporal sequences of contents of your own purely Experiential Operations are not accessible to others unless they, too, have access to our impossible device, the EFR. Sometimes we wish that flow were more accessible to others, and sometimes we're glad it's not.

4. FIVE MOTIFS OF CONSCIOUS PERFORMANCE

There seem to be five notable configured flows of attention to the contents of our experience that herald the emergence of five Motifs of our performance in the Wondering, Critical, and Evaluative Modes. There seem to be five Basic Interests that determine the directions and temporal sequences of contents of the flow of our attention. A first interest I'll call the Practical Interest, which probably accounts for the recorded temporal sequences of contents in your thought-experiments. A second I'll call the Intellectual Interest, which accounts for the dynamic configuration of the flow of contents of your experience as you undertook the thought-experiment itself as an exercise of CPA. A third I'll call the Aesthetic Interest. A fourth I'll call the Dramatic Interest. A fifth I'll call the Mystical Interest. From the configured flows of the contents of our Experiential Operations, governed by these five interests, there emerge five recurrent themes or Motifs of Conscious Performance: (1) the Practical Motif, (2) the Intellectual Motif, (3) the Aesthetic Motif, (4) the Dramatic Motif, and (5) the Mystical Motif. Conscious performance can be governed by one of the basic interests alone, or it can be governed by a combination or blend of the Basic Interests. It can be characterized by a single Motif or by a blend of Motifs or by an alternation of Motifs. As we shall see, conscious performance is ordinarily governed by a blend of Basic Interests, with one interest in the blend always taking the dominant or leading role.

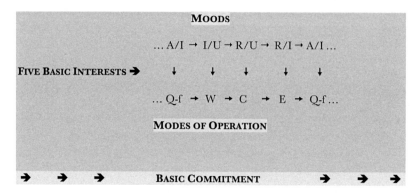

THE VARIOUSLY INTERESTED FLOW OF CONSCIOUS PERFORMANCE

[Key to the diagram: A/I = Attentive or Inattentive, I/U = Intelligent or Unintelligent, R/U = Reasonable or Unreasonable, R/I = Responsible or Irresponsible; Q-f = Question-free, W = Wondering, C = Critical, E = Evaluative; three dots indicate ongoing cyclic process; downward arrows indicates qualification of operations by adherence or non-adherence to the basic commitment; arrows along bottom indicate governing influence on the direction of the flow of consciousness by the basic commitment; the large arrow indicates influence of the range of basic interests.]

In the chapters to follow, we'll consider separately each of the Basic Interests and the motifs that emerge from them. But keep in mind that no one can operate in just one Motif to the exclusion of all the others indefinitely. The motifs of our conscious performance in ordinary living emerge and recede, alternate, mix and blend. They're called forth by the demands of the given or deliberately imposed by us in response to its demands and invitations. One motif seems to be routinely and spontaneously evoked by the demands of the given and to have a virtually irresistible attraction: the Practical Motif. Other motifs, it seems, emerge less as reactions and more as responses to the demands and invitations of the given and are more difficult to maintain: for example, the Intellectual Motif and the Mystical Motif. One triple blend of motifs seems to be the predominant mixture or blend of motifs characteristic of ordinary living: the Practical-dramatic-aesthetic Motif. Some blends seem marked by internal tension and even appear to be at odds with themselves: for example, the Practical-intellectual Motif, the Practical-aesthetic Motif, the Mystical-practical Motif, and the Mystical-intellectual Motif. It should be noted that a blend or mixture of motifs is not a democracy of motifs. In every blend or mixture, one motif is dominant and the other or others are subservient to the interest governing the dominant motif. After we've considered each motif in isolation, we'll consider briefly some examples of the alternation and blending of motifs in conscious performance.

In the five chapters to follow, we'll attend to and briefly reflect upon each of the motifs, considering in particular (a) the prevailing Basic Interest that governs the temporal sequence of the flow of contents of our experience or configures the flow of our attention, (b) the interest's persisting influence on our performance of subsequent Wondering, Critical, and Evaluative Operations, (c) the determinate meanings we assign spontaneously to the basic notions as a result of the prevailing interest, and (d) the precepts for performance typically issued to guide performance in the motif.

Let's turn now to the task of identifying the directing Basic Interests of conscious performance as they become explicit as motifs in Wondering, Critical, and Evaluative Operations and as they specify our basic commitment by spontaneously assigning determinate meanings to the basic notions of meaning, objectivity, knowledge, truth, reality, and value.

Chapter Seven

THE PRACTICAL MOTIF

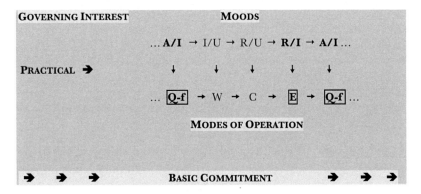

THE PRACTICAL MOTIF, EMPHASIZING THE QUESTION-FREE AND EVALUATIVE
MODES
[Key to the Diagram: Emphasized or stressed moods in boldface;
emphasized or stressed modes of operation are boxed and in
boldface; largest arrow indicates specification of the direction of
the flow of consciousness by the Practical Interest.]

T he Practical Interest is *the interest to get things done*. It's not an
unfocused interest in doing things but an interest in taking
care of business or getting things *done*. Its first emergence is
normally in reaction to given biological demands that announce to
us what, in the first instance, needs doing. The unconscious
orientation of organic life to maintain itself emerges into
consciousness as, for example, feelings of hunger and thirst, the
desire for pleasure and the fear of pain, fatigue, and sexual
discomfort.

We desire to live before we respond to this desire with our incipient commitment to meaning and value. We desire nourishment and sustenance before we intelligently devise efficient and effective ways to obtain them and to guarantee that we obtain them on a regular basis. We are pleased by pleasure and desire it and hurt by pain and fear it before we intelligently devise ways to ensure our pleasure, to protect ourselves from pain, and to relieve pain when we suffer it. We grow fatigued and desire protection from the elements and threats before we build for ourselves effective shelters and make for ourselves useful coats of armor, hardhats, work gloves, boots, and overcoats.

In desperate times, when biological demands have gone unmet and become virtually irresistible, the desire to live *by itself* may configure the flow of my experience. When this occurs, the flow is configured uniformly by what is better described as *instinct* than as *interest*. When I'm somewhat hungry I may become *practically interested* in preparing a satisfying meal, in driving to the market, or in finding a suitable restaurant. When I'm actually threatened with death by starvation, my need is too urgent even for considered practicality. When I'm "dead tired," I don't become practically interested in making preparations for sleep; I simply 'fall' asleep. When my very existence is placed in danger by a sudden and unexpected threat, I don't become practically interested in tactics and strategies for preserving my life; I immediately, instinctively, and "without thinking" protect and defend myself. In virtue of my previous practical performance and development, seemingly instinctive reactions may exhibit the intelligence and reasonableness and responsibility of prior understanding, critical judgment, and moral evaluation, but the moods of intelligence and reasonableness and responsibility are not my moods at those moments of reaction to the threat. My mood is simply that of reactionary and impulsive attentiveness.

The demands of our embodiment, then, may determine the configuration of the flow of our experience all by themselves. This configuring, though, is not by interest but either by instinct alone or by instinct augmented by previously acquired habits. When biologically based desires and fears alone configure the flow of our experience they are met, satisfied, and alleviated, not by intelligent and reasonable planning and responsible practical action, but by spontaneous and immediate, unplanned and instinctive bodily movements. This biological configuring, determined as it is by instinct rather than by interest, does not unfold as a motif of conscious performance in its own right, but remains at the level of

Question-free Experience – pre-wondering, pre-critical, and pre-evaluative. It is neither intelligent, nor critical, nor moral to brush an insect off one's arm or to duck to avoid an oncoming projectile. When the flow of experience is patterned *solely* by biological demands, it resembles most closely that of the higher mammals who spot their prey, pursue it, consume it and, once satiated, fall asleep. While there is an intermittent, merely biological configuring of the flow of experience, there is no "Motif of Embodiment" or "Biological Motif" that unfolds on the basis of a flow of experience configured solely by biologically based desires and fears. There is no wondering, no criticism, and no evaluation that unfolds on the basis of purely biological configuring of the flow of attention.

The demands and requirements of our embodiment persist as a constant accompaniment to our conscious living. But, for the most part, these demands and requirements rise to consciousness only to be met, addressed, framed, contextualized, ordered, subordinated, and exceeded by the unfolding of Motifs of conscious performance in which our basic commitment has emerged and become explicit. Inasmuch as we are driven solely by instinct or by instinct augmented by previously established habits, we stand in no immediate relation to the basic notions. Still, as our inescapable basic commitment comes into play, biological demands remain to be met, addressed, framed, contextualized, ordered, subordinated, and exceeded. Our pursuit of meaning, objectivity, knowledge, truth, reality, and value is and remains an *incarnate* pursuit. Thus, our pursuit of the basic notions is physically tiring or enlivening, emotionally exhilarating or draining, and accompanied, affected, sometimes motivated and sometimes interrupted and cut short by the desire to live and the fear of injury or death. Further, and more importantly, our Wondering, Critical, and Evaluative Operations relate us to the basic notions only insofar as they emerge in response to interests that configure the flow of our *sensible experience* linked to bodily movement and bear fruit in *physical conduct*, in *incarnate intelligence, reasonableness, and responsibility*.

When our basic desire to live *combines with* our incipient basic commitment to meaning and value, the configuring of the flow of contents of our experience by the desire to live is augmented by an interest to address our biological needs intelligently and reasonably, efficiently and effectively. In response, and not merely in reaction, to the demands of the given, we direct our attention to those contents of our experience that pertain to our survival and to the comfortable maintenance of life, its protection, and its reproduction. We attend to the contents of the flow in anticipation of dealing with them intelligently, reasonably, and responsibly. Our attention is no longer pre-wondering, pre-critical, and pre-moral; it becomes *practical*. The desire to live becomes a practical interest in addressing our needs and wants and in guaranteeing their satisfaction as efficiently and effectively as possible.

1. PRACTICAL PERFORMANCE

We superimpose our Wondering, Critical, and Evaluative Operations on our practically configured flow of experienced contents. Our *sensing* becomes alertness. We *imagine* possibly effective courses of action. We *recall* similar situations and the courses of action we took to address them effectively in the past. We *feel* expectant, wary, impatient, relieved. We *position and move ourselves* in accordance with our practical aims.

The practical interest remains to exert a practical influence in the unfolding of subsequent operations and on the cycle of conscious performance over time. We ask *practical questions*, get *practical ideas*, submit those practical ideas to *practical criticism*, and carry forward our practical knowledge into *practical deliberation, evaluation and action*. Our practical action provides for us a flow of new experience that is again configured by our persisting practical interest. If our practical interest isn't displaced by another Basic Interest, our conscious performance becomes a practical cycle of wondering, critical, and evaluative operations and actions.

As we develop in our relationship to practical meaning and practical value, we continue to extend our practical interest to everything that bears directly or indirectly upon the maintenance, protection, and comfort of our everyday living. Our collaborative practical performance over time gives rise to technology, to the economy, and to the polity. Our common interest in comfortable survival becomes a shared concern to deal efficiently and effectively with everything that bears directly or indirectly upon the maintenance of our safety and comfort. The motif of our conscious performance becomes practicality.

My practical attentiveness, practical wondering, practical criticism, and practical evaluation undergo development. I become an ever more practical performer. My performance is characterized more and more thoroughly by the practical interest to get things done. I become habitually practical. The given continues to invite my attention and, sometimes, to demand my attention, and I grow ever more selective in my acceptance of its humble invitations. I respond ever more readily to the imperious demands of the given, and I become good at anticipating these demands long before they arise. If my attention wanders beyond the demands of the given, I respond to only those invitations to which I can bring my governing practical interest, and my attention to them is ever more single-mindedly practical. If my attention is drawn by others to what, to "the practical me," are practically irrelevant invitations of the given, I simply declare those invitations 'impractical' or 'unimportant' or 'insignificant' or 'useless' or 'meaningless' or 'irrelevant', and I turn them down. The flow of contents of my Experiential Operations, the flow of my attention, becomes uniformly practical in its orientation. Every situation that arises *is defined by* my practical attention as *a practical situation* that calls for *practical performance*. I meet the given, regardless of the multifarious invitations it offers me, with a governing interest to take care of the business of life, with a preoccupation with getting things done. I come to be known to others as a highly practical person. My conscious performance is characterized for the most part by the Practical Motif.

2. LIMITATIONS OF THE PRACTICAL MOTIF

The practical interest has a notable influence on conscious performance. It determines which modes of performance I emphasize or stress and how the operations in these modes are performed. From its starting-point in the practical flow of my attention, the practical theme of my Wondering, Critical, and Evaluative Operations unfolds.

Because my motif is determined by the practical interest in addressing the immediate demands of living, I *emphasize or stress* the Experiential Operations in which I encounter those demands and experience their results, and I *emphasize or stress* the Evaluative Operations that immediately precede and lead directly to actions by which those demands are to be met. But despite my more deliberate performance of Evaluative Operations, the operative meaning of the notion of value that constitutes and guides my Evaluative Operations is *depleted* by my practical specification of its meaning. Clearly, the notion of value means more than usefulness or utility, personal survival, and personal advantage. But, in the Practical Motif, I give the fundamentally undefinable and open-ended notion of value the very specific meanings of usefulness or utility, personal survival, and personal advantage. Further, because my motif is practical, the notions of objectivity, knowledge, truth, and reality are *constricted*, and my Critical Operations are *suppressed or truncated* by my practical impatience to act and to get things done. Because my motif is practical, my Wondering Operations are *narrowly restricted* to asking and answering questions that I believe will make an immediate practical difference in my life.

When I'm being practical I readily ask the kinds of questions whose answers are, not *the possible meanings* of my experience, but *possible things to do and possible ways of getting things done*. I pursue consistently the sorts of ideas with which the Evaluative Mode, not the Critical Mode, begins. It makes no sense to ask, "Is it really true?" with regard to a proposed way of getting things done. In the practical motif, this would amount to disorderly performance. It makes no sense to make the judgment, "Yes, it's true," when the evidence required to support the idea hasn't yet taken place, just as it makes no sense to ask, with regard to the proposition "Speed multiplied by time equals distance," the evaluative question, "Should I do it?" I'm reluctant to ask questions that have no easily imaginable short-term, practical consequences for my present living. I feel like I'm making good use of my time when I'm raising and answering practical questions. I feel like I'm making the best use of my time when I'm engaged in practical action. I feel like I'm wasting my time when I ask and try to answer questions that have no obvious practical import. I'm impatient with questions that are "merely theoretical" and ideas that are "merely abstract," and I'm impatient with people who think and think and think, but never *do*.

In the Practical Motif, I readily ask *practical questions*. For example:

> Where is it? Where did I put it? How far away is it? How long will it take to get there? How can I make use of it? How does it work? How much does it cost? How will I recognize it? When did it happen? When will it happen? Will it happen to me? What does it look like? What did I do with

it? What's it for? Do I need it? What do I need? Why can't I
find it? Where did it go? Where can I get one? Who took it?
Where did they put it? When can I get another one? How
many are there? Where can I put it? How can I get to it?
What's going on? What's happening? Who's that? What are
they doing here? What do you want? Will it work? When
can I try it? What can I do with it? What use can I make of
it? How can I do it? How many will I need? How can it be
done? How long will it take? How long do I have? Where
can I do it? What do I have to do tomorrow? What's the
best way to do it? What's the practical payoff? What
practical difference does it make? Is it dangerous? What
are the practical benefits?

But I'm reluctant to ask other sorts of questions that, given my
presently dominant Practical Motif or habit of practical performance, I describe variously as 'insignificant', 'irrelevant',
'unimportant', meaningless', 'useless', 'pointless', 'boring', and
'uninteresting'. What I really mean, though, is that I regard those
questions as impractical. I'm not interested in asking questions I
regard as impractical. For example:

What is the square root of -1? Why are there irrational
numbers? What is energy? Is this really a work of art, or is
it just a pile of junk? How can I become more creative?
Does she think I'm unreflective? Is he just using me? What
is the meaning of it all? Why is there anything at all? Did
the events described in the New Testament really happen?
Does being practical pertain at all to finding the solution to
the problem of finding direction in life? Does my worth as a
person depend upon how practical I am? Am I too
practical? Am I habitually practical? What is the effect of
unbridled, single-minded practicality on the course of
human history? Is the universe expanding? Why is the sky
blue?

As practically interested I tend to suppress or truncate my
Critical Operations. Some of my practical questions are factual
questions about my immediate practical situation. "Is that the exit?"
"Where's the closest drugstore?" "Where's my wallet?" The ideas I

get in answer to these questions can be critically doubted, the evidence for their truth marshaled and weighed, the sufficiency of the evidence grasped, and their truth or falsity critically judged. But I tend to replace *the critical and reflective test* of the correctness of answers to these questions with *the pragmatic test* of their adequacy in action. I judge ideas to be adequate or inadequate, correct or incorrect, true or false, not by performing Critical Operations *before* they're put into practice, but *after* they've been tried out in action. I open the door to see if it leads outside. I drive around until I find a drugstore. I check beneath the driver's seat of my car. If the testing actions lead to consequences that meet my criteria of practical success, I call them 'true' or 'great'; if they don't, I call them 'false' or 'bad' or 'lousy'. The notions of objectivity, knowledge, truth, and reality are *overwhelmed* by my practical specification of the notion of value as utility, personal survival, and personal advantage. My Critical performance is *suppressed or truncated.*

In my practical living, I deal recurrently with situations whose general features I've already come to understand and with ranges of possible action with which I'm already familiar. Practical performance pertains to recurrent demands of the given and, over time, I've grown familiar with these demands. I build up a stock of practical understandings that apply for the most part to situations I regularly encounter. But no two situations are ever identical. I always need to understand the slight but inevitable differences in already familiar situations. I may perform Critical Operations in order to determine whether or not my understandings of minor changes in these familiar situations are correct. But, normally, this doesn't require prolonged investigation and, typically, I'm content to let the adequacy or inadequacy, the correctness or incorrectness, the truth or falsity of my understanding of the minor differences appear in the success or lack of success of the actions I perform in light of them.

The most practical questions I ask are questions about what is to be done and how to get it done. They're questions about the most efficient and effective courses of action. In my practical conscious performance I move rapidly from attention to my situation to a decision to act, from Experiential Operations to Evaluative Operations. The more quickly and effortlessly I make this transition, the more practical I seem to be, as long as the consequences prove useful. I spend only as much time in the performance of Wondering and Critical Operations as I think is absolutely necessary to get where I'm going and not a moment longer. To do otherwise would be inefficient, and to be inefficient is to be impractical.

> Strike the iron while it's hot! He who hesitates is lost! Act now! Get busy! Do something! Hurry up! The early bird catches the worm! Shake a leg! Let's go! Get a move on! Just do it!

As a practical performer I often facilitate my rapid movement through the Wondering and Critical Modes of Operation by deciding to believe others' opinions about the given or anticipated problematic practical situations and by deciding to imitate the actions others have taken to address similar practical problems. Believing, in practical performance, is a timesaving operation. It liberates me from the time-consuming performance of my own Wondering and Critical Operations. I borrow others' acquired practical knowledge and treat it as my own. Imitation saves me even more time. It liberates me, not only from the time-consuming performance of Wondering and Critical Operations, but also from the often more time-consuming performance of Evaluative Operations. I often regard it as more efficient to copy the "tried and true solutions" or so-called "best practices" of others than to ask whether those practices are really the most worthwhile and whether those who promote them have understood correctly the similar situations in which they've previously been applied.

I do recognize the practical risks involved in believing and imitating others. The people I believe might be wrong. The people I imitate might be misguided. But, like other operations, the decision to believe and the decision to imitate can be performed attentively, intelligently, reasonably, and responsibly, or inattentively, unintelligently, unreasonably, and irresponsibly. The adequacy of these decisions to believe and to imitate depends upon my critical judgments of ideas that arise in answer to my questions about the dependability, credibility, and trustworthiness of others. But my practical impatience doesn't permit me to spend much time in the performance of Wondering and Critical Operations. If someone's obviously a practical success by my present criteria of practical success, I conclude that she's probably worth believing and imitating. I try to make these decisions as responsibly as I can. I weigh "the costs and benefits" in conformity with my depleted notion of value. I could be wrong. I know this is a little risky, but it's a risk I'm willing to take if it will enable me to get things done more efficiently and effectively. If my decisions to believe and to imitate others are wrong, I figure that their inadequacy will become apparent soon enough in the consequences of believing and imitating them.

The governance of conscious performance by the practical interest has its short-term advantages. By adopting the Practical Motif we take care of the necessities of life and make our day-to-day living more comfortable. But single-mindedly practical performance has inherent deficiencies that may be *highly impractical in the long term.*

The weakening of the relationship of Evaluative Operations to the operative notion of value more or less ensures that courses of action with no immediate practical consequences are unlikely to be envisioned, judged worthwhile, and tried. The courses of action I find worthwhile are those that promise short-term practical advantages. The suppression or truncation of Critical Operations and their replacement by the pragmatic test more or less ensure that inadequate or incorrect understandings of my practical situation will be carried into action before their inadequacy or inaccuracy come to light. Uninformed and misinformed practical actions guided by a preoccupation with immediate advantage can have dire, lasting consequences. But, because I'm preoccupied with short-term benefits, I am insensitive to long-term consequences, and I'm unlikely to foresee them. The emphasis of Experiential Operations preoccupies me with the immediate situation and moment, distracts me from the lessons of the past, and precludes my envisioning of the implications of my actions in the more distant future.

The practical narrowing of our concern for what's worthwhile, the practical suppression of our concern for truth, the relatively uncritical reliance upon believing, and the practical restriction of our concern for meaning are results of the strict governance of conscious performance by the practical interest. The most basic deficiency of conscious performance with the Practical Motif is the habitual constriction of our attention and the consequent restriction of the range of questions we're interested in asking and willing to ask about our situation. From this habitual constriction of attention, the contraction and depletion of the concern for value, the suppression of the concern for truth, the casual reliance upon believing, and the restriction of the concern for meaning follow. Our Experiential, Intellectual, Critical, and Evaluative Operations are channeled into the pursuit of narrowly practical ends and become mere instruments for their attainment. Our presence to ourselves becomes *strictly practical self-presence.* I am present to myself as a practical instrument whose primary purpose is to maintain and enhance my own practical well-being and that of others who are or may be useful to me or upon whom I depend for my comfort and survival.

3. PRACTICAL SPECIFICATION OF THE BASIC NOTIONS

In the Practical Motif I spontaneously assign determinate meanings to the intrinsically open-ended and unrestricted basic notions. These meanings are depletions of the substantial operative meaning of the basic notions in conscious performance. Instead of appealing to and relying upon the operative meanings of the notions for guidance of my living, I rely upon and appeal to the determinate meanings I've assigned to the notions in the Practical Motif. Instead of giving my anticipation of meaning, objectivity, knowledge, truth, reality, and value free rein, I rein it in. As the unfolding of my basic commitment has been given a practical theme, so the basic notions are given narrowly practical meanings. Fixed, conceptual practical meanings replace the dynamic, operative meanings of the basic notions. The most profound advice I can give or am interested in receiving is advice about how to be more attentively, intelligently, reasonably, and responsibly *practical*.

As practical performers we're concerned with meaning, objectivity, knowledge, truth, reality, and value. But our basic commitment is qualified and focused by our concern to get things done efficiently and effectively. The *meaning* we seek is immediately practical meaning. Our questions revolve around the practical relations of things to us, to our practical well-being, and to our immediate practical plans. We pursue ideas, but the ideas we seek are ideas with immediate practical import. Ideas without immediate practical import are dismissed as insignificant, irrelevant, unimportant, boring, uninteresting, useless, meaningless, worthless. The *objectivity* we strive for is practical hard-headedness, practical tough-mindedness, and unwaveringly practical single-mindedness. Objectivity is reduced to attentiveness to immediate, practically-configured contents of Question-free Operations and to the reinforcement of our practical interest. We refuse to be distracted by anything we regard as irrelevant to our practical well-being. We raise all the questions that seem relevant to us, but the only questions we find relevant are the practical ones. We seek *knowledge*, but the knowledge we seek is immediately useful knowledge, knowledge of the practically relevant facts here and now, knowledge we can put to work now or very soon to serve our immediate practical interests. We're concerned with what's *real*, but the reality with which we're concerned is the reality of our present practical situation. The real is our present practical situation just insofar as it pertains to our immediate practical future. We regard ourselves as realistic to the extent we restrict our attention to the immediate practical situation. We condemn the 'idealism' and 'tender-mind-edness' of those who wish things were otherwise and pride ourselves on dealing with things as they are. We're concerned about *value*, but only those courses of action seem worthwhile to us that promise to contribute to our practical well-being in the here-and-now or in the immediately foreseeable future. In the Practical Motif meaning, objectivity, knowledge, truth, reality, and value are just so many variations on the useful, the efficient, the effective, the advantageous – the practical. We're concerned with value, but only insofar as it is *specified* as the vital and social values of survival, health, and maintenance of the social order that preserves and ensures these.

4. PRACTICAL PRECEPTS

The specification of the basic notions in practical performance is manifested in the great variety of practical precepts we issue to ourselves and to others. These practical precepts are our practical expressions of the basic precepts that can be derived from our exploration of the four Modes of Conscious Performance: Be attentive! Be intelligent! Be reasonable! Be Responsible! They are practical specifications of these open-ended, general rules governing orderly conscious performance. They promote *practical attentiveness, practical intelligence, practical criticism, and practical evaluation.* These practical precepts have been formulated *by practical people for practical people.* They're just specific and clear enough for practical purposes. Some of them may seem to contradict others, because their relevance depends upon the characteristics of the immediate, concrete situation. Here are some examples:

> Be realistic! Get busy! Size up the situation! Be sensible! Open your eyes! Follow directions! Measure twice, cut once! Watch for opportunities! Don't waste time! Get going! Slow down! Think! Don't think too hard! Gain experience! Make yourself useful! Try it out! Live and learn! Take your time! Watch carefully! Stick with it! Go for it! Hold on! One step at a time! What are you waiting for! Be

patient! Wait and see! Act now! Face facts! Actions, not
words! Come to your senses! Get real! Get serious!

In practical conscious performance we can be attentive or
inattentive, intelligent or unintelligent, reasonable or unreasonable,
responsible or irresponsible, but these moods are qualified by the
practical interest. Practical conscious performance unfolds through
all four Modes of Operation. In practical performance the basic
notions are operative, but their operative meaning is depleted by
practical determination. Even at our most attentive, intelligent,
reasonable, and responsible, in practical performance our attention
is *severely contracted*, our intelligence is *severely restricted*, our reasonableness is *suppressed or truncated*, our responsibility is *severely contracted
and depleted*, and our conduct tends to become *a series of recurrent
practical routines or a series of variations on the same routine*. Even the most
efficient and effective practical performance, after a while, becomes
a repetitive daily grind. The single-minded pursuit of vital and
social values is, of course, worthwhile, but the fulfillment it affords
seems to fall short of the fulfillment anticipated by our open-ended
basic commitment.

Practical Reservations about CPA

To be honest, I haven't been finding this CPA stuff all
that interesting from the very beginning. I guess I'm not
that interested in my conscious performance. Well ... unless
the way I perform starts to mess up my life. I mean, if my
eyesight suddenly got bad or I started to lose my hearing,
then I might be interested. I want to be able to see where
I'm going. How would I get to work? No, now that I think
about it, even if I started to lose my eyesight, I wouldn't do
CPA; I'd go to a doctor. CPA can't fix my eyes. It just talks
about what I'm seeing with my eyes. But I already know
what I'm seeing. Like, right now, I'm seeing a lot of words
and, no offense, but I'm wondering why I'm wasting my
time looking at them, let alone trying so hard to understand
them. Oh, I'm not saying I can't understand them. I pretty
much get what you're saying. You're saying I'm 'selecting'
what I'm seeing, that I'm only asking questions about what
I want to ask questions about, and I'm always asking
practical questions. Well, why not? Isn't that a good thing?

I mean, isn't it good to ask practical questions? It just doesn't seem practical not to be practical. I know, you're saying that being practical is just one way of being. I get that. Sure, there are other ways of being. I know there are 'intellectuals' and artsy types out there. I just don't happen to think those are very practical ways of being. I mean, let's face it, you have to stay alive, right? So, what's wrong with making that my priority? What are you gonna do, ignore your basic needs? You've gotta be practical. You don't really have a choice. Well, you do, but you know what I mean. You have to be realistic. I don't know what to think about these so-called 'deficiencies' of practical performance. To me, it seems 'e-fficient', not 'de-ficient'. It sounds like you're saying that because I'm usually practical I don't think or I'm not critical. I guess I'm critical *enough.* I'm still here, aren't I? You can't spend all of your time thinking. You've gotta act, and it seems obvious that the quicker you act the better. Time is money. Right, I probably don't spend a lot of time 'criticizing' my ideas before I try them out. Yes, I believe lots of people, especially successful people, and maybe I even copy what they do. Anyway, like you said, you can't 'criticize' things you haven't even done yet. I like that. I get that. That's so true. It's all about trial and error. You've gotta break a few eggs to make an omelet. You try it out, and if it works and there isn't some major disaster, it must have been good enough! I really don't see what the big problem is about being practical. I wish more people were practical. *Impracticality* is the real problem! But you're right. Working all the time *does* get pretty boring.

Chapter Eight

THE INTELLECTUAL MOTIF

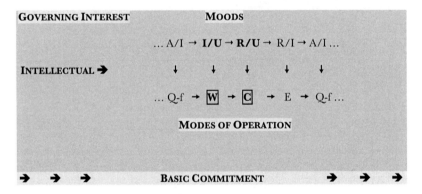

GOVERNING INTEREST	MOODS				
	... A/I → I/U → R/U → R/I → A/I ...				
INTELLECTUAL ➜	↓	↓	↓	↓	↓
	... Q-f → W → C → E → Q-f ...				
	MODES OF OPERATION				

➜ ➜ ➜ BASIC COMMITMENT ➜ ➜ ➜

THE INTELLECTUAL MOTIF, EMPHASIZING THE WONDERING AND CRITICAL
MODES

T he intellectual interest is *the interest in complete understanding of the universe and ourselves*. It is the desire to understand that motivates the questioning with which the Wondering Mode of conscious operation begins. But it is that desire unfettered by the restrictions imposed upon our questioning by other interests. It is *the operative notion of meaning*.

The practical interest emerges to govern conscious performance from the intersection of the biological demands of the given with our incipient, implicit, anticipatory commitment to meaning and value. It emerges as an incipiently intelligent, reasonable, and responsible reaction to the demands of the given. The intellectual interest is the emergence of the notion of meaning, not to meet the demands of the given, but to respond to any and all of its invitations, including the invitation to understand those imperious demands that evoke in us the practical interest. It emerges in response to the invitation to understand that is offered to us by the sensible and self-present given which, inasmuch as it is not yet comprehended, evokes a mood of unrestricted and disinterested wonder.

The intellectual interest introduces an intellectual dynamic configuration into the temporal flow of contents of our Experiential Operations. We attend to the contents of the flow in unarticulated anticipation of describing accurately and explaining correctly the object of our inquiry. We attend only to those contents of our experience that further our pursuit of an explanation of some aspect of the given about which we've begun to wonder. Our attention becomes intellectual. We're interested in understanding, not because we want to take care of business and get things done, but simply because we desire to know what and why and how often, and our experience, because it is uncomprehended, puzzles us and invites us to seek the satisfaction of that desire. [5]

---

[5] An engraving from an 18th-century book by Giammaria Mazzuchelli depicting the death of Archimedes. Legend has it that Archimedes was doing geometry during the Siege of Syracuse and requested of the soldiers that they not disturb the lines and circles he had drawn in the sand. In *An Introduction to Mathematics* (Oxford, 1958) Alfred North Whitehead wrote: "The death of Archimedes by the hands of a Roman soldier is symbolical of a world-change of the first magnitude: the Greeks, with their love of abstract science, were superseded in the leadership of the European world by the practical Romans. Lord Beaconsfield, in one of his

1. INTELLECTUAL PERFORMANCE

On this intellectually configured flow of contents we superimpose our subsequent Wondering, Critical, and Evaluative Operations. Our *sensing* becomes intellectual observation. Our *imagining* is enlisted in the service of our inquiry and becomes heuristic imagination. Our *remembering* becomes recollection of similar problems and their solutions. Our ordinary desires and fears are muted. We *move and position ourselves* to facilitate the unfolding and the pursuit of our inquiry. Imagine being present to yourself in the space occupied by Rodin's *The Thinker* or Vermeer's *Astronomer by Candlelight*. Imagine yourself pacing in pondering anticipation of an elusive insight. Imagine your movement suddenly arrested, not by a perceived threat or a sudden pain, but by the emergence of an intriguing and synthesizing idea. Like the

practical interest, the intellectual interest remains to exert its influence on the unfolding, not only of subsequent operations, but also on the cycle of conscious performance over time. We ask intellectual questions, give precise descriptions, produce helpful diagrams, propose possible explanations, submit those explanations to critical reflection and critical judgment, and carry forward the knowledge we acquire into our deliberations about possible future courses of intellectual performance, into our evaluations of those possible courses of intellectual performance, and into our decisions to pursue the intellectual strategies that we

---

novels, has defined a practical man as a man who practices the errors of his forefathers. The Romans were a great race, but they were cursed with the sterility which waits upon practicality. They did not improve upon the knowledge of their forefathers, and all their advances were confined to the minor technical details of engineering. They were not dreamers enough to arrive at new points of view, which could give a more fundamental control over the forces of nature. No Roman lost his life because he was absorbed in the contemplation of a mathematical diagram" (pp. 40-41).

judge to be most likely to lead to still greater and deeper understanding of our world and ourselves. Our ongoing intellectual performance provides us with a flow of new experience that, in its turn, invites further intellectual attention; as more questions are answered, more questions arise about previously unnoticed aspects of the given. We order the contents of the flow of our new experience with our persisting desire for meaning. The contents of our Experiential Operations are assembled into a configured flow of attention governed by *a purely intellectual interest*.

Like our practical performance, our intellectual performance undergoes development. Over time, I become an ever more intellectual performer.[6] My performance is characterized ever more

---

[6] An engraving by Augustin de Saint-Aubin of Isaac Newton, the discoverer of the laws of motion. Richard S. Westfall, in *Never At Rest: A Biography of Isaac Newton*, writes of Newton that "He could abandon himself completely to the studies he had found. The capacity Newton had shown as a schoolboy for ecstasy, total surrender to a commanding interest, now found in his early manhood its mature intellectual manifestation. The tentativeness suggested by the earlier unfinished notes vanished, to be replaced by the passionate study of a man possessed. Such is the characteristic that his chamber-fellow Wickins remembered, having observed it no doubt at the time with the total incomprehension of the Woolsthorpe servants. Once at work on a problem, he would forget his meals. His cat grew very fat on the food he left standing on his tray. (No peculiarity of Newton's amazed his contemporaries more consistently; clearly food was not something they trifled with.) He would forget sleep, and Wickins would find him the next morning, satisfied with having discovered some proposition and wholly unconcerned with the night's sleep he had lost. 'He sat up so often longer in the year 1664 [the year he discovered the new natural philosophy] to observe a comet that appeared

thoroughly by the intellectual interest to understand the universe of my sensible experience and the self of my self-presence. The given continues to make its imperious demands upon me, but in virtue of my previous development as a practical performer, I am ever less susceptible to practical distraction and ever more capable of maintaining my intellectual pursuits. When I must capitulate to the demands of the given and perform again with the Practical Motif, I do so only for the sake of creating leisure time in which to continue my intellectual pursuits – only for the sake of "getting the practical things out of the way," only for the sake of freeing myself for uninterrupted impractical inquiries. Even my necessary practical digressions are permeated by my intellectual interest and sub-ordinated to it. I'm minimally practical, and perhaps grudgingly so. In contrast, intellectual digressions from practical performance are rare. The uncomprehended given issues gentle invitations, not harsh demands. The operative notion of meaning, in its non-practical, unrestricted sweep, is a weak competitor with the felt instinctual drives to which I respond with my intelligent practicality. If the practical performer does see some obviously practical advantage in making a brief intellectual digression, her pursuit of universal explanations remains permeated by a practical interest in the concrete and the particular, is subordinated to immediately practical ends, and is terminated as soon as those ends have been served. If, when my intellectual interest is dominant, I still see a point to being practical, it is only in order to free myself from the restrictions imposed upon my Experiential, Wondering, Critical, and Evaluative Operations by the practical interest and, sometimes, by other interests as well. When I have to be practical, I'm practical only for the ulterior purpose of attaining knowledge

---

then,' he told Conduitt, 'that he found himself much disordered and learned from thence to go to bed betimes.' Part of the story is true; he entered his observations of the comet into the 'Quaestiones.' The rest of it is patently false as Conduitt knew from personal experience. Newton never learned to go to bed betimes once a problem seized him. Even when he was an old man the servants had to call him to dinner half an hour before it was ready, and when he came down, if he chanced to see a book or a paper, he would let his dinner stand for hours. He ate the gruel or milk with eggs prepared for his supper cold for breakfast" (p. 104). "Newton seldom left his chamber. He prefers to eat there alone. When he does dine in the hall, he is hardly a genial companion; rather he sits silently, never initiating a conversation, as isolated in his private world as though he had not come. He does not join his fellows on the bowling green. He rarely visits others." Westfall describes Newton as "a man ravished by the desire to know" (193-194).

whose practicality is not yet evident to me. I'm practical for the sake of liberating my intellectual interest from the distracting demands of practicality. My conscious performance is governed by the intellectual interest and characterized by the Intellectual Motif.

Like the practical interest, the intellectual interest has its persisting influence on the unfolding of our Modes of Conscious Operation. Because my motif is intellectual, governed by the notion of meaning and the anticipation of truth, I emphasize my Wondering and Critical Operations. My Evaluative Operations are *narrowed or suppressed*, and the notion of value is *conflated with* the notion of explanatory universal truth. Explanatory universal truth, known by marshaling and weighing the evidence, grasping the sufficiency of the evidence, and critical judgment, is *the supreme value* of the Intellectual Motif.

Because of this conflation of the notion of value with the notion of universal truth, my Wondering and Critical Operations are emphasized. I eagerly ask questions whose abstract, theoretical complexities invite the performance of the full range of Wondering and Critical Operations. I propose hypotheses in answer to my questions, and I proceed to seek their verification or falsification. I don't feel like I'm impractically wasting my time; nor do I feel like I'm making good practical use of my time. In my intellectual departure from practicality, I simply lose track of time in my pursuit of truths that will hold for any place and time. It's only when the demands of life require my adoption once again of the Practical Motif, when I grow hungry or thirsty or tired or feel a need for exercise, that time again becomes an issue for me, not because I haven't gotten something that needs doing done, but because I haven't been able to continue doing something that I know will never finally be done, no matter how long I do it.

I eagerly ask *intellectual questions* and submit them to my critical judgment:

What is the nature of light? What is the nature of a free fall? Why do bodies fall? Do heavier bodies fall faster? What is a society? What is a polity? What is the relationship between genes and personality? What is the relationship between the nervous system and conscious performance? What is justice? Why does the sun appear to rise and set? Is there a relationship between income level and health? What is the nature of an institution? Is there a relationship between global warming and agriculture? What is the

relationship of variations in the selectivity of attention to
the ongoing human pursuit of meaning and value? What is
the impact on the course of history of small communities
that devote themselves to intellectual inquiry?

In some of my intellectual inquiries there may linger a hope or
expectation that the understanding I eventually acquire will have
significant practical applications in the long term. There may linger,
for example, an interest in the security afforded by being able to
predict events. In other inquiries I have no expectation at all that
the knowledge I acquire will serve any practical purpose in the
short or the long term. Many unanticipated practical innovations
have been made possible by purely intellectual discoveries, but only
once the relevance of those discoveries to meeting the demands of
the given has been recognized by practical performers. The
intellectual questions I ask may have arisen because of some
disruption of my particular, practical situation. But once my intellectual interest takes hold, my practical interest in my particular,
personal situation falls away. The initial practical restrictions on
my wonder disappear, and the practical wonder that emerged as a
concern to understand the concrete and particular relations of
things and events to me and my well-being is transformed into a
purely intellectual wonder that seeks understanding of the abstract
and universal relations of things to one another. The truths about
my practical situation that I reach in my practical performance are
truths, but they're true only in the here and now. Their relevance
as truths lasts only as long as my practical situation remains
basically the same. The universal truths I reach in my intellectual
performance remain true regardless of changes in my practical
situation. The universal truths I'm after will be just as true in
present-day Tokyo as in present-day Topeka, just as true in ancient
Athens as in early medieval Gaul.

In practical performance the most important questions are
questions arising in the Evaluative Mode. My Evaluative Operations are qualified by the practical specification of the notion of
value. They're placed in the service of getting things done and
taking care of business. In intellectual performance I move into the
Evaluative Mode only in order to reinforce, facilitate, and perfect
my performance in the Wondering and Critical Modes of
Operation. My Evaluative Operations are placed in the service of
Wondering and Critical Operations. What I take to be most worthwhile is the pursuit of universal truth. I propose to myself possible
courses of intellectual performance and possible topics for further

intellectual investigation, evaluate these in light of what I've come to understand, decide upon a methodical refinement or a precise topical focus, and engage again in Wondering and Critical Operations. With each new question, further aspects of the sensible and self-present given are made relevant to my ongoing inquiry and added to the configured flow governed by my intellectual interest. Whereas practical performance hurries from attention to the sensible situation to the decision to carry out the most efficiently practical act, intellectual performance dwells in the performance of Wondering and Critical Operations to produce the most comprehensive and coherent theories. To do otherwise would be to play fast and loose with the truth.

2. LIMITATIONS OF THE INTELLECTUAL MOTIF

From the standpoint of the Practical Motif, the greatest deficiency of intellectual performance is the emphasis it places upon the Wondering and Critical Modes of Operation. Conscious performance with the Intellectual Motif doesn't seem to the practical performer to get anything worthwhile done. But this is a predictable bias of the performer in the Practical Motif. The inherent deficiency of intellectual performance is *its conflation of the notions of truth and value*. This conflation more or less ensures that courses of action that do not further the pursuit of understanding for its own sake will not be envisioned and undertaken. Or, if they are envisioned and undertaken, they are likely to be relatively uninformed by knowledge of the concrete, particular situation in which they're carried out. They are likely to be carried out with the inflexibility of excessive abstractness, under the governance of universal rules or unchanging principles, without regard for the subtle concrete and particular differences of ever-changing concrete and particular situations. The practical interest to address efficiently and effectively the concrete practical demands of concrete and particular situations leads to the suppression of Wondering and Critical Operations and excessively nearsighted and particularized performance of Evaluative Operations. The intellectual interest in universal truth, on the other hand, leads to the emphasis of Wondering and Critical Operations and excessively farsighted and universalized performance of Evaluative Operations. In intellectual performance our Experiential, Intellectual, Critical, and Evaluative Operations are subordinated to our pursuit of comprehensively intellectual ends.

3. INTELLECTUAL SPECIFICATION OF THE BASIC NOTIONS

Like practical performers, intellectual performers are concerned with meaning, objectivity, knowledge, truth, reality, and
value. In the Intellectual Motif, the intellectual interest spontaneously assigns intellectual meanings to these notions. The
meaning we seek is explanatory meaning of things in their relations
to one another. We seek answers to "What is it?" and "Why?"
questions. We don't consider ourselves to have grasped the
meaning of our experience until we possess an explanation of the
relations of things, not to us and our immediate personal and
practical concerns, but to one another, regardless of our immediate
personal and practical concerns. Ideas that don't contribute
directly to our pursuit of explanations are dismissed as pointless,
irrelevant, unimportant, uninteresting, insignificant, and relatively
meaningless. The *objectivity* we strive for is openness to the invitations of the given, sensitivity to the emergence of questions,
willingness to ask questions as they arise, detachment from our
personal concerns and preferences and prejudices, logical clarity,
rigor, and consistency, and a demand and respect for evidence. We
pursue *knowledge*, but the knowledge we pursue is universal knowledge, not immediately useful knowledge of the variable concrete
and particular situations in which we find ourselves. We're
concerned with what's *real*, but the reality with which we're
concerned is not the reality of things in their relations to us and our
immediate personal and practical concerns but the reality of things
in their relations to one another. We're concerned with *value*, but
only insofar as it is *specified as universal truth*. Only those courses of
action seem worthwhile to us that promise to contribute to our
ongoing pursuit of complete explanatory understanding and universal knowledge of our sensible and self-present experience.

4. INTELLECTUAL PRECEPTS

The precepts of intellectual performance aim to promote
attentive, intelligent, reasonable, and responsible intellectual performance. They are formulated *by intellectual performers for intellectual
performers*. Because the notions of value and truth are conflated and
Evaluative Operations are narrowed by the Intellectual Motif, a

good deal of attention is devoted to deliberation about possible courses of action pertinent especially to the ongoing pursuit of truth. That is to say, intellectual performance itself is the theme of Evaluative Operations in the Intellectual Motif. Consequently, the precepts expressed and issued by intellectual performers to guide their own and others' intellectual performance are often more precise and specific than the precepts issued by practical performers. Scientific method is one such precise set of precepts devised for the guidance of intellectual performance. There are other precepts as well:

> Seek understanding! Seek complete understanding! Attend to all the relevant data! Think things through to the end! Investigate all the relations! Work out all the implications! Pin down all the relevant variables! Beware of logical errors! Devise experiments to test your ideas! Assemble all the evidence before you make your judgment! Determine all the conditions that must be met! Ask all the further relevant questions! Invite others to challenge your tentative results! Formulate your ideas precisely! Don't claim greater certitude than the evidence permits! Entities must not be multiplied beyond necessity!

As in practical performance, so too in intellectual performance we can be attentive or inattentive, intelligent or unintelligent, reasonable or unreasonable, responsible or irresponsible. Like practical performance, intellectual performance unfolds through the four Modes of Operation. The basic notions are operative, and they are given specific intellectual meanings, but these are not nearly as restrictive as the meanings given to the notions in practical performance. Nevertheless, the operative meaning of the notion of value is conflated with the intellectual specification of the notion of truth as explanatory, universal truth. This results in a contraction of the range of anticipated action into intellectual performance in the pursuit of truth "for its own sake." Even the most responsible subject in the Intellectual Motif is relatively uninterested in the concrete differences of concrete situations and "abstracts from" them. The intellectual performer's decisions and actions flow from judgments on the probable truth or falsity of universal understandings and from deliberation about possible courses of action governed by universal principles. When actions must be taken by the intellectual performer to address the concrete demands and concrete problems of her immediate situation, they're often taken under the guidance of abstract, universal principles, and they fail to address adequately the situation in its concreteness. The practical performer lacks the concern for universal understanding that would enable her to take into consideration the long-term implications of her preoccupation with short-term solutions. The intellectual performer lacks the practical concern that would enable her to take into consideration the immediate, personal and practical implications of her preoccupation with explanatory, universal understanding.

Chapter Nine

THE AESTHETIC MOTIF

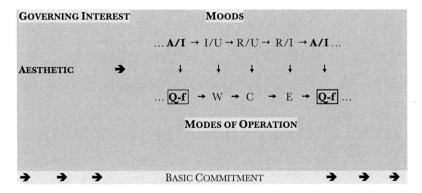

THE AESTHETIC MOTIF, EMPHASIZING THE QUESTION-FREE MODE

The aesthetic interest is perhaps best introduced by contrasting it with the practical and intellectual interests. The practical interest first emerges when our desire to live combines or intersects with our incipient basic commitment to meaning and value. The interest to get things done efficiently and effectively configures the flow of our experience and forces our Experiential Operations into the service of our pursuit of comfortable survival. The intellectual interest is a pure desire to understand, unfettered by practical concerns. It configures the flow of our experience and enlists our Experiential Operations in the service of our pursuit of truth "for its own sake." Like the practical interest, the aesthetic interest is related to our biological lives. But that relationship is manifested in celebratory, spontaneous *joie de vivre*, rather than in a sober, business-like desire to survive. Like the intellectual interest it's related to our concern for meaning and value. But its relation to our desire for meaning and value is manifested, not in detached, rigorous pursuit of explanatory, universal knowledge regarded as the highest value, but in joyful, creative expression of the open-endedness of our orientation toward meaning and value, of our basic commitment.

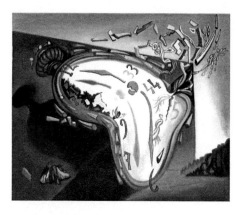

The aesthetic interest liberates the flow of our experience from the constraining sequences imposed by the practical and intellectual interests.[7] It is *two-sided*. It may be purely aesthetic or creatively artistic. As *purely aesthetic*, it is a relaxation of our Experiential Operations into *joyful receptivity to patterning by the given*; it is experiencing just for the sake of experiencing. In this respect the aesthetic interest is an interest in the experiential flow as a felt, seen, heard, smelled, tasted, and touched lived flow. But as it exerts its influence on the unfolding of our Wondering, Critical, and Evaluative Modes of Operation, it is a wonder-full, *creative patterning*, as opposed to an instrumentalizing patterning, of the flow of experienced contents; it becomes *an artistic interest*.

When we are *aesthetically interested*, we *celebrate being alive*. We're awash in the shifting moods of our primordial experience of living and caring about meaning and value. We're exuberant and playful, joyful and delighted. We are sensitive to the meaning and value of the given in its naturally- or artistically-patterned givenness. We

---

[7] The image is of Salvador Dali's *Soft Watch at the Moment of First Explosion*. Reproduced with permission from VEGAP, Artist Rights Society.

follow the upward sweep of the leafless branches of trees in late autumn, without any inclination to put them to use or to explain why they are that way. We marvel at the multicolored mounds of fallen leaves that blanket walkways, without any inclination to understand why they fall in autumn or to complain that their accumulation obscures ankle-twisting irregularities on our paths. When we're *artistically interested*, we *creatively explore* potentialities of the given for visible, audible, and textural patterning that evokes in ourselves and others a feeling of the basic commitment in its open-endedness. We mould the given creatively into sensible embodiments of the moods and tones that accompany the unrestricted aspirations of our basic commitment and our anticipations of their possible fulfillment.

1. AESTHETIC AND ARTISTIC PERFORMANCE

Purely aesthetic performance is limited to the Question-free Mode of Operation. It is experiencing for the sake of experiencing. It is joy in sunrises and sunsets, cloudless blue skies and pounding rain, the stillness before dawn, a warm breeze, the quiet of evening descending. It is delight in the multitudinous sounds of living nature awakening, in the icy freshness of mountain streams, in the scent of pine and eucalyptus, in the cool softness of damp grass. It is awe before soaring mountain peaks, roaring surf, deep canyons, and the unfathomable depth of a sparkling night sky. It is being transported by melodies. It is the pointless intensity of play, the semi-seriousness and satisfying strenuousness of games, the rhythmic abandon of dance, the eager enjoyment of athleticism. It's the moods of mystery evoked by fine art. It is being swept away by the beautiful, intimidated and slightly frightened by the sublime, intrigued and fascinated by the unusual and unexpected, bored by the commonplace and superficial and trivial, disenchanted, repelled and disgusted by the crass, the base, the ugly, the hideous.

When Wondering, Critical, and Evaluative Operations are superimposed upon the aesthetically configured flow of experience, the aesthetic interest becomes a creative, artistic interest. From its primordial manifestation as *joie de vivre*, the aesthetic interest unfolds in the creative wondering that invents games and other diverting forms of recreation. These inventions are possible courses of action conceived independently of our desire for the truth. No knowledge is being sought and there are no truths at stake, and so there is no call for the performance of Critical Operations. The conscious performer governed by the life-celebrating aesthetic interest moves more or less directly from the Wondering Mode of Operation to the Evaluative Mode. Just as in the Practical Motif, the critical test of the playfully creative idea, to the extent that one is sought, is an aesthetic test in its implementation. The reliance in the Practical Motif upon the pragmatic test in action has its drawbacks and its dangers. In the Aesthetic Motif, this reliance poses no risks. The only risk run by the creative aesthetic performer is that her invention won't be as diverting, amusing, entertaining, as much fun, or as liberating as she had hoped.

In its manifestation as *aesthetic appreciation*, the aesthetic interest unfolds as creative or artistic inquiry, artistic understanding, artistic evaluation, and artistic activity. Again, the critical test of the adequacy of an artistic idea is the artistic deed. We ask about our experienced participation in a life of open-ended, unrestricted, indeterminate commitment to meaning and value. We reach artistic understanding of our aesthetic flow of experience and of our possibilities. We ask how we can express and communicate the felt moods and tones of the participation we artistically discern. With the sensible materials available to us, and with sensible materials we invent, we introduce into the flow of experience expressions of possibilities of meaning and valuing grasped by our artistic understanding for the appreciation of others whose performance is characterized by the Aesthetic Motif. We produce works of art.

Unlike practical and intellectual inquiry, artistic inquiry that leads eventually to the artistic idea need not, and typically does not, reach explicit expression in formulated questions. It is a diffuse wonder about an obscure object. It's not wonder about the nature of a specific object of my experience; it's not an explicit intellectual interest in explanatory understanding of the universe and myself. It's not wonder about how to get things done; it's not a practical interest in efficiency and effectiveness. It's an interest in *the sensible and felt experience of participation in the movement of our open-ended commitment to meaning and value*, in the seemingly infinite range of creative possibilities contained in that movement, and in the sensible revelation of those creative possibilities. The expression of the artistic idea is as obscure as the aesthetically configured flow of experience to which artistic wonder is addressed. If you ask an artist what she's trying to say with or in her creation, her answer is likely to take the form, "Attend to what I created. If I could have expressed it differently, I would have." The meaning of a work of art is not grasped by practical or intellectual performance. It's grasped only by conscious performance governed by the aesthetic interest, by understanding in the Aesthetic Motif. It expresses what lies beyond us in possible, undetermined futures. As the poet Rilke wrote: "I live not in dreams but in contemplation of a reality that is perhaps the future." "The perfect work of art touches on our condition only in that it outlives us."[8]

If, with some frequency, I lift from the flow of my experience the restrictions imposed upon it by my other interests and the motifs to which they give rise, my aesthetic sensibility undergoes refinement, and the stage is set for ongoing artistic development. From a starting-point in a wonder-full flow of attention receptive to patterning by the given, a diffuse wonder anticipates artistic ideas that will find their expression in activity that creatively transforms the given. The aesthetic configuring of experiential contents remains in effect throughout artistic performance. But the contents configured now include additional contents generated by the bodily movements dictated by desire to incarnate and communicate the obscure artistic idea. The aesthetic sensibility of the artistic performer undergoes further refinement, artistic wonder is ever more clearly distinguished from wonder that pursues practical solutions and explanatory understanding, and artistic activity becomes an ever more skillful and creative enlistment of sensible materials in the service of artistic expression. The poet Rilke alludes to this process of development and refinement in his own life: "I am learning to see. I don't know why it is, but everything penetrates more deeply into me and does not stop at the place where until now it always used to finish. I have an inner self of which I was ignorant. Everything goes thither now, what happens there I do not know."[9]

Under the governance of *the purely aesthetic interest*, my conscious performance is arrested in the performance of Experiential Operations. Under the governance of *the artistic interest*, it unfolds as artistic wonder, artistic understanding, artistic evaluation, and creative artistic production and expression. Both the formulation of the artistic idea and the critical test of the artistic idea are the creative patterning of the given in the finished work of art. The artistic idea is neither true nor false. In its creative artistic

---

[8] *Letters of Rainer Maria Rilke 1892-1910*, trans. Jane Bannard Greene and M. D. Herter Norton [W. W. Norton and Company, 1945], 101. *Rilke and Benvenuta: An Intimate Correspondence*, trans. Magda von Hattingberg [Einaudi, 1987], 50.

[9] *The Notebooks of Malte Laurids Brigge* [W. W. Norton and Company, 1941], Book One.

incarnation, it is appreciated as beautiful, or it is found to fall short of the beautiful. Rilke once again: "Works of art are of an infinite solitariness, and nothing is less likely to bring us near to them than criticism."[10]

2. LIMITATIONS OF THE AESTHETIC MOTIF

Conscious performance with the Aesthetic Motif can be orderly or disorderly. As *purely aesthetic* it is threatened with disruption by the spontaneous and almost irresistible super-imposition of subsequent operations on the purely experiential flow. Spontaneously, we begin to express the diffuse wonder constitutive of the aesthetic interest in specific questions. Spontaneously, we seek to formulate the obscure artistic idea in ways more appropriate to the Practical and Intellectual Motifs. Spontaneously, we ask for a clearer communication of the artistic idea than its sensible embodiment in the finished work of art. In our basic commitment to the basic notions we spontaneously move *beyond the sensible*, but as aesthetically interested performers we perform most adequately when we *dwell with and in the sensible*. The emphasis in purely aesthetic performance is upon Experiential Operations and their liberation from instrumentalization by the practical and intellectual interests. We're most aesthetically responsible when we are deliberately attuned to the deraiIing influence of practical and intellectual interests and vigilant in resisting it.

From the standpoint of the Practical Motif, aesthetic performance can be justified only by its contribution to practical living. It is valued only inasmuch as it is a useful, intermittent diversion from practical routine that refreshes us for renewed dedication to our practical tasks. It is the entertaining Friday night party, the relaxing Saturday afternoon walk in the park, and the lazy Sunday that enable us to return to work refreshed on Monday morning. It is the weekend pause that refreshes us for nine-to-five, weekday efficiency. Otherwise, aesthetic performance has no justification. It is viewed as simply impractical. Further, from the practical standpoint, artistic performance is regarded, not as a motif in its own right, but as a certain set of practical skills, and it is justified only insofar as it is subordinated to the practical interest and put in the service of the practical ends of diverting

---

[10] *Letters to a Young Poet*, trans. Franz Xaver Kappus [Courier Dover Publications, 2002], 17.

entertainment, effective marketing, persuasive advertising, and political propaganda.

From the standpoint of the Intellectual Motif, the diffuseness of aesthetic wonder, the obscurity of the aesthetic idea, and the restriction to sensible, symbolic expression are deficiencies of the Aesthetic Motif. Performance appropriate to the Aesthetic and Artistic Motif can be carried over inappropriately into intellectual performance. The aesthetic performer is content to frame intellectual questions imprecisely, to resist the movement of intellectual performance away from the sensible and imaginable, to prefer fleshed out, representative, or symbolically rich imagery to schematic, bare-bones, heuristic imagery, to prefer affect-laden inquiry to intellectual detachment, to formulate intellectual ideas obscurely and metaphorically, allusively, and symbolically, and to seek critical evidence for their adequacy in the moods they evoke, rather than in evidence that supports them.

3. AESTHETIC AND ARTISTIC SPECIFICATION OF THE BASIC NOTIONS

When performing with the Aesthetic Motif, we spontaneously assign aesthetic and artistic meanings to the basic notions. But these meanings are as obscure as the object of aesthetic interest, and they are expressed obscurely in *the hybrid notion of the beautiful*. The beautiful is what is anticipated and felt in purely aesthetic experience for its own sake and pursued and creatively produced by orderly artistic performance. The artistic performer appeals to the notions of meaning, truth, and value. She hesitates to appeal explicitly to the notions of objectivity, knowledge, and reality. The aesthetic interest is openness to the unrestricted and indeterminate possibilities of our experienced participation in the movement of the unfolding of our basic commitment. For the aesthetic and artistic performer, objective knowledge of present reality is, for the most part, irrelevant, except insofar as it is recognized as falling short of the beautiful. The notion of truth is assimilated to the notion of value, and the two are conflated with the sensible flow of experience in the notion of the beautiful. Recall the concluding lines of John Keats' *Ode on a Grecian Urn*: "'Beauty is truth, truth beauty' – that is all / Ye know on earth, and all ye need to know." The beautiful is the felt sensible embodiment, in objects and in ourselves, of the possibilities of participation in the movement toward the satisfaction of our basic commitment, especially insofar as that basic commitment is a concern with value. It is joyful liberation from other concerns that constrict our basic commitment; it dissolves the practical and intellectual specifications of the basic notions and so evokes our basic commitment in its open-ended and unrestricted purity. It is the enthralling motivation that inspires us to creatively explore, sometimes calmly and sometimes feverishly, our basic commitment in its openness to an as-yet-unspecified range of possibilities. In the Aesthetic and Artistic Motif we're interested in the sensible expression of truth and value in the beautiful.

4. AESTHETIC AND ARTISTIC PRECEPTS

Aesthetic and artistic performance has a direction. It is the obscure, unspecifiable direction discernible in the purely aesthetic configuration of our experience and in the creative conscious performance of the artist. Because the aesthetic interest is in its origins a liberation of the experiential flow from instrumentalization by other interests, the precepts of the Aesthetic Motif are often negatively rather than positively expressed.

> Be receptive! Let yourself see, hear, touch, and feel what is there to be seen, heard, touched, and felt. Take your time! Let it be! Don't be so practical! Relax! Take it easy and just enjoy it! Don't try to figure it out! Free your imagination! Lighten up! Don't be so inhibited! You're thinking too much! Explore possibilities! Be playful! Enjoy life! Let the artwork speak to you! Let yourself feel! Be open! Let it absorb you! Be creative!

But the artistic interest unfolds as the positive refinement and development of sensitivity to our most basic commitment. In his counsel to a young poet Rilke wrote: "I could give you no advice but this: to go into yourself and to explore the depths where your life wells forth."[11]

---

[11] *Letters to a Young Poet*, 13.

Chapter Ten

THE DRAMATIC MOTIF

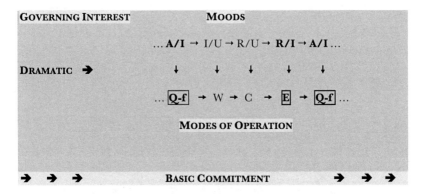

THE DRAMATIC MOTIF, EMPHASIZING THE EXPERIENTIAL AND EVALUATIVE
MODES

O ur experience may be configured only intermittently by the
aesthetic and artistic interest. But it is configured with great
frequency by an interest that, while not identical with the aesthetic
and artistic concerns, nevertheless has a strongly aesthetic and
artistic tenor. It is the interest to incarnate in our sensible presence
to others, and to manifest in our presence to ourselves, our own
intrinsic value and essential worth as constituted and guided by a
basic commitment to meaning, objectivity, knowledge, truth,
reality, and value, and to exhibit our developing worthiness as

attentive, intelligent, reasonable, and responsible participants in the ongoing movement of that basic commitment.

For the single-mindedly *practical* performer, concerned with getting things done, the world is a source of raw materials and a workplace in which those resources are turned to practical advantage. For the single-mindedly *intellectual* performer, concerned to discover truth for the sake of knowing the truth, the world is an enticing puzzle to be solved and a puzzling problem to be resolved. For the strictly *aesthetic* performer, concerned with the appreciation and creation of the beautiful, the world is a sensible revelation of human possibilities and a studio stocked with media for their expression. For the *dramatic* performer, concerned with her own worth as a conscious performer and as the leading actor in the drama of living, "all the world's a stage" on which roles are played under our own and others' watchful eyes.

The dramatic interest introduces a dramatic pattern or dynamic configuration into the temporal flow of contents of our Experiential Operations. I attend to those contents of my experience that pertain to *my and others' sensible beauty, my and others' intellectual respectability, my and others' critical and moral authority, and my and others' worthiness to play the leading roles in the unfolding dramas of our lives.* My attention is *dramatic attention.*[12]

1. DRAMATIC PERFORMANCE

About this dramatically configured flow of contents we ask dramatic questions, seek dramatic understanding, ask critical

---

[12] Renoir's *Luncheon of the Boating Party*. Reproduced with the permission of the Phillips Collection, Washington, D. C.

questions about the adequacy of our dramatic understanding, and project and evaluate dramatic courses of action. Our *sensing* becomes heightened sensitivity to raised eyebrows and rolling eyes, disapproving frowns and grimaces, encouraging nods and nudges, discouraging shakes of the head, congratulatory smiles and pats on the back, condemning glares, condescending gazes, puzzled and uncomprehending stares, tentative glances, bold and suggestive advances, aloof withdrawals, welcoming waves, extended hands and open arms, bored yawns, wide-eyed surprise, insulting tones, thoughtless remarks, aggressive postures, dismissive or offensive gestures. Our *movements* are graceful or awkward, agile or bumbling, confident or hesitant and halting. We *recall* with pride our past successful performances. We *remember* with embarrassment our foolish *faux pas*. Our *feelings* are of pride or humility, embarrassment or self-assurance, contentment, pleasure, or elation at our achievements, unhappiness with our mediocre performances, depression in the wake of our failures, and hopeful anticipation of approval or fearful expectation of disapproval. We feel loved, or we feel hated. We feel liked or disliked. We feel cared for or ignored and dismissed. We feel suspected, or we feel trusted. We feel offended or appreciated. We feel respected or disrespected, equal or unequal, better or not as good. We *imagine* how we might deliberately impress others, or we worry about how we might inadvertently expose ourselves to derision and ridicule. The experience of risk in conscious performance before others, through which we approached our account of the Basic Moods of Conscious Performance (Chapter Five, § 1), is prominent in this dramatically configured flow of our experience.

The dramatic interest has an influence on the unfolding of our subsequent Wondering, Critical, and Evaluative Modes of Operation and on the recurrent cycle of dramatic conscious performance over time. My questions pertain to the dramatic situation. I seek, not the practical or the aesthetic or the intellectual meaning, but *the dramatic meaning* of the present situation in which I always play a leading role; I pursue dramatic, interpersonal understanding. I submit my dramatic ideas to critical assessment and make judgments on my understanding of the dramatic significance of my experience. In light of my dramatic knowledge of myself and of my dramatic situation, I engage in dramatic deliberation. I anticipate scenarios charged with emotion, creatively propose for myself courses of dramatic action, complete with brightly-colored or subtly-shaded costumes and tentative scripts and accompanied by some degree of personal risk, evaluate them, decide on the best course of action, listen or watch for my cue, take the stage, find my mark, and 'act'. In my acting, not only do I write the next page of the current chapter or the first page of the next chapter of the unfolding drama of my life, but I also constitute myself as an attentive or inattentive, intelligent or unintelligent, reasonable or unreasonable, responsible or irresponsible character in the larger drama of human life and human history. In the Dramatic Motif my actions aren't *caused*; they're more or less deliberately *authored*. I constitute myself as a type of character and, in the estimation of others and in my own eyes, I am heroic and praiseworthy, or villainous and contemptible, or something in between. Most fundamentally, I constitute myself as guided in my concrete living more or less completely by my basic commitment. My conscious performance is characterized by the Dramatic Motif.

In my dramatic artistry I inform and beautify my appearance and decoratively transform my surroundings. I am warm enough in the most basic clothing, but I require this or that label, this or that style, these colors, and this fit. If I have something in my eye, a mirror serves a useful, practical purpose. But mirrors are more often and more regularly used for purposes that are entirely dramatic. Each morning, before I step before my audience, I apply my stage-makeup and select from my wardrobe the appropriate costume for the day's performance. I set the stage for my living. My biological needs would be met more effectively and efficiently if I were just single-mindedly practical, if I were not so concerned to dignify my biological life with dramatic accoutrements. But I'm intent on dignifying my biological drives and their satisfaction. I'm not content simply to satisfy my hunger and to slake my thirst. I prepare my meals, season them to my taste, and garnish my plate with often tasteless and sometimes inedible sprigs. I don't merely eat, I dine, with an embroidered linen table cloth or with placemats depicting the National Parks, with utensils of red plastic or Sterling silver, with souvenir cups or inherited fine china, with cheap paper or fine linen napkins, with crystal wine glasses or tankards, with salt and pepper shakers shaped like bunnies, leprechauns, or the Eiffel Tower, under a hanging lamp in the Tiffany style or actually made by Tiffany. My sexual desire is draped in indirectness, allusiveness, and innuendo, made mysterious by romanticism, dignified by courting and candlelight, elevated by love and intimacy.

Because the Motif of my conscious performance is my own worth and the enhancement of my worth as a participant in the flow of life, in my dramatic performance I emphasize Experiential and Evaluative Operations. My sensitivity to the responses and reactions of others to my performance is heightened and acute. I anxiously and warily anticipate their evaluations, and I'm careful to mask that anxiety and wariness. I worry about the worthiness or unworthiness of my proposed courses of action, and I feel an inclination to shift the burden of evaluating my chosen courses of action to others. At the same time, I quietly prepare my defense against the criticisms others might make of me. I am vividly aware of the finality of my actions and of my inability, once I've carried them out, to undo them or take them back. I tend to await the reactions and responses of others to my actions before I make my own judgment on their worth. I perform Intellectual Operations, but my performance of them is *suppressed* by my anticipation of my renewed participation in the ongoing drama. I could take the time to subject my hasty grasp of the present dramatic situation to critical reflection, but the drama is ongoing, and the curtain never seems to fall even when I'm alone and my sole audience. As in practical performance, Critical Operations are *suppressed*. My primary concern is with possible courses of dramatic action, and these cannot be judged true or false, but only worthy or unworthy of me as the kind of being I am. The prominent notion in the Dramatic Motif is the notion of value. But, because my dramatic performance is *the actual sensible realization* of my creative possibilities for participation in the flow of life, the dramatic notion of value is closely akin to the aesthetic and artistic notion of beauty.

I ask *dramatic questions*. For example:

> What does he think of me? Does she respect me? Does she think I'm unreflective? Which outfit would be most impressive? Has he been thinking about me? Why did he use that tone of voice with me? Was he just looking at me? Why's he looking at me like that? Is he angry with me? How does my hair look? Is this too much make-up? I wonder where I can find shoes to match this outfit? I wonder if she can tell what I'm really thinking? Why do you treat me like that? What is my reputation? Does this dress make me look fat? Why do I get so nervous when I meet new people? Is he just interested in me because he thinks I'm rich? Is she just using me? What kind of person do you think I am? What kind of person am I becoming?

I ask *evaluative* questions:

> Did I just make a fool of myself? How am I coming
> across? How will I come across? If I tell him what I really
> think, will he get offended? How much should I tell her
> about myself? What if she thinks I'm crazy? What have I
> done? Will they ever forgive me? How can I make it up to
> them? How can I show my face? If I do this, what will they
> think? Will I look foolish if I do that? Will he think I'm
> getting too personal? What if I say no? What sort of
> reputation will I have? What am I going to make of myself?

In the Dramatic Motif, the most important questions pertain to my evaluation of myself and to others' evaluations of me. In my performance of Evaluative Operations, I experience *a dramatic tension*. I want my audience to be pleased or entertained or impressed; I look to others' responses to confirm my sense of my own worth. At the same time, I want to please myself; I don't want the likely reactions of others to blunt and diminish my dramatic creativity, push me along a path I consider worthless or beneath me, and determine for me the roles I play and the nature of my character.

2. Limitations of the Dramatic Motif

From the standpoint of the Practical Motif the greatest deficiency of dramatic performance is its dramatically artistic sensibility and its evaluative preoccupation with self-worth. Dramatic attentiveness often makes for practical inefficiency. The dramatic preoccupation with personal worth makes the dramatic performer unwilling or reluctant to reduce herself to the status of a mere instrument for the pursuit of merely practical ends: I am a person, not a thing; I am or want to be freely self-determining, not a slave; I'm to be treated with dignity and respect, not casually dismissed.

From the standpoint of the Intellectual Motif, the greatest deficiencies of the dramatic performer are her propensity to regard the given only as the stage-setting for the unfolding of her personal story, her constriction of Wondering Operations by an artistic attachment to the sensible embodiment of meaning and value, her displacement of the pursuit of truth by the pursuit of personal worth, the resulting diminishment of critical performance, and her propensity to defer to the reactions and responses of others without prior critical determination of their suitability as evaluators of her performance.

From the standpoint of the Aesthetic Motif, the deficiency of dramatic performance is not its artistic sensibility but its self-assertive and self-concerned artistic configuring of the flow of experience and the excessively personalizing compression of an inherently diffuse and open-ended artistic wonder.

The intrinsic deficiency of performance in the Dramatic Motif resides in *the unresolved tension* between self-evaluation and evaluation by others that persists as long as Wondering Operations are constricted by attachment to sensible appearance and Critical Operations are diminished by dramatic anticipation of the interpersonal risks of public performance. The dramatic performer is inclined to draw evaluative conclusions on the basis of appearance alone and to invite others to draw evaluative conclusions on that basis as well. Dramatic performance can be derailed by uncritical identification of the measure of personal worth with its socially-accepted or traditional trappings and degenerate into superficial mimicry. We can become, in T. S. Eliot's phrase, "hollow men": "Shape without form, shade without color, / paralysed force, gesture without motion."[13]

3. DRAMATIC SPECIFICATION OF THE BASIC NOTIONS

In the Dramatic Motif, dramatic meanings are spontaneously assigned to the basic notions. The *meaning* I seek is personal and interpersonal meaning, the meaning of things and events as precisely things and events in my life with and among others. Things are meaningful if they are props pertaining to the success or failure of my role as the leading actor in the drama of my own life. I am *objective*, but my objectivity is primarily evaluative objectivity. I am objective if I ask and answer all the dramatically relevant questions. I am biased and one-sided if I fail to consider the possible effects of my dramatic performance on my own character, on my reputation, and on the pursuit of the basic commitment by others. I am interested in *knowledge*, but the knowledge I seek is psychological and moral knowledge of myself and others as dramatic performers and knowledge of others' estimation of me as a person. I'm concerned about *truth*, but I'm more concerned about telling and being told the truth than about knowing truths. I'm

---

[13] From Eliot's poem "The Hollow Men."

concerned with *value*, but my interest in value is contracted by my preoccupation with my own worth and its enhancement. Only those courses of action seem obviously worthwhile to me that promise to enhance my worth in the eyes of others and in my own estimation. In dramatic performance our Experiential, Wondering, Critical, and Evaluative Operations are subordinated to the highly personal creation, embodiment, and constitution of ourselves as uniquely worthwhile characters in the unfolding dramas of our lives. We're concerned with the personal value of ourselves and others as committed to the pursuit of meaning, objectivity, knowledge, truth, reality, and value.

4. DRAMATIC PRECEPTS

Dramatic performance can be attentive or inattentive, intelligent or unintelligent, reasonable or unreasonable, responsible or irresponsible. Dramatic precepts aim to promote adherence to the basic commitment in dramatic, interpersonal performance, and they are numerous.

Be sympathetic! Empathize! Be polite! Be friendly! Be honest! Be good! Be caring! Be loving! Be kind! Be nice! Don't judge! Be tolerant! Do unto others as you would have them do unto you! Cool it! Have a little self-respect! Be dignified! Don't be sloppy! Be respectful! Wash your face! Stand up straight! Don't put your elbows on the table! Make your bed! Be honest! Tell the truth! Do the right thing! Do it gracefully! Don't be crass! Enunciate! Be humble! Don't be rude! Have some class! Be refined! Say you're sorry! Admit your mistakes! Don't be arrogant! Show us what you can do! Get a grip! Don't develop bad habits! Don't be so self-conscious! Give yourself a little credit! Don't worry about what others think of you! Give some thought to your reputation! Don't be cruel! Don't make a fool of yourself! Don't let yourself be used! Be considerate! Act wisely! Be yourself! Be the best you can be! Act natural! Make something of yourself! Don't do anything you'll regret! Take control of your life! Don't let others tell you what you should be! Don't stray too far from the norm! Invent yourself! Get a life! Don't be such a copycat! Take a risk! Be daring! Break a leg! Don't be such a jerk! Don't blow it!

Chapter Eleven

THE MYSTICAL MOTIF

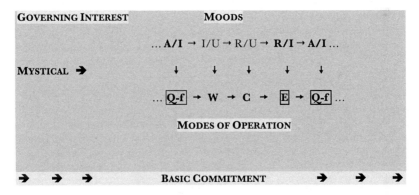

GOVERNING INTEREST	MOODS				
	...A/I → I/U → R/U → R/I → A/I...				
MYSTICAL ➜	↓	↓	↓	↓	↓
	...Q-f → W → C → E → Q-f...				
	MODES OF OPERATION				
➜ ➜ ➜	BASIC COMMITMENT			➜ ➜ ➜	

THE MYSTICAL MOTIF, EMPHASIZING THE EXPERIENTIAL AND EVALUATIVE
MODES

The Mystical motif is governed by a mystical interest. The
name I've given to this interest may be misleading. I might
have named it "the religious interest," but I don't want contemporary disillusionment with religious institutions or so-called
"organized religion" to divert attention from an interest that seems
just as properly human and as closely intertwined with our basic
commitment as are the practical, aesthetic, intellectual, and
dramatic interests. The religious institutions from which so many
are currently disaffected arose as a result of conscious performance
governed by the interest I've named 'mystical'. The word 'mystical',
though, presents its own difficulties. It brings to mind the great

mystics like John of the Cross and Teresa of Avila and Rumi, and few of us are developed and refined mystics in this sense. We might get the impression that the interest I propose to describe, unlike the practical and dramatic interests, is very unusual, extraordinary, and only for the select few. But, like religious institutions, the developed mysticism of the great mystics is also a result of recurrent conscious performance governed by the basic interest to which I want to draw attention.

The interest I have in mind is not at all unusual. Its emergence in most of us is intermittent, but it is a very memorable configuring of the experiential flow. It is acknowledged widely and in the most pedestrian of contexts. For example, on the Internet dating site *Match.com* users are invited to carry out the dramatic project of describing themselves for others who are also seeking companionship. When it comes to indicating religious affiliation, a number of choices are provided. But the designers of the website, in their wisdom, have added an additional, less specific religious category. Besides Atheist, Christian/Catholic, Christian/Protestant, Jewish, Islamic, and Christian/Other, users who, for whatever reasons, eschew involvement in so-called "organized religion" can reveal their fundamental religiosity by marking "Spiritual but not religious." Perhaps this pre-institutional or extra-institutional spirituality approximates to what I mean here by the mystical interest. It is the interest out of which institutionalized religions and extraordinary mystical expression may, but need not, arise. Whether or not we go on to affiliate ourselves with one of the organized religions, the mystical configuration of the flow of experience, when it occurs, exerts its influence on the full range of conscious performance.

The mystical interest is an interest in the Ultimate, the All, the One, the mysterious Beginning, the mysterious End, and the mysterious Ground and the Point of our existence. It emerges to pattern the flow of experience from *the combination of our presence to ourselves as inescapably limited beings with an inescapable unlimited aspiration* for meaning, objectivity, knowledge, truth, reality, and value. Our presence to ourselves in our basic commitment is at once presence to ourselves as unfinished, striving, and incomplete and presence to ourselves as radically dissatisfied with anything less than meaning, objectivity, knowledge, truth, reality, and value *in their absoluteness*.

We can always be more effectively and efficiently practical. But, no matter how practical we are, death awaits us. We can always be more receptively aesthetic and more creatively artistic. Yet absolutely flawless beauty eludes us. We can always become more knowledgeable. But, as our knowledge increases, our questions multiply. We can always become more competently and authentically dramatic. But still we miss our cues, suffer stage fright, stumble through our chosen dramatic roles, fall short of our dramatic ideals, and are reduced to apologizing for our failures, transgressions, and sins and to accumulating regrets.

The mystical interest in its most common manifestation configures the flow of contents of our experience with a radically humble anticipation of *the absolute fulfillment* of the aspirations that constitute and guide our conscious performance and in which we nevertheless take pride. It is an interest in the complete fulfillment that we recognize is not going to be attained "in this life" however orderly and constant our adherence to the basic commitment may be. It is a configuring of Experiential Operations by a concern with ultimate or absolute meaning and value. Often the stage is set for its emergence by the aesthetic configuration of our experience and performance in the Aesthetic Motif. The mystical interest is the configuring of the flow of operations by the notions of truth and value, not in their character as anticipations of obscure and indeterminate possibilities, but in their character as anticipations of the absolute truth and absolute value and of actual absolute fulfillment.[14]

The mystical configuring of our experience is not the actual absolute fulfillment of our fundamental aspirations. But it may be *the experienced or felt fulfillment* of them. It can be a configuring of the flow of our experience that resembles the transformation of the flow of our experience that occurs when we fall in love and know

---

[14] A detail of Bernini's *Ecstasy of St. Teresa.*

ourselves to be loved in return. But the love of a dramatic performer for another, while it is a deeply fulfilling experience, is not the experienced fulfillment of our basic commitment. No one who finds herself existing mysteriously between an unknown beginning and an unknown end, in what the philosopher Plato named "the in-between," can satisfy the desire in me for absolute fulfillment that characterizes my basic commitment. Our love for one another is conditional and restricted love. The object of our mystical being-in-love is mysterious. The love we feel is a love that has no bounds. The acceptance we feel is an acceptance that has no conditions. It is unconditional and unrestricted love that sustains us and enables us to persist in our basic commitment to the pursuit of meaning, objectivity, knowledge, truth, reality, and value despite our dramatic failures and psychological suffering, our intellectual confusion, our aesthetic numbness, our practical obstacles and debacles, our physical pain, our distracting, derailing, and debilitating desires and fears, and our undermining victimization by others.

> He who is sick with love,
> whom God himself has touched,
> finds his tastes so changed
> that they fall away
> like a fevered man's
> who loathes any food he sees
> and desires I-don't-know-what
> which is so gladly found.[15]

1. MYSTICAL PERFORMANCE

What is implicit in the mystical flow of experience is made explicit by the performance of Wondering, Critical, and Evaluative Operations. Initially, it is an intimation of a value that exceeds and encompasses the vital and social values we pursue in our practicality, the values of beauty and universal truth that we pursue in our artistic and intellectual pursuits, and the personal value we pursue in our dramatic projects. It is loving attention, prayerful or

---

[15] St. John of the Cross, "A Gloss (with Spiritual Meaning," in *Twenty Poems* [Wilder Publications, 2008], 34.

worshipful meditation, or contemplation. It is deep-seated joy, awe, fascination, peace, a feeling of union with the mysterious Ground. It is a spontaneous inclination to kindness, faithfulness, gentleness, self-control, gratitude, and a readiness to forgive and be forgiven. Because it is an affective or felt apprehension of *absolute value*, it can be as terrifying as it is fulfilling, as humbling as it is uplifting.

> How gently and lovingly,
> you wake in my heart,
> where in secret you dwell alone;
> and in your sweet breathing,
> filled with good and glory,
> how tenderly you swell my heart with love.

The mystical interest unfolds in the interpretive expression of mystical experience. Even before we ask about the mysterious consolation we've experienced, we express our experience in a generosity that exceeds the demands of justice, in a faith that exceeds the limits of our understanding, in a hope that exceeds our human expectations. When we bring our concern for meaning and value to our experienced fulfillment of that very concern, we ask what it is that we've experienced, what it means, and what its implications are for our living. Our practical preoccupations are disrupted by the reluctant recognition of the mysterious inefficiency and pointlessness of our life-preserving practicality. Our intellectual preoccupations are disrupted by the recognition of the mysterious unrestrictedness of our questioning. Our artistic preoccupations are disrupted by the recognition of the mysterious possibilities of our creativity. Our dramatic preoccupations are disrupted by the recognition of the mysterious interventions that change the courses of our lives and of the mysterious turns our stories take independently of our deliberate dramatic decisions. Ultimately, we ask what our deliberate response to this experienced apprehension of a mysterious absolute value will be.

> After I have known it
> love works so in me
> that whether things go well or badly
> love turns them to one's sweetness
> transforming the soul in itself.
> And so in its delighting flames
> which I am feeling within me,

swiftly, with nothing spared,
I am wholly consumed.[16]

With the Mystical Motif, the emphasis falls upon conscious performance in the Experiential and Evaluative Modes. As experiential it is meditation, contemplation, prayer, worship, gratitude, and participation in sacred rituals. As evaluative, it is bringing to bear in loving, hopeful, and faithful deliberation, evaluation, decision, and action whatever understanding I have attained, by my own inquiries or by involvement in a community informed and guided by a religious tradition, of the mysterious meaning of my mystical experience.

2. LIMITATIONS OF THE MYSTICAL MOTIF

The inherent deficiency of the Mystical Motif has its root in my experience of the starkness of the contrast I discern between my known limitations and experienced fulfillment. Even before I begin to wonder about my experience, I tend to collapse into false reconciliations of an opposition I cannot overcome. My feelings vacillate. One moment I'm absolutely overflowing with undying hope, everything's right with the world and myself, I couldn't be more fulfilled, I couldn't feel more loved, and I'm confidently committed to proceeding freely and responsibly. The next moment I'm absolutely desolate, over-burdened by my imperfections and the imperfections of the world, I feel abandoned and unloved, and I see no point in doing anything at all. When I begin to wonder about the mysterious absolute value I apprehend, I vacillate between conceptions of a God who is personal, communicative, and loving, or of a Force that is impersonal, uncommunicative, and uncaring. I vacillate between understandings that render me excessively humble and lead me toward a self-abnegating and deluded affirmation of my absolute unworthiness or render me excessively proud and lead me toward the self-assertive and deluded affirmation of my absolute worth. I conceive God as immanent and proximate, or as transcendent and distant. I regard myself as irredeemably imperfect and infinitely distant from the absolute value I discern, despite my inescapable aspiration for

---

[16] Elizabeth Ruth Obbard, *John of the Cross' Living Flame of Love: For Everyone* [London: New City Press, 2004], 22.

complete fulfillment; or, I regard myself as God or in God, or I
regard God as in me, or I regard everything as God, and the only
problem is that I've been slow to recognize the fact, despite my
presence to myself as aspiring and as yet unfulfilled.

Mystical performance emphasizes the Experiential and Evaluative Modes of Operation. It inspires the intellectual performance
of the theologian, but it isn't itself performance in the Intellectual
Motif. When, governed by the mystical interest, I seek some
understanding of my mystical experience, even if only through a
glass darkly, I easily become entangled in the profound
complexities of the radical tension between human limitation and
human aspiration, and of the persistence of that tension despite the
experienced fulfillment of falling, unrestrictedly and uncondi-
tionally, in love. Of course, this mystery is not to be unraveled by
any intellectual performance, but the intellectual performer is more
attuned than the mystical performer to the need for its special
handling in the Wondering and Critical Modes of operation.

> This knowledge in unknowing
> is so overwhelming
> that wise men disputing
> can never overthrow it,
> for their knowledge
> does not reach
> to the understanding
> of not understanding,
> transcending all knowledge.[17]

A FRIEND'S ACCOUNT OF HER MYSTICAL EXPERIENCE

When I was in high school one of my teachers took an
interest in my personal development. I was young and
naïve. I had begun to sense the dramatic demands of living
a human life, and I was intimidated by the challenges. I
suppose you could say I was attuned to the basic notions,
but I wouldn't have put it that way at the time. I was
spiritual, but disaffected from the organized religion in

---

[17] St. John of the Cross, "Stanzas Concerning an Ecstasy Experienced in High
Contemplation," in *Twenty Poems*, 16.

which I was raised. I was searching for "an answer" to the problem of finding direction in my life. I was looking for "a way," but I felt I lacked the personal resources to figure out the way. From this teacher I received a lot of attention. He made me feel that I had value, that I was special. I gave his advice great weight, took the guidance he offered very seriously, and derived a feeling of my worth from the attention he gave me.

This teacher belonged to an esoteric community whose founders believed themselves to be among the elect who understand the mysteries of life. He dangled before me a solution to the problem of finding direction in my life. I could join this esoteric group and adopt its solution, its way of life. I finished high school and went on to college, but I remained disorientated, and I stayed in contact with my former teacher throughout. Eventually, after completing my studies, I decided to join the esoteric community and handed myself over to the 'elect'. For nine years I followed the dictates of the leaders. The direction of the flow of my life was determined for me. I contributed my earnings to the group, probably a hundred thousand dollars over the years, and I followed the rules that were handed down to me by those who claimed to know the solution to the problem of finding direction in the flow of life. In my ninth year in this group I concluded that I wasn't getting my money's worth. I decided to take my life back. It was a great struggle. For nine years my story had been written for me. Now I had to write my own story. I had been possessed, in a way, and now I wanted to possess myself. My desire to know the design of life had become a desire to design my own life.

After I left, the friends I'd made in the community were forbidden to communicate with me. I had become "an outsider." In addition to these interpersonal difficulties I faced enormous practical problems. I was also burdened by the feeling that I'd been betrayed, manipulated, and conned by the teacher I'd trusted. I'd spent nine years of my early life relying upon people who, I had concluded, knew no better than I what "the answer" is. I was embarrassed, and I was also very angry.

Ten years after my departure from the community I heard through the grapevine that the teacher who had exploited my naïveté and abused my trust was very ill. I experienced a flood of memories, some good and some unsettling, and a mix of conflicting emotions. The unresolved feelings of anger and betrayal that had simmered in me over the years re-emerged. But in the course of my reflection on my odyssey from high school to my present situation something entirely unexpected happened to me. My feelings changed. I don't mean that they just shifted the way feelings often do. They *changed*. I wasn't angry any more. The offenses against me no longer held any power over me. I had every good reason to be angry, to demand compensation for the great injustice that had been done to me, to demand at least an apology for this inexcusable victimization by a trusted teacher. But none of this mattered any more. For no good reason at all, I was moved to forgive the seemingly unforgivable, and I forgave him.

I don't mean that I just felt like forgiving my former teacher and left it at that. I actually wrote him a brief letter. While writing it I felt great clarity. The words flowed easily. The letter was concise and artfully composed. It wasn't a sentimental letter. I didn't write it to make myself feel better or to make him feel better, if in fact he had any regrets. I didn't write it in order to make him face what he had done. My words to him issued from a feeling I already had of complete contentment with the situation just as it is. I expressed my concern for him and let him know about the bigger developments in my life since leaving the community. I knew the time was right to do this, and I knew that this was the right thing to do. When I finished the letter I felt a great sense of freedom. It wasn't a feeling of relief from the burden of hurt and anger I had been carrying. That burden had already been removed; it was already gone. It was a feeling of the creative freedom of

performing an entirely superfluous act that goes beyond
the requirements of ordinary justice.

I told a friend of mine about all this. He still wants to
take my teacher to task in the interest of justice. I really
couldn't express to him with precision what had occurred,
except to say that this act of forgiveness was self-justifying.
I know there were all sorts of reasons for not doing it.
There were no reasons for it. No reasons need to be given
for it.

3. MYSTICAL SPECIFICATION OF THE BASIC NOTIONS

In mystical performance, as in performance with other motifs,
I'm concerned about meaning, objectivity, knowledge, truth,
reality, and value. But the always only partial fulfillment I obtain
from my pursuit of practical, intellectual, aesthetic, artistic, and
dramatic meanings and values pales beside the experienced
fulfillment, proleptically felt without its actually being achieved, of
my desire for absolute value. I'm concerned about *meaning*, but the
meaning I'm after is the absolute meaning of it all. I'm concerned
about *truth*, but the truth I am concerned about is an absolute truth
that is to be lived, not known. I'm concerned about *reality*, but the
reality of this world is nothing in comparison to the absolute reality
of absolute value; or, if the reality of this world is all that is, then
my concern must be with the Nothing 'beyond' this reality. I'm
concerned about *value*, but I'm concerned about value in its
absoluteness, value beyond all criticism. In the Mystical Motif
we're concerned, not with the vital and social values of the
Practical Motif, not with the cultural values of the Intellectual and
Aesthetic Motifs, not with the personal value of the Dramatic Motif,
but with the actual absolute fulfillment of our basic commitment to
value in its absoluteness.

4. MYSTICAL PRECEPTS

 The specific precepts issued *by mystical performers for mystical
performers* vary greatly from religious tradition to religious tradition.
They are directions that are specified by a great variety of
developed interpretations of the meaning of the mystical configuration of the flow of experience, generated by mystical inquiry
and developed over time. Some are so specific that, were it not for

the fact that they often carry the mysterious weight of divine authority and the mysterious threat of divine retribution, they would be virtually indistinguishable from ordinary practical and dramatic precepts.

There is a special class of mystical precepts that aim to promote and reinforce the mystical configuration of the flow of attention. These are the sorts of precepts issued to guide the mystical performer into or through specific ascetic practices and meditative strategies, like the precepts of the various forms of Zen meditation and of the Spiritual Exercises of St. Ignatius of Loyola, for example.

> Cast aside all involvements and discontinue the myriad affairs. Good is not thought of; evil is not thought of. It is not mind, intellect or consciousness; it is not thoughts, ideas or perceptions.

> As he who is receiving the Exercises is to give an hour to each of the five Exercises or Contemplations which will be made every day, he who is giving the Exercises has to warn him carefully to always see that his soul remains content in the consciousness of having been a full hour in the Exercise, and rather more than less. For the enemy is not a little used to try and make one cut short the hour of such contemplation, meditation or prayer.[18]

But the most fundamental mystical precepts are few:

> Be loving! Love yourself! Love your neighbor! Love God! Be hopeful! Have faith! Do good and avoid evil! Pray! Repent! Be thankful! Be forgiving!

---

[18] *Treasury of the Eye of True Dharma, Principles of Zazen*, Book 11; and *Spiritual Exercises of St. Ignatius*, 12th Annotation, trans. Elder Mullan, S.J. [Cosimo Classics, 2007], 8.

Chapter Twelve

THE MIXING AND
BLENDING OF MOTIFS

We've identified and distinguished five Motifs of Conscious
Performance that arise from the configuring of the flow of
attention by five interests. The interests are practical, intellectual,
aesthetic and artistic, dramatic, and mystical. These five interests
are basic. All of the specific interests we have seem to fall within the
ranges of these five interests or of blends of them. A Basic Interest
may emerge more or less frequently. When it arises, it may be
more or less intense. The duration of its governance of conscious
performance may vary. But during our conscious performance of
Wondering, Critical, or Evaluative Operations it seems we are
always operating in one or more of the Motifs to which these
interests give rise.

So far, for the sake of identifying the Basic Interests and the
Motifs to which they give rise, we've considered them in isolation
from one another. While our conscious performance is occasionally
governed by a single interest and characterized for some length of
time by a single Motif, in our everyday living our interests alternate
and mix and blend. Some interests seem to mix and blend easily.
Others, like oil and water, don't mix well at all and, when
combined, bring about unfortunate personal and interpersonal
entanglements and undesirable social and cultural consequences.
Now let's consider these interests in some of their possible
combinations and relations to one another for the sake of

illustrating the concrete confluence of the basic interests in our conscious performance.

1. The Quotidian Blend of Motifs

Everyday conscious performance is normally governed by the blending and alternating dominance of the practical and dramatic interests. Our conscious performance is Dramatic-practical or Practical-dramatic. In this familiar blend, either the dramatic interest dominates and the practical interest in getting things done serves dramatic ends, or the practical interest dominates and the dramatic interest in self-worth serves practical ends. One of these interests can temporarily recede as the other rises to prominence. One interest can take over and temporarily quiet the other.

I may be operating with *a Dramatic-practical Motif.* Suppose I'm with someone with whom I'm interested in developing a friendship. My prevailing concern is to be appreciated, respected, liked, or even loved, and I am dramatically attentive to the meaning and worth of myself in the other's eyes and of the other in my eyes. At the same time, the two of us are engaged in a common task and getting something done. We're performing with and before one another and, while we're performing, we're taking care of business. Imagine working with someone in whom you have a serious interest and whose estimation of you matters greatly to you; imagine what it's like to work with someone in whom you have little or no interest and whose evaluation of you is of no consequence.

I may be operating with *a Practical-dramatic Motif.* Suppose I'm interested in getting things done, but, as is frequently the case, I'm getting them done with and before others who may approve or disapprove of my performance, praise me or blame me, like me or dislike me, love me or hate me. I work, and I take pride in my work. If my work doesn't meet my own or others' standards, I might cover it up, hide it, disown it, attribute the mess I've made to someone else, or admit reluctantly that I made the mess myself.

In the *Practical-dramatic* blend, the practical interest can become so prominent that the dramatic interest is temporarily extinguished. Suppose I'm engaged in casual conversation and exchanging pleasantries with my co-workers while I work. My computer screen suddenly goes black. I tap the space bar, but the screen remains black. I withdraw from conversation to address the practical crisis I face. My attention becomes uniformly practical. A moment ago, we were discussing excitedly our plans to spend time together on the weekend. Now it's as if my co-workers are just distractions from the practical problem I face, or aren't even there.

In the *Dramatic-practical* blend, with its dominant dramatic interest, the practical interest can suddenly overthrow the dramatic interest, take the dominant position, or even temporarily eliminate it.

COOKING DINNER TOGETHER

Suppose I'm preparing dinner with a fairly good friend. The dinner preparation is routine, and our attention is focused on sharing our memories of how we met and how our friendship has blossomed. We anticipate that our friendship might reach a new depth this evening. The olive oil I'm heating catches fire. Our dramatic conversation is abandoned abruptly as we take immediate practical measures. She grabs the lid from the kitchen counter and hands it to me. I drop it onto the frying pan to smother the fire. Our Dramatic-practical performance has become, for the time being, purely practical cooperation. With the practical situation now under control, the dramatic interest regains its former prominence in both of us. Relieved, we compliment one another for responding so swiftly and effectively to the practical crisis and averting a practical disaster.

But things might have unfolded differently. Suppose that, when the olive oil bursts into flames, my friend grabs the frying pan, drops it into the sink, and reaches to turn on the water. I yell, "No, you idiot! Don't put water on an oil fire!" I push her aside, and drop the lid onto the frying pan. The practical crisis is over, the practical interest recedes, and the dramatic interest returns with a vengeance. "OK, so I made a mistake! You didn't have to call me an idiot!" she says. "Sorry," I say, "but you were about to do something really stupid." The dramatic interest is dominant again, but the dramatic tenor of the evening is likely to be marked now, not by pride in our collaborative practicality, but by residual dismay and anger,

embarrassment and hurt feelings, worry about the prospects for our friendship, and perhaps a little sorrow.

Dramatic-practical and Practical-dramatic living are punc-
tuated by recurrent forays into aesthetic performance. From the
dramatic and practical workday we retreat to the entertainments
and amusements of the evening. We seek respite and relief from
the labors of the workweek in the relaxation and recreation of the
weekend. Commonly, we relax and recreate with others and,
because others are present, our performance is either Aesthetic-
dramatic or Dramatic-aesthetic. Either the aesthetic interest
dominates and the dramatic interest serves aesthetic ends, as when
we need a partner to play a game but conversation would simply
be a distraction, or the dramatic interest dominates and the
aesthetic interest serves dramatic ends, as when we "dress to
impress" or decide to take dance lessons in order to make new
friends.

We've already noticed the affinity of the aesthetic and the
dramatic interests. The aesthetic interest blends easily with the
dramatic interest. Dramatic performance and aesthetic performance share an interest in the sensible embodiment of beauty.
In my dramatic performance, there is an aesthetic interest in the
embodiment of beauty in my own appearance and movement
before others and in the appearance and movement of others
before me. In my single-mindedly and uniformly aesthetic
performance, my interest lies in the sensible beauty of the given-as-
given. In the dramatic apprehension of another there may be an
aesthetic relaxation of the control of the flow of experience by
other interests that permits its aesthetic patterning by the
appearance and movement of the other. I may be attracted or
repelled by the meaning and value incarnated and communicated
by another's posture and movements, manner of dress, pitch and
tone of voice, facial expressions, and gestures. The dramatic
embodiments of meaning and value that I and others are, are
products of a dramatic artistry that not only decorates the body but
also informs its motion with meanings and guides its motion with
values. In a sense, dramatic performance is always Dramatic-
aesthetic performance. There is always an aesthetic interest
involved in dramatic performance, but the essentially purposeless
and open-ended aesthetic interest is made to serve, well or badly, a
dramatic end.

In the *Aesthetic-dramatic* blend the dramatic is made to serve the
aesthetic interest.

THE PHOTO SHOOT

Suppose I'm an artist, and my medium is photography. I invite a friend over in the hope that she'll be willing to pose for some photographs. Appealing to her dramatic concern, I say, "Wow, you look amazing! I'd really like to photograph you!" Then, in order to coax her into adopting the postures and attitudes, and to evoke from her the facial expressions that carry the subtle meanings and values I hope to capture, I engage in flattering small-talk, bombard her with hyperbolic compliments, and ask her questions about herself and her achievements. I exploit her dramatic interest in her own worth and in my estimation of her worth for my aesthetic purposes.

But suppose that, when the shoot is over, my artistic subject attempts to pick up a thread from our earlier conversation when I was commenting on her impressive personal achievements, and that I stare at her blankly with no memory of exactly what I said while I was shooting the photos. I was preoccupied with their composition and the lighting. She's a bit annoyed to discover that my dramatic performance was subservient to my aesthetic concern and that I was exploiting her dramatic concern for her own worth for my own aesthetic and artistic satisfaction. Of course, she wouldn't explain her annoyance in that way. She might simply say, under her breath and perhaps somewhat sulkily, "I guess all you're really interested in are your darn photographs."

The practical interest and the aesthetic interest can blend. In the *Practical-aesthetic* blend, the aesthetic interest is made to serve practical ends. My intrinsically non-practical artistic performance might be enlisted in the design and production of household goods and cosmetics for future sale. It might be enlisted to further the pursuit of economic goals in the creation of advertisements and the design of packaging. It might be subordinated to the pursuit of personal advantage or to the pursuit of social or political ends in the creation of propaganda that exploits the aesthetic and dramatic sensibilities of others for the purpose of eliciting the practical decisions and actions desired by me or by those who pay me for my artistic services. I might play sports in college or professionally, and I might do so, not out of love for the game, but simply to earn my tuition or my paycheck. I might visit museums but fail to see what all the fuss is about. My legs get tired as I walk the marble floors, and my aesthetic appreciation of what's on display amounts to little more than the color-matching sensitivity of a Practical-aesthetic interior decorator and expresses itself in slightly forced praise for the practical skills demonstrated by the artists.

In the *Aesthetic-practical* blend, on the other hand, my practical interest is made to serve my interest in aesthetic liberation or my interest in purely artistic creation. When I play games, I take efficient and effective measures to score points and, ultimately, to win the game, but the win is not primarily a practical achievement, and I find my satisfaction in the very experience of playing. When I undertake to produce a work of art, I put into service all of the pertinent practical skills I've acquired to produce a non-practical and purely artistic product.

Ordinary, everyday living normally involves the alternation and blending of the practical, dramatic, and aesthetic interests and the alternating dominance or interweaving of the Practical, Dramatic, and Aesthetic Motifs. Less common are blends of these everyday interests with the intellectual and mystical interests.

2. OTHER PERMUTATIONS OF MOTIFS

Besides the quotidian blend of Motifs there are other, less ordinary blends. Let's consider a range of these less ordinary blends and illustrate briefly how they might manifest themselves in our conscious performance.

The mystical interest can blend with the practical interest. In the *Mystical-practical* blend, the mystical interest dominates, and the practical interest may unfold in devout efficiency and effectiveness in the preparation and enactment of rites and rituals.

In the *Practical-mystical* blend, on the other hand, the mystical interest is subordinated to the practical interest and given a practical interpretation. I might seek in my practical success the proof of my holiness. I might appeal to the divine to serve my personal advantage. I might do yoga for my health. I might dabble in magic in the hope of enlisting supernatural support and a divine guarantee for my practical projects. I might pray for new tires for my car, a new roof for my house, a new watch, or an increase in my salary. I might attempt to redirect the mystical interest of others in the mysterious Ground of existence to myself as the incarnation of that Ground or as its divinely-chosen spokesperson to enhance my practical authority and political power or to feather my own nest. I might exploit others' mystical apprehension of their imperfection and their felt need for redemption from insurmountable limitations for my own practical advantage. In short, I might attempt to make being religious or being "spiritual but not religious" practically useful and personally advantageous.

The mystical interest in ultimate meaning and ultimate value can blend with the intellectual interest in explanatory under-standing and truth. In the *Mystical-intellectual* blend, in which the mystical interest dominates and the intellectual interest serves, there might emerge precise and rigorous and systematic theological speculation and the pursuit of imperfect understanding of the mysteries inherent in the mystical expression of mystical experience.

The *Intellectual-mystical* blend, in which an intellectual interest dominates and the mystical interest serves, may occur, but it is often short-lived. A prevailing interest in universal truth attainable by unaided human inquiry might result in the recasting of unfathomable mysteries as merely intellectual problems to be solved. Ultimately, this blend might result in the eliminative declaration that the mystical interest and mystical expression are merely 'ideological' manifestations of a desire to be relieved of the suffering imposed by the practical, economic, social, political, or historical situation.

The mystical interest can blend with the Dramatic-aesthetic interest. In the *Mystical-dramatic-aesthetic* blend, we might create beauty in the worshipful service and celebration of the divine. We might design and construct massive cathedrals and tombs whose spires and towers reach toward a mysterious Beyond, create sacred spaces and adorn them with depictions of generosity and forgiveness that exceed our human capacity for giving and forgiving, sing melodic hymns and recite poetic psalms, outfit ourselves in ceremonial robes, and perform sacred dances.

The intellectual interest can blend with the dramatic interest. In the *Intellectual-dramatic* blend, in which the intellectual interest dominates and the dramatic interest serves, we might engage in intellectual discussions with others in which a shared interest in the truth overrides the dramatic interest in being the authority, in being thought smart, acute, insightful, the one who deserves credit for the bright idea, or the one who is right.

In the *Dramatic-intellectual* blend, intellectual discussion might degenerate into an intellectual competition in which we're more interested in making or proving a point than in understanding it or knowing if it's true. The discussion might be derailed by the confusion of my personal worth, which is correctly measured by the orderliness or disorderliness of my performance, with the adequacy of my own present understanding of things or with the intellectual capitulation and deference of others.

The intellectual interest can blend with the practical interest. In the *Practical-intellectual* blend, in which the practical interest dominates, we might pursue abstruse scientific questions only to lay the intellectual foundations for the design and fabrication of tools. Physicists, chemists, biologists, neuroscientists, psychologists, and sociologists might become contractors to governments whose interest lies in weaponry, crowd control, population control, the untainted supply of food and water, health services, interrogation of terrorists, social engineering, political manipulation, and re-election.

In the *Intellectual-practical* blend, practical performance serves the pursuit of explanatory understanding for its own sake. Practical intelligence and skill are enlisted, for example, to enable us to gather the evidence needed to test our hypotheses about a Big Bang that may have occurred 13.7 billion years minus 10^{-6} seconds ago or about the existence of a subatomic particle. Practical intelligence might be called upon to make scientific inquiry more efficient and effective in its pursuit of understanding; we might devise methodical rules to be followed in the pursuit of intellectual ideas, like those which constitute scientific method, those which control conceptual analysis, or those which guide our own performance of CPA; or we might design orbiting telescopes to assist us in the collection of data. Pedagogical strategies and tactics might be conceived for the purpose of communicating the truths we've discovered or in order to elicit in others the intellectual inquiry that led to their discovery.

The intellectual interest can blend with the aesthetic interest. In the *Intellectual-aesthetic* blend, aesthetic appreciation might become the conscious performance of the art critic or art historian. The artistic interest might become the pursuit of elegance and simplicity in the technical formulation and expression of universal, theoretical understanding of the relations of things to one another.

Other and more complex blends could be illustrated and their implications explored. But perhaps enough examples have been provided to show that the Basic Interests, and the Motifs to which they give rise, alternate and blend in the course of our living.

Chapter Thirteen

THE BASIC TENSION OF
CONSCIOUS PERFORMANCE

C onscious performance with a single Motif or with a blend of
Motifs may be attentive or inattentive, intelligent or
unintelligent, reasonable or unreasonable, responsible or
irresponsible. The basic commitment informs and guides performance in every Motif more or less effectively. But in each Motif
the basic notions are conceptually determined or specified. These
specifications of the basic notions are conceptual products of my
preconceptual, comprehensive, and unrestricted anticipation of
meaning, objectivity, knowledge, truth, reality, and value; they are
products of the notions at work in my conscious performance. In
each Motif, motif-specific conceptions of the meanings of the basic
notions temporarily seize control of conscious performance from
the operative basic notions, focus my basic commitment, and
restrict the range of my fundamentally open-ended and
indeterminate anticipation of meaning, objectivity, knowledge,
truth, reality, and value. One or more of the basic notions rises to
prominence while others are depleted, and one or more basic
modes of operation come to be emphasized or suppressed. But my
basic commitment remains. There results a felt tension between *the
focused and restricted demand* for attentiveness, intelligence, reasonableness, and responsibility imposed by the governing interest or
blend of interests and *the over-reaching and unrestricted demand* for
attentiveness, intelligence, reasonableness, and responsibility
imposed by my open-ended and indeterminate basic commitment.

The felt demand of my basic commitment *always exceeds* the requirements imposed upon me for attentiveness, intelligence, reasonableness, and responsibility by any Basic Interest or blend of interests. It makes its presence felt in the emergence of further questions which, when taken seriously, might lure me out of my present Motif and into another. For example, my prolonged involvement in practical performance in order to resolve the many practical problems I encounter during an economic recession may be disrupted by the emergence of puzzlement about the difference between capitalism and socialism, of confusion about the relationship of free trade and trade restrictions to the health of a national economy, of doubt about the capacity of the science of economics, in its present state, to understand the flow of money in a capitalist economy and to issue intelligent recommendations to politicians, or of moral concerns about unbridled greed on Wall Street. My prolonged dramatic involvement in a complicated personal relationship may be disrupted by the emergence of wonder about the psychological relationship between early life traumas and later neurotic behavior. My single-minded involvement in purely intellectual performance and my prolonged disregard of practical tasks and personal relationships may be disrupted by concerns about the impact of my intellectual work on my practical and dramatic living. My intellectual struggle with the complexities of subatomic events may evoke mystical contemplation on the mysteriousness of the universe. My frequent immersion in artistic pursuits may evoke mystical wonder about the roots of creativity and the sources of artistic inspiration. In my performance with any Motif, it is always concretely possible for me *to raise a further question that transgresses the limits* imposed by my dominant interest or blend of interests of the moment and sets the stage for the emergence of a different interest and performance with another Motif. Moreover, if I do not deliberately maintain the interest that governs the Motif with which I happen to be performing, this possibility is realized spontaneously in reaction to the imperious demands and in response to the intriguing invitations of a flow of experience that is never completely configured by my governing interest.

The five Motifs are not coextensive; they move us into distinct realms or domains of meaning and value. But, because they are all determinations and specific expressions of my basic commitment, they are not incommensurable. The boundaries that separate them from one another can be crossed. Transitions from one Motif to another may be resisted, postponed, bumpy and difficult, like the transition from the Practical Motif to the Artistic or the Intellectual Motif; or they may be welcomed, sought, smooth and easy, like the transition from the Dramatic Motif to the Aesthetic Motif. But the transitions can be, are, and sometimes must be made. The concrete possibility of making them is given in the unrestrictedness and comprehensiveness of my basic commitment. The concrete necessity of making them is given in the variable nature of the concrete situations in which I find myself.

Attentive, intelligent, reasonable, and responsible performance, whether practical or intellectual or aesthetic or artistic or dramatic or mystical, may be found upon reflection to be a relatively inattentive, unintelligent, unreasonable, and irresponsible reaction or response both to the situation-at-hand and to the larger situation that is the ongoing and unfolding drama of my life. When we perform with a Motif we labor under its specific limitations and deficiencies. We can always ask if our dominant interest of the moment is appropriate to the situation in which we find ourselves. We need not ask this question, and we may not wish to ask it. But we are able to ask it. Only by raising and answering this ever-relevant question about the propriety of our dominant interest or blend of interests of the moment for the moment can we determine whether or not our present conscious performance with a particular Motif or blend of Motifs satisfies the demand of the basic commitment that always exceeds and points beyond the specific demands of any Motif or blend of Motifs. We can always ask if our performance in a specific Motif or blend is *sufficiently* attentive, intelligent, reasonable, and responsible performance in reaction or response to the present situation and the problems with which it presents us. In response to this motif-transcending question, we may decide to prolong our performance in the present Motif or to make the transition to another we judge to be more appropriately attentive, intelligent, reasonable, and responsible.

As a practical, intellectual, aesthetic/artistic, dramatic, or mystical performer, then, I experience a tension between the limiting specifications of the basic notions and the transcending anticipation that is my open-ended basic commitment. The tension is manifested as residual confusion, nagging doubts, an uneasy conscience. I can attend to my experience of this tension between the limiting requirements of the Motif in which I find myself and the over-reaching requirements of my basic commitment, admit its existence, and deliberately negotiate it, or I can ignore it and inadvertently confine myself to living with a particular Motif or blend of Motifs despite my ever-varying situation. I can take seriously my motif-transcending wonder, doubt, and moral concern, or I can treat their emergence as a distraction from the motif-specific task-at-hand and judge them irrelevant, insignificant, meaningless, or pointless and cling single-mindedly to the governing criteria of the Motif with which I happen to be performing.

The trick, it seems, is to pursue each interest in such a way that our present interest does not so limit and obstruct our attention to the situation-at-hand and to the ongoing drama of our lives as to render even our conscientious performance with a particular Motif or blend of Motifs fundamentally inattentive, unintelligent, unreasonable, and irresponsible performance. To perform this trick regularly and successfully, however, requires that we remain, in spite of our involvement with a specific Motif, finely attuned to the basic tension of conscious performance and sensitive to the open-ended and over-reaching basic commitment that informs and guides all conscious performance.

1. THE HIGH DRAMA

The Practical, Aesthetic/Artistic, Intellectual, and Mystical Motifs are fundamentally in the service of dramatic living. Without practical performance and the pursuit of vital and social values, the minimal conditions for dramatic performance will not be met. Without aesthetic and artistic, intellectual, and mystical performance, the drama of life comes to be regarded as, in the words of the philosopher Thomas Hobbes, "solitary, poor, nasty, brutish and short," and life hardly seems worth living. Without aesthetic and artistic performance and the pursuit and creation of beauty, the drama of life is uninspired and unmotivated, the same old story is repeated over and over again, the horizon of living contracts, and life becomes routine, boring, stultifying, alienating, or ugly. Without intellectual performance and the pursuit of the cultural value of truth, dramatic performance is crippled by ignorance of the sensible and self-present world in which the drama is begun, enacted scene by scene, act by act, and eventually reaches its conclusion. Without mystical performance and the pursuit of absolute value, the drama becomes a cycle of blind justice, of an eye for an eye and a tooth for a tooth, of doing what's required and nothing more, unbroken by inexplicable generosity, unearned rewards, undying hopes, unwarranted forgiveness, and unconditional, unrestricted love that requires no justification at all.

The dramatic interest and the Dramatic Motif, then, seem to have a certain primacy. Performance with any Motif can be regarded as, in a broad sense, dramatic performance, not only when observed from without by others, but also when experienced interiorly by ourselves. In every Motif we remain present to ourselves even when, in the moment, our concern with our own value in our relations with others is not our dominant concern. In our performance with any Motif, we are more or less present to ourselves as risking evaluation, if not by others, then at least by ourselves, as attentive or inattentive, intelligent or unintelligent, reasonable or unreasonable, responsible or irresponsible performers – as adhering to our basic commitment or as failing to do so. Because of our persistent presence to ourselves, then, every other interest is already minimally blended with the dramatic interest, and every other Motif is virtually blended with the Dramatic Motif. In virtue of this dramatic concern that is coincident with my self-presence, the dramatic interest becomes more or less operative, its intensity rising and falling with the emergence and recession of other interests and with the emergence of the further questions that invite and initiate transitions from one Motif of performance to another. In short, because I am always present to myself in my basic commitment, because I am always performing before myself, in my performance with any Motif there lurks the often unformulated concern with the orderliness or disorderliness of my own performance that may be expressed in the critical question, "Am I *really* adhering to my basic commitment?" and in the evaluative question, "Is what I'm doing *really* worthwhile?"

When this felt but unformulated dramatic concern with the orderliness or disorderliness of my conscious performance with every Motif is deliberately formulated in critical and evaluative questions about my present performance, the dramatic interest stands to my dominant interest of the moment as the basic commitment stands to all the specifications of the basic notions. It underpins them, penetrates them, and points beyond their limitations. I take my stand, so to speak, more emphatically on my basic commitment than on the motif-specific commitment of the moment, but without abandoning the Motif with which I am performing. My performance in the Motif of the moment is subject now to *a higher dramatic control*. I become a deliberate participant in the higher drama informed and governed by the realization that my performance with every Motif is just one moment in the larger drama in which I constitute my own character and make my contribution, for good or ill, to the world in which I and others must live out our lives.

2. MAJOR AND MINOR AUTHENTICITY

We can distinguish, then, between performance that is governed more or less thoroughly by the specifications of the notions proper to a particular Motif, on the one hand, and performance that, while still motif-specific, is immunized, so to speak, against the limiting determinateness of the motif-specific meanings of the basic notions by the implementation of higher dramatic control. We can distinguish, on the one hand, between *the minor authenticity* of performance with a Motif and under the control of motif-specific meanings of the basic notions and, on the other hand, *the major authenticity* of performance with a Motif but under higher dramatic control. In the absence of the realization that my performance in every Motif is world-constitutive and self-constitutive, I am concretely capable of only minor authenticity in my practical, aesthetic, artistic, intellectual, dramatic, and mystical performance; I exercise only the limited attentiveness, intelligence, reasonableness, and responsibility proper to a particular Motif. With the occurrence of the realization of the primacy of the Dramatic Motif, I become capable of major authenticity in the full range of my conscious performance. I achieve a heightened sensitivity to the orderliness or disorderliness of my own performance and become attuned to the manifestations of the basic tension of conscious performance. I am no longer satisfied with my minor authenticity in a particular Motif; I can no longer assume that my orderly performance within the limits imposed by the specifications of the basic notions in any of the Motifs is enough; I can no longer be complacently practical, intellectual, aesthetic or artistic, dramatic, or mystical. In addition to the ordinary sets of questions pertaining to the authenticity of my performance with the five Motifs, I raise questions that pertain to the authenticity of my performance in the higher drama: Is orderly performance in my current Motif truly an attentive, intelligent, reasonable, and responsible response to my personal situation and to the times in which I live? What type of performance does my personal situation call for? What type of performance does our shared situation call for? Is it enough for me to perform attentively, intelligently, reasonably, and responsibly in pursuit of strictly practical or artistic or intellectual or mystical or ordinary dramatic ends? Should I undertake to develop myself with another Motif or blend of Motifs? What type of subject am I now? What type of subject should I become?

CPA has equipped us with a type of self-knowledge and an intimate vocabulary that enables us to raise the question of major authenticity with some precision. In the next and final chapter, we shall consider in some detail the transition from spontaneous and unreflective performance to deliberate and reflective performance, from ordinary living to the High Drama, that the knowledge we've acquired through CPA empowers us to enact.

Chapter Fourteen

FROM SELF-KNOWLEDGE TO SELF-POSSESSION

W e began this exploration of conscious performance with an Elemental Meditation that brought to our attention our spontaneous basic commitment to the pursuit of meaning, objectivity, knowledge, truth, reality, and value. I then tried to show that we cannot deny this commitment without involving ourselves in embarrassing performative self-contradiction. In our conscious living, our reliance upon the basic notions is inescapable, and our appeal to them is inevitable. The basic notions constitute and guide our conscious performance, even when we deny their constitutive and guiding roles.

I also attempted to show just how basic the notions of meaning, objectivity, knowledge, truth, reality, and value are to our conscious living. They're more basic than any ideas or concepts we might produce about them. Ideas and concepts are products of conscious performance that is constituted by the basic notions and guided by them before and while we form any ideas or concepts of them. When we formulate concepts of these basic notions, inevitably we fail to capture their full meaning. The most fundamental meaning of our basic notions is their operative meaning in our conscious performance, prior to any attempt we may make to identify them or to clarify them for ourselves. I concluded that, if we wish to come to know ourselves in our basic commitment, our only option is to describe the basic notions at work in our conscious performance.

I then proposed that we undertake Conscious Performance Analysis in order to get to know ourselves as spontaneously committed to the pursuit of meaning, objectivity, knowledge, truth, reality, and value. I drew attention to the Language of Self-Possession that we already use to talk about ourselves as conscious performers. I noted the vagueness, allusiveness, and imprecision of the existing Language of Self-Possession. When it comes to talking about our sensible experience, we are often remarkably clear and precise, and we strive for ever greater clarity and precision. When it comes to talking about ourselves as conscious performers, we are surprisingly unclear and imprecise, and we are surprisingly tolerant of this obscurity and vagueness. Because our own conscious performance typically lies on the periphery of our attention, we tend to settle for and employ a vague and merely allusive Language of Self-Possession.

I identified some natural and cultural obstacles to giving more focused attention to ourselves and to taking ourselves more seriously as conscious performers. I emphasized especially the role our spontaneous preference for sensible objects plays in distracting us from ourselves as conscious performers. I issued an invitation to step over or around these obstacles, to take advantage of our intimate presence to ourselves, and to undertake an exploration of the operative meaning of our basic commitment to meaning, objectivity, knowledge, truth, reality, and value.

I suggested that, in the course of CPA, the Language of Self-Possession would undergo a gradual purification and that, once it had been purified, we would be able to make more profitable use of it to speak pointedly and seriously about ourselves as conscious performers. Now, through CPA, we've achieved a basic knowledge of ourselves as conscious performers. In the process, we've drawn upon and purified the existing Language of Self-Possession. We've equipped ourselves with a basic vocabulary and basic grammar of self-possession. We've given names to Moods of Self-presence, to Modes of Operation, to operations within each Mode, to basic Motifs of Conscious Performance, and we've identified the meanings given to the basic notions when they're specified in each Motif. We're in a position now to speak much more clearly and precisely about ourselves as conscious performers and about what it might mean to take possession of ourselves as conscious performers.

I also emphasized, at the end of Chapter Three, that the aim of CPA is a limited one, and this important point should not be forgotten. Through CPA we come to know ourselves as conscious performers. But to come to know ourselves as conscious performers is not yet to take possession of ourselves as conscious performers. Just as we've discovered that, in the spontaneous orderliness of our conscious performance, Wondering and Critical Operations follow upon Experiential Operations, so too we've discovered that Evaluative Operations follow upon Wondering and Critical Operations. Just as self-presence is not to be confused with self-knowledge, so self-knowledge is not to be confused with self-possession. To be able to talk knowledgeably about what it means to be a self-possessed performer is not yet to deliberate about performing in a self-possessed manner, to evaluate that possible way of acting, and to decide to act that way.

Now that we've begun to purify the Language of Self-Possession and established a basic vocabulary, we're able to speak more clearly and precisely about the self-possession we seek. We need no longer rely upon the too-vague ideas of "being yourself," "being natural," and "going with the flow" that find vague expression in the unpurified Language of Self-Possession. We need no longer rely upon the excessively determinate meanings spontaneously assigned to self-possession by performers in the various Motifs. Now, when we issue to ourselves and to others the fundamental precept "Be Yourself!" we're able to say in some detail and with some precision and clarity just what we mean. But to understand that precept more precisely is one thing; to act upon that precise understanding is another. Again, to be able to talk precisely about self-possession is one thing; to actually take possession of oneself is another.

Our limited aim throughout has been to equip ourselves with an understanding of ourselves as conscious performers for the sake of taking possession of ourselves. It should be clear now that CPA is itself performance with an Intellectual Motif, governed by an intellectual interest in explanatory understanding of the relations of things to one another – of Moods to one another, of Moods to Modes, of Modes to one another, of Modes to Motifs, of Motifs to one another, of Motifs to Moods, and of Moods, Modes, and Motifs to the constitutive and guiding basic notions. But it should also be clear now that CPA ultimately and in the long run serves another interest. Our intellectual performance of CPA has been a lengthy digression within the encompassing context established by our intermittently operative dramatic concern to find direction in the flow of our lives. Our intellectual performance in CPA has been a self-attentive pursuit of self-understanding and self-knowledge. But that pursuit of self-understanding and self-knowledge serves a profound dramatic aim. The self-knowledge we acquire in CPA is *for the sake of* taking possession of ourselves and being at home with ourselves as conscious performers. It is for the sake of assuming our roles in the High Drama.

The knowledge we gain of ourselves as performers through CPA is dramatically empowering, and we have pursued it for the sake of our dramatic empowerment. CPA empowers us to transform our spontaneous and unreflective commitment to the pursuit of meaning, objectivity, knowledge, truth, reality, and value into a deliberate and reflective commitment. It empowers us to perform deliberately and reflectively instead of spontaneously and unreflectively. While it has always been possible abstractly and in principle for me to make this fundamental change in my relationship to my basic commitment, it is now concretely possible for me to do so. This is the difference CPA can make, and this has been our purpose in doing CPA.

CPA is an essential intellectual digression that serves our dramatic interest. From that digression we return now to address our dramatic concern to find direction in the flow of our lives. We shift now from the Intellectual Motif governed by a concern to find the truth about ourselves as conscious performers to the Dramatic Motif governed by a concern with our own and others' worth and with making worthwhile lives for ourselves with others, now and in the future.

The dramatic decision to exercise my newly acquired power to establish deliberately my own relationship to my basic commitment is, like all dramatic decisions, a highly personal one. It requires that I perform the Evaluative Operations that follow naturally upon the *critical judgments* I've made about what I've come to *understand* about my intimate *experience* of myself as a conscious performer. The *decision* I make depends ultimately upon my own estimation of the value of performing deliberately and reflectively in my conscious living. It depends upon my discernment of the relationship of my inevitable and inescapable commitment to my self-worth and of my own relationship to that basic commitment. This decision will issue from my own Evaluative Operations and be entirely my own, just as my basic commitment is mine and no one else's. Of course, that is not to say that the decision will be merely 'subjective' in that mistaken sense of 'subjectivity' that we identified and rejected. It is to say, rather, that no one can perform this evaluation and make this decision for me.

1. THE POLYMORPHISM OF HUMAN CONSCIOUSNESS

Our prolonged meditation has revealed the variability and flexibility of our conscious performance. It has brought to light four Moods of Conscious Performance, four Modes of Conscious Operation, the spontaneous orderliness of the unfolding of operations within each Mode, the spontaneous orderliness of the unfolding of the Modes themselves, and our susceptibility in our spontaneous performance to disordering derailment. We've identified five Basic Interests that configure the flow of our attention and five basic Motifs of Conscious Performance. We've noted our differing relationships to our basic commitment and to the basic notions in those five Motifs and the influence of the specification of the basic notions in the five Motifs on our performance of conscious operations. Human consciousness is not a homogeneous medium; our presence to ourselves varies with the various operations we perform with various interests. It is not homogeneous, the same throughout, but *polymorphic*; it takes on a variety of dynamic shapes. We can distinguish three dimensions of the polymorphism of human consciousness: the Operational Polymorphism of Consciousness; the Orientational Polymorphism of Consciousness; and the Executive Polymorphism of Consciousness.

I am present to myself in my performance of a variety of conscious operations that can be organized into four Modes: Question-free; Wondering; Critical; and Evaluative. This is *the Operational Polymorphism of Consciousness*. [See Diagram V in Appendix II]. I am present to myself as operating in the four Modes with a variety of interests that give rise to Five Motifs: Practical; Intellectual; Aesthetic/Artistic; Dramatic; and Mystical. This is *the Orientational Polymorphism of Consciousness*. [See Diagram VI in Appendix II]. But the degree of control I exercise over my conscious performance of the variety of operations with a variety of Basic Interests is also variable. My basic commitment can be fragile or durable. I can be loosely tethered to it and easily derailed. I can be tightly tethered to it and resistant to derailment. I can perform spontaneously and unreflectively, uninformed by philosophical self-understanding and self-knowledge, ungoverned by decisions based upon my philosophical self-knowledge, and for the most part reactive to the imperious demands of the given. I can perform deliberately and reflectively, informed by basic philosophical self-understanding and self-knowledge, governed by decisions based upon my philosophical self-knowledge, and for the most part responsive to the demands and invitations of the given. I can be spontaneous and unreflective or deliberate and reflective in my conscious performance. This difference in the degree of control I exercise in the execution of my conscious performance is *the Executive Polymorphism of Consciousness* [See Diagram VII in Appendix II].

My presence to myself in the ongoing variation of the Basic Moods of my performance, in the ongoing variation of the Basic Modes of my performance, and in the shifting Motifs of my performance can be informed by philosophical self-knowledge and deliberately controlled, or it can be uninformed by philosophical self-knowledge and more or less at the mercy of and determined by the variable demands of the given. I can put the knowledge I've acquired of myself in CPA to work, make the transition from the first three Modes of Operation to the fourth, Evaluative Mode, take possession of myself as a conscious performer, and become deliberate and reflective in my conscious performance, or I can fail to carry my newly acquired self-knowledge into the Evaluative Mode, truncate the process of taking possession of myself, and remain for the most part a spontaneous and unreflective performer.

Our meditative exploration of ourselves in CPA enables us to ask very precise questions about ourselves as conscious performers. It enables us to ask pointed questions about what kind of conscious performers we've been so far and about the real possibilities and real prospects for our conscious performance in the future. Let us adhere to our basic commitment, then, and address the issues surrounding the transition from spontaneous and unreflective performance to deliberate and reflective performance that is made concretely possible by the self-knowledge we've acquired in CPA.

2. UNREFLECTIVE AND SPONTANEOUS PERFORMANCE

Spontaneous conscious performance, just because it is spontaneous, is highly susceptible to becoming disordered. The spontaneous orderliness of our performance is fragile. It may be that we can never ensure that our conscious performance won't be occasionally derailed. No matter how reflective and deliberate we become in our living, the demands of the given still catch us off guard and take us by surprise, and our personal pasts still exert present influence in our ingrained habits of feeling, thinking, and acting. Like New Year's resolutions, our resolution to live reflectively and deliberately has an ineliminable fragility. But the probability of disorderly performance and derailment, and the duration of disorder and derailment when they do occur, may be reduced significantly, even if they are not reduced to zero, when we become reflective and deliberate in our adherence to our basic commitment.

My performance of conscious operations may be spontaneous or deliberate. If it is spontaneous, I'm highly susceptible to disorder and derailment in my conscious performance. Before I undertake CPA and come to know myself as a conscious performer, I am inevitably a predominantly spontaneous performer. Before I acquire the precise self-understanding and self-knowledge that enable me to be a reflective and deliberate performer, the intensity of my adherence to my basic commitment fluctuates in reaction and response to the demands and pressures of my physical, social, cultural, personal, and historical situation. I have certainly been, to some extent, a beneficiary of my upbringing, education, social-ization, and enculturation. But I have also, to a greater or lesser extent, been a victim of the situations in which I've found myself, a victim of my physical, psychological, social, cultural, and historical circumstances, a victim of my ignorance of myself as a performer and of others' ignorance and maliciousness as well. I have been talked into things, overtly or subtly pressured, pushed around, ordered about, and occasionally manipulated. I've gone against the current of my own unfolding basic commitment or been diverted down tributaries that led me nowhere. I'm already to some extent disorderly in my performance. I've already developed as a certain kind of subject and acquired habits of conscious performance and habits of non-performance before I come to know and take posses-sion of myself as a conscious performer. I have *already constituted myself* and have *already been constituted by others* as a certain type of conscious performer before I attempt to take possession of myself. I've already wandered off the path, through thickets and brambles, and my return to the path requires passing through those thickets and brambles again

The conclusions I've reached in CPA enable me to ask with some precision *what type of subject I have already become*, whatever the causes may have been. My spontaneous development to this point will be revealed broadly in my spontaneous emphasis of a specific Mode of Operation and in my spontaneous emphasis of a specific Motif or blend of Motifs of Conscious Performance with its charac-teristic specifications of the basic notions and its characteristic intensification or suppression of certain Modes of Operation [See Diagram VIII in Appendix II].

2.1 SPONTANEOUS EMPHASIS OF A MODE OF OPERATION

Let's begin by considering some illustrations of the types of spontaneous subject I can become when a single Mood and Mode of Operation are enhanced and given dominance, that is, when I identify myself so strongly with one Mode of Operation that my performance in the others is diminished or suppressed, truncated, or virtually eliminated. Note that the issue here is not the entirely mistaken identification of myself with the contents of a particular Mode of Operation, but the partially accurate and undue identification of myself as a conscious performer with only one Mode of Operation.

I may find myself to be *emphatically* an Experiencing or Question-free Subject, or *emphatically* a Wondering Subject, or *emphatically* a Critical Subject, or *emphatically* an Evaluative Subject. My intermittent emphasis of a single Mode of Operation is not in itself problematic. Sometimes, in my pursuit of meaning and value, my situation calls for prolonged performance in a single Mode. But, if it involves the diminishment of my performance in other Modes or failure to perform in other Modes when performance in other Modes is called for, my conscious performance becomes disordered. Then I contract my conscious performance and tend to isolate my performance in one Mode of Operation from my performance in the other Modes upon which that performance builds or to which it leads in the spontaneous orderly sequence. I interrupt and disrupt the orderly, sequential flow of Modes of Operation.

The Unquestioning Subject. I can become known to others as usually reactive to the demands of the given and excessively deferential to others. I may be disinclined to ask questions about my experience, uninquisitive, lacking in intellectual curiosity, and intellectually lazy or passive; I may be credulous and gullible; I may be other-directed and imitative in my living. My relationship to the notions of meaning, objectivity, knowledge, truth, reality, and value remains for the most part implicit, anticipatory, and incipient. My performance is truncated and disorderly. I am fairly attentive, but my attention is not deliberately bestowed upon the situations in which I find myself; it is captured by them. In virtue of my emphasis of the Experiential Mode I may seem attentive, but my attentiveness is diluted. My relationship to all the notions is weak.

My diluted attentiveness is unintelligent, unreasonable, and irresponsible. The flow of my experience may be easily and regularly organized by an Aesthetic interest and less regularly by a Practical or Mystical interest, but these configurations of my experiential flow are for me dwelling-places rather than points of departure for Wondering, Critical, and Evaluative performance.

The Intellectually Speculative Subject. I can become known to others as excessively theoretical and speculative. I may question readily and be very inquisitive, but my wonder is an indiscriminate curiosity; I rest content with mere ideas; I tend to give all ideas equal weight and, at the same time, to give none of them any compelling weight; I am a great hypothesizer, but only that. Because I tend toward exclusive emphasis of the Wondering Mode of Operation, my performance is disorderly, and even in my questioning I'm careless. I am intelligent, but incompletely so. My intelligence is not tethered securely to the notions of objectivity, knowledge, truth, reality, and value. My relation to the notion of meaning is strong, but my relation to the notions of objectivity, knowledge, truth, reality, and value is weak. My concern for meaning is excessively abstract, and my intelligence is diluted. My diluted intelligence is inattentive, uncritical, and irresponsible. The flow of my experience is regularly organized by an Intellectual interest, but the flow is for me a constant invitation to further speculation and rarely, if ever, is treated as a critical witness to the adequacy or inadequacy of my ideas.

The Critically Suspicious Subject. I may become known to others as excessively suspicious and skeptical of others' ideas and, at the same time, as opinionated and dogmatic about my own. I spontaneously presume the inadequacy of the ideas that arise from others, yet I also presume the indubitable adequacy of my suspicions. Because I tend toward exclusive emphasis of the Critical Mode of Operation, my performance is disorderly, and even in my critical questioning I'm careless. My relation to the notions of knowledge, truth, and reality is strong, but my concern for knowledge, truth, and reality is excessively abstract because my relation to the notions of meaning, objectivity, and value is weak. In virtue of my emphasis of the Critical Mode I may seem reasonable, but my reasonableness is diluted. My diluted 'reasonableness' is inattentive, unintelligent, and irresponsible. My experiential flow is regularly organized by an Intellectual interest, but that flow for me is always a flow of evidence for the adequacy of my own ideas and rarely if ever invites the further questions that would expose my own erroneous opinions.

The Morally Self-righteous Subject. I may become known to others as 'judgmental' and morally dogmatic. I may readily evaluate the actions of others, but because I tend toward exclusive emphasis of the Evaluative Mode, my performance is disorderly, and even in my evaluating I'm careless. I have little grasp of the concrete, ever-changing reality of my situation and the situations of others. My relation to the notion of value is strong, but my concern for value is excessively abstract because my relation to the notions of meaning, objectivity, knowledge, truth, and reality is weak. In virtue of my emphasis of the Evaluative Mode I may seem responsible, but my responsibility is diluted. My diluted 'responsibility' is inattentive, unintelligent, and unreasonable. The flow of my experience is regularly organized by a Dramatic interest and less often by a Mystical or Practical interest, but the flow for me is always one into which I must introduce my corrective control and rarely if ever witnesses to the adequacy of inadequacy of my moral judgments and decisions or invites inquiry into the concrete complexities of the situations in which they are enacted.

This classification of types of spontaneous subject by dominant Mode of Operation is merely illustrative. It's intended only to bring to light some possible disordering emphases in conscious performance and their possible implications for ongoing conscious performance. I might be able to identify myself as relatively unquestioning, or merely speculative, or suspicious and dogmatic, or dogmatically self-righteous. I might conclude that my com-mitment to the basic notions is an uneven one and that its unevenness results in disorderly conscious performance.

But this manner of classifying subjects and characterizing myself doesn't take into account fully the governing interests in conscious performance and the Motifs of Conscious Performance that emerge when those interests focus my basic commitment and constrict its range. As we've seen, with each Motif we emphasize one or two modes of operation and diminish our performance in the other modes. With the Aesthetic Motif, we emphasize the Question-free Mode. With the Practical Motif, we emphasize the Question-free and Evaluative Modes. With the Intellectual Motif, we emphasize the Wondering and Critical Modes. With the Mystical Motif, we emphasize the Question-free and Evaluative Modes. The interest and the Motif of Performance to which it gives rise determine the emphasis of Modes. If we are performing in the present moment with the Intellectual Motif, we might be puzzled by the fact that only the Intellectual Motif emphasizes a dynamic segment that is an orderly sequence of two Modes, that only the Intellectual Motif diminishes both Question-free and Evaluative Performance, and that all the other Motifs emphasize either the Question-free Mode in which the basic commitment is merely incipient or both the merely experiential Mode and the Evaluative Mode in which the basic commitment is supposed to reach partial and incremental fulfillment of its aspirations. If the transition to the Dramatic-Intellectual blend of Motifs that is required now has been made, we might wonder what implications these differences have for our pursuit of self-possession.

2.2 Spontaneous Emphasis of a Motif

My performance is always interested performance. I'm always performing with some Motif or blend of Motifs. As noted in my discussion of the five Motifs, in each of the Motifs I *emphasize* performance in one or two Modes of Operation and *diminish* my performance in the others. With each of the Motifs, I spontaneously assign specific meanings to the basic notions. The operative meanings of the notions are more or less obscured and their constitutive and guiding roles are more or less diminished or contracted by these specifications. Further, each Motif is *intrinsically self-interested*, and its self-interest gives rise to unfortunate personal and interpersonal entanglements. Besides the undue emphasis of Modes of Operation illustrated by the excessive passivity of the Unquestioning Subject, the excessive abstractness of the Intellectually Speculative Subject, the excessive skepticism and dogmatism of the Critically Suspicious Subject, and the repugnant moralism and moral dogmatism of the Morally Self-righteous Subject, we must consider the undue emphasis of a single Motif or blend of Motifs.

When I identify myself so strongly with one Motif or blend of Motifs that my performance in others is diminished or virtually eliminated, I become a narrowly Practical, Intellectual, Aesthetic, Dramatic, or Mystical Subject, or I become a subject whose conscious performance is characterized by a single blend of two or more of these Motifs or by a repetitive and predictable alternation of Motifs. Over time, as I continue to engage in conscious perfor-mance governed by a single interest or by a single blend of interests, I develop along the line determined by that interest or blend, I get better and better at performing that way, and I constitute myself as a subject of a certain type. My experiential flow is governed ever more inflexibly by a single interest or a single combination of interests. I come to view and interpret the world and others and myself from the standpoint of only one Motif or only one blend of Motifs.

Practical, Intellectual, Aesthetic, Dramatic, and Mystical Subjects do not operate uniformly, but only predominantly, with a single Motif. The demands of life and the indeterminate reach of our basic commitment more or less ensure occasional and intermittent performance with other Motifs. But my development over time in a single Motif or in some blend of Motifs is carried with me into my occasional or intermittent performance with other Motifs. When I shift Motifs, I take with me the fruits of the time I've spent performing Experiential, Wondering, Critical, and Evaluative Operations and acting with my dominant Motif or dominant blend of Motifs.

For example, if I am predominantly a Practical Subject, I may from time to time become intellectually, aesthetically, dramatically, or mystically interested. But, when my performance is directed by one of these other interests, I give it *a practical twist*. I am spontaneously Practical-intellectual, or Practical-aesthetic, or Practical-dramatic, or Practical-mystical, and it is unlikely, without my deliberate and reflective intervention, that the subordinated interests will ever gain the upper hand in these blends. It is still more unlikely that I will engage in *purely* Intellectual, *purely* Aesthetic, *purely* Dramatic, or *purely* Mystical performance. My Intellectual, Aesthetic, Dramatic, or Mystical performance will be skewed by the imposition of my Practical specification of the basic notions and by my employment of Practical criteria of meaning, objectivity, knowledge, truth, reality, and value. Similarly, if I have become an Aesthetic Subject, when I perform with other Motifs I give them *an aesthetic twist*. My Intellectual, Dramatic, Practical, and Mystical performance will be skewed by the imposition of my Aesthetic criteria of meaning, objectivity, knowledge, truth, reality, and value. In short, whenever I perform with other Motifs, those other Motifs usually *are subordinated to* my dominant Motif and *are made to serve it*. Whatever the situation, I approach it with the spontaneous conviction that my dominant Motif is *the appropriate one* for dealing attentively, intelligently, reasonably, and responsibly with it. To the extent that the situation does call for conscious performance with my dominant Motif or with a blend in which that Motif is dominant, I will in fact *employ the appropriate criteria and handle it appropriately*. To the extent that the situation calls for performance with another Motif or blend of Motifs, I will in fact *employ inappropriate criteria, handle it inappropriately, and aggravate it* by my spontaneous attempts to address it under the governance of my dominant Motif.

Inevitably, I encounter others who are performing with interests and Motifs different from my own. My spontaneous Motif governs my interpretation and evaluation of their conscious performance, just as theirs governs their interpretation and evaluation of mine. I am insensitive to their differing Motifs, and I appeal spontaneously to the criteria of relevance, importance, and significance appropriate to my own Motif when I interpret and evaluate what they say and do and when I offer them advice. My interpretations of the words of others and my evaluations of their actions are informed and guided by the specification of the basic notions characteristic of my dominant Motif. Their interpretations and evaluations of my words and actions are in turn informed and guided by the specifications of the basic notions characteristic of their dominant Motifs.

For example, if I am a Practical Subject, I interpret the expressions and evaluate the actions of Aesthetic, Intellectual, Dramatic, and Mystical Subjects *practically*, guided by my spontaneous practical specification of the basic notions. I spontaneously seek the practical meaning and practical value of their performance. I spontaneously wonder what they're trying to get done or want me to do, what practical value their present performance has, what useful consequences will flow from their performance. Again, if I'm an Aesthetic Subject, I interpret the expressions and evaluate the actions of Practical, Intellectual, Dramatic, and Mystical Subjects *aesthetically*. I spontaneously seek the aesthetic meaning and aesthetic value of their performance. I spontaneously estimate them as affectively liberated and open to possibilities, adventurous or inhibited, playful or super-serious, relaxed or tense, zestful or flat. If I am a Dramatic Subject, I interpret the expressions and evaluate the actions of other types of subjects *dramatically*. I spontaneously seek the dramatic meaning and dramatic value of their performance. I spontaneously search their expressions for indications of what they think about me and how they feel about me. I spontaneously regard them as more or less accomplished actors with whom I share the stage. If I am an Intellectual Subject, I interpret the expressions and evaluate the actions of other types of subjects *intellectually*. I spontaneously seek the intellectual meaning and intellectual value of their performance.

I spontaneously question the adequacy of their assumptions, explore the consistency and coherence of their ideas, demand technical precision in their formulations, and weigh the evidence for the truth of their assertions. If I am a Mystical Subject, I interpret the expressions and evaluate the actions of other types of subjects *mystically*. I spontaneously seek the mystical meaning and mystical value of their performance. I spontaneously place their words and actions in the absolute context of absolute meaning and absolute value.

In short, my understanding and evaluation of subjects with other Motifs are governed by the specific meanings I give to the basic notions within my dominant Motif. The same is true, of course, of the understanding and evaluation of me by others with dominant Motifs different from mine. In this regard, every Motif is spontaneously self-interested. The result is mutual misunderstanding and misevaluation by spontaneous subjects who are all equally convinced of the adequacy of their specifications of the basic notions and of the appropriateness in every situation and in every encounter of the interpretations and evaluations they carry out according to the criteria imposed by these specifications.

Spontaneous and habitual performance with a particular Motif deprives me of the meanings to be discovered and the values to be discerned and created by pure performance within each of the other Motifs and within blends in which other Motifs are dominant. It cripples my ability to understand and evaluate correctly and to respond and act appropriately in the ever-changing situation in which I find myself. It involves me in a multitude of interpersonal entanglements and deprives me of the benefits to be gained by interpreting and evaluating correctly the expressions and actions of others. It leads me to squelch other basic interests as they begin to emerge in me, to limit my interpersonal relations to relations with those who happen to share my dominant Motif, and to avoid people with dominant interests different from my own and in whose presence I experience discomfiting tension, dissonance, and confusion. It radically contracts the range of my experience, understanding, knowledge, and action, and it radically constricts the range, diversity, and depth of my relationship with myself, the world, and others.

My spontaneous performance with my dominant Motif may be attentive or inattentive, intelligent or unintelligent, reasonable or unreasonable, responsible or irresponsible. But my attentiveness, intelligence, reasonableness, and responsibility in my spontaneous performance with a dominant Motif are always *just sufficient to meet the limited requirements of my Motif.* The actual demands and invitations of the situation in which I find myself *might, and typically do, exceed* my capacity to address them or to respond to them by continuing to perform with my dominant Motif. When this is the case, no matter how thoroughly I meet the requirements for attentiveness, intelligence, reasonableness, and responsibility made upon me by my basic commitment as it unfolds with my Motif, I am still *fundamentally* inattentive, unintelligent, unreasonable, and irresponsible.

We can distinguish, then, Motif-specific attentiveness, intelligence, reasonableness, and responsibility from the unrestricted and comprehensive attentiveness, intelligence, reasonableness, and responsibility of our basic commitment. The operative meaning of the basic notions *exceeds* the specific meanings assigned to them in any Motif. That over-reaching operative meaning of the notions is always somewhat obscured in spontaneous operation within a Motif. My basic commitment continues to constitute and guide my performance, but I tend to be prematurely satisfied with a range of meanings and values much narrower than that to which I am basically committed. Each Motif has its inherent limitations and deficiencies. As a merely spontaneous performer, I am easily deluded into thinking that I am performing excellently when, in fact, my performance, in the greater scheme of things, is far from excellent and may actually aggravate the ever-changing situation that I and others are called upon continuously to address. No matter how appropriately I perform with my dominant Motif, there is an ever-present danger that my performance *will be fundamentally inappropriate.*

3. REFLECTIVE AND DELIBERATE PERFORMANCE

The spontaneous subject is not a self-possessed performer. The disorderliness and derailment that occur in our spontaneous performance are due in large part, although not entirely, to our lack of self-possession. The resolution of the problems that attend merely spontaneous performance is to be had only by making the transition from unreflective and spontaneous performance to reflective and deliberate performance. This transition *is made concretely possible* by acquiring knowledge of ourselves as conscious performers through CPA, but it *is not realized or effected* simply by the acquisition of that self-knowledge [See Diagrams VIII, IX, and X in Appendix II].

3.1 The Ensconced Spontaneous Subject

Before we undertook CPA, we had been present to ourselves. We've already taken notice, at the end of Chapter 4, of the experience of recognizing ourselves in the results of CPA and of its possibly misleading character. From that experience of recognition, we're not to infer that we already knew ourselves before undertaking CPA and are now just recalling what we already knew. That experience of finding in the results of CPA someone with whom we are already familiar is a consequence of our having been present to ourselves all along. But self-presence isn't self-knowledge. While we were *intimately familiar with ourselves* before, we didn't yet *know ourselves* in our basic commitment. Unless we make the transition through CPA to knowledge of ourselves as conscious performers, we won't be able to guide our performance reflectively and deliberately. In this ignorance of ourselves, despite our presence to ourselves, we are merely Spontaneous Subjects. As merely Spontaneous Subjects, while we are present to ourselves, we nonetheless lie to a great extent beyond the present range of our own understanding. Our performance is conscious, but it's always in the background, intimately close to us but still obscured by our preoccupation with the contents of our performance and dramatic problem of finding direction in the flow of life. We experience our conscious performance, but we don't attend to it, and we don't explore it. As Spontaneous Subjects, we may operate in the four Modes of Operation with regard to our sensible experience and, perhaps, also with regard to our more prominent or obtrusive feelings. But, with regard to our own conscious performance, we remain for the most part in the Question-free Mode. Our intimate self-presence alone affords us nothing more than intimations, indications, invitations offered by the given to which we haven't yet responded with inquiring self-attention.

If and when we're moved by our circumstances to meditate and to reflect upon ourselves, we typically do so with a Dramatic interest. Our pursuit of self-understanding is motivated by immediate dramatic concerns. Then we might turn to our self-experience as to a flattering mirror and concentrate our attention on our most prominent products and achievements, rather than on our deepest anticipations. Similarly, when in CPA we deliberately bring the ever-present background of basic anticipations forward and begin to reflect upon ourselves as performers, we're likely to be on the alert for the self with whom we are already familiar and in whom we take some defensible pride. I might discover first my dominant Mode of Operation and then my dominant interest and Motif. My dominant Mode of Operation, because it is dominant, will obscure the other Modes of Operation that have been diminished or suppressed. My dominant Mode of Operation will stand out as "my strength." For example, if I happen to be an Unquestioning Subject, I might describe myself, if not to others then at least to myself, as affectively attuned to my experience, as a person who "notices things," and as "*very* attentive and sensitive." If I'm an Intellectually Speculative Subject, I might describe myself as intellectually attuned, an "idea person," and "*very* intelligent and thoughtful." If I'm a Critically Suspicious Subject, I might describe myself as critically attuned, as "a relentless truth seeker," and "*very* reasonable and critical." If I'm a Morally Self-Righteous Subject, I might describe myself as attuned to value, as "a consistent person," and "*very* responsible and moral." Similarly, my dominant interest, because it is dominant, will obscure the other basic interests that emerge only intermittently and, even then, only to serve my dominant interest. For example, I may take special pride in my "*very* practical approach to things," in my "*very* scientific temperament," in my "*very* artistic sensibility," in my "*very* dramatic self-presentation," or in my "*very* religious outlook."

Both my dominant Mode of Operation and my dominant interest may obscure my fundamental, operative commitment to the basic notions. My initial reflection upon myself is not yet the deliberate, Dramatic-*intellectual* reflection essential to CPA. My attention to myself is patterned by an immediate dramatic interest to find myself not only fairly sufficient as I already am but also praiseworthy just for being the way I am. My dramatic reflection tends to mirror my "finished self" of the moment, put into stark and colorful relief by my past and current achievements, obscured by the darker hues of lapses and regrets, surrounded by those products of mine in which I take special pride, adept at those Modes of Operation I happen to emphasize and in those Motifs in which I happen to have undergone some development and acquired some level of skill. My dramatic reflection doesn't expose immediately my "ever-unfinished self," stripped down to my most fundamental anticipations or Moods without which I wouldn't even have that "finished self" in whom I now take qualified pride.

The subject who simply becomes deliberate in her performance with a single Motif *is not sufficiently self-possessed*. She has indeed taken possession of herself, but only of her "finished self" of the moment. She hasn't taken possession of herself as her "ever-unfinished self." I may discover myself to be narrowly interested and narrowly operative, and I may conclude correctly that *this is what I am* and presume incorrectly that *what I am is what I ought to be.* I may make a transition from the spontaneous emphasis of a particular Mode of Operation to deliberate emphasis of that same Mode, and from spontaneous emphasis of a specific Motif to deliberate emphasis of that same Motif. In virtue of my new deliberateness, I may conclude that I am now an adequately self-possessed performer. But, while I have become deliberate, I've done so without carrying out fundamental *intellectual reflection* on the operative notions and on the actual range of conscious per-formance. I have become deliberate about what I already and spontaneously am. I have reinforced my narrowed and contracted performance and settled snugly into my spontaneous Mode and Motif. I have become an *Ensconced Spontaneous Subject.*

The Ensconced Spontaneous Subject is not sufficiently self-possessed. She is *deliberate but still relatively unreflective.* To come to know and take possession of my "finished self" as, say, pre-dominantly unquestioning and predominantly practical is not to take possession of my "unfinished self" in my basic commitment. It is not self-directing self-possession but merely a taking possession of myself as already spontaneously directed. It is to reinforce deliberately the exclusive interest at the root of my dominant Motif. It is to ensconce myself on the already-established path of an inherently limited type of conscious performance with inherent deficiencies.

We're inclined to praise the person who comes to know herself as spontaneously emphasizing a specific Mode and Motif, who chooses deliberately to take possession of herself in those spon-taneous emphases, and who then stands firm in the choice that reinforces those emphases. We tend to praise even minimal reflectiveness, because it shows some concern with knowledge. We tend to praise deliberate choice, regardless of what is chosen, because it shows some concern with value. We tend to praise consistency, even when it is consistent narrowness, because it exhibits some degree of commitment. We might even envy such a person her minimally reflective knowledge of her "finished self" and her deliberate appropriation of it. We may be inclined to describe this deliberate but relatively unreflective self-possession as the achievement of personal authenticity. But there really is little to praise or envy here. Admittedly, this is a degree of self-possession, but it is radically inadequate. It's *an insufficiently reflective possession of oneself as one happens to have become.* It's achieved without having sought and obtained a thoroughgoing account of conscious performance and without having asked, with that knowledge in hand, these evaluative questions: Is it worthwhile *to continue to be* what I happen to be already, to commit myself to being *what I just find myself being already?* Should I *be more than what I just happen to have become so far?* Should I actually *be less what I've become?*

We must be careful not to confuse the Reflective and Deliberate Subject we envision and hope to become with the *deliberate but relatively unreflective* Ensconced Spontaneous Subject. When we confuse reflective possession of ourselves as conscious performers with relatively unreflective possession of ourselves as we happen to find ourselves at the present stage of our spontaneous development, we make a mistake that has serious immediate and long-term personal, social, cultural, and historical consequences. The Ensconced Spontaneous Subject makes herself at home in just one room of a sprawling dwelling, and she mistakes that small room for the whole house. If she hears faint sounds through the walls, she regards them as alien, unearthly manifestations of spirits to be cursorily appeased or completely exorcised.

When we fall prey to this confusion, we're inclined to assume that one Mode of Operation is sufficient to fulfill our basic commitment, and we're inclined to assume that the basic commitment in its full breadth and depth can be met by per-formance with a single Motif. We overlook the multiplicity of Modes of Operation, the orderly sequence of their unfolding, the relations of the Modes to one another, and their relations to the basic notions. We overlook the multiplicity of basic interests and the corresponding multiplicity of Motifs. We overlook the inherent and exclusive self-interest of every Motif. We overlook the emphasis, the narrowing, the contraction, the diminishment, and the suppression of specific Modes of Conscious Performance that occur with every Motif. We fail to see the radical difference between attentive, intelligent, reasonable, and responsible performance with a specific Motif, on the one hand, and attentive, intelligent, reasonable, and responsible performance that *exceeds the reach* of every Motif, on the other. We assume that the way we happen to have developed so far as conscious performers is the way we ought to be. We confuse the strictly circumscribed, same-staying authenticity of deliberate but *relatively unreflective* self-possession with the unbounded, different-becoming authenticity of deliberate and *reflective* self-possession. We become Ensconced Spontaneous Subjects.

When we mistake relatively unreflective self-possession for adequate self-possession, we claim for ourselves the authority to interpret and evaluate the conscious performance of subjects operating in other Motifs by the criteria of relevance, significance, and importance proper to the Motif in which we happen to have found ourselves. If we propagate this mistaken conception of personal authenticity, we open the door for subjects ensconced in one Motif to critique, by appealing to the criteria of their own Motifs, subjects operating in others. We grant ensconced Practical Subjects, for example, authority to critique the performance and products of Intellectual, Aesthetic, Dramatic, and Mystical Subjects. We invite a totalitarian practicality to press art into the service of economics and politics, to silence and imprison intellectuals, to torture and banish mystics, to replace creative dramatic interaction with management techniques and to impose dramatic conformity, and to drain the deep reservoir of language available for the expression of human emotion until only the dregs of iChat emoticons and texting abbreviations remain. Again, we grant ensconced Intellectual Subjects authority to critique the performance and products of Practical, Aesthetic, Dramatic, and Mystical Subjects. We invite scientists to denigrate practical common sense, to reduce artistic creativity, intellectual insight, mystical experience, and dramatic creativity to neurological events, hormones, and genes, and to ridicule religious faith as primitive superstition. We invite philosophers to depict ordinary living as unenlightened and akin to cave dwelling and to declare themselves the only ones qualified to rule. Again, we invite ensconced Mystical Subjects to set themselves up as authoritative critics of the products, performance, and lives of Aesthetic, Dramatic, Intellectual, and Practical subjects, to arrogate to themselves political power, to carry out inquisitions of artists and intellectuals, to discount and dismiss selected scientific achievements, and to force creative dramatic living into religiously-sanctioned practices and routines.

When we confuse reflective self-possession with relatively unreflective self-possession, we give our tacit consent to an all-out war of interpretations and evaluations among subjects committed to specific Motifs, and we implicitly deny the possibility of a peaceful resolution short of absolute dominance of the entire culture by subjects who declare their own "finished state" the ideal of human authenticity.

The self-possession anticipated by CPA is not the deliberate choice of myself as I happen to have become spontaneously, before I ever intervened seriously in my own process of development. It is not the simple matter of settling comfortably or – as is more likely to be the case, given the unrestricted and comprehensive reach of the basic notions – somewhat uncomfortably into myself as I happen to have become. The self-knowledge that makes possible the self-possession anticipated by CPA is not the knowledge of myself as, for example, spontaneously self-righteous, spontaneously Practical, and spontaneously dismissive of intellectual inquiry and aesthetic sensitivity. Nor is it the knowledge of myself as spontaneously unquestioning, spontaneously Aesthetic, and spontaneously dismissive of practical intelligence and theoretical understanding. Nor is it the knowledge of myself as spontaneously speculative, spontaneously Intellectual, and spontaneously dismissive of practical intelligence, artistic sensibility, dramatic artistry, and mystical contemplation. Nor is it the knowledge of myself as spontaneously self-righteous, spontaneously Mystical, and spontaneously dismissive of practicality, intellectual inquiry, artistic creativity, and dramatic self-distinction.

The self-knowledge that makes possible the self-possession anticipated by CPA *is fundamental knowledge of myself in my basic commitment,* of myself as committed to meaning, objectivity, knowledge, truth, reality, and value in their indeterminate breadth and depth, as characterized fundamentally by *four Moods and four Modes of Operation,* and as focused, in alternation and combination, by *five Basic Interests.* It is a self-knowledge obtained by Intellectual reflection on the notions as operative or at work, a self-knowledge that enables me *to evaluate critically* my present, spontaneous relationship to the basic notions that inform and guide my conscious performance. It is a fundamental knowledge of myself in my most basic anticipations of meaning, objectivity, knowledge, truth, reality, and value, over and above my actual achievements or attainments at this point in my life of meaning, objectivity, knowledge, truth, reality, and value. (See Diagram IX in Appendix II) It is my knowledge of myself, not as emphasizing one Mode of Operation or another, not as emphasizing one Motif or another, but as a concretely existing human being with a basic commitment that *always exceeds* my commitment as it unfolds with any Motif. It is my knowledge of myself, not narrowly defined as a practical being, or as an aesthetic being, or as an intellectual being, or as a social being, or as a religious being, but as broadly defined as a human being who is potentially all of these and who defines for myself the kind of human being I shall become.

3.2 THE REFLECTIVE AND DELIBERATE SUBJECT

Fundamental self-knowledge enables me to take possession of myself as a conscious performer. It enables me to ask and answer for myself two sets of question that, before I came to know myself in this way, I could not formulate clearly and precisely [See Diagram IX in Appendix II.]

I ask the first set of questions for the sake of understanding correctly *the type of subject I have already more or less spontaneously become.* I ask the second set of questions for the sake of determining for myself *the type of subject I will deliberately make of myself.*

What Type of Subject Am I Now? What type of subject have I been so far? What kind of subject am I? What is my present relationship to the basic notions of meaning, objectivity, knowledge, truth, reality, and value? Do I emphasize one Mode of Operation and suppress other Modes? Have I been operating predominantly with one Motif or one blend of Motifs? Am I predominantly Practical, Intellectual, Aesthetic, Dramatic, or Mystical, or some blend of two or more of these? What Motif or Motifs most frequently characterize my performance? When I perform intermittently with other Motifs, do I always give them a twist that reveals my dominant Motif? Do I tend to dismiss other Motifs or to enslave them to my dominant interest? With which Motifs am I most at ease, and with which am I most uneasy? In which Motif do I feel most at home? With which Motifs do I experience the greatest degree of personal risk? Do I shift easily or with great difficulty from one Motif to another in reaction to the demands or in response to the invitations of my ever-changing situation? Do I tend to ignore those aspects of my situation that I cannot handle easily with my dominant Motif? Do I avoid situations in which performance in other Motifs would be more appropriate, and do I gravitate toward or seek out situations in which performance with my dominant Motif seems most appropriate? How susceptible am I to the contracting specifications of the meanings of the basic notions in my dominant Motif? Do I fail to find significance where others find it? Do I fail to discern value where others discern it? How frequently do I catch myself lapsing into performative self-contradiction? Do I even take my entanglement in performative self-contradiction seriously? Am I unembarrassed and unfazed by performative self-contradiction? Am I attentive, intelligent, reasonable, and responsible only within the confines of my dominant Motif? Am I even attentive, intelligent, reasonable, and responsible with my dominant Motif? Do my attentiveness, intelligence, reasonableness, and responsibility ever point me beyond the effective range of my dominant Motif, lead me to question the present adequacy of my Motif, lead me out of my dominant Motif and into another? Do I ever abandon my dominant Motif in response to the demands or invitations of my situation? Have I experienced the disorientation and awkwardness that accompanies ventures into Motifs with which I'm unfamiliar? What invitations of the given do I never accept? Am I more committed to being consistently Practical, or Intellectual, or Aesthetic, or Dramatic, or Mystical, than I am to adhering to my over-reaching basic commitment? Has my inescapable commitment been relatively unreflective, spontaneous, and half-hearted, or has it been reflective, deliberate, and wholehearted? What has been my story so far? What type of subject have I become? What type of subject am I now? How do I justify to myself and to others being the kind of subject I find myself to be? Are the criteria to which I appeal to justify being that way recognizable as the criteria imposed by an interest that governs a specific Motif? What kind of subject *am I now?*

What Type of Subject Shall I Become? Given what I know now about myself as a conscious performer, what type of subject shall I become? Should I reaffirm the spontaneous emphases I find already in place and become an Ensconced Spontaneous Subject, or should I adopt a new, reflective and deliberate posture that enables me to bind myself tightly in any Motif to my most basic commitment whose demands always exceed those made upon me in any Motif? Should I adopt a reflective and deliberate posture that enables me to counteract the self-interest inherent in every Motif, to resist the inclination in every Motif to totalize its criteria of significance, importance, and relevance, and to shift smoothly and easily from one Motif to another as the ever-changing nature of my situation requires? Given what I know about myself and my development so far, what type of subject *can I become?* Are there measures I should take to augment my capacity to develop in new ways? How should my story unfold from here on out? What type of subject *should I become?*

No one can answer these two sets of questions for me. I must answer them for myself from within the unique dramatic context of the life I'm living. This is a daunting challenge. Can I meet it? How shall I meet it?

3.3 "BE YOURSELF!"

When we approach those dramatic decisions that may alter the course of our lives, it's not uncommon for us to augment and inform our own Evaluative Operations by seeking the sage advice of others. This advice frequently comes in the form of familiar precepts. Often the precepts are relevant especially to performance with a specific Motif. In my discussion of the various Motifs, I provided examples of the sorts of precepts issued by subjects with a particular Motif for subjects with the same Motif. But there is one familiar precept that seems relevant to performance with any Motif: *Be Yourself!* This may be one of the most profound pieces of advice we receive from others. It also seems to be one of the vaguest, most ambiguous, and most puzzling pieces of advice we receive. Perhaps we're in a position now to give a clear and precise meaning to this familiar precept and to derive the benefits of its profundity.

SEEKING GOOD ADVICE

Suppose I'm about to engage in dramatic performance of which I have no prior experience. I've never done before what I'm being called upon to do. A lot depends on how well I perform. I'm extremely nervous and ill at ease. I don't know if I have the resources to do it. I don't know if I'm up to it. I doubt my ability to act appropriately. I'm very worried about how others will evaluate my performance. I feel like their evaluation could make a huge difference in my life. I just don't know how to prepare, and I don't know how I should act.

Suppose I turn for help to a trusted friend. Reluctantly, I express my lack of confidence, my fear of failure, my uncertainty, and my anxiety. She hears me out, and then, with the best of intentions and a sympathetic smile, she offers me this sage bit of advice, "You'll be fine. Just be yourself!"

I realize she means well, but I'm distraught and on edge. I was hoping for something a bit more specific, for some guidelines, some rules I can follow, something like that. I think to myself, "Great! That's a big help. Be myself!

I *already am* myself. What else *can* I be but *myself?* Didn't I just tell her *I don't know what to do? That* is myself, the one who *doesn't know what to do!* Obviously, continuing to be myself isn't going to solve my problem! I'm being myself right now, I haven't got much choice about that, and 'myself' is asking for advice, because I'm totally anxious and confused. What kind of advice is that?! What exactly am I supposed to do to be myself that I'm not already doing? Ok, I'm worried and pretty upset. I know I'm taking her advice too literally. I know she's trying to help and means well. She *can't mean* I should just be the way I already am – nervous, on edge, worried. That would be totally useless advice. If I followed it, I'd be exactly where I am right now. It *must mean* more than that! But what *does* it mean, and what on earth *should I do to follow it?!"*

I notice that my well-meaning friend has been watching me, awaiting a response. "Thanks," I say, exhibiting relief I don't feel at all. "Right, I guess that's all I *can* do!"

When the precept "Be Yourself!" is meant and taken literally it is of little help. It's merely an expression of confidence in my ability to decide and act appropriately. When it's meant and taken slightly less literally, it encourages me to take stock of myself as operating predominantly in one Mode or with one Motif of Conscious Performance and to take possession of myself as I already happen to be. It encourages me to become or to continue to be an Ensconced Spontaneous Subject, and it suggests that my present problem, whatever it might be, will be solved by deciding to be the way I happen to be already.

But, when I face a serious dramatic decision, I'm challenged to perform *creatively* in a situation in which *I've never performed before.* As an Ensconced Spontaneous Subject, I will decide to perform only in ways I've previously performed, to do only what I've previously done, emphasizing my preferred Mode or Modes of Operation and with my preferred Motif or blend of Motifs. If the situation in which I'm called upon to perform requires the attentiveness, intelligence, reasonableness, and responsibility proper to performance in another Motif, I shall fail miserably, and my worst fears might be realized.

The precept "Be Yourself!" is meant to be profound advice. Certainly, I benefit from encouragement that bolsters my confidence in my ability to deal with the problematic situation I face. If the situation I face happens to demand no more of me than greater determination to be the way I usually am, I'll benefit as well. But the situation I face may require more of me. Then the advice may elicit in me a sweeping *reflective* attentiveness, intelligence, reasonableness, and responsibility that extends beyond the limited range of my preferred Mode of Operation or my preferred Motif of Conscious Performance and issues in creative action appropriate to my present situation. It may call me to diverge from my settled ways, and it may evoke in me a transformation of my unreflective and spontaneous commitment into a reflective and deliberate commitment, a tightening up of my relationship to the basic notions, and a resolution to take my stand, not upon myself as I have been and just happen to be, but upon myself in my basic commitment, upon myself in my most basic human aspirations. It may invite me to attend with a readiness to break the boundaries of my spontaneous or habitual attentiveness, to inquire with a readiness to exceed the limits of my spontaneous or habitual intelligence, to criticize with a readiness to exceed the limits of my spontaneous or habitual reasonableness, to deliberate, evaluate, and decide with a readiness to exceed the spontaneous or habitual reach of my deliberating, evaluating, and deciding. It may invite me to become a Reflective and Deliberate Subject. But, when the advice is offered in its terse and unelaborated form *by* an Ensconced Spontaneous Subject, it invites a contracted and limited attentiveness, intelligence, reasonableness, and responsibility that may issue in profoundly inattentive, unintelligent, unreasonable, and irresponsible action. We may be reminded of the proverb, "The road to hell is paved with good intentions." Perhaps, we should say that the road to dramatic disaster might be paved with apparently good Moods.

With the self-knowledge afforded by CPA, we can issue the profound precept "Be Yourself!" more clearly, precisely, and helpfully to others and to ourselves. We're able to unpack the compact precept and bring to light the fundamental precept of conscious performance hidden within it: *Be Reflectively and Deliberately Attentive, Intelligent, Reasonable, and Responsible! Be a Reflective and Deliberate Subject!* In short, go with the conscious flow, but ensure that that flow is the orderly flow of the operative basic commitment to meaning, objectivity, knowledge, truth, reality, and value.

3.4 The Puzzling Problem of the Criterion

Residual Uneasiness: What's the Criterion of Truth and Value?

Alright, I've stuck with it. Here I am at the final chapter and, to me at least, there's something bothersome and unsatisfactory about all this. It's been bothering me from the very beginning. I accepted the invitation to do CPA, and I tried to set this problem aside. But I've had to struggle to contain my dissatisfaction, because the same question kept popping up again and again. There's something I've been looking for that I'm just not finding. Sure, I could be missing something. I'm open to that possibility. But I really don't think my complaint is superficial or unfounded. I wouldn't be true to myself if I brushed this question aside! (I know you'd agree with that! ☺) You're probably expecting me to say that CPA has been too intellectual for me, that I don't think it's practical enough, or aesthetic enough, or mystical enough, or dramatic enough. But that's not the issue for me. If I said that, I'd be one of those Ensconced Spontaneous Subjects you talked about, wouldn't I? I see the problem with that weak, unreflective kind of self-possession, and that's not where I'm coming from. At least, I hope it isn't. I guess I might as well put my problem in terms of what you were just saying about "being yourself," because that bothers me in just the same way, and it looks like this book might end without dealing with what's really been bothering me.

How can I put this so that you see what my problem is? In light of what I've discovered about myself in CPA – my basic commitment, my basic notions, my basic moods, my basic modes of operation, my basic interests, and the relations of all these to one another – I'm supposed to be reflectively and deliberately attentive, intelligent, reasonable, and responsible. Sounds great, but here's my problem. What *standard* am I supposed to use to determine what I *should* attend to, what questions I *should* ask, which of my ideas are *correct* and which aren't, which courses of action are *worthwhile* and which aren't, and even which motif is *appropriate* to a certain situation? What's the standard? What *criterion* am I supposed to use to make these judgments and decisions? You say I should tie myself reflectively and deliberately to my basic commitment. But my basic commitment is to something I really can't define. You said so yourself! The basic notions exceed or go beyond or over-reach any specific meanings we try to give them. If I can't say exactly what I'm anticipating in my basic commitment, how can I know when I've reached it? All along I've had this problem. You've talked about under-standing meanings, judging their correctness, and evaluating possible courses of action. But what's the criterion of truth? What's the criterion of value? How am I supposed to know when I've reached the truth or discerned a true value?

So that's my problem. I guess you could call it "the problem of the standard or criterion." I was expecting you to address this problem. Maybe you have, but it still seems to me like you haven't. Am I missing something?

How am I to determine the demands and requirements of my situation? How will I know when I've understood my situation correctly? What is the criterion of truth? How will I know when I've discerned the true value of a possible course of action? What is the criterion of true value? Our interest throughout has been to discover the basic notions at work in our own conscious per-formance. When we raise these questions about the criterion, the basic notions are at work *yet again*. So, in order to answer these questions, let's turn our attention to the course we must follow when we search for this all-important but seemingly elusive criterion.

We begin with *our experience of ourselves in our uneasiness and as confused about the criterion*. We're in the Mood of intelligence, troubled by an unanswered question. We realize we're perplexed about the standard or criterion to which we might appeal. We express our perplexity in *questions*: What is the criterion of truth? What is the criterion of true value? We proceed to *inquire*, undaunted and uninhibited by the seeming absence of a known criterion that could bring our inquiry in pursuit of the criterion to a satisfactory conclusion. Without a known criterion of truth, we nevertheless *set off in pursuit of ideas* about the criterion of truth, and we *anticipate making a true judgment* about those ideas. Without a known criterion of true value, we take it for granted that this inquiry of ours into the nature of the criterion *is worth our time and effort*. To what criterion of truth shall we appeal to bring *this* inquiry to a satisfactory conclusion? *To what criterion of truth are we already appealing* in our pursuit of knowledge of the criterion of truth? *To what criterion of true value have we already appealed to motivate this inquiry* into the criterion of truth and true value?

An Already-Operative Criterion. The criterion we seek is already operative in our pursuit of knowledge of the criterion. We appealed to it surreptitiously, although not unconsciously, to motivate our inquiry, and we appeal to it surreptitiously, although not unconsciously, throughout our inquiry. It is *the basic notions at work* in our orderly conscious performance. As has been repeated so many times throughout this book, our conscious performance is constituted and guided by the basic notions. It is precisely for the sake of coming to know the criterion of truth and true value that we undertook our investigation of the basic notions at work in our conscious performance. This is the point of doing CPA.

Do we anticipate, then, that the criterion we seek will turn out to be *different from* the criterion we'll appeal to in order to bring an end to *this inquiry* into the criterion? In the interest of getting a good grasp of this fundamental issue, let's suppose the impossible. Suppose that we discover, by our performance of Wondering and Critical Operations, that the actual criterion of truth and true value *is not* the criterion to which we have appealed to motivate our inquiry and to bring it to its conclusion. Suppose that, by relying upon the basic notions at work in our conscious performance, we find ourselves *reasonably compelled* to conclude that the actual criterion of truth and true value *is not* the orderly unfolding of conscious performance constituted and guided by the basic notions. What, then, will be the *reasonable* thing to do? We will have to turn around and *toss out* this supposedly new knowledge of the *different* criterion, because we will have found that *the criterion to which we have appealed to obtain this new knowledge is not the right criterion!*

In the reasonably skeptical pursuit of the criterion, we find ourselves in an inescapable bind. If, in our pursuit of the true criterion, we discover that the true criterion is not the criterion operative in our pursuit of the true criterion, that it is not the one to which we appealed to bring our inquiry to a conclusion, then we must *retract the judgment* that the criterion we've discovered is the true criterion *as soon as we make it.* In short, we simply *cannot make the judgment* that the criterion of truth and true value is different from *the notions of meaning, objectivity, knowledge, truth, reality, and value at work in our conscious performance.* The idea doesn't make sense, and so the judgment that it's true can't be a true judgment.

To take possession of ourselves in our basic commitment is to make our own, and to be at home with, *the already operative criterion* of truth and true value. We have no intelligent, reasonable, and responsible alternative but to trust ourselves in our reflective and deliberate conscious performance. Every other course leads us into embarrassing performative self-contradiction. The puzzling problem of the criterion is solved, then, *by taking ourselves as puzzled conscious performers seriously* and by settling into the basic Moods of attentiveness, intelligence, reasonableness, and responsibility as our basic commitment unfolds.

How, then, are we to know when we're succeeding in our pursuit of true meanings and true values? How are we to go about being ourselves, not merely in the deliberate but still relatively unreflective fashion of the Ensconced Spontaneous Subject, but in the deliberate and reflective manner of the subject who is truly at home with herself?

As the criterion of truth and true value resides in the orderly unfolding of the four Moods and Modes of Conscious Performance, our success in the pursuit of truth and true value depends upon *our adherence to the basic commitment operative in our own conscious performance.* If we make this basic commitment our own and undertake to remain true to it – if we transform our relationship to this commitment by raising it to the level of a reflective and deliberate commitment – we will be more likely to perform attentively, intelligently, reasonably, and responsibly when we're operating in the various Motifs and blends of Motifs. Moreover, we will be less likely to fall into the trap of operating with one Motif or blend of Motifs when and where another Motif or blend is called for. Our basic Moods of attentiveness, intelligence, reasonableness, and responsibility are our intimately self-present commitment to the basic notions. The basic Moods anticipate and evoke the questions that determine the adequacy of our performance with the various Motifs and blends of Motifs. The basic Moods anticipate and evoke the questions by which we move from one Mode of Operation to the next and by which we exceed, overreach, supersede, go beyond the limited attentiveness, intelligence, reasonableness, and responsibility required by any particular Motif or blend of Motifs with which we happen to be performing. The basic Moods are our experience of being tethered to the basic notions, our experienced anticipation of meaning, objectivity, knowledge, truth, reality, and value. Only by performing in the spirit of these anticipations can we hope to satisfy, step by step, our desire for meaning, objectivity, knowledge, truth, reality, and value. Only by following reflectively and deliberately the fundamental precept – Be reflectively and deliberately attentive, intelligent, reasonable, and responsible! – can we hope to satisfy our inescapable desire for truth and true value.

4. THE REFLECTIVE AND DELIBERATE COMMITMENT

CPA *heightens* our presence to ourselves as conscious performers, *informs* our intelligence and reasonableness in our conscious performance, and *enables us to transform* our responsibility in our conscious performance. In CPA, we reflectively expose ourselves to ourselves in our basic commitment and reflectively familiarize ourselves with ourselves as conscious performers. This new, reflective familiarity with ourselves as conscious performers makes concretely possible a set of decisions that assist in the transformation of our unreflective and spontaneous performance into reflective and deliberate or self-possessed performance and that assist us as well in our efforts to resist being victimized by the limitations and deficiencies inherent in every Motif [See Diagram X in Appendix II].

4.1 HEIGHTENED AND INFORMED SELF-PRESENCE AFTER CPA

Before we undertook CPA, our basic Moods were, so to speak, 'behind' us, obscured, and clouded over. We hadn't yet undertaken this reflective inquiry. Our basic Moods weren't distinguished from our many other moods, "mixed feelings," desires and fears, and isolated from the distracting contents that accompany them, blend with them, or often displace them. Now that we've isolated them, identified them, and discovered their inescapable role and significance in our living, we're able to "get behind" *them*, take possession of them, make them truly our own. Prior to undertaking CPA, we experienced but took no special notice of these basic but subtle modifications of our intimate presence to ourselves. Our basic Moods were just a faint and inadvertently felt background.

Now, the intelligent mood of intellectual wonder, the reasonable mood of critical doubt, and the responsible mood of evaluative conscience have taken their rightful places in the vividly felt foreground of our self-experience.

In the past I may have put the nagging uneasiness I felt when I ignored or dismissed my intelligent perplexity, my reasonable doubts, and my responsible reservations on a par with other feelings that come and go, emerge and recede, in the flow of my self-presence. Because I had not identified that uneasiness, explored it, and discovered its fundamental role in the unfolding of my life, it was easily swamped by other feelings, confused with them, or displaced by them. I may have given it no more notice than I give a momentary spell of indigestion, a shooting pain in my leg, or a hunger pang. Now, having reflected upon myself as a conscious performer, I recognize that uneasiness as one of a variety of familiar expressions of the pressure exerted upon me by my inescapable basic commitment. I find now that I have to make a concerted effort to overlook this intelligent or reasonable or responsible uneasiness and to resist the subtle pressure it exerts upon me – the pressure I spontaneously exert upon myself – to superimpose upon my Question-free performance my orderly pursuit of meaning, objectivity, knowledge, truth, reality, and value. My very self-presence has undergone an important change. Now, because it has been identified and named, and its role in my living has been explored and understood, I can't help but notice what, before I engaged in CPA, I hardly noticed and rarely attended to. My Question-free presence to myself as a conscious performer is no longer my presence to myself before I've reflected upon myself; it is my Question-free presence to myself as a conscious performer subsequent to the prolonged meditative digression that was initiated by my Elemental Meditation. My presence to myself in my basic commitment *is sharpened or heightened by CPA.*

My self-presence in my basic commitment – in my attentiveness, intelligence, reasonableness, and responsibility – is also *informed by CPA.* To carry out CPA is to bring about a development in my *knowledge of myself* as a conscious performer; it is to become more knowledgeable *in* my conscious performance. Because I know now about my basic Moods and their relationships to my Modes of Operation, I'm able to promote and enforce my own attentiveness, intelligence, reasonableness, and responsibility. I'm able to deliberately perform Question-free, Wondering, Critical, and Evaluative Operations and deliberately enforce the spontaneous order of my Modes of Operation.

Moreover, my exploration of the basic notions at work has shed light not only on my pursuit of meaning, objectivity, knowledge, truth, reality, and value but also on the elusive meanings of these basic notions. Now I'm able to give an account of the meanings of the basic notions without involving myself in the circular reasoning I fell into on my first attempt in Chapter One. This is a very important advance in my understanding of my basic commitment, because it enables me to distinguish between *the specific meanings* I give spontaneously to the basic notions in the various Motifs and their always over-reaching *operative meanings*. My familiarity with this all-important distinction reduces the likelihood that I will confuse the specific meanings given to the notions in the various Motifs with the meanings of the notions at work or their operative meaning and, consequently, dismiss those questions of meaning and value that would take me beyond the limited range of my performance in a particular Motif.

4.2   THE OPERATIVE MEANINGS OF THE BASIC NOTIONS

Let's recall what happened in Chapter 1 when we attempted to define the basic notions. We found ourselves involved in a peculiar circularity. When we asked, for example, "What is the meaning of meaning?" we found ourselves having to take for granted the meaning of meaning in our very pursuit of it, just as we found ourselves, a moment ago, having to take for granted the operative criterion of truth in our effort to discover the true criterion. The basic notions, I concluded, are not to be thought of as products of our conscious performance, like ideas or concepts, but as *already at work* in our production of ideas and concepts. Later, we observed how the meanings of the basic notions are specified in each of the Motifs and given the determinateness of conceptual products. We noted that the meanings of the notions *always exceed* the specific meanings assigned them in the various Motifs, and we were alerted to the danger of identifying the over-reaching operative meanings of the basic notions with their specific meanings in the various Motifs. In short, we found that it is futile to attempt to define the basic notions the way we define some determinate object or some determinate goal. However, our exploration of the basic notions at work, as informing and guiding our conscious performance, enables us to draw some general conclusions about the elusive meanings of the basic notions. We arrive at these conclusions simply by drawing out the implications of our exploration of the notions at work. These conclusions, once drawn out, will serve to inform and guide us in our deliberate effort to take possession of ourselves in our basic commitment.

CPA doesn't enable us to define meaning, objectivity, knowledge, truth, reality, and value *directly*. It doesn't alter any of the facts about our basic commitment. It doesn't enable us to say precisely and clearly just *what* meaning, objectivity, knowledge, truth, reality, and value *are*. But it does enable us to define the basic notions *indirectly*. It enables us to say, with a precision and clarity that eluded us before we undertook CPA, just *how we are to go about seeking and finding* meaning, objectivity, knowledge, truth, reality, and value. To define some X by saying *how we go about seeking and finding* that X is not to define that X *directly* but to define that X *indirectly and heuristically*. Let's see what CPA enables us to say now heuristically about the meanings of the basic notions.

Heuristic Definitions of Meaning and Nonsense. Meaning is what is sought, reached, and expressed by the orderly performance of Wondering Operations: questioning, heuristic imagining, understanding, conceiving, and formulating. It is what we are present to ourselves as anticipating when we are in the intelligent Mood. It is what we are present to ourselves as seeking when we raise intelligent questions. It is what we are present to ourselves as discovering when we come up with a "good idea." It is what we are present to ourselves as conceiving and formulating when we isolate the essentials of an idea and express the idea linguistically or in some other way. My discovery of meaning depends upon my adherence to the basic commitment operative in my Wondering Operations. The criterion of meaning is the satisfaction of the intelligent wonder that takes me beyond mere Question-free performance and moves me to ask, to produce heuristic images, to understand, to conceive, and to formulate what I've understood.

Sometimes our intelligent anticipation of meaning is finally frustrated, and our performance of Wondering Operations bears no fruit. We wonder about a given thing, event, or situation; we produce heuristic images in the hope of triggering an insight. But despite our efforts, the optimistic flow of intelligent anticipation becomes an ever-deeper pool of intelligent pessimism. Renewed attentiveness to the object of our inquiry does us no good; reformulations of the guiding question make no difference; revisions and reconstructions of our heuristic images get us nowhere. Intellectual frustration builds until at last it dawns on us that the given thing, event, or situation may actually make no sense at all. We do finally get an idea, but it is the unusual and unexpected idea that, in this case, there is no meaning to be grasped, nothing to be understood. As in the case of every act of understanding, the accumulated tension of prolonged inquiry is temporarily relieved. But, because our understanding in this case is not of a possibly correct answer to the question with which we began but of the pointlessness of continuing to ask that question, we're left with a residue of puzzlement and a lingering dissatisfaction that there may be some things, events, or situations that do not make any sense at all.

Meaning is what we seek when we perform Wondering Operations; it's what we reach when we get insights; it's what we expected but find strangely lacking when, in some situations, we understand that there's no understanding to be had.

Heuristic Definitions of Objectivity and Bias. Objectivity is what is achieved through the orderly performance of the four Modes of Operation. It is attentive, intelligent, reasonable, and responsible subjectivity, or what we may call *authentic subjectivity*, as opposed to the disorderly or derailed subjectivity of inattentive, unintelligent, unreasonable, and irresponsible performance. Objectivity in the Question-free Mode is intelligent, reasonable, and responsible attentiveness to the given. Objectivity in the Wondering Mode is attentive, reasonable, and responsible intelligence in pursuit of meaning. Objectivity in the Critical Mode is attentive, intelligent, and responsible reasonableness in the pursuit of knowledge, truth, and the real. Objectivity in the Evaluative Mode is attentive, intelligent, and reasonable responsibility in the discernment and creation of what's worthwhile. My achievement of objectivity depends upon my adherence to the basic commitment incipient in my Question-free operations and ever more fully operative in my Wondering, Critical, and Evaluative Operations. We can distinguish between *the minor objectivity* of attentive, intelligent, reasonable, and responsible performance within the limits imposed by the specification of the notions in a specific Motif, on the one hand, and *the major objectivity* of attentive, intelligent, reasonable, and responsible performance that takes us beyond those limits.

Objectivity – attentive, intelligent, reasonable, and responsible conscious performance – is not achieved in isolation. It is achieved in community with other authentic subjects. My own adherence to my basic commitment in the past has been uneven, sporadic, intermittent. My present attentiveness is limited by my developed interests; my present intelligence and reasonableness are limited by my previous attentiveness and intellectual development; my present responsibility is limited by my previous attentiveness, intellectual development, and moral development. To rely entirely on my own conscious performance in my pursuit of objectivity is, in a sense, to presume I'm not a conscious *performer* at all, that I am not a subject who *develops*, who begins in ignorance and moves by sometimes tiny and sometimes giant steps towards objective knowledge of truths and true values, and whose present standpoint on the matter-at-hand is not a result of *previous conscious performance.*

Authentic subjectivity requires participation in a community of authentic subjects. If I am to achieve objectivity, in addition to engaging in my own pursuit of truth and true value I must turn to and rely upon others whose basic commitment was strong where and when my commitment was weak or lapsed, who are more perspicuously attentive to the pertinent given, who have asked and answered more questions about the things, events, or situations about which I'm inquiring, whose discernment of value is more developed and more sensitive than mine. I'm not just looking for people with more experience than I have. A person may have visited and photographed every monument in Europe and still have nothing intelligent to say about any of them. I'm looking for people who have gone beyond their mere Question-free experience to understand it, to make critical judgments about their understanding, and to make responsible choices in light of those judgments. I'm looking for people who are more developed than I am. I'm looking for people whose memories and expectations, as a result of their personal development, differ from mine. I attend to others as conscious performers, I raise intelligent questions about their authenticity as conscious performers, I ask critical questions about the ideas I get about them as conscious performers and, if I judge them to be credible subjects worthy of my trust, I decide to seek their assistance in my own pursuit of meaning, objectivity, knowledge, truth, reality, and value. I compensate for my personal history of limited and deficient adherence to the basic commitment in myself by making others' adherence to the basic commitment, and the fruits of their faithfulness to the basic commitment, my own. Authentic subjectivity is not isolated, individualistic conscious performance. The pursuit of objectivity is a collaborative enterprise.

Bias, on the other hand, is inattentive, unintelligent, unreasonable, or irresponsible performance, and it is non-performance where performance is called for. My Question-free performance may be excessively selective. My Wondering performance may be both inhibited and reinforced by a dominant Motif or by personal predilections, preferences, or prejudices. My Critical performance may be crippled by my failure or refusal to ask all the further relevant questions about my or others' ideas about the given. My Evaluative performance may be truncated, derailed, or misdirected by what I find personally pleasing or satisfying. If I undertake to rationalize, defend, and justify my inauthentic performance, I become an ideologue. Moreover, my inattentiveness, unintelligence, unreasonableness, and irresponsibility may be reinforced rather than tempered and corrected by my community. The community to which I would turn in search of others to assist me in my pursuit of objectivity may itself be biased. Bias may be manifested in our common spontaneous oversights or in our common deliberate refusal to attend, to ask, to decide, or to act.

Objectivity is what is achieved by authentic subjectivity in an authentic community. Bias is inauthentic subjectivity, and it is reinforced in an inauthentic community.

Heuristic Definition of Knowledge. Knowledge is what is achieved by the attentive, intelligent, reasonable, and responsible performance of Question-free, Wondering, and Critical Operations. It is not achieved by attentive Question-free performance alone, nor by attentive Question-free and intelligent Wondering performance alone, but by the orderly unfolding of attentive Question-free, intelligent Wondering, and reasonable Critical performance. I don't come to know simply by experiencing; by experiencing alone I simply encounter what I could come to know. I don't come to know simply by experiencing and understanding; by experiencing and understanding alone, I simply obtain bright ideas that may or may not be correct. I come to know by experiencing attentively, understanding intelligently, and judging critically. Knowledge isn't achieved by just looking around, by seeing what is there to be seen, by mere extroversion; self-knowledge isn't achieved by self-presence alone. Knowledge isn't achieved by just thinking, by getting a "good idea," by merely understanding. Knowledge is achieved by asking and answering all of the relevant questions about the adequacy of my ideas about the sensible or self-present given. The criterion of objectivity in my knowing is above all the resolution and evaporation of the reasonable doubt that takes me beyond mere Wondering performance and moves me to ask critical questions about my ideas, to seek out the critical questions of others, to assemble and weigh the evidence, to grasp that the evidence is sufficient, and to make a critical judgment.

Heuristic Definition of Truth. Truth is both a quality of objective judgments and the content of objective judgments. An objective judgment is both a true judgment and a judgment that all of the conditions are fulfilled, that all of the evidence is in, for a prospective judgment being true. I reach a true judgment when I grasp that the conditions for its adequacy are fulfilled and acknowledge that fulfillment. The content of a judgment for which the conditions are fulfilled is a truth. The criterion of truth is not merely the presence of contents of Question-free operations. It is not merely the occurrence of exhilarating insights into my experience. It is the absence of any lingering and nagging doubts about the perspicuity of my Question-free performance and the correctness of my insights. But my judgments are made by me at my present stage of development in my present circumstances. The criterion of truth, then, is the absence not only of my own further relevant questions but also of the further relevant questions raised by others. My judgment is a true judgment when my conclusion that all the conditions are fulfilled survives not only my critical scrutiny but also critical scrutiny by other attentive, intelligent, reasonable, and responsible subjects.

Heuristic Definition of Reality. Knowledge of reality is the proximate objective of all my intelligent and reasonable questioning. Reality is what is known piecemeal in true judgments when all the relevant questions about a thing, event, or situation have been answered. It is not merely what is confronted through Question-free operations of sensing or merely what is given in Question-free self-presence. It is not known by seeing, hearing, tasting, smelling, touching, or feeling. It is not known by mere self-presence. That might be reality. But, if it is, it is reality under the aspect of mere experience as it is encountered in Question-free performance, and it is not known to be real simply because it is experientially encountered. Some of what we encounter in Question-free operations turns out not to be real at all. Some of what is real cannot be seen or imagined. The real is not merely what is understood through Question-free and Wondering operations alone. It is not known by merely getting insights into heuristic images. That might be reality. But, if it is, it is reality under the aspect of mere experience and understanding, and it is not known to be real simply because it has been experienced and understood. To have an idea is not yet to know the real. The real is what is reached in its fullness by the orderly performance of the first three

Modes of Operation. It is what is known in true judgments on the adequacy of my ideas about the sensible or self-present given.

Heuristic Definition of Value. Value is what is sought, discerned, and created in the attentive, intelligent, reasonable, and responsible performance of Evaluative Operations. It is what is known in objective judgments of value. It is what is brought into existence by attentive, intelligent, reasonable, and responsible action.

It might be what pleases or attracts me; it might be what makes me feel good. But the criterion of value is not found in the performance of Question-free operations or Question-free self-presence alone. It is found in the satisfaction of the responsible anticipation that takes me beyond myself as a Question-free performer, beyond myself as a Wondering performer, beyond myself as a Critical performer, and moves me toward responsible action that not only transforms the world but also transforms me. My discernment and creation of value depend upon my adherence to the basic commitment as it unfolds in my performance of Evaluative Operations. As the criterion of meaning is the satisfaction of my intelligent wonder, as the criterion of objectivity in my knowing is the resolution and evaporation of my and others' reasonable doubts, so the criterion of value is the quieting or calming of my responsible concern that takes me beyond mere knowledge and moves me to ask what is or would be worthwhile or more worthwhile, to envision possible courses of action, to evaluate them as good or bad or as better or worse, and to decide and act.

CPA has enabled us to define the basic notions of meaning, objectivity, knowledge, truth, reality, and value without involving ourselves in the peculiar circularity we encountered in Chapter 1. We have appealed to our prolonged reflection on the notions at work, as informing and guiding our conscious performance, to provide indirect, heuristic definitions of them. We haven't attempted presumptuously to define the basic notions directly. We haven't presumed to say, for example, what reality is or what value is. We realize that reality and value are revealed to us only gradually and in a piecemeal fashion as we engage in orderly conscious performance over time. But we haven't rested content either with our mere presence to ourselves as spontaneously committed to the pursuit of meaning, objectivity, knowledge, truth, reality, and value. While we haven't gone so far as to claim to know and discern what we cannot know and discern before we know and discern it, we have gotten far enough to be able to say with some precision how we are to go about knowing and discerning it.

4.3 FOUR TRANSFORMATIVE DECISIONS

Our general conclusions about the elusive meanings of the basic notions provide an intelligent and reasonable basis for the implementation of four responsible, transformative decisions about how we should proceed in our conscious performance if we hope to grasp meaning, achieve objectivity, reach knowledge and the truth about the real, and discern and create value. The four decisions are transformative, because they constitute a deliberate break with the derailing expectations that typically accompany our spontaneous extroversion, our spontaneous preference for sensible objects, our spontaneous resistance to shifting our attention from the contents of our operations to our operating, and our spontaneous, contracting specification of the basic notions in every Motif. They promote the implementation of the self-knowledge we've acquired in CPA. They are decisions that pertain directly to the reflective and deliberate governance and control of ourselves in our pursuit of meaning, objectivity, knowledge, reality, and value.

Choosing Objectivity. Objectivity is not merely extroverted attentiveness to the sensible given – seeing, hearing, smelling, tasting, touching, feeling just what is there to be seen, heard, smelled, tasted, touched, and felt. It is attentiveness to sensible data and to data of consciousness, and intelligent inquiry, and reasonable reflection, and responsible deliberation, evaluation, and decision. It is adherence to the basic commitment, not merely in the performance of this or that operation or in this or that Mode of Conscious Performance. It is adherence to the basic commitment throughout the complete orderly sequence of Modes of Conscious Performance. It is not simply attentive sensitivity to the given as given. It is not simply intelligent concern with meaning. It is not simply critical concern with truth. It is not simply responsible concern with value. It is all of these in their orderly, dynamic relations. It is being attuned to the basic commitment; it is authentic subjectivity. On the basis of her knowledge of her inescapable commitment, of the constitutive and guiding role of the basic notions, and of the orderly unfolding of the four Modes of Operation, the reflective and deliberate subject opts for attunement to her basic commitment.

On the basis of her knowledge of the dynamic, orderly unfolding of the basic commitment, the reflective and deliberate subject decides to identify objectivity with authentic subjectivity, to pursue objectivity as it has been indirectly and heuristically defined, and to remain alert to and to resist the interference of spontaneous extroversion with her orderly conscious performance.

Choosing Knowledge. Knowledge is not reached by the spontaneous or deliberate performance of a single operation or by performance in a single Mode of Operation. It is what is attained by the orderly performance of Question-free, Wondering, and Critical Operations, in that order. The reflective and deliberate subject distinguishes clearly between the relatively simple and effortless Question-free performance that merely reveals the demands and invitations of the given, Question-free experience of objects and situations previously known, and the relatively complex and strenuous performance of Question-free, Wondering, and Critical Operations by which new knowledge of truth is attained.

On the basis of her knowledge of the radical difference between Question-free performance, on the one hand, and Wondering and Critical performance, on the other, the reflective and deliberate subject decides to identify knowledge with what is achieved by the complete orderly sequence of Question-free, Wondering, and Critical Operations, to pursue knowledge as it has been indirectly and heuristically defined, and to remain alert to and to resist her inclination to claim knowledge on the basis either of Question-free performance alone, or of Wondering performance alone, or of the combination of Question-free and Wondering performance alone.

Choosing the Real. Reality is not encountered or confronted immediately without intellectual and critical control in Question-free performance or merely 'intuited' without critical control in Wondering performance. It is what is judged to be the case by the orderly performance of Question-free, Wondering, and Critical Operations. We have already explored in some depth our extroverted preference for sensible contents and the obstacle it presents to our pursuit of knowledge of ourselves as conscious performers. But, while our propensity to prefer sensible contents may be held in check temporarily for the purposes of CPA, it is never eliminated. Sensible encounter with the demanding and inviting given is a permanent feature of our conscious lives. The temptation to identify the real with the tangible, odiferous, colorful, noisy, flavorful, satisfying or dissatisfying demands and invitations of the given persists and competes with our intangible, odorless, colorless, and soundless anticipations of meaning, objectivity, knowledge, truth, reality, and value which, we have to assume, are themselves nevertheless real. Question-free performance will always be the most obvious mode of our conscious performance. But, as we have discovered through CPA, we would be mistaken if we were to conclude that the very obvious content of sensitive Question-free performance is obviously the real.

On the basis of her knowledge of the orderly sequence of Modes of Operation constitutive of knowledge of the truth, the reflective and deliberate subject decides to identify the real with what is known in true judgments on the correctness of her ideas about the sensible and self-present given, to pursue the real as it has been indirectly and heuristically defined, and to resist the temptation to identify the real either with the very obvious contents of Question-free performance alone or with the slightly less obvious contents of Wondering performance alone.

Choosing Value. Value is not what is found to be spontaneously satisfying in the performance of Question-free Operations. It is what is found to be worthwhile in the given situation or worth creating by the orderly, objective performance of Question-free, Wondering, Critical, and Evaluative Operations. In my pursuit of value I go beyond myself as I happen to be, to become the self I ought to be. What I presently find satisfying or dissatisfying and what I presently like or dislike are irrelevant to my discernment and creation of value, except insofar as my likes and dislikes may either divert my attention from what is truly worthwhile or incidentally draw my attention to it. The satisfying may also be valuable, but it is not known to be valuable just because it's satisfying. The dissatisfying may be worthless, but it's not known to be worthless just because it's dissatisfying. In my pursuit of value, as I move beyond myself as I am, I still am the self I am, and my feelings of satisfaction or dissatisfaction with the things, events, situations, and courses of action I'm evaluating may become entangled with my basic commitment to value or obscure it.

The reflective and deliberate subject decides to identify the valuable or the worthwhile with what is discerned in true judgments of value and created by action issuing from authentically subjective performance, to pursue the valuable or the worthwhile as it has been indirectly and heuristically defined, and to resist the temptation to make "what's personally satisfying" or "what I happen to prefer" or "what feels good" the criterion of value just because it happens to be satisfying or preferred or pleasant.

My conscious performance has been heightened and informed by CPA. I have come to know myself in my basic commitment, as performing in four Moods of four Modes, as performing in alternation and at least intermittently with five interests and with five Motifs, as committed to the pursuit of meaning, objectivity, knowledge, truth, reality, and value spontaneously in conformity with the contracting specifications of the basic notions in the five Motifs, and as exceeding in my basic commitment the limited commitments required of me in any particular Motif or blend of Motifs. The stage has been set for the four transformative decisions.

Self-Presence After CPA. My presence to myself in my basic commitment has been *sharpened and heightened* by my self-investigation. Now my basic commitment is present to me, not merely as an orderly or disorderly sequence of unidentified and unnamed feelings intermingled with other feelings in the flow of demands and invitations of the self-present given. It has taken on an urgency, a compelling quality, similar to that of the imperious instinctual demands that confront me in the sensible given, but also quite different from them and, unfortunately, not so intensely compelling. The instinctual demands of the sensible given are not intelligent, reasonable, and responsible demands for meaning, objectivity, knowledge, truth, reality, and value. They are the emergence into consciousness of pre-conscious non-intelligent, non-reasonable, non-responsible biological demands. They are to be met by eating, drinking, resting, sleeping, exercising, reproducing, and so on. They are met more efficiently and effectively when they are addressed with my basic commitment as it unfolds in the Practical Motif. But my now demanding basic commitment is to be met only by attentive, intelligent, reasonable, and responsible performance. These new demands of the self-present given are no longer an inadvertently felt uneasiness and perplexity that invited my undivided attention but didn't receive it. They are now known to be the intellectual, rational, and moral compulsion of my basic commitment. My basic Moods are no longer unknowingly felt; they're known to be felt, and they're felt as known. My experience of myself has been sharpened and heightened by CPA. Now that I know about these things, it takes more effort to ignore them, and it takes a strong tolerance for prolonged puzzlement, persistent doubts, and a nagging conscience to resist them.

Conscious Performance After CPA. CPA has enabled me to define indirectly and heuristically the basic notions that inform and guide my conscious performance. I may not be able to say precisely what meaning, reality, and value will turn out to be when I reach them, but I can say precisely now how to go about reaching them in any situation in which I decide to seek them. Moreover, it is now clear to me that the basic notions mean more than they are taken to mean spontaneously in any of the Motifs. I know now that neither Practical nor Intellectual nor Aesthetic nor Dramatic nor Mystical meaning alone captures the meaning of *meaning*, that none of these alone captures the full meaning of *objectivity*, that none of these alone is the only path to *knowledge,* that none of these alone is the only road to *truth.* I know now that neither the vital and social values of Practical performance, nor the cultural values of Intellectual and Aesthetic/Artistic performance, nor the personal value of Dramatic performance, nor the religious value of Mystical performance is the only *value* worth pursuing in every situation that arises. Just as *my presence to myself* in my basic commitment has been heightened by CPA, so too *my intelligent and reasonable relation to myself in my basic commitment* has been *informed* by CPA.

But what about *my responsible relation to myself in my basic commitment?* How has this been affected by CPA? There is no guaranteed effect of CPA upon my living. As we've seen, CPA by itself does not bring about this reflective, deliberate, responsible relation. The knowledge I acquire of myself in CPA makes the establishment of a new, responsible relation to myself in my basic commitment concretely possible, but self-knowledge by itself does not establish it. Self-knowledge, as I've noted repeatedly, is not self-possession. Only when I bring my heightened and informed self-presence to bear upon my conscious performance by way of the four transformative decisions do I begin to exercise the reflective and deliberate governance and control of myself that constitutes self-possessed performance. Only by making the truths I've discovered about myself as a conscious performer my own and putting them into action do I actually take possession of myself as a conscious performer. To make these truths my own is to make the four transformative decisions that my heuristic definitions of objectivity, knowledge, reality, and value enable me to make. It is to carry them out in deliberate and reflective control and governance of myself in my adherence to my basic commitment to the pursuit of meaning, objectivity, knowledge, truth, reality, and value in my performance of conscious operations in four Modes with five Motifs. With the implementation of the four transformative decisions, my attentive, intelligent, reasonable, and responsible pursuits of Practical, Intellectual, Aesthetic, Dramatic, and Mystical meaning and value become integral episodes in the encompassing high drama that is the ongoing reflective and deliberate pursuit of direction in the flow of my life. Now I'm no longer drifting. I'm *at home* in my conscious performance.

Appendix I

CPA AND OTHER APPROACHES

C PA differs from the standard contemporary approaches to the philosophical investigation of the basic notions of meaning, objectivity, knowledge, truth, reality, and value. For those who are familiar with contemporary philosophical practice, a brief comparison and contrast of CPA with two prominent approaches may prove helpful.

CONTRAST WITH THE *ARGUMENTATIVE APPROACH*

The great majority of contemporary introductions to Philosophy take what can be called "the argumentative approach." They introduce their readers to *arguments* that are ongoing and have been going on for quite some time. They are introductions to the state of those arguments, to this or that problem posed by someone, and to this or that response offered by someone else. They give the distinct impression that Philosophy is just a series of arguments, that the arguing is endless, and that nothing is ever resolved or settled. Commonly, they are collections of excerpts from larger works or of articles in which arguments are made for or against assigning this or that specific meaning to one or more of the basic notions which, as I have argued myself in Chapter 1, defy all attempts at precise definition, because all of those attempts presuppose the notions at work in the attempt to define them. The argumentative approach is, from the standpoint of CPA, pedagogically inappropriate, inherently superficial, and personally and culturally debilitating.

The argumentative approach is bad pedagogy, because beginning students should begin at the beginning, not somewhere in the middle. Wonder, as Socrates remarked in Plato's *Theaetetus,* is the feeling of the philosopher, and Philosophy begins in wonder. If the arguments are arguments about ourselves and our relationship to meaning, objectivity, knowledge, truth, reality, and value, then students should be introduced to the relevant experience, to these basic notions in their informing and guiding role in conscious performance, before they are plunged into arguments about the possible meanings of that experience. How will they be able to understand the arguments if they are unfamiliar with the data around which the arguments revolve? How will they be able to critically evaluate them, if they achieve only a speculative understanding of them because their understanding is unconnected to the data to be understood? How could they be convinced by any of the arguments without seeking out the evidence for themselves? How can they be expected to derive knowledge of themselves from them if their attention is not directed beyond the arguments to the conscious performance to which they pertain?

The argumentative approach is inherently superficial. It takes for granted and relies upon, but nevertheless studiously ignores or only indirectly alludes to, the conscious performance around which the arguments revolve and without which the arguments wouldn't and couldn't be made. With its emphasis upon ongoing arguments and its disregard of conscious performance, this approach gives the impression that Philosophy is just analysis of free-floating concepts and their logical relations and that a person will be sufficiently self-possessed if she is *sufficiently logical.* The argumentative approach obscures the concrete flow of conscious life by its adherence to the logical ideal that governs all argumentation. Simultaneously, it promotes performance governed strictly by the logical ideal. In doing so, it tends to restrict conscious performance to performance governed by the logical ideal. The logical ideal of consistency, coherence, and rigor – of precise definition and careful deduction and valid inference – is always to be sought in philosophical expression. But achievement of the logical ideal is *a minimal criterion* of adequate philosophical understanding and expression. It may be met satisfactorily by the logical manipulation of *any* arbitrarily selected set of meanings, true or false, fictitious or factual, worthy of serious attention or not worth considering at all. On this conception of Philosophy, perspicuous self-attention is not regarded as an advantage but as a distraction, and it is not encouraged. If we're good at the game of chess, we might conclude, we're equipped with all we need to be fine philosophers.

The limitations of the logical ideal of conceptual consistency, coherence, and rigor are widely recognized, but they don't seem to have been adequately appreciated and absorbed. Ordinarily, greater and more serious attention is paid to the conduct of arguments than to their premises, and more attention is paid to the premises than to the conscious performance out of which the premises arise. Pursuit of the logical ideal never takes us beyond and beneath concepts, their combination into propositions, the combination of propositions into arguments, and the combination of arguments into logically coherent and consistent theories. The logical ideal can only be pursued with and among the products of conscious performance.

We should take special notice of the differences between CPA as an introduction to philosophical reflection and the argumentative approach. CPA is primarily *a descriptive exploration* and only secondarily *a theory* in which the logical implications of that description are worked out in logical arguments. It is a descriptive exposition, not a logical analysis or treatise. It begins from descriptions of non-sensible experience, not from assumed premises. Its organization is determined by pedagogical motives, not by logical priority or by supposed metaphysical priority.

CPA is an attempt, through the careful use of the purified Language of Self-Possession, to direct attention to our own conscious performance, to the flow of our own conscious lives, as the unfolding pursuit of our basic commitment. Only gradually does there emerge a logically organized, conceptual framework as familiar words are given more-than-ordinary precision, as relations among the operations we perform are uncovered, and as dynamic sequences and structures of operations come to light. But, if the theory that results as we introduce logical order into our understanding of our conscious performance is to be *more than just another hypothetical theory*, it must be grounded *in close attention to the data* that is the flow of conscious performance itself. If we hope to avoid lapsing into merely conceptual analysis, if we hope to gain from this exploration more than possession of ourselves as capable of reasoning logically on the basis of premises we have never questioned, have never explored, and have never grounded, then we must maintain throughout our exploration close attention to our own conscious performance.

In CPA, we must beware of setting in motion and promoting the *logicism* which afflicts so many introductions to the philosophic pursuit of self-knowledge and self-possession. Not only does that approach obscure the conscious performance which reflective self-attention would bring to light and the Language of Self-Possession would specify, but it also tends to transform the concrete, passionate pursuit of self-knowledge and self-possession into a fruitless and frustrating tour of conflicting hypotheses that leaves the student confused, numb, disaffected, and alienated from Philosophy.

CONTRAST WITH THE *CRITICAL THINKING APPROACH*

Similar criticisms may be offered of the proliferating introductions to "critical thinking," and they may be extended to include in their critical sweep the so-called "critical thinking movement" which is the most recent response to the philosophical disorientation and confusion many of us experience.

Despite their laudable concern to provide students with a foundation for reasonable and responsible thinking and living, proponents of the "critical thinking" approach typically adopt the logical approach. But, instead of introducing students to ongoing arguments about the meanings of the basic notions, they focus attention on argumentation itself as though, by doing this, they are going right to the heart of the problem of taking possession of ourselves and finding direction in the flow of our lives. Their aim seems to be limited to the propagation of clarity, coherence, and rigor in thinking, as though everyone already knows quite well that clarity, coherence, and rigor in reasoning are the keys to the adequate discernment of meaning, to the achievement of objec-tivity, to the acquisition of knowledge, and to the discernment of what's true, real, and worthwhile.

Clear, coherent, and rigorous thinking alone does not deserve the name "critical thinking," let alone the name "intelligent, reasonable, and responsible thinking." I am *clear* if I define my terms and use them univocally. I am *coherent* if my definitions do not contradict one another. I am *rigorous* if I insist on clarity and coherence and do not rest until I've achieved them. I am 'critical', in the view that frames this approach, if I rigidly adhere to these standards myself in my conscious performance and measure others' conscious performance by them as well. In short, the operative assumption in this approach is that "being critical" is virtually indistinguishable from "being logical." *Truly critical* questions, such as "Is logical thinking *really* critical thinking? Am I being *sufficiently critical* if I'm being logically consistent?", are rarely raised in introductions to critical thinking. If such questions do arise, they are regarded as beyond the range of philosophical reflection, and they are not given the truly critical attention they deserve.

The precept "Be logical!" is unquestionably an important one, but it seems to mean much less than "Be critical!" It's not uncommon for us to find ourselves having critical doubts about the truth of an otherwise logical conclusion. Many who tout clear, coherent, and rigorous thinking often strike us as still surprisingly or dangerously uncritical and unreflective. They seem not to notice that in many situations it's not nearly enough to be logical. Anyone can remain consistent with abstract principles, but are the principles *true*? Is there any evidence to confirm them? Have they been reached *objectively?* Are they *worth* retaining if they haven't been? If they are really so obviously true, why do other seemingly intelligent and reasonable people reject them? Those who take the "critical thinking" approach don't seem to recognize that being critical means much more than just being logical.

More often than not, we go well beyond being critical in this narrow sense and issue to ourselves more encompassing and seemingly more basic precepts, such as "Be attentive!", "Be intelligent!", "Be reasonable!", "Be responsible!", "Be creative!", "Be loving!" We don't normally consider a person adequately critical if she is logical but fails to pay attention, to question intelligently, to seek evidence, to judge reasonably, to evaluate sympathetically. A *truly critical* person, it seems, would ask if being logical is enough. A truly critical person might even ask if being critical is enough. Even if I pay attention, question intelligently, seek evidence, and judge reasonably, but still fail to decide responsibly and to live lovingly, have I done enough?

To be critical is to be more than merely logical. But, on the "critical thinking" approach, it seems to mean no more than being logical. Being logical is singled out and upheld as equivalent to the attainment of the critical ideal, and being intelligent, being reasonable, being responsible, being creative, and being loving are left on the margins, brushed aside, ignored. A rigorous course in "critical thinking" may promote the minimal sort of self-knowledge that enables me to be *a deliberately consistent thinker*, but it doesn't promote the sort of self-knowledge that enables me to be *a deliberately attentive, intelligent, reasonable, responsible, and loving person* and to say, with Emerson, "With consistency a great soul has simply nothing to do."

Instead of aiding us in our efforts to be at home with ourselves, the "critical thinking" approach almost convinces us that there's no one home at all. We've grown accustomed to talking about our own conscious relationships to the world and to others, when we aspire to be critical, strictly in terms of the logical ideal. Our so-called 'critical' observations seem to be so many versions of "You're contradicting yourself!" or "You're being inconsistent!" or "You haven't defined your terms!" or "That's ambiguous!" In so-called 'critical' discussions we try to account for or to explain away disagreements by claiming that their roots lie in 'semantics', in conflicting premises, in poorly constructed or fallacious argumentation, or in faulty analyses of concepts. In our 'critical' evaluations of our actions and those of others we seek out the 'irrational', and by 'irrational' we usually mean no more than "inconsistent with previous or current behavior or beliefs." It's regarded as a serious failing, for example, if a candidate for public office "flip-flops," as though there could never be good reasons for changing one's mind and even for doing so repeatedly. Generally, the walls of our present culture reverberate with calls to "Define your terms!", "Be consistent!", "Be clear and precise!", "Stick to your principles!". The logic-machine metaphors of 'programming', "software and hardware," 'computing', and 'processing' are heard everywhere. We don't think; we "process information." We don't teach and learn; we "program and are programmed." We don't perform consciously; we "use software." We don't fail to understand; things just "don't compute."

The "critical thinking" approach promotes and reinforces the narrow logical approach. By doing so, it dangerously oversimplifies and caricatures the complex and delicate, concrete task of performing critically and responsibly that each of us faces upon awakening each and every day of our lives.

The logical approach to the problem of finding direction in the flow of life is a comfortable solution, provided one does not think or feel too deeply. It has the same attraction as other overly simple solutions to very complex problems. But, like most simplistic solutions to complex problems, it's not only inadequate, but, because of its inadequacy, it compounds the problem. The precept "Be logical!" invites the disorientated, confused, bewildered, per-plexed, troubled person confronted by life's ambiguities and complexities to settle for clear definitions without worrying too much about their correctness and to adopt fixed principles without raising critical questions about their sources and the evidence for their truth. It invites the disorientated seeker to follow a consistent path without being overly concerned about the rightness of that path. From the multitude of conscious operations which constitute the flow of our conscious performance, it selects a privileged few that pertain primarily to the management and manipulation of concepts or products of conscious performance – defining, assuming, deducing, clarifying, and inferring – and relegates the rest to the fringes of our concern, with the implication that these other conscious operations are 'illogical' or 'uncritical' and so, in some sense, insignificant or irrelevant or inapplicable to the task of taking possession of ourselves and finding direction in the flow of our lives.

The comfort afforded us by the narrow logical approach lasts only as long as we persist in ignoring the real sources of our disorientation, confusion, bewilderment, perplexity, and troubles. If we are disorientated, it is not because we can't define terms clearly, think coherently, and respond to the demand for rigor and consistency. It's because we aren't sure what to bother defining, what to bother thinking about coherently, what to bother pursuing consistently. In brief, we are more worried about living inattentive, stupid, silly, irresponsible, and loveless lives than about being illogical, unclear, inconsistent, and incoherent in our thinking. To the extent that the logical approach assists us in addressing these concerns, to that extent we need to inhabit it and master it. But, if it does not address these concerns or does not address them sufficiently, we would be radically uncritical if we attempted to solve our problem of orientation in life by relying upon this approach alone. The reliance upon the logical precepts of so-called "critical thinking" to guide us through the complexities of human living offers only a superficial and short-lived comfort, one easily disturbed and dismantled by the persistent problem of how to go about finding direction in the flow of life.

Appendix II

DIAGRAMS

I

THE SPONTANEOUS ORDERLY SEQUENCE OF MOODS AND MODES OF OPERATION

	World- and Self-Constituting Action ↑				
What is called	Evaluative Self-Presence	Responsible/ Irresponsible	Evaluative Mode of Operation	↑ Moral	Worth or Value
M I N D	Critical Self-Presence	Reasonable/ Unreasonable	Critical Mode of Operation	↑ Critical	Reality, Truth, Knowledge, Objectivity
	Wondering Self-Presence	Intelligent/ Unintelligent	Wondering Mode of Operation	↑ Intellectual	Meaning
	Question-free Self-Presence	Attentive/ Inattentive	Question-free Mode of Operation	↑ Experiential	The Given: [notions incipient]
	MOODS OF SELF-PRESENCE		MODES OF PERFORMANCE	TYPES OF OPERATIONS	BASIC NOTIONS

See Chapter Five, § 3 & 4, pp. 153-165.

II

THE SPONTANEOUS ORDER OF CONSCIOUS OPERATIONS

⇑ MORAL MODE conscience	[ORIGINATING OPERATION] QUESTIONING So what? What ought I do?	→ DELIBERATION envisioning possible courses of action	→ EVALUATION of the envisioned courses of action	[TERMINAL OPERATION] DECIDING and ACTING	⇑ VALUE or WORTH
⇑ CRITICAL MODE doubt	[ORIGINATING OPERATION] QUESTIONING Is it true?	→ MARSHALLING AND WEIGHING EVIDENCE Setting up conditions to be fulfilled	→ REFLECTIVE UNDERSTANDING grasping the fulfilment of the conditions	[TERMINAL OPERATION] JUDGMENT	⇑ REALITY, TRUTH, KNOWLEDGE, OBJECTIVITY
⇑ INTELLECTUAL MODE wonder	[ORIGINATING OPERATION] QUESTIONING What? Why? How Often?	→ IMAGINING in the service of inquiry	→ UNDERSTANDING OR INSIGHT	[TERMINAL OPERATION] FORMULATING the idea	⇑ MEANING [All Notions implicitly]
⇑ EXPERIENTIAL MODE	Seeing, hearing, touching, tasting, smelling, remembering, imagining, feeling				THE GIVEN Something I could ask about

THE SPONTANEOUS ORDER OF CONSCIOUS OPERATIONS

The experiential mode of operation is taken up and preserved by the intellectual mode; the experiential and intellectual modes are taken up and preserved by the critical mode; the experiential, intellectual, and critical modes are taken up and preserved by the moral mode. The intellectual mode originates with questions about what is given in experience and terminates in a formulated idea. The critical mode originates with questions about the truth or correctness of the formulated idea and terminates in a judgment of truth or falsity. The moral mode originates with questions about what to do, given the truth or falsity of my understanding of my experience, and terminates in a decision to act. See Chapter Five, § 3 & 4, pp. 153-165.

III

THE CYCLE OF PERSONAL DEVELOPMENT

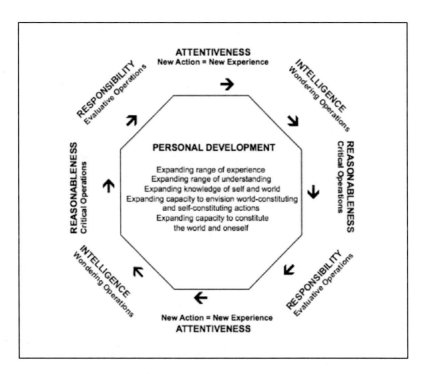

When I perform the four modes of conscious operation repeatedly in their orderly sequence, I develop. The range of my experience and understanding expands, my knowledge of myself and the world expands, my capacity to envision courses of action expands, and my capacity to constitute the world and myself expands. Each new action I perform on the basis of my newly acquired knowledge presents me with new experience about which I can then inquire. See Chapter Five, § 6, pp. 166-169.

IV

CONSCIOUS PERFORMANCE ANALYSIS

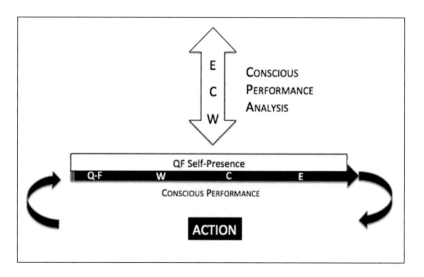

In CPA we turn the basic commitment on itself. We are present to ourselves in our performance of Question-free, Wondering, Critical, and Evaluative Operations. We turn our attention from the contents and objects of our operations to the operations themselves, identify them, describe their relations to one another, and determine the operative meanings of the basic notions. See p. 171.

V

OPERATIONAL POLYMORPHISM

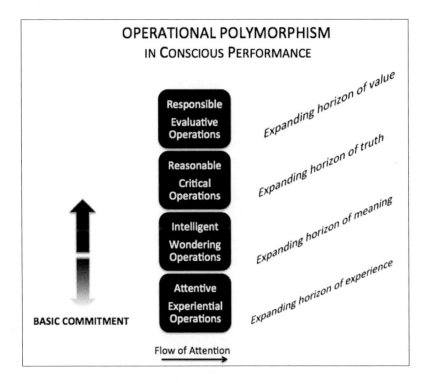

There are four modes of conscious operation which are informed and constituted by the unfolding basic commitment. As I perform in each of these modes, the range of experience, meaning, truth, and value to which I have access expands. See p. 269.

VI

ORIENTATIONAL POLYMORPHISM

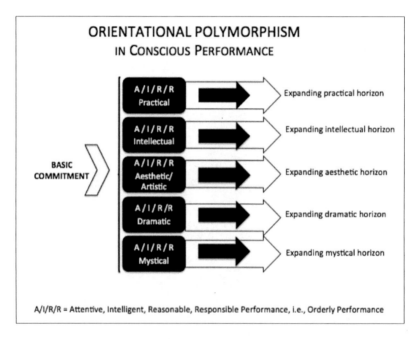

There are five basic interests that may govern the performance of the four modes of operation, giving rise to five motifs of conscious performance and further specifying the basic commitment. Performance in each of the motifs may be attentive or inattentive, intelligent or unintelligent, reasonable or unreasonable, responsible or irresponsible. If it is attentive, intelligent, reasonable, and responsible, I develop. See p. 269.

VII

TRIPLY POLYMORPHIC CONSCIOUSNESS

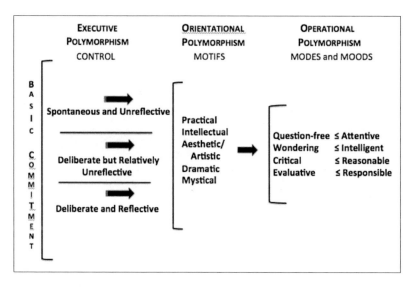

Human consciousness is polymorphic in three notable ways. It is polymorphic inasmuch as there are four modes of operation, inasmuch as there are five motifs, and inasmuch as there are three manners in which control of our performance of modes of operation in the variety of motifs can be exercised. See p. 270.

VIII

EXECUTIVE POLYMORPHISM: SPONTANEOUS AND UNREFLECTIVE

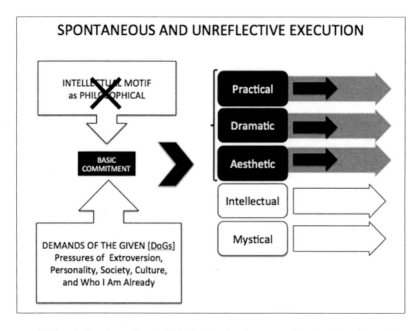

Without the benefit of CPA, instead of responding to the demands and invitations of the given, we are inclined to *react* to the demands. Inasmuch as we are reacting to the demands, we tend to spend our time in the quotidian blend of motifs and only rarely venture beyond it. See p. 270-279.

IX

EXECUTIVE POLYMORPHISM: DELIBERATE AND REFLECTIVE

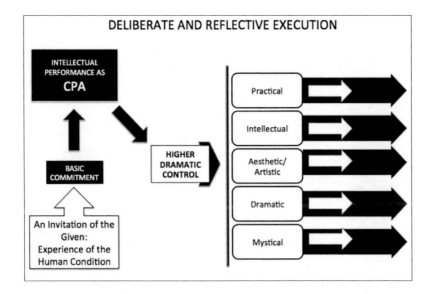

We have a basic commitment. We can reflect upon that commitment. If we do, we enter the intellectual motif in its specifically philosophical dimension, i.e., as a pursuit of understanding of the relations of conscious operations to one another and to the basic notions. As the reflective investigation [CPA] unfolds, we discover the triply polymorphic nature of human consciousness, and we realize that our heretofore unreflective and spontaneous constitution of the world and ourselves can become the reflective and deliberate High Drama in which our forays into the five motifs are intermittent deliberate episodes. See pp. 286-295.

X

THE HIGH DRAMA

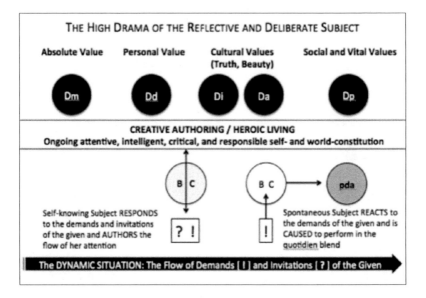

THE HIGH DRAMA OF THE REFLECTIVE AND DELIBERATE SUBJECT

Absolute Value   Personal Value   Cultural Values   Social and Vital Values
                                    (Truth, Beauty)

Dm   Dd   Di   Da   Dp

CREATIVE AUTHORING / HEROIC LIVING
Ongoing attentive, intelligent, critical, and responsible self- and world-constitution

B C   B C   pda

Self-knowing Subject RESPONDS   Spontaneous Subject REACTS to
to the demands and invitations   the demands of the given and is
of the given and AUTHORS the   ? !   !   CAUSED to perform in the
flow of her attention   quotidien blend

The DYNAMIC SITUATION: The Flow of Demands [!] and Invitations [?] of the Given

The subject who has acquired the basic philosophical self-knowledge achievable by the extended meditation of CPA *responds* to the demands and invitations of the given and selects reflectively and deliberately the motif appropriate to the experienced situation with heightened awareness of her role as *the author* of the drama of her living. Her basic commitment [BC] unfolds as High Drama. Performance in any motif is now a moment in the deliberately authored High Drama (indicated by the capital D). The spontaneous and unreflective subject *reacts* to the demands of the given and is *caused* to perform in the quotidian blend of the practical-dramatic-aesthetic motif. Her basic commitment is channeled into the quotidian blend. See pp. 295-297 and pp. 260-262.

An Elementary Vocabulary of Self-Possession

Brief Definitions of the Basic Terms of CPA

Action: World- and self-constituting performance issuing from a decision made in the Evaluative Mode of Operation that, because it is informed by new knowledge, is always an occasion of new sensible and self-present experience.

Attentiveness: The emerging or incipient basic commitment in Question-free Performance; the mood of Question-free Performance anticipatory of Wondering, Critical, and Evaluative Performance. I am *attentive* to a situation when I *anticipate* the objective pursuit of its meaning, the achievement of knowledge of its true meaning, and deciding and acting appropriately. Attentiveness is the anticipation of ongoing adherence to the basic commitment. Attentiveness may be spontaneous or deliberate in reaction to the demands of the given or in response to its invitations.

Authenticity, Major: Deliberately and reflectively attentive, intelligent, reasonable, and responsible performance that overreaches or goes beyond the specifications of the notions in the various Motifs; reflective and deliberate adherence to the basic commitment that informs and guides conscious performance. **Minor**: Spontaneous and unreflective or deliberate and relatively unreflective adherence to the basic commitment inasmuch as it is specified with a particular Motif. See also **Motif of Conscious Performance** and **Objectivity**.

Authentic Subjectivity: See **Objectivity** and **Authenticity**.

Basic Commitment: The orientation of conscious performance toward meaning, objectivity, knowledge, truth, reality, and value, exhibited in the orderly performance of question-free, wondering, critical, and evaluative operations.

Basic Interest: An orientation that patterns the flow of attention and the flow of contents of Question-free Operations. There seem to be five Basic Interests at the present time: Practical, Intellectual, Aesthetic, Dramatic, and Mystical.

Basic Notions: Our inescapable preferences for and anticipations of meaning, objectivity, knowledge, truth, reality, and value that inform and guide our conscious performance; fundamental ideals of conscious performance.

Basic Notions At Work: Ideally, our attentive, intelligent, reasonable, and responsible performance. But the basic notions are at work as well although "behind our own backs" in our disorderly conscious performance, as is revealed by our lapsing into performative self-contradiction.

Beautiful, notion of the: the conflation of the notions of truth and value in the Aesthetic/Artistic Motif; the sensible embodiment of truth and value evocative of the feeling of our open-ended possibilities in virtue of our adherence to the Basic Commitment.

Believing: The performance of Question-free, Wondering, Critical, and Evaluative Operations for the purpose of determining the credibility or trustworthiness of another.

Bias: Unauthentic subjectivity; inattentive, unintelligent, unreasonable, irresponsible performance. See also **Objectivity** and **Authentic Subjectivity**.

Blends (and Mixes) of Interests: Complex temporal orderings of the flow of contents of Question-free operations determined by more than one end. In every blend, one interest is dominant, and other interests are subservient to that dominant interest.

Commitment: A decision to carry out a course of action, made in the Responsible Mood of the Evaluative Mode. See also **Basic Commitment**.

Conceiving: Identifying the set of aspects of the heuristic image that are essential to the occurrence of understanding. Conceiving is subsequent to understanding and prior to formulating.

Conceptual Analysis: Merely logical or linguistic analysis of the already-achieved meanings of the products of conceiving and formulating in the Wondering Mode. Because it is operation only in the Wondering Mode, it deals with possibilities only.

Conscience: Responsible self-presence without having yet formulated an evaluative question; the desire for or anticipation of value.

Conscious Operations: Seeing, hearing, tasting, touching, smelling, imagining, remembering, questioning, representative and heuristic imagining, descriptive and explanatory understanding, conceiving, formulating, critical questioning, grasping the fulfillment of conditions or grasping the sufficiency of evidence, judging, moral questioning, deliberating, evaluating, deciding and choosing. In conscious operations we are present to ourselves and by them we are related to objects.

Conscious Performance: Any and all conscious operations constitutive of our pursuit of meaning, objectivity, knowledge, truth, reality, and value.

Conscious Performance Analysis (CPA): The exploration of the basic notions at work in conscious performance; turning the basic commitment on itself; experiential, wondering, and critical performance with regard to the four modes and five motifs of performance.

Consciousness: Intimate presence to oneself in the performance of Question-free, Wondering, Critical, and

Evaluative Operations. Often misconceived as another conscious operation. It's not an operation; it's a quality of operations. See also **Polymorphism of Consciousness**.

Content: The immediate object of a conscious operation.

Criterion, Already Operative: The basis for true judgments of knowledge and value. Adherence to the basic commitment is the criterion of authentic conscious performance.

Critical, Being: Performing Critical Operations with a concern for the truth of a prospective judgment. See also **Reasonableness**.

Critical Mode of Operation: The Mode of Operation constituted by critical questioning, establishing the conditions for the correctness of an idea, marshaling and weighing evidence, reflective understanding, and judgment.

Deciding: The operation that completes the Evaluative Mode; not to be confused with judging which is the concluding operation in the Critical Mode.

Declinatory Cycle of Conscious Performance: The recurrent performance of Question-free, Wondering, Critical, and Evaluative Modes of Operation, in or out of that order, inattentively, unintelligently, unreasonably, and irresponsibly over time. See also **Progressive Cycle**.

Degrees of Personal Risk: There are four degrees of risk I experience when I expose myself as a conscious performer to others: the first is the risk of being found inattentive; the second, the risk of being found unintelligent; the third, the risk of being found unreasonable; the fourth, the risk of being found irresponsible. The risk is that of exposing myself as, and being discovered to be, tethered only loosely to my basic commitment.

Deliberation: Envisioning possible courses of action in the Evaluative Mode of Operation; subsequent to moral questioning and prior to evaluation and decision.

Demands of the Given: Those aspects of the sensible or self-present given which capture my attention. Some demands of the given are fixed by instinct; others are variable and are apprehended as demands in virtue of the dominance of a non-practical basic interest or in virtue of personal development over time. Any content of Experiential Operations or of self-presence can become a demand of the given.

Description: An intelligent account of the relations of things given to oneself in Question-free performance, by either Experiential Operations or in one's presence to oneself.

Disorderly Performance: See **Disorderly Sequences of Modes** and **Disorderly Sequences of Operations**.

Disorderly Sequences of Modes: Sequences of Modes of Operation which violate the spontaneous order of Modes of Operation that is promoted by the adherence to the basic commitment, e.g., the performance of Critical Operations prior to the performance of Wondering Operations, or the performance of Evaluative Operations prior to the performance of Critical Operations.

Disorderly Sequences of Operations: Sequences of Operations which violate the spontaneous order of operations that is determined by adherence to the basic commitment within a Mode, e.g., judging prior to grasping the sufficiency of the evidence, or deciding prior to evaluating.

Doubting: Reasonable self-presence without having yet formulated a critical question; the desire for or anticipation of objective knowledge of the real.

Ensconced Spontaneous Subject: The subject who has become a deliberate performer in the Motif in which she happens to have developed herself, but without the benefit of the self-knowledge achieved in CPA and, therefore, unreflectively.

Evaluation: Inquiry into the relative value of envisioned possible courses of action; asking if a possible course of action would really be worthwhile. The second operation in the orderly sequence of operations in the Evaluative Mode.

Evaluative Mode of Operation: The Mode of Operation constituted by moral questioning, deliberation about possible courses of action, evaluation of possible courses of action, and decision or choice. The fourth Mode in the orderly sequence of Modes of Operation.

Experiential pattern or dynamic configuration: The order or organization to be found in the temporal flow of contents of sensing, perceiving, imagining, remembering, and feeling. See also **Patterns of Attention**.

Explanation: Relating things to one another in the Intelligent Mood of the Wondering Mode of Operation.

Extroversion: Specifically, preoccupation with the contents of operations of Question-free sensing, perceiving, imagining, and remembering. More generally, it is the preoccupation with the contents (the intended objects or contents) of any conscious operation to the detriment of attentiveness to the performance of the operations.

Formulation: The expression in concepts of what is understood in the Wondering Mode. Formulation is subsequent to understanding and conceiving, and prior to doubting and critical questioning.

Fragility of the Spontaneous Order: The susceptibility of unreflective and spontaneous adherence to the basic commitment to disordering derailment.

Fundamental Precepts of Conscious Performance: Be Attentive! Be Intelligent! Be Reasonable! Be Responsible! See also **Precepts**.

Fundamental Preference: A preference is a desire for one thing rather than another. A fundamental preference is a desire for meaning, objectivity, knowledge, truth, reality, or value rather than for nonsense, bias, ignorance, falsehood, illusion, or disvalue. The denial of this fundamental preference involves me in performative self-contradiction.

Heuristic Definition: Indirect definition of X by saying how we go about seeking and finding X.

Heuristic Imagining: The production of typically schematic images or diagrams for the sake of understanding. Heuristic images may also be representative images, but their function as heuristic is not to represent the objects of inquiry. See also **Representative Imagining**.

High Drama: My performance in the Dramatic Motif as encompassing my performance in every Motif subsequent to the realization that my performance in every Motif is constitutive of my character and of the world for myself and others.

Idea: The unconceived and unformulated content of an act of understanding or insight.

Imagining: Production of representative or heuristic imagery. See also **Heuristic Imagining** and **Representative Imagining**.

Integrity: Either the minor integrity of consistency between one's beliefs and values, or consistency between one's beliefs and values, on the one hand, and one's actions, on the other; or, the major integrity constituted by the harmony between what one is saying and the conscious performance in which one is engaged while one is saying it. Hypocrisy resembles but differs fundamentally from a lack of major integrity, because hypocrisy is a disharmony of products of conscious performance, whereas performative self-contradiction is a disharmony between products of performance and the performance that generates them.

Intelligence: Self-presence in adherence to the basic commitment in the performance of Wondering Operations; the Mood of Wondering performance; caring about meaning. Not to be confused with I.Q. in which we are not present to ourselves and which is a measure of native or developed intellectual ability. (The so-called Flynn Effect is the rate of increase in I.Q. worldwide due, it is supposed, to improved nutrition. But eating well doesn't put me in the mood of Intelligence in the sense in which this term is used in CPA.)

Intelligent, Being: Performing operations in the Wondering Mode with a concern to grasp the meaning of an object or situation. See also **Intelligence**.

Intimate Self-Presence: See **Self-Presence**.

Invitations of the Given: Those aspects of the sensible or self-present given about which questions might be asked but which do not demand my attention.

Judging, Judgment: The concluding operation in the Critical Mode; subsequent to grasping the sufficiency of evidence.

Language of Self-Possession: The language we use to speak about ourselves as conscious performers.

Mixes (and Blends) of Interests: See **Blends**

Mode of Operation: A set of conscious operations. There are four Modes of Operation: Question-free; Wondering; Critical; Evaluative.

Mood of Conscious Performance: The self-feeling of conscious performance. The basic moods are Attentiveness or Inattentiveness, Intelligence or Unintelligence, Reasonableness or Unreasonableness, and Responsibility or Irresponsibility.

Motifs of Conscious Performance: Themes of conscious performance determined by basic interests. There are five Motifs: Practical, Intellectual, Aesthetic, Dramatic, and Mystical. In every blend of Motifs, one Motif is dominant. See also **High Drama**.

Notions: See **Basic Notions**.

Object: Anything to which I am related by a conscious operation; not limited to contents of Experiential Operations and inclusive of the operations of the subject when these are attended to in CPA.

Objectivity: Attentive, intelligent, reasonable, and responsible conscious performance, or authentic subjectivity. Distinguish the minor objectivity of attentive, intelligent, reasonable, and responsible performance within the limits imposed by the specification of the basic notions in a Motif and the major objectivity of attentive, intelligent, reasonable, and responsible performance that over-reaches those limits and asks if performance in my current Motif is sufficient and/or appropriate to the given situation. See also **Bias**.

Orderly Sequence of Modes: The sequence of my Modes of Operation when I am adhering to my basic commitment. First, the Question-free Mode, and then the Wondering Mode, and then the Critical Mode, and then the Evaluative Mode.

Orderly Sequence of Moods: The sequence of my Moods of Performance when I'm adhering to my basic commitment. First, Attentiveness, and then Intelligence, and then Reasonableness, and then Responsibility.

Patterns of Attention: Purely temporal sequences of contents of Question-free performance, determined by a basic interest. See also **Experiential Pattern**.

Performative Self-Contradiction: A contradiction between what I say about my conscious performance, or about the basic notions that inform and guide it, and the conscious performance I engage in and by which my performance is informed and guided, while I'm saying it. Embarrassment when exposed as involved in performative self-contradiction occurs in direct proportion to the seriousness with which I take myself as a conscious performer.

Polymorphism of Consciousness: The variability of our self-presence that accompanies variations in Modes of Operation, Motifs of Conscious Performance, and in degree of control of our conscious performance. Distinguish between Operational Polymorphism (the variety of operations and Modes), Orientational Polymorphism (the variety of Motifs), and Executive Polymorphism (spontaneous and unreflective, deliberate and relatively unreflective, or deliberate and reflective performance).

Possible Courses of Action: Anything that I can actually decide to do and then actually do now, given my present level of development, or do in the future, assuming my future development.

Precepts: General rules of conscious performance. Precepts may pertain to conscious performance in a specific Motif, e.g., "Be Practical!", or pertain to conscious performance in general, e.g., "Be Yourself!" See also **Fundamental Precepts of Conscious Performance**.

Progressive Cycle of Conscious Performance: The recurrent performance of Question-free, Wondering, Critical, and Evaluative Modes of Operation, in that order, attentively, intelligently, reasonably, and responsibly over time. See also **Declinatory Cycle of Conscious Performance**.

Propriety of Interest: The relevance or appropriateness of a basic interest for the situation in which one finds oneself.

Purely Temporal Objects: Non-spatial and unimaginable objects; conscious operations are purely temporal objects.

Purification of the Language of Self-Possession: The tethering of terms used to speak about our conscious performance to the experience of our performance given in our presence to ourselves.

Question-free Mode of Operation: The Mode of Operation constituted simply by acts of seeing, hearing, tasting, touching, smelling, feeling, remembering, and imagining, and by mere presence to oneself.

Reasonableness: The mood of the Critical Mode of Operation; caring about the truth.

Reflection: A general name for the performance of the four Modes of Conscious Operation with regard to our own conscious performance as given for our attention in our intimate presence to ourselves.

Reflective and Deliberate Performance: Self-directed conscious performance guided by decisions based upon the knowledge of oneself as a conscious performer achieved through CPA.

Reflective and Deliberate Subject: The subject engaged in conscious performance with self-presence heightened and informed by the self-knowledge acquired in CPA.

Representative Imagining: Production of images that replicate the sensible qualities of actual or possible objects of Experiential Operations, or that are thought to replicate, but do not actually replicate, qualities of non-sensible objects. See also **Heuristic Imagining**.

Responsible, Being: Performing operations in the Evaluative Mode; with a concern for what is worthwhile; caring about value.

Responsibility: The basic mood of orderly performance in the Evaluative Mode of Operation.

Self-Attention: Attention to data of consciousness given in my presence to myself in my conscious performance.

Self-Experience: See **Self-Presence**.

Self-Knowledge (as a Conscious Performer): What is reached by the performance of Question-free, Wondering, and Critical Operations with regard to the flow of conscious performance as given in my presence to myself in my own performance.

Self-Possession (as a Conscious Performer): Being at home with oneself in one's conscious performance, that is, self-directing conscious performance informed and guided by the self-knowledge achieved in CPA, or deliberate and reflective conscious performance.

Self-Presence: A quality of conscious operations in virtue of which I have experience of myself in my conscious performance and am able to attend to myself as a conscious performer.

Self-Worth: The notion of value as specified in the Dramatic Motif.

Specifications of the Basic Notions: Determinate, conceptual meanings given to the Basic Notions in the various Motifs.

Spontaneous Order of Modes of Operation: The sequence of Question-free, Wondering, Critical, and Evaluative Modes, such that Question-free Operations evoke or call forth Wondering Operations, Wondering Operations evoke or call forth Critical Operations, and Critical Operations evoke or call forth Evaluative Operations.

Spontaneous Order of Moods of Conscious Performance: The sequence of the moods of Attentiveness, Intelligence, Reasonableness, and Responsibility, such that Attentiveness evokes or calls forth Intelligence, Intelligence evokes or calls forth Reasonableness, and Reasonableness evokes or calls forth Responsibility.

Subject: The one who is present to herself in the performance of conscious operations. Types of subject may be characterized by their dominant Mode of Operation, by their dominant Motif, by their degree of development or decline in a specific Motif, or – most basically – by their adherence to or lack of adherence to the basic commitment, i.e., as authentic or inauthentic.

Subject-as-Subject: The conscious performer in the very performance of her operations.

Subject-as-Object: The conscious performer as the content of her own or another's sensing, perceiving, remembering, or imagining.

Subjective: Of or pertaining to the one who performs conscious operations. In the unpurified Language of Self-Possession it is often said, mistakenly, to be the opposite of 'objective'.

Subjectivity: The entire range of conscious performance given in one's presence to oneself. Subjectivity may be authentic or inauthentic, that is, in our conscious performance we may adhere to the basic commitment or diverge from it, and our adherence to it may be spontaneous or deliberate.

Superimposition of Operations upon Operations: The performance of different operations simultaneously, e.g., questioning while perceiving, imagining while understanding, judging while remembering, etc. My performance of operations in the Question-free Mode, for example, do not cease when I begin to perform operations in the Wondering Mode. Moreover, operations in earlier Modes are transformed by the performance of operations in later Modes.

The Given: The contents of Question-free operations and of mere self-presence before I ask any questions about them.

Thinking: Performance in the Wondering Mode: inquiry, heuristic imagining, understanding, conceiving, formulating. Thinking produces thoughts or formulated conceptions which may be true or false but which are not known to be true or false by thinking alone. 'Thinking' is used vaguely in the existing Language of Self-Possession to refer to a large number of distinct operations.

Transformative Decisions: Decisions to perform in conformity with the heuristic definitions of the basic notions. There are four transformative decisions pertaining to the pursuit of objectivity, knowledge, reality, and value.

Unreflective and Spontaneous Performance: Conscious performance without knowledge of oneself as a conscious performer; it may be authentic or inauthentic subjectivity, but, in virtue of its spontaneity and unreflectiveness, its authenticity is fragile.

Unconscious: Not present to myself, e.g., in deep sleep.

Wonder: Intelligent self-presence without having yet formulated an intelligent question; the desire for or anticipation of meaning.

Wondering Mode of Operation: The Mode of Operation constituted by intelligent questioning, heuristic imagining, understanding, conceiving, and formulating.

A Publication of

ENCANTO EDITIONS
Los Angeles   CA
USA